Demystifying the European Union

ADDITIONAL PRAISE FOR THE FIRST EDITION

"Ginsberg's book is indispensable for students and scholars seeking a clear, accurate, and readable account of how the European Union works. He traces the organization's history, clarifies its institutions and procedures, and critically assesses a vast amount of literature on the subject. This comprehensive and reader-friendly text is the best I've seen."

—Michael Sodaro, George Washington University

"A clear, in-depth account of the process of European integration. . . . Very well written and extremely well organized, Ginsberg's book provides students of European integration with a fresh approach to issues such as political unity, political thought, decision-making, and international security. . . . A must read for anybody interested in European studies."

—Gabriela Marin Thornton, EU Center of Excellence, Texas A&M University

"Roy Ginsberg is the premier American scholar on the European Union. Better than anyone, he has elaborated the sui generis nature of an institution in which independent Member States have pooled their sovereignty in certain areas and retained it in other areas. But in his newest book, he has emphasized how this unique regional integration has grown over time, not just in the number of Member States, but in the development and maturity of its institutions. The breadth of his scholarship and his impact on transatlantic relations are astonishing. This book is yet another of his seminal works and a must read for anyone interested in understanding one of the most important and least understood institutions in the world, the European Union."

—Stuart E. Eizenstat, former U.S. ambassador to the European Union, undersecretary of state, and deputy secretary of the treasury

"*Demystifying Europe* is a rare and wonderful find—a highly readable, provocative textbook full of useful and usable information. I thoroughly enjoyed the approach, which thankfully gets away from some of the traditional textbook format. Ginsberg's aim to 'demystify' the EU through an interdisciplinary and comparative approach is to be greatly commended. His comparison of EU governmental institutions to those of the United States sheds much light on the governmental features unique to the EU. A must read for students and instructor alike."

—Glenda G. Rosenthal, Columbia University

"Ginsberg's text is deliberately pedagogic, with welcome concluding sections in each chapter on review, key concepts, study questions, and recommendations for further reading. . . . Exemplary in providing the simple analytical building blocks—supranationalism, intergovernmentalism, *acquis communautaire*, *acquis politique*, multispeed Europe, outputs, comitology, and the like—and then showing how blurred these concepts become as political clashes and pragmatic compromises unpredictably mix bits of each approach. . . . The beginning student could hardly find [a] better guide to the unique construction of the European Union than [this] introductory text."

—Elizabeth Pond, *Internationale Politik*

Demystifying the European Union

The Enduring Logic of Regional Integration

SECOND EDITION

Roy H. Ginsberg

ROWMAN & LITTLEFIELD PUBLISHERS, INC.
Lanham • Boulder • New York • Toronto • Plymouth, UK

Published by Rowman & Littlefield Publishers, Inc.
A wholly owned subsidary of The Rowman & Littlefield Publishing Group, Inc.
4501 Forbes Boulevard, Suite 200, Lanham, Maryland 20706
http://www.rowmanlittlefield.com

Estover Road, Plymouth PL6 7PY, United Kingdom

British Library Cataloguing in Publication Information Available

Library of Congress Cataloging-in-Publication Data

Ginsberg, Roy H.
  Demystifying the European Union : the enduring logic of regional integration / Roy H. Ginsberg.—2nd ed.
    p. cm.
  Includes bibliographical references and index.
  ISBN 978-0-7425-6691-0 (cloth : alk. paper)—ISBN 978-0-7425-6692-7 (pbk. : alk. paper)—ISBN 978-0-7425-6693-4 (electronic)
  1. European Union. 2. European Union—Decision making. 3. European Union countries—Economic integration. I. Title.
  JN30.G553 2010
  341.242'2—dc22

                                                                              2009053022

♾ ™ The paper used in this publication meets the minimum requirements of American National Standard for Information Sciences—Permanence of Paper for Printed Library Materials, ANSI/ NISO Z39.48-1992.

Printed in the United States of America

Dedicated to the Memory of
Dr. Nicholas Nyaradi (1905–1976)
Hungarian Statesman
Beloved Professor and Mentor

Contents

Illustrations

Tables

Boxes

Figures

Maps

Images

Acknowledgments

As a professor, I have been privileged to work with young people during their college careers. Over the past twenty-five years, my students at Skidmore College have been a source of inspiration as I developed and taught a course—Political Economy of European Integration—that focused on why the European Union is important to their understanding of how nation-states who had been at war for so long can make a lasting peace. My research assistants for the first edition, Joshua Hutchinson, Kenny Olmstead, and Shubha Gokhale, who represent the best and brightest of their generation and of Skidmore, helped not only with research, writing, collecting and verifying data, graphic work, and editing, but with articulating why European integration is important to their cohort. My research assistant for the second edition, Mihaela David, was truly Herculean in her efforts to update the volume to take into account changes in the European Union over the past five years, especially those brought about by the enactment of the Treaty of Lisbon. Mihaela represents the best of her native Romania and of the new and young face of today's European Union. It seemed very appropriate for a textbook on European integration to be based on such intensive and mutually beneficial faculty-student collaboration.

Colleagues at Skidmore provided invaluable assistance, especially Professors Patricia-Ann Lee (History), Mehmet Odekon and Joerg Bibow (Economics), and Mary-Beth O'Brien (German), who critiqued individual chapters. This book also reflects the knowledge I have gained on the topic of European integration from many astute thinkers over many years, among them Lily Gardner Feldman (American Institute for Contemporary German Studies), Christopher Hill (Cambridge University), Henry R. Nau (The George Washington University), Donald Puchala (University of South Carolina), and Glenda G. Rosenthal (Columbia University).

My wife, Kirsten Elizabeth Mishkin, and daughter, Monica Jane Ginsberg, proved again to be meticulous editors and critics. Moreover, they were patient and supportive when I would disappear for weeks at a time to our log cabin in Newcomb, New York, deep in the central Adirondack Mountains, to write what I had taught over the length of a professional career.

Preface

In 1958, the Treaties of Rome entered into force, laying the foundations for the European Union (EU), the most important peacetime development in modern international relations. From the perspective of a half-century later, such a milestone affords the opportunity to reflect on the nature and evolution of European integration from early postwar reconstruction and interstate reconciliation through the Cold War to the present.

This book introduces students to European integration so that they may begin to assess what the EU means to them and to the world. One goal of the text is to construct, deconstruct, and reconstruct the European Union to ensure that the reader's understanding of the EU rests on a solid foundation. The book's interdisciplinary and comparative approaches help demystify the EU for both new and seasoned students. No one discipline has a monopoly on knowledge of the EU; therefore, this study of European integration draws on history for context; on law, economics, and politics for structure; on institutions and leaders for concepts of agency or influence; and on internal and external public opinion to test relevancy and effect. Moreover, the study of EU governance is informed by the field of comparative government. Since the EU and the United States have in common certain federal governmental features, EU governmental institutions are compared to those of the United States to illuminate the governmental features unique to the EU.

Students will find that the most effective method for studying the EU is to place themselves at the intersection of theory and practice and of history and contemporary reality. This busy and exciting intersection is where students can put to use what they learn, first by analyzing and critiquing the effects of EU policies and practices and then by weighing different problem-solving options—just as EU and national decisionmakers do before they act. The author has enjoyed the benefits of marrying theory with practice, having had careers in college teaching and in the federal government, where as an analyst in the Foreign Agricultural Service, the Office of Management and Budget, and the International Trade Commission he covered United States economic relations and issues with the then European Community.

This book is based on the author's experience of teaching an interdisciplinary course on European integration at Skidmore College—Political Economy of European Integration—introduced twenty-five years ago as the first of its kind in the United States. When the author was a college student, he was introduced to the novelty of Franco–German reconciliation, in contrast to centuries of European warfare, by his mentor at Bradley University—Dr. Nicholas Nyaradi (1905–1976), Hungary's postwar minister of finance. The author's graduate school professors at The George Washington University, particularly Drs. Henry R. Nau, Howard M. Sachar, and George Stambuk, encouraged him to demystify what was then the European Common Market. The notion of interstate reconciliation appealed to his youthful outlook on a world that could be made better. It still does.

Although it is often fashionable to dismiss the EU as something less than the sum of its parts, the author's interest in the theory and practice of European integration has not been dampened by the skeptics and naysayers. His sustained interest in interstate reconciliation came naturally to his generation, a generation that succeeded to the sacrifices of others during and after the Second World War. His father-in-law, Henry George Mishkin (1909–1994), served in Patton's Third Army, which landed at Omaha Beach to begin the Allied liberation of Europe from the Nazis. Many other members of this generation of heroes fought in Europe during the war, liberated the death camps run by the Germans and their collaborators, helped with postwar reconstruction, and provided the security within which the seeds of modern European integration took root. These men and women are twentieth-century heroes, and we—their children, grandchildren, and great-grandchildren—are heirs of their legacy of sacrifice.

One of those men who helped with postwar reconstruction was the author's father, Lt. Jerome Solomon Ginsberg (1928–1962), who served in the American Army of Occupation in western Germany in the early 1950s. That Allied military presence, which removed Nazis from power and created democratic institutions, gave the fledgling Federal Republic of Germany the chance to establish a lasting democratic order that its predecessor, the Weimar Republic (1918–1933), did not enjoy. In other words, America and its allies who won the war and stayed to win the peace ought to be proud of their sacrifices for a democratic Germany in a uniting Europe. One shudders at the thought of what Europe and the world would be like today had the Nazis remained in control of much of Europe.

The EU has proven to be a powerful antidote to the horrors of war, genocide, and the pernicious effects of hypernationalism that developed after the Thirty Years War and gathered momentum in the nineteenth and twentieth centuries until Europe lay in ruins in 1945. It proves that the lessons of Europe's past can be learned. Many scholars of international politics tend to pay more attention to the study of why nations go to war. In this book, the author is primarily interested in why and how nations make peace. There is enough time for young people to grow skeptical of what can be achieved in international politics, but the author has found that the more he has learned about the European Union, with all its imperfections and shortcomings, the more he has come to appreciate its unique value in a rough and tumble world.

Acronyms Related to the European Union

ACP	African, Caribbean, and Pacific States of the Cotonou Agreement
AFSJ	area of freedom, security and justice
ASEAN	Association of Southeast Asian Nations
AU	African Union
Benelux	Belgium, Netherlands, and Luxembourg
BiH	Bosnia-Herzegovina
BRICs	Brazil, Russia, India, and China
CAP	Common Agricultural Policy
CCP	Common Commercial Policy
CEE	Central and Eastern Europe
CET	Common External Tariff
CFI	Court of First Instance
CFP	Common Fisheries Policy
CFSP	Common Foreign and Security Policy
COPA	Committee of Agricultural Organization
CoR	Committee of the Regions
COREPER	Committee of Permanent Representatives
CIVCOM	Committee for Civilian Aspects of Crisis Management
CSDP	Common Security and Defense Policy
DG	Directorate-General
DRC	Democratic Republic of Congo
EAGGF	European Agricultural Guidance and Guarantee Fund
EC	European Community
ECA	European Court of Auditors
ECB	European Central Bank
ECHO	European Community Humanitarian Office
ECJ	European Court of Justice
Ecofin	Economic and Financial Affairs Council
ECSC	European Coal and Steel Community
EDA	European Defense Agency

EDC	European Defense Community
EDF	European Development Fund
EEA	European Environmental Agency
EEAS	European External Action Service
EEC	European Economic Community
EESC	European Economic and Social Committee
EFSA	European Food and Safety Agency
EFTA	European Free Trade Association
EGF	European Gendarmerie Force
EIB	European Investment Bank
EMS	European Monetary System
EMU	economic and monetary union
ENP	European Neighborhood Policy
EP	European Parliament
EPC	European Political Cooperation
ERDF	European Regional Development Fund
ERM	Exchange Rate Mechanism
ESCB	European System of Central Banks
ESDP	European Security and Defense Policy
ESF	European Social Fund
EU	European Union
EUMC	European Union Military Committee
EUMS	European Union Military Staff
Euratom	European Atomic Energy Community
Eurodac	European Dactylographic System
EUFP	European Union Foreign Policy
EUISS	European Union Institute for Security Studies
Eurojust	European Judicial Cooperation Unit
Europol	European Police Office
EUSR	European Union Special Representative
FAC	Foreign Affairs Council
FIFG	Financial Instrument for Fisheries Guidance
FSAP	Financial Services Action Plan
FTA	free trade area
GAC	General Affairs Council
GATT	General Agreement on Tariffs and Trade
GCC	Gulf Cooperation Council
GDP	gross domestic product
GSP	Generalized System of Preferences
HOGS	Heads of Government and State
HR	High Representative of the Union for Foreign Affairs and Security Policy
IAEA	United Nations International Atomic Energy Agency
ICC	International Criminal Court
ICTY	International Criminal Tribunal for Former Yugoslavia
IDP	internally displaced person
IGC	Intergovernmental Conference

ILO	International Labor Organization
IMF	International Monetary Fund
IPE	International Political Economy
JHA	Justice and Home Affairs
KEDO	Korean Energy Development Organization
MEP	Member of the European Parliament
MEPP	Middle East Peace Process
Mercosur	Common Market of the South
MFN	most-favored-nation
MONUC	United Nations Organization Mission in the Democratic Republic of the Congo
NAFTA	North American Free Trade Agreement
NATO	North Atlantic Treaty Organization
NGO	nongovernmental organization
NNPT	Nuclear Nonproliferation Treaty
NTB	nontariff barrier
OCA	Optimum Currency Area
ODA	official development assistance
OECD	Organization for Economic Cooperation and Development
OAPEC	Organization of Arab Petroleum Exporting Countries
OEEC	Organization for European Economic Cooperation
OJ	Official Journal of the EC
OLAF	Office Européen de Lutte Anti-Fraude; European Anti-Fraud Office
OMC	Open Method of Coordination
OSCE	Organization for Security and Cooperation in Europe
P.A.	Palestinian Authority
PCA	Partnership and Cooperation Agreement
PSC	Political and Security Committee
QMV	Qualified Majority Voting
RRF	rapid reaction force
SAA	Stabilization and Association Accord
SCA	Special Committee on Agriculture
SEA	Single European Act
SGP	Stability and Growth Pact
SIS	Schengen Information System
TAC	total allowable catch
TACIS	Trade Assistance for the Commonwealth of Independent States
TECS	Europol Computer System
TEU	Treaty on European Union
UNMIK	United Nations Mission in Kosovo
UNRWA	United Nations Relief Works Agency
VAT	valued added tax
VIS	Visa Information System
WEU	Western European Union
WFP	World Food Program
WMD	weapons of mass destruction
WTO	World Trade Organization (formerly GATT, General Agreement on Tariffs and Trade)

Note to Instructors

Based on many years of experience teaching courses on European integration to undergraduates at Skidmore College, this book distills all the lessons I and my students have discovered in the process of exploring and explaining the EU. Written expressly with active student learning in mind, the book offers study questions and key concepts and events after each chapter. For each key concept and event, students should provide a clear definition, plus a date and an example when appropriate, and they should explain *why* that concept or event is relevant to the study or practice of European integration. If students learn why key concepts and events are significant, they are more likely to remember the definitions. Key concepts and events are bolded and defined in each chapter. Although key concepts are listed after the chapters where they are first mentioned, most also appear—with examples—elsewhere in the book. Therefore, students may wish to use the index to find additional references to key concepts and events when working on their definitions and seeking examples. The glossary focuses on major institutions and policies of the European Union.

Please consult the book's website at http://www.rowman.com/isbn/0742566927, where you will have access to a variety of assignments in the form of "think piece" questions—provocative and probing questions that stimulate students to think and write creatively about what they are learning—as well as debate and roundtable topics, which also lend focus to students' learning by engaging them in classroom exercises about current topics. I have found that students are more likely to engage actively in learning about European integration when they are asked to think on their own about how Europeans—decisionmakers and citizens alike—deal with European Union issues and how scholars attempt to explain what the EU is and where it is likely to go.

It has been my experience that students are more inclined to embrace the study of European integration by coupling discussion of EU current events with the readings in the text. At the start of each lecture, a student is assigned to share with the class major developments in the European Union. My students and I have found that the combination of reading *The Financial Times* and the Luxembourg-based daily newsletter, *Bulletin Quotidien Europe*, is ideal for covering current events and generating more interest in the content of the course.

Professors and students are welcome to contact me with comments and questions at rginsber@skidmore.edu. I hope you find this book as rewarding to read and teach as I found it to write.

Introduction

The Importance of the European Union to the World

For many in Europe, and still more abroad, the EU is a mystery—little understood, at times maligned, and wrongly evaluated on the basis of standards reserved for nation-states, which the European Union is not. The EU is often known more for its fits than its starts—its blemishes than its clear complexion. Demystifying the European Union, which this book sets out to do, requires a panoramic view of European integration that reveals a transformation in the behavior of states toward one another. Evaluating this significant change in the behavior of states, the reader understands how and why nations make peace and knows what the European Union is.

The EU is more than a conventional international organization—it has sovereignty in some areas usually reserved for states. In other areas, it shares sovereignty with its member states. At the same time, the EU is less than a state—it is not responsible to an electorate for the defense of territory. Without precedent in international affairs, the EU is establishing a precedent for overcoming interstate hatreds and war. It remains a great experiment in international cooperation in a region that was home to the First and Second World Wars. Since it is sui generis as an international phenomenon, studying, traveling, living, or working in the European Union is worthwhile and different. Indeed, if the lessons of Europe's past are to matter over time—to have universal appeal—they must be applied outside Europe.

What makes the European Union an object of study for those in troubled regions of the world locked in deep-seated conflict is that its model of peace and reconciliation through economic and political integration could help to free those troubled regions from the chains of hatred and despair. In this book, **interstate reconciliation** refers to a process by which states, previously engaged in conflict, engage with one another in order to come to terms with the past, work through differences, negotiate and make amends and restitutions as needed, and agree to establish a new relationship based on structural (institutionalized) peace and mutual respect.[1] The EU is the world's first example of the success of interstate reconciliation on a large scale. However, to have any meaning for the wider world, the notion of interstate reconciliation must have relevance to other regions in trouble. For example, a water or energy community between Israel and her neighbors, should future conditions permit, could do for the Levant what the coal, steel, and iron community, the forerunner of the European Union, did for Germany and her neighbors after World War II.[2]

As an experiment in regional peace and prosperity and as a provider of stability, the European Union is a magnet for countries along and near its external borders. The EU is the world's largest donor of foreign aid. For example, the EU and its member states contribute sixty percent of all official development assistance (ODA), benefiting 160 countries. Furthermore, the EU and its member states have deployed twenty-two military and civilian missions to help countries prevent war, end war, and rebuild after war. The EU has been important to the success of various democratic transitions and consolidations in Central and Eastern Europe (CEE). It also seeks to foster stability and prosperity in the wider European neighborhood from the eastern Mediterranean to the Caucasuses. Candidates for EU membership—Turkey, Croatia and Macedonia—are making major constitutional, political, economic, and other changes required of them by the EU. The EU has important special relationships and strategic partnerships with countries in every region of the world, for examples, Brazil, Russia, India and China (the BRICs). At the same time, the EU is important to Europeans, Americans, and Europeans and Americans together.

FOR EUROPEANS

The EU is important to Europeans because it has so drastically influenced the international relations of the continent, as well as the domestic politics of the member states, that the resurgence of war among them is unimaginable. In only half a century, these nation-states have overcome centuries of internecine warfare to create a structure of democratic peace and reconciliation. Moreover, the Europeans have forged a single continental economy that rivals in size that of the United States. The euro that they created has become the world's second reserve currency. The EU members have established a body of treaty law—accepted as binding by national and local judiciaries—that imposes obligations and responsibilities on member governments, confers rights on individuals, and creates common practices and institutions to negotiate new areas of cooperation while managing what has already been agreed upon. At the same time that the Europeans have developed a union of values and institutions to structure peace and stability, they have managed to preserve the diversity of their separate states and peoples within the unity of collective and complementary interests.

The EU offers a scale of cooperation in economic, political, legal, social, educational, environmental, and other realms of public life that enhances the welfare of the member citizens, strengthens the individual member state governments and their interests at a new European level of governance where national and collective interests coalesce, and lends more weight to common or complementary interests abroad than when the constituent states act alone.

The EU matters in international affairs. It has **powers of attraction** for what the EU is (normative power), what the EU does (empirical power), and what the EU is becoming (putative power). The EU has the power to attract countries who wish to join, associate with, or partner with it. This is not just because the EU is the world's largest and richest internal market and economic and monetary union of states, but because the EU is a union of values and norms that resonate on a global scale. The EU has the power to attract attention for what it does: pressing Iran to stop uranium enrichment and submit its facilities to international inspection; deploying observers to monitor a fragile peace on an international political fault-line, such as that which exists between Georgia and Russia; providing leadership for international negotiations on climate change and criminal justice issues; and pursuing an end to capital punishment worldwide. The EU also has the power to attract the world's attention for what it is becoming. It is gaining traction as a leading player in the fight against transnational crime and terrorism and in deploying military and civilian forces to enhance security and stability in troubled lands.

The idea of European unity is as old as the Roman Empire. However, most forms of unity have been achieved not by voluntary association, but by force leading to involuntary union—the Roman Empire, Charlemagne's Frankish Empire, the Austro–Spanish Habsburg Empire, and the Holy Roman Empire, Napoleonic Europe, the Nazi Third Reich, and the Soviet bloc. Compacts or unions by generally voluntary association are far less frequent and have included the Hanseatic League (twelfth through seventeenth centuries), the Concert of Europe (nineteenth century), the customs union (Zollverein) of Germanic states (1820s–1870s), and the Benelux Customs Union of Belgium, the Netherlands, and Luxembourg (1948). The European Union has staying power because it gains legitimacy as an association by voluntary means and is a pole of attraction for prospective and associated members. The EU has already lasted longer than the Napoleonic, Nazi, and Soviet conglomerates of forced unity— because it is free and voluntary—and it has become much deeper and broader in form and function, breadth and depth, than the Hanseatic League.

Over time, Europeans have had to band together when faced with external security threats such as those posed by the Ottomans in the sixteenth century, the Soviets in the twentieth century, and al Qaeda and other transnational terrorists in the twenty-first century. At times the external enemy divided and ruled the Europeans; at other times it forced them to unite. And yet Europe can also be its own worst enemy. Europe was all too frequently at war with itself, when an empire such as Napoleonic France or Hitlerite Germany tried to impose its dominion over the rest. Yet disunity and disintegration during a period of continental war have been followed by a collective European reflex to cooperate, and opposing states unified to defeat the common enemy, thus establishing conditions for postwar cooperation and a new period of relative unity (for example, the Congress of Vienna after the Napoleonic Wars). Thus, the study of European integration must always be punctuated by the study of European disintegration, which can never be dismissed, given the history of Europe.

The shadow of Europe's atrocious past—from Flanders Fields in the west to Buchenwald and Srebrenica in the east—still hovers over the European Union and its neighbors and shapes the values important to Europeans at home and abroad. However, the specter of external threat and internal conflagration or the logic of economic and political scale do not alone capture the idea of European unity, recurring since the fall of the Roman Empire. Hugo Grotius, William Penn, Immanuel Kant, and Winston Churchill—among many others—have called for or predicted the eventual unification of Europe based on the continent's common heritage. Yet it was not until the 1950s that the Europeans finally found and acted on their voice. World War II set in motion a fundamental break with the centuries-old habit of interstate conflict in Europe, given the unprecedented scale of human suffering during and after the war and the loss of global power sustained by each of the leading European states.

The lead voice for a new postwar order was neither an intellectual nor a politician but a French wine merchant from Cognac: Jean Monnet had a vision of how to keep the European peace through a process of economic integration. The first step would be the unification of the coal, steel, and iron industries of France and West Germany. Monnet, with Robert Schuman and Konrad Adenauer, the postwar French and German leaders, formed what became a chorus for change that finally ended the cacophony of Franco–German relations. Reconciliation between France and West Germany, the pivot around which the EU grew, was the twentieth century's single most important peacetime event.

A mistaken Europe has learned the lessons of its past. Still, the EU's accomplishments of the past half-century will not be sufficient to garner the interest of young Europeans during the next half-century. Significant confusion over or skepticism toward the EU exists. If the EU is to matter to Europeans in its next half-century, its member governments and common institutions will have to be more responsive to the needs of citizens. Europeans will need to learn more about their union if they are to distinguish myth from reality. Europeans of all ages should care about their union, particularly young Europeans reading this book, who will spend the bulk of their lives in the EU's second half-century. They will need to learn more about the EU to evaluate what it means to their interests. They will learn in this book that EU decisions affect the way they will live, work, and play. For example, the EU

- raises standards for safe drinking water and ensures food safety;
- improves standards of living and economic prospects for its least developed regions;
- ensures legal rights and privileges for all citizens of the EU, from equal pay for equal work to legal recourse when individuals are directly affected by EU law, and from the right to vote in the elections for the European Parliament (EP) wherever they are in the EU to access to the diplomatic/consular services of any EU member state's embassy or consulate abroad;
- ensures that Europeans may work, study, and live anywhere across the EU and travel across EU national frontiers freely;
- encourages students to study in each other's universities in programs such as ERAS-MUS, the EU-sponsored program named for the sixteenth-century Dutch humanist and theologian;
- reduces roaming charges to users of mobile phones for text messaging and surfing the internet while those users travel around the EU; and
- eases travel and trade—and decreases the costs of doing each—in the Eurozone since the introduction of the EU's currency, the euro.

In short, the EU matters to Europeans, especially young Europeans, in ways few thought possible fifty years ago when their grandparents came of age. The union will likely matter more to young Europeans in the next fifty years as the EU grapples with socioeconomic, demographic, energy, environmental, health, global criminal and terrorist, and other challenges of the twenty-first century; as the EU grows in membership and attains borders adjoining areas of opportunity and risk; and as the EU is called on to take a more concerted approach to world affairs, especially in providing security in regions in need of Europe's experience and resources.

FOR AMERICANS

The EU is important to Americans and others around the world because they too have a deep stake in its success. Twice in the twentieth century, Americans, Canadians, other citizens of the British Commonwealth, and many others outside Europe gave their lives to free Europe from tyranny. During the period of postwar reconstruction, especially from 1947 to 1952, the United States was not just present at the creation of the European Coal and Steel Community (ECSC), forerunner of today's European Union, but actively garnered, cajoled, and underwrote support in France and Germany for its creation.

Cultural and ethnic ties; deep-seated commitments to the rule of law, representative democracy, human, civil, and minority rights; and highly interdependent commercial interests so deeply connect American and European civil societies that no one difference over policy or personality is likely to unravel those bonds. The EU economy matters in the international economy. The EU constitutes one-quarter of the world's gross national product. The EU is the largest source of foreign investment in the United States, the largest importer of U.S. goods and services combined, and the largest foreign generator of jobs in the United States. EU companies employ about 3.6 million Americans (and American firms employ a similar number of Europeans). Many individual U.S. states depend not only on trade with the EU, but on job-creating inward investment from the EU. EU-based firms are the largest investors in forty-five U.S. states. That said, the EU, like other capitalist commercial partners of the United States, is a competitor for markets. Disputes, which occur over trade rules, barriers to trade, and regulations, do exist, but they tend to be dwarfed by the flow of commerce between the United States and the EU, which remains unscathed by controversy.

Although the glue that held Americans and Europeans together during the clarion battles against Fascism and Communism from the 1940s through the 1980s has now worn thin, far more still unites Americans and Europeans than divides them. The richest group of advanced democracies in the world—the EU and its members—are critical interlocutors of the United States when confronting global problems. No group of like-minded states other than the EU has the economic and political scale, experience, resources, and willingness to remain engaged on a global basis and to cooperate with the United States to address global problems too big for any one state or union of states to do alone. A weak and divided Europe is good neither for Europe nor for the United States because it leaves to the Americans too much responsibility and too much power, within a vacuum of international leadership.

Americans are at times too quick to dismiss the EU as less important than its member states. They err in this dismissal because the EU in many respects strengthens the individual member states at a collective level, and this gives the EU staying power. Young Americans, like their European counterparts, will spend the bulk of their lives in the EU's second half-century. They too need to understand what the EU is and how it works in order to assess the impact of EU policies on their interests.

FOR EUROPEANS AND AMERICANS TOGETHER

The European Union is important to Europeans and Americans together because both have a deep stake in the ability of the EU to

- provide leadership in the functioning of a fluid, stable, and growing global political economy critical to political stability and economic growth for the developed and developing countries; and
- respond effectively with its member states to real and evolving global security threats—transnational crime and terrorism, the spread of weapons of mass destruction (WMD) and the means to deliver them, environmental degradation, and the myriad humanitarian disasters that accompany pandemics, collapsed states, civil wars, forced migrations, genocide, ethnic cleansing, and natural disasters.

When two-way trade and investment are combined, the United States and the EU are each other's largest commercial partners. Bilateral trade amounts to €1.7 billion a day. Foreign direct investment by EU firms in the United States and by U.S. firms in the EU has exceeded €257 billion. The EU and the U.S. share a common interest in maintaining order and growth in the international political economy with other major trading countries such as the BRICs, Canada, and Japan. Together, the EU and the United States account for roughly 42 percent of world services trade and 33 percent of world merchandise trade. Foreign direct investment by EU firms in the United States and by U.S. firms in the EU exceeds €257 billion.

In many areas of international security—from police and juridical cooperation in response to global crime and terror to stabilization of war-torn regions—the EU accomplishes certain tasks that many of its member states would not be able to implement on their own. The more the EU, with its combined political and economic scale, can act with speed, efficiency, and effect in international affairs, the better it is for the United States and the world. Why is this? The United States needs an interlocutor of scale, like the EU, to confront global challenges too large for any one state or region to address alone. Given the complementarity of many European and American values and interests related to democratic government, the rule of law, market economics, and human rights, the scope for cooperation between the United States and the European Union has never been broader. This is especially true in recent years as the EU gains experience and develops capabilities for the deployment of military and civilian operations abroad that enhance international stability and human security.

Young people in Europe and America should relate to one another and, together, to the world's greatest experiment in international cooperation—the European Union. The world will be less secure if America rides roughshod—and Europe remains passive—in international politics and security. America and Europe need each other to help manage a dangerous world because (1) they have relative strengths to bring to global problem solving; and (2) their cooperative relationship is based on complementary values and interests. It is because the European Union is important to Europeans and Americans and to the rest of the world that this introduction to European integration has been written.

The Structure of the Book

The EU is introduced in this book as a unified construct, then deconstructed into its separate pieces for detailed examination before being reconstructed in a final evaluation. The book is organized into three parts: (1) the foundational elements of European integration; (2) the contexts, functions, and policies of the EU as a decision-making political system or polity; and (3) the effects of the EU on its member governments and citizens and on the outside world.

Part I situates the book where it ought to begin. It constructs the introductory study of the EU on the basis of three foundation blocks—history, law, and economics. The EU is no accident of history. The more we place the EU in historical perspective, the more we avoid the pitfalls of viewing the victories and defeats of European integration as singular events in history. Chapter 1 surveys the incarnations of unity and disunity that haunt and shape today's European Union. Individuals—what they thought and did—mattered in how the EU eventually started and evolved. Chapter 2 introduces readers to the history of political thought and political theory associated with European integration and provides a brief overview of major watersheds in the EU's development over the past half century. In weighing the explanations and predictions of theory against the record of European integration, readers begin to evaluate the relative power of different explanatory concepts. To have application, theory should never be an afterthought of history. Since economics and law together have most shaped the supranational elements of European integration, Chapter 3 introduces the economic and legal foundations and principles of European integration, and in doing so rounds out and completes the introductory chapters of Part I.

Part II places you squarely at the intersection of theory and practice—to apply what you have learned of history and theory to the formulation and execution of EU governmental decisionmaking and to the outcomes (or effects) of EU policies. The chapters of Part II deconstruct the EU into its key individual elements in order to examine them carefully in relation to one another and to the whole. Chapter 4 introduces you to the contexts of EU governmental decisionmaking and Chapter 5 to the structure and function of the institutions of the EU, which together comprise a most unusual, if not unprecedented, polity. Chapters 6 and 7 introduce you to the outputs of EU governmental decisionmaking in the internal dimension of European integration—key policies designed to enhance the common welfare and security of EU citizens at home (Chapter 6) and to enhance common foreign and security policy interests of the EU states (Chapter 7).

Part III reconstructs the EU as a single polity in order to evaluate its effects on its member governments and citizens and on the world outside. Chapter 8 evaluates the impact of internal policies on EU citizens and member states, and Chapter 9 evaluates the impact of external policies on the world and on the EU itself. Chapter 10 summarizes the main findings of the book.

In this book you are challenged to transform assumptions about war and peace, integration and disintegration, and what is possible in the relationships of states to one another. Since the European Union is a work in progress, you will be able to assess theory and practice long after you have finished reading this book. You will come to know if the lessons of Europe's past will have universal or limited meaning for the world's troubled regions. You will live the epic that is about to unfold in the EU's second half-century.

Key Concepts

interstate reconciliation
powers of attraction

Study Questions

1. Why is the European Union important in a global context?
2. Why is the European Union important to Europeans and Americans together?

Selected Readings

The official website of the Delegation of the Commission of the European Union to the United States: http://www.eurunion.org
The official website of the European Union: http://europa.eu/index_en.htm
The official website of the U.S. mission to the European Union: http://useu .usmission.gov

Part I

FOUNDATIONS

Part I, which stresses the context and foundation of the European Union, introduces readers to the history, political thought and theory, economics, and law of modern European integration. The European Union developed through an uneven and messy historical process. Its logic is rooted in welfare and peace gained by economic integration, and fortified and shaped by the rule of law.

Part I is a passport to the study of how the EU works in practice—the focus of Parts II and III. As we begin to explore the foundations of the European Union, a thumbnail sketch of its major institutions and their functions is offered here, even though a full scale examination is covered in Part II.

The EU is perhaps the most complicated system of government in the world because it adds a layer of government onto the member states and has arcane and baffling decisionmaking procedures, some far removed from the scrutiny and understanding of voters. Moreover, since the EU is a political work in progress—it goes through a metamorphosis each time it expands in membership or amends the Treaty—it is a moving target for those who wish to describe and explain how it works. A hybrid, still young, and incomplete polity, the EU consists of the following components:

- A supranational bureaucracy and executive: The European Commission is Treaty guardian and policy initiator, implementer, overseer, administrator, enforcer, and manager. Its eyes are on what can be done to advance European interests in the context of national prerogatives. Its President shares executive tasks with the President of the European Council.
- An intergovernmental executive and legislator: The Council of the EU represents national interests through member-government ministers who legislate. Representatives of governments to the Council and the Council's own Secretariat share an

9

ethos of getting things done at the European level that often helps move governments to compromise in order to conclude agreements.

- A democratically elected, transnational colegislator with supranational features: The Members of the European Parliament (MEPs) have important legislative, budgetary, and oversight powers.
- An intergovernmental summit: The European Council—comprising the Heads of Government and State (HOGS)—sets broad policy guidelines and strategic directions and makes overarching unionwide decisions. The President of the European Council has the authority to lend leadership and vision to the EU at home and abroad.
- An independent auditor: The European Court of Auditors (ECA) seeks to assure that EU funds are being expended effectively and efficiently and in accord with the law.
- A supranational central bank: The European Central Bank sets interest rates.
- A supranational judiciary: The Justices of the European Court of Justice interpret and rule on EU law.

The complexity of EU governmental decisionmaking is the net result of fifty years of compromise among states that naturally wish to retain sovereignty and, concomitantly, cooperate on the bases of economies and politics of scale. Therefore, the EU polity has features that are

- Federal: There is a distribution of political power among European, national, and subnational units in the formulation and execution of common policies and laws.
- Supranational: There is a body of law that is supreme over national law, and there are EU bodies that have powers independent of member governments, powers delegated to the former by the latter at Treaty junctures. Decisionmaking is based on majority voting on most areas of the internal market and monetary union.
- Interinstitutional: EU bodies interact and bargain with one another over proposed legislation. In many instances they share an ethos of advancing European interests amidst differing national prerogatives and with regard to their own institutional interests in the EU governmental decisionmaking system.
- Intergovernmental: Governments of sovereign states make decisions based on national interests in a European context. Decisionmaking is based on unanimity or consensus on such issues as defense, treaty reform, and admission of new member states.
- Transnational: Members of the EP share legislative enactment powers with the Council on most areas of the internal market. MEPs are organized by and vote with European political parties. They are not governmental representatives.

Thus, the EU is an amalgam of different governmental features. It is a sui generis partially completed polity whose traditions draw from a unique and troubled history of nation-states in times of cooperation and conflict. It is to that history we now turn.

CHAPTER 1

Unity and Disunity

Preview

The European Union is not an accident of history. It is an outgrowth of previous attempts at unity. It is a response to the deafening silence of tens of millions of Europeans who perished when the continent suffered the perils of disunity, disintegration, and war. European integration is by no means a linear process. Even during periods of unity or integration, there were periods of uncertainty and regression. Students need a panoramic view of the peaks and troughs of European unity over time to better situate and assess today's EU and to avoid a single snapshot of any one time. The EU represents a response by its member states to the cumulative impact of the history of conflict.

Chapter 1 introduces the themes of European unity–disunity and integration–disintegration that have appeared and reappeared since the Roman Empire. The chapter defines these terms in relation to today's European Union. Central to the study of the EU, these terms are used broadly to depict ideal and simplified versions of the scope of peace and conflict—and of stability and instability—that have alternately benefited and plagued Europe. Centripetal and centrifugal forces have brought Europe together and pulled it apart. Voluntary European integration as an antidote to war draws on the **common denominators** of geography, history, religion, economy, and civilization among like-minded states to foster peace, security, stability, and prosperity. The chronology of Europe's experiences with unity and disunity is offered through the eyes of a political scientist to situate today's European Union in historical context.

Presence and Absence of Regional Unity and Integration

Unity is an ideal term that rarely exists among sovereign states. It may refer to a political or economic union of states (e.g., confederation, customs union, monetary union, political union) or it could refer, more loosely, to a state of mind or a preference for common ideals and interests linked to peace and cooperation across a single region by the states that inhabit it (Concert of Europe in 1815, Hague Congress in 1948). Unity is associated with peace and stability when states come together voluntarily, but when unity is forced onto states by a regional hegemon, there is resistance, and peace and stability are less likely to take root (Napoleonic France, Soviet orbit). Disunity implies a breakdown of a common order or association in which instability, and perhaps war, could follow (the decline of Charlemagne's Holy Roman Empire or the unraveling of the Concert of Europe).

Regional integration and disintegration depict broadly simplified versions of the scope for peace and conflict, stability and instability. Regional integration, generally a form of stability, is linked to and could lead to unity, but need not do so. **Regional integration** broadly refers to a process by which highly interdependent, like-minded states in a region, which have a degree of economic and political complementarity, engage in intensive and binding cooperation in selected areas of common interest. Integration may extend to areas of intense cooperation and thus have multiple terminuses, or it could lead to a form of functional or political union.

Integration is associated with a desirable form of cooperation when it helps heal wounds between formerly warring states. Although often associated with positive notions of regional peace and security, integration could spur a nationalist backlash if there is a sense that the integration process is impinging too deeply on the sovereignty of the state. France boycotted the EU in 1965–1966 for this reason. The choice of regional integration—a union run primarily by states (intergovernmentalism), common institutions and elite groups (supranationalism), or both (institutionalism)—is a defining battle fought in every twist and turn of today's European Union, as it was at the time of the French empty chair.

Disintegration—the polar opposite of integration—is a form of disunity that could lead to instability and conflict. It refers to the breakdown of extant cooperation and order among states in a given region. It has a negative connotation because it conjures up the potential results once order among a group of states falls apart and habits of cooperation and common interests vanish. The classical "balance of power" international order established at the 1815 Congress of Vienna had disintegrated by the late nineteenth century and was followed by the First World War. Disintegration of the "collective security" international order established by the 1919 League of Nations had occurred by the mid-to-late 1930s and was followed by the Second World War.

At its inception and during its early years, the EU promoted peace and stability to stave off war and instability. The EU drew on traditions fostering unity and integration from previous incarnations. At the same time, the EU and its members remained haunted by a collective memory of the horrors of war that have resulted from disunity and disintegration. Aversion to war is embedded in the psyche and ethos of the EU, and it has served as an integrating force as well as the basis of distinctly European values (of conflict prevention/resolution and humanitarianism) in international society. The instinct to make the EU work continues to drive European integration, whether in introducing a new currency, welcoming new members, or finalizing a new constitution. The fear of failure—the fear of disunity and disintegration that lingers in the collective European memory—remains.

Which process, integration or disintegration, unity or disunity, will prevail in Europe? It is impossible to be certain, since the study and theory of European integration is not a hard science. The EU is a union with a highly diverse membership of twenty-seven nation-states comprising many more nations within states, ethnicities, and regions with their own rich identities and cultures. Can the European Union preserve diversity (of states and peoples) in unity (of common interests) and stave off the ghosts of wars past? It appears to have done this in its first half-century. In the EU's second half-century, there is reason to think it will, overall, manage diversity within unity, although not without difficulty. The integration process is firmly planted in the body of common and binding laws, agreements, and practices—known as the *acquis communautaire*—that stretches over fifty years. However, the *acquis* does not itself guarantee growth in cooperation beyond existing agreement. In the next fifty years, there may be neither integration nor disintegration but periods of stagnation and status quo or of consolidation. Thus you, as a student of European integration, will want to keep one eye fixed on Europe's present, the other on Europe's past. Since Europe's past casts a long shadow over today's European Union, it is where we begin. Box 1.1 lists the major developments in Europe's experience with periods of unity and disunity, providing an historical overview for the chapter sections that follow.

Incarnations and Ghosts

This section explores the incarnations of European unity and disunity over the past twenty centuries. The Roman Empire, whether by hook or by crook, established a European unity by force between the first century BCE and fifth century CE that extended 3,000 miles from Iberia and England to northern Africa and deep into the Near East. Map 1.1 compares the borders of the EU in 2007 with those of the Roman Empire at its zenith. Germany lay largely outside the reach of the Roman Empire and of Roman law; this historical-geographical observation may shed light on why Germany experienced so much difficulty in integrating peaceably into Europe until the last half of the twentieth century.

The Roman Empire extended to areas south and east of the Mediterranean, but the EU has more of a northern center, with areas far to the northeast of the territory of the Roman Empire. Both unions—the Roman Empire and the European Union—covered all or most of the northern littoral of the Mediterranean Basin. The Roman Empire extended to northern Africa and the Near East, whereas the EU does not. However, the EU has extended its influence to the entire southern and eastern shores of the Mediterranean Basin in what it now calls its wider European neighborhood. It is no accident of history that the Mediterranean Basin has been an object of great interest to both the Roman Empire and European Union.

Christianity gave Europe a common religion, culture, and spiritual unity. The Roman Empire gave Latin to Christianity, and Christianity gave Latin to Europe. Although the EU is an association by voluntary means, its heritage from the Roman Empire includes a number of concepts and practices:

Box 1.1. Twenty Centuries of European Unity and Disunity: A Chronology

1st century BCE– 5th century CE	Roman Empire
8th–9th centuries	Carolingian Empire
9th century	Spread of Feudalism
1054	Division of Christianity into Roman and Greek Churches
1066	Norman Conquest
1095–1192	Crusades (First through Third)
12th–17th centuries	Hanseatic League
1337–1453	Hundred Years War
14th century	Spread of bubonic plague
1492	Reconquest of Spain, expulsion of the Jews and Muslims
15th century	Era of exploration followed by colonialism
15th–16th centuries	Renaissance
16th century	Consolidation of the Holy Roman Empire by the Habsburgs
16th century	Reformation and splintering of Christendom
1618–1648	Thirty Years War
1648	Peace of Westphalia
1750s	Beginning of Industrial Revolution
17th–18th centuries	Enlightenment
1789	French Revolution
1799–1814	Napoleonic Wars
1815	Congress of Vienna and the Concert of Europe
1834	Start of the Zollverein
1854–1856	Crimean War
1866–1871	Wars of German National Unification
1899, 1907	Hague Peace Conferences
1914–1918	World War I
1919	Treaty of Versailles
1920	League of Nations
1938	Munich Agreement
1939–1945	World War II
1942	Final Solution
1945	United Nations

- The idea of a common civilization and a geographical definition;[1] the notion of "diversity within unity" (i.e., a union may comprise very diverse autonomous cultural and regional groups).
- The practice of expanding markets by establishing and maintaining trade routes, and a system of commerce with an intricate network of roads.
- A common currency.
- A common language root (Latin) and a predominant religion (Christianity).

Map 1.1. The Roman Empire (Fifth Century) and the European Union (Twenty-first Century)

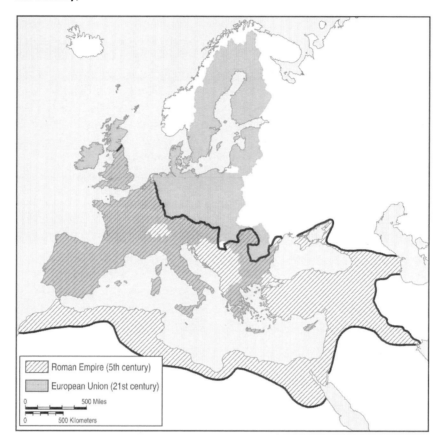

- Legal principles incorporated into written law that remain basic tenets of Western law and, by extension, EU law. For example, individuals are innocent until proven guilty, cannot be tried twice for the same crime, and cannot be convicted under a law passed after the act they committed.

The decline of the Roman Empire by the fifth century left Europe vulnerable to attack from Vikings and Germanic tribes. The Roman Empire failed to reconsolidate in the face of threats to and breaches of its security. It had become too diffuse, decentralized, and overstretched to respond effectively. Instability and fragmentation followed disunity and disintegration for the next three centuries. The inability of the Roman Empire to fend off foreign attacks and to assimilate large populations of "outsiders" resonates through history as a lesson Europeans ignore at their peril.

Unity and Disunity in Christian Europe

As the Roman Empire declined, local Frankish, Germanic, and other tribes replaced the authority of the Roman governors. As the Catholic Church expanded its temporal authority over increasingly large portions of Western Europe, cooperation gave way to competition between secular and religious authorities. In the west, three centuries of European disintegration followed the fall of Rome. In the eighth century, the king of the Franks, Charles the Great or Charlemagne, built up a superstate of lands that stretched from the Pyrenees in the west to the Danube in the east and from Hamburg in the north to Sicily in the south.

As map 1.2 indicates, the Holy Roman Empire comprised all or parts of the original six charter members of the EU—France, Italy, Germany, Belgium, the Netherlands, and Luxembourg. Charlemagne's capital, Aachen (Aix-la-Chapelle), is not far from Brussels, the "capital" of today's EU. It is no accident of history that the borders of Charlemagne and the EU charter members were broadly similar, given their common denominators: geography, history, religion, economy, and civilization.

The Holy Roman Empire rose to prominence as the ideal of political authority, and it gained the blessings of the Catholic Church when Charlemagne was crowned

Map 1.2.   Charlemagne's Europe (800 CE) and the EEC (1958)

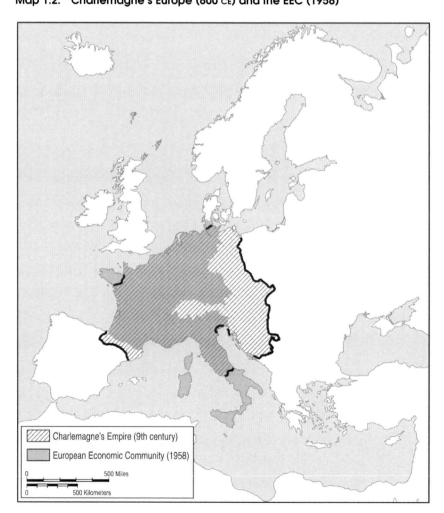

Holy Roman Emperor in 800 CE. The Holy Roman Empire grew in unity and strength under Charlemagne. Whereas the Roman Empire excluded Germany, the Holy Roman Empire included much of Germany, thus sparking a long-term process, punctuated by many setbacks, of integrating Germany into Western Europe.

In this period of European unity, there was a revival of stability, and education and culture flourished. Charlemagne actively expanded the empire's borders by force, but he was also held in esteem by inhabitants on both sides of the Rhine—Franks and Germans—who distinguished him as the "father of Europe." Unity lasted during the forty-six years of Charlemagne's rule, but after his death, Charlemagne's Frankish Empire began to decline; his heirs carved up the empire into separate kingdoms in the ninth century. By the tenth century the empire had already been divided into different territories governed by descendants of Charlemagne or other princes. A universal Christian commonwealth remained an aspiration among some but did not take the centralized form it had during the Carolingian period. Bands of marauding Vikings, Magyars, Saracens, and other tribes plagued Western Europe from the eighth to the tenth centuries. The Holy Roman Empire that in theory limped on until the mid-seventeenth century actually lacked the unity of the Carolingian period to maintain its borders against external attack.

The breakup of Charlemagne's Frankish Empire was followed by the advent of Feudalism. Feudalism, an economic order of small political units of lords and serfs, and Christendom, the transnational idea of religious unity of Western Europe linked to the papacy, continued through the Middle Ages. However, the church was not able to maintain an effective unity beyond the idea of universal Christian authority. Instead, what developed was a feudal and fragmented Europe in the ninth to eleventh centuries consisting of smaller local political units such as towns and duchies. These polities grew into modern centralized states in the fourteenth through seventeenth centuries, by which time Feudalism had fallen into decline. The seventeenth century saw the rise of powerful states that eclipsed Feudalism and transnational Christendom. Even earlier, by the time of the Hundred Years War, England and France had already become centralized national states, which eroded the feudal order in their countries. The centralized states of the seventeenth century became modern nation-states by the nineteenth and twentieth centuries.

Two events in the eleventh century had major effects on unity and disunity. The Norman invasion and defeat of the English at the Battle of Hastings in 1066 brought England into the European feudal system, presaging Britain's integration into the EU 900 years later. In 1054, Christianity was formally divided into its Roman Catholic and Greek Orthodox churches. This splintering of Christian unity would later weaken Europe as it faced the growing resolve and power of the Ottoman Empire. While the Ottoman Turkish threat exposed Europe's lack of unity and integration, it also catalyzed the Europeans to repel the attacks, but not before the Ottomans extended their control over the Balkans and the Middle East. The Ottomans captured Constantinople, thus ending the Byzantine Empire, and repeatedly laid siege to Vienna. European Christians sometimes joined to fight the Ottoman Muslims. A European army, led by the Polish general and king Jan Sobieski and consisting of troops from Poland, the Holy Roman Empire, and Austria, repelled the Turks on the outskirts of Vienna in 1683.

A Christian Europe found a new enemy around which to unify itself—Islam. The

Crusades (1095–1192)—a common European-Christian experience that involved alliances among church, kings, and princes—were designed to take Christian sites from Muslim rule in the Levant. The battles between European Christians and Muslims in the Middle East during and after the Crusades still cast a shadow on the Islamic world's perception of Europe today. The expulsion of the Muslims and Jews from Spain in 1492 solidified European Christian identity as distinct from Muslim and Jewish identities and had fateful consequences for relations between Christian Europe and the Muslim and Jewish worlds that still resonate.

Meanwhile, there were concomitant bursts of unity and disunity in the period between the fourteenth and fifteenth centuries. A divided Europe was at war with itself and with the Ottoman Empire. The English–French Hundred Years War (1337–1453) was symptomatic of an epic conflict. War was accompanied by the fourteenth century's bubonic plague, which may have killed between one-quarter and one-third of the European population. The plague began to break down the hierarchical, feudal structure of medieval Europe, which opened Europe to new economic possibilities for an emerging mercantile class. (This great natural disaster hit Germany the hardest and is thought to have delayed the modern political development and national unity of Germany centuries beyond that of Britain and France.)

Exploration and colonization, beginning in the fifteenth century, introduced conflict among the competing European colonial empires, yet the rise of Europe as a center of world trade and technology and as ruler of the high seas allowed European civilization to dominate others. Colonization and imperialism were common to the major European countries from the fifteenth to the twentieth centuries.

The Holy Roman Empire, which came under the domination of the Austrian and Spanish Habsburg dynasty in the 1500s, grew to comprise 25 percent of the European population of 105 million and controlled wide swaths of territory from Gibraltar in the west to Poland in the east by the early 1600s. The Holy Roman Empire was consolidated in 1519 when Spain's Charles V was selected Holy Roman Emperor and the Austrian and Spanish Habsburgs united. The two separate branches of the Habsburg dynasty cooperated with each other to dominate much of Europe. Map 1.3 depicts the territorial breadth of the Holy Roman Empire in 1648. Although close to establishing a European-wide hegemony and, with the Roman Catholic Church, a Christian commonwealth, the Habsburg dynasty was subject to the same fragmenting forces that weakened the Roman Catholic Church—the Reformation, the rise of modern sovereign secular states, and the Renaissance. The Reformation frontally challenged Vatican authority. The rise of modern states preceded the start of, and was confirmed by, the Thirty Years War. The humanism and rationalism of the Renaissance had opened up new ways of thinking about identity and faith.[2]

The sixteenth century's Reformation divided and destroyed Christian unity, despite the efforts of the church in the Counter-Reformation to recapture control. Martin Luther began translating the Bible from Latin into German in 1521, a development that marked the beginning of the end of the universal use of Latin by the educated European elite. At the same time, secular states and societies independent of the rule of the church were gaining ground. In 1555, the authority of the Holy Roman Empire was weakened by the Treaty of Augsburg, which permitted each prince of the Holy Roman Empire to determine the religion of his subjects. The loss of Christian unity in Europe led again to a period of disintegration and conflict.

Map 1.3. Holy Roman Empire (1648)

The Thirty Years War (1618–1648) between the northern European Protestant states, supported by Catholic France, and the Catholic Habsburgs and the papacy left Central Europe in ruins. No firm figures are available for the total number of war deaths (civilian and military) during the Thirty Years War, but it is known that many millions died. Germany again suffered the most. By some estimates, up to 75 percent of the German population may have perished, shrinking the population from 16.5 million to 4 million; other estimates suggest a population decline of 33 percent, from 21 million to 13.5 million.[3] The depopulation of Germany twice in 300 years served only to further distance Germany from her western neighbors in terms of the evolution of national unification and constitutional government. At the end of the conflict, at the Peace of Westphalia, the Holy Roman Empire as a political entity was finally destroyed and was replaced by a loose German confederation (which became the modern German state 223 years later).

As the idea of a European Christian commonwealth gave way to a divided system of sovereign secular states, Christendom gave way as well to the notion of "Europe." The Peace of Westphalia is significant for students of the EU because it ended a period of transnational religious unity in Europe and ushered in a new and ultimately very unstable period of competitive sovereign secular and highly centralized states in a fragmented Europe. The loyalty of citizens shifted from the church to the state and ultimately to the nation-state. Unity was followed by disunity and disintegration. For example, the Seven Years War (1756–1763) involved France, Austria, Saxony, Russia, and Sweden against Prussia, Hannover, and Britain in conflicts over Austria's attempt to regain Silesia from Prussia and over French and British colonial issues in North America and India.

The Renaissance, the Hanseatic League, and the Elements of Unity

There were exceptions to European disunity and disintegration after the Reformation and during and after the Thirty Years War. The Renaissance (fifteenth and sixteenth centuries) and the Enlightenment (seventeenth and eighteenth centuries) were European phenomena that did not stem the tide of interstate conflict but did make Europe and its common civilization a base of influence on a global scale.

During the Renaissance, Europeans rediscovered classical learning and languages. The flourishing of learning, thought, art, literature, cultural heritage, and science was accompanied by the establishment of great universities. By the time of the Renaissance, the old feudal order was giving way to a new European economic system—mercantilism—in which states actively traded in preindustrial products (precious metals) and sought colonies to further their trade goals. In pursuit of state interests based on *raison d'état*, governments subsidized and otherwise supported privileged firms to attain export markets.

The Enlightenment challenged assumptions about religion, science, the rights of the governed, and the legitimacy and distribution of political power. It is no accident that the Hanseatic League (1159–1669), a nonsectarian trade organization of independent sovereign cities, grew to prominence and enjoyed success at the height of the Renaissance and then was eclipsed by the rise of the modern state system and changes in international trade. The league, influenced by the Renaissance and by the new openness to change, helped spread ideals of the Renaissance. The league thought and acted in European terms. Its members and their trading partners stretched from London, Bergen, and Lisbon in the west to Novgorod in Russia in the east. Its seven major city-state members secured and enjoyed tariff cuts with one another and with others with whom the league negotiated preferred terms of trade. Trade in salt, herring, cloth, and tin were among the commodities of interest to the member cities. The development and eventual eclipse of the Hanseatic League by modern centralized European states are described in box 1.2.

The Industrial Revolution of the 1750s, which led to the growth of new factories and industries, such as textiles, and the eventual use of breakthrough technologies (mass production as in steel), was accompanied by a new European economic system. Capitalism, first analyzed in Adam Smith's *Wealth of Nations*, emerged from mercan-

Box 1.2.   Rise and Eclipse of the Hanseatic League

The Hanseatic League established a European trading order whose market objectives and many of whose city-state members are present in today's European Union. There was tariff-free trade among the city-states of the league. The league had agreements with other cities that provided for some tariff cuts and other means to free trade, but also allowed monopolies in certain areas.

Like the EU, the league preferred diplomacy as the primary means of dispute settlement (war disturbed trade). Unlike the EU, the league at times condoned the use of force by its traders to open up new markets, and had no centralized bureaucracy and authority but instead was a diffuse organization of trading entities supported by their city-state governments.

The eventual decline of the Hanseatic League was caused by the rise of modern nation-states that imposed rule on the league cities; the loss of cuts from certain tariffs and the end of monopolies; and the decline of trade in raw materials in favor of manufactures. Modern centralized states assumed the commercial functions of the old Hanseatic League by offering special treatment and protection for privileged firms to seek and maintain markets in Europe and abroad. The economic system by which newly centralized state governments actively supported the foreign commerce of their major economic units became known as mercantilism, which lasted roughly from the mid-sixteenth century to the start of the Industrial Revolution 200 years later.

In this new European-wide economic order, governments of such states as the Netherlands provided special treatment, such as tax breaks and subsidies, to companies like the Dutch East Indies Company, in order to expand foreign trade as a priority of the state. Mercantilism replaced the less modern commercial forms of the league. Over the next couple of centuries, a small class of merchants and craftspeople gained more importance in the economy of European cities. They and unskilled workers who migrated to European cities from the countryside began to form the pool of labor that, together with capital and technology, made possible the Industrial Revolution in an increasingly urbanized Europe.

tilism. A capitalist economy is one in which the relationship between supply and demand determines prices and production. In other words, market forces, not centralized governments, regulate economic activity.

The Industrial Revolution as a European phenomenon aided in establishing a European economy in the eighteenth and nineteenth centuries, but it also introduced much more deadly instruments of war. In addition, due to the Industrial Revolution, interstate conflict focused on regions of Europe rich in raw materials needed to fuel or build industry, such as coal, steel, and iron along the Franco–German frontier. New breakthroughs in transportation (rail, steamship) and communication (telegraph) brought European states closer together, but states also used these technologies to establish control over colonies and to fight one another. For better or worse, Europe became the fulcrum of a global economy enabled by its technological prowess to impose European rule on and exploit much of the rest of the world. The European Union today is an advanced industrial and service-oriented economy with roots in the Industrial Revolution. The economic system of its member states is a substantially refined variant of eighteenth-century capitalism—that is, social market economics (known also as social democracy), in which the government intervenes fairly broadly in the market to achieve social goals, such as health care, education, and the protection of the environment.

REVOLUTION, WAR, AND PEACE

The 1789 French Revolution propagated the Enlightenment's liberal principles of individual rights and freedoms and of representative government, which were at odds with the conservative-absolutist German, Austrian, and Russian monarchies. These states feared the liberal tide in their own countries and sought to turn back revolution. In the early nineteenth century, Napoleonic France sought to export its revolutionary ideas to the rest of Europe and, at its zenith, either conquered or brought into its sphere of influence all of non-Russian Europe except parts of Iberia, the British Isles, and a few other pockets of fully independent states, as depicted in map 1.4.

Napoleonic France introduced on a European scale its own legal system (Napoleonic Code) and the principle of a meritocracy—that government jobs would be open to applicants based on merit rather than on privilege or by sale—for the newly centralizing bureaucracies of the European states. The prevailing European economy based on Feudalism, or the remains thereof, was largely put to rest in France during the revolution and in those countries that Napoleon occupied or influenced. In other words, Napoleonic France not only engineered a political and military conquest of Europe but drove major continental economic changes as well. Regional and local economies were merged into modern national economies; national tariffs and import quotas were raised to protect domestic production; a uniform system of weights and measures was established, as were new legal rules for trade; new infrastructure was constructed in the national economies; serfdom was abolished; and citizenship was granted to European Jewry. (Russia ended serfdom in 1861.)

The forced unity France tried to bring to Europe was met eventually by a successful coalition of powers (Austria, Britain, Prussia, and Russia) that forced the French back within their prewar borders by 1814–1815. Estimates of combined French civilian and military deaths during the 1799–1815 Napoleonic Wars range from 500,000 to 2.4 million. Russia fared very poorly, as did other countries, but figures are hard to come by. In the 1812 Russia campaign, it is estimated that only 10,000 Russian troops returned from 453,000 sent to battle. With the Napoleonic Wars over, the European powers for the first time devised a new international system based on unifying principles that provided for a long period of relative stability, principles that influence today's international system in general and occupy central features of the EU in particular. The Treaties of Paris (1814–1815) dealt with the terms of French defeat, and the Congress of Vienna (1815) was a series of conferences that gave birth to a new international order based on new principles and practices.

The Treaties of Paris restored France to its pre-Revolutionary frontiers. None of the victors sought to impose a **punitive peace** on the vanquished. France was neither

Map 1.4. Napoleonic Europe (1810)

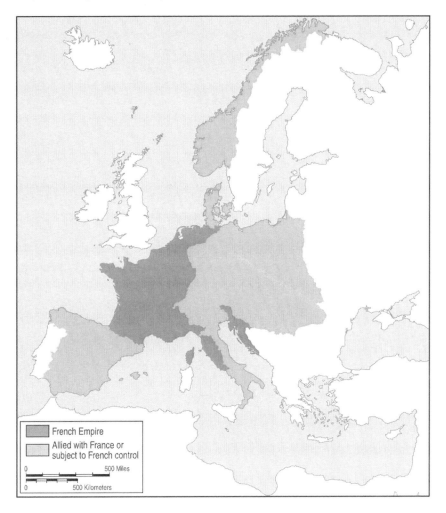

French Empire
Allied with France or subject to French control

0   500 Miles

0   500 Kilometers

partitioned in an act of revenge nor prevented from representing itself at the Vienna negotiations. As demonstrated below, this contrasts sharply with Germany's treatment of France in 1871 and France's treatment of Germany in 1919. Even though France had ridden roughshod over Europe for fifteen years, none of the victors questioned the right of France to exist as an independent state so long as France returned to a conservative monarchical government. The victors needed a like-minded government in France to help secure a new system based on a balance of power, which they were forming as a means to achieve stability after a long period of instability. No postwar arrangement in Europe could be made and kept without France because of its geographical and political position relative to the other major powers.

For those who preside over postwar settlements—that is, those who hover at the intersection of war and peace—the most profound lesson of the Vienna system is the prescription not to impose a punitive peace on the vanquished, for a punitive peace mortgages the postwar international order.[4] The reincarnation of the principle of a just and lasting postwar settlement came in 1951 with the reconciliation of Germany with her neighbors in the European Coal and Steel Community (ECSC). The principles of international relations introduced at Vienna that have been incorporated into and developed by the EU are listed in table 1.1. At Vienna, the eight participating states established what became known as the classical balance of power—a broad collective security model of international systems by which roughly equal major powers balance one another—and agree on a set of principles that generally manage the overall peace, such that if one of their number or another power upsets the balance achieved, the others will intervene to reestablish the balance. In short, the great powers took on the responsibility of policing one another to maintain the postwar territorial status quo, much as the UN Security Council was designed but failed to do in the Cold War period.

Vienna also established international legal norms related to modern diplomacy and diplomatic procedure and the use of force. Closely equated with the classical balance were the principles of territorial status quo and nonintervention in the internal affairs of states. The powers agreed not to accept any change in frontiers by the use of force and to avoid intervening in the domestic affairs of one another, in other words to respect each other's full sovereignty. Any breach of the territorial status quo was to be opposed by the other signatories. A German confederation was established to succeed the moribund remnants of the Holy Roman Empire and a neutral Switzerland was guaranteed.

Unlike their predecessors, the leaders of Europe also agreed to meet periodically to review the structure of peace they set up. The conference participants agreed to establish a Concert of Europe. The Europeans rehabilitated France during the first of the summits of the Concert of Europe in 1818 at Aachen, thus conjuring up the image of Charlemagne and his period of European unity a millennium earlier. Occupation troops were withdrawn, reparations were settled, and full sovereignty was returned to France. The Concert of Europe is a common ancestor of today's European Council, the summit of EU Heads of Government and State (HOGS), as well as other exercises in summitry—the G-8 and the annual EU-U.S. Presidential Summit. Alas, the Concert of Europe weakened in the 1820s when Britain removed itself from full cooperation,[5] although summits and conferences of the great powers were held intermittently in the nineteenth century, usually to prevent conflict or deal with postconflict situations. The legacy of the Concert of Europe for the European Union is not in its ultimate demise but in the establishment of the principle of interstate cooperation at the highest levels of national governments in order to maintain a structural interstate peace and address common security and other interests.

The classical balance of power provided a framework for peace and stability at the European level for ninety-nine years, although conflict between states grew after the Crimean War (see p. 27). The classical balance of power had a unifying principle, collective security—a broad commitment to maintaining overall European stability to avoid another pan-continental conflict. Vienna advanced the principle of sovereign equality, by which the large states accepted the participation of smaller states. At Vienna, France and the Quadruple Alliance members (Britain, Austria, Prussia, and Russia) were joined by smaller states—Sweden, Portugal, and Spain. Seven of the eight participants at Vienna joined the EU a century and a half later. The EU today consists of many more smaller member states than larger ones, and each state, no

Table 1.1: Principles of International Relations and Organizations Established in 1815: Legacy for the European Union

Principles	Objectives	Legacy for European Union
(Classical) Balance of Power	prevent war/promote stability	war made unfathomable among EU members
territorial status quo	no borders changed by force	war made unfathomable among EU members
no punitive peace	establish new stable postwar order	Franco-German reconciliation
reintegrate the vanquished	establish new stable postwar order	Franco-German reconciliation
nonintervention in internal affairs	protect state sovereignty	national veto in EU Council of Ministers
Concert of Europe	police the peace	European Council
interstate summitry	regularize meetings of leaders	European Council
sovereign equality	rights of small states honored	influence of small states; national veto
functional cooperation	respond to human needs collectively	multiple sectors of policy integration
international organization	establish means to promote cooperation	European Commission
collective security	commitment to common security	preference for multilateral conflict prevention
international legal norms	codification of rules of diplomacy, neutrality	European Court of Justice
ideology of the like-minded	promote conservative authoritarianism	requirement of market economy/political pluralism

matter how small, has the right to exercise the national veto when it feels compelled by its vital national interests.

Vienna introduced modern international organization. The first international functional organization was set up at Vienna: the Central Commission for the Navigation of the Rhine, which was designed to ease trade by eliminating tolls among the eight countries through which the Rhine ran. The Central Commission meets the conventional definition of **international organization**: an organization of three or more member states who together address a common need or function. The organization has a permanent base, with international civil servants who do not report to member governments, and it holds periodic or regular meetings. The Central Commission for the Navigation of the Rhine is the common ancestor of all subsequent international organizations, including the European Union.

The international functional bodies of the nineteenth century flowed from the Rhine River Commission: the Central Commission for the Control of the Danube (1856), the International Telegraphic (now Telecommunications) Union (1865), and the Universal Postal Union (1874), among others. The League of Nations sought to relate these and other new functional bodies, such as the International Labor Organization (1919), to one another under the League of Nations rubric but did not succeed. However, the UN Charter of 1945 folded most international functional bodies into its Economic and Social Council. The EU is also an heir to these nineteenth- and early twentieth-century functional bodies, albeit with more sophistication and breadth than its ancestors.

Political ideology was present at Vienna just as it was at the EU's founding. The Vienna protagonists, with the exception of Britain, were all conservative authoritarian monarchies, many dynastically interrelated and most of them eager to stem the tide of democracy and liberalism unleashed by the French Revolution. Three of the four great powers, Prussia, Austria, and Russia, were members of the Holy Alliance designed to perpetuate Christian authoritarianism in Central and Eastern Europe. When liberal revolutions took place in Europe in 1830 and 1848, Germany's conservative princes and kings—and the despots of Austria and Russia—suppressed the purveyors of democratic change rather than move toward constitutional monarchies and parliamentary systems, as was happening elsewhere in Western Europe, particularly in the Low Countries, Britain, and France. The EU founders were all anticommunist pluralistic democracies supportive of social market capitalism.

The nineteenth century was a century of technological change that brought Europeans closer to one another. Discovery of the telegraph (1832) revolutionized international communication. International banking continued to fuel cross-border trade and investment, and international transportation made Europe seem smaller, with many positive effects. Expansion of the railway also added to the upsurge in international interdependence among the European states. However, the economic interdependence that grew among European states did not stem the tide of war in 1914, and one would be naive to think that interdependence alone is the future guarantor of European or universal peace.

Repeal of the British Corn Laws in 1846 lifted restrictions on agricultural imports to ease exports of British manufactures. This began to free up international trade through the end of the nineteenth century. Indeed, trade liberalization (reductions in tariffs and other barriers to trade) occurred between such countries as France and

Britain with the entry into force of the Cobden-Chevalier Treaty (1860). The treaty reduced all British import tariffs for French products (except wine) and granted French industry access to less expensive and higher quality British iron and coal. French import tariffs for British goods, such as pig iron, were reduced to no more than 25 percent. More significantly, however, was the treaty's inclusion of a most-favored-nation treatment, or MFN clause—a commitment not to offer nonsignatories terms of trade better than those they offered one another. This principle of nondiscriminatory trade was later enshrined in the General Agreement on Tariffs and Trade (GATT, 1947), the forerunner of today's World Trade Organization (WTO). The Cobden-Chevalier Treaty stimulated other trade liberalization treaties between European states in this period, and as a result, Europe enjoyed an increase in trade.

The rise and spread of nationalism in mid-nineteenth-century Europe eroded the Vienna compact and the French, Piedmont/Italian, Russian, Prussian/German, Serbian, and Austrian leaderships began undermining the international system that had helped keep peace and stability for a half-century. The balance of power showed its first crack in the Crimean War (1854–1856). Russia invaded Turkey; Britain and France came to the defense of Turkey to defeat Russia in order to regain the delicate balance of power in the eastern Mediterranean. Crimea undermined but did not end the classical balance of power. France began to weaken the classical balance of power system on which its own security was based when its power was enhanced at the expense of Russia's. As the next section shows, the balance of power system was so eroded that no great powers bothered to reestablish the system when France and Germany went to war a few years later.

EXTREME NATIONALISM AND DISINTEGRATION

Early in the nineteenth century a structure of peace based on the classical balance of power, collective security, and international cooperation was tried after a pan-European war. The Vienna system eschewed close military alliances, since the Great Powers would themselves manage the peace and challenge each other if one tried to upset the classical balance of power. The results were relative peace and stability for several decades and no pan-European war for ninety-nine years. As this section shows, in the century's twilight and at the dawn of a new one, the Europeans at The Hague tried again to manage the peace, but their efforts were not enough to stem the tide of war. Between the 1880s and the early twentieth century, European collective security was replaced by an international system based on collective self-defense alliances whose secretive terms bound signatories to aid one another when facing enemy mobilization or attack. In stark contrast to the classical balance of power, the system based on collective self-defense fragmented Europe in ways that did not enhance overall security.

Europe was again at war with itself in 1799–1815 (Napoleonic Wars) and 1914–1918 (World War I). In these instances, there was no external threat to the security of Europe. Disunity and disintegration brought about cataclysms resulting in efforts to reclaim unity and stability. The Vienna system lasted ninety-nine years; its successor, the League of Nations, lasted twenty.

The rise and spread of extreme forms of nationalism put further distance between the unity of the Vienna system and the disunity associated with the behavior of increasingly nationalistic states. Nationalism refers to the affinity of a nation—people united by such common features as geography, ethnicity, history, religion, and language—to its state. In its moderate form, nationalism helps states to develop a central economy, common political institutions, and a common security capability. However, in its immoderate form, **extreme nationalism** is a major cause of interstate conflict. Extreme forms of nationalism or hypernationalism that can trigger war include chauvinism (a nation thinks it is superior to another), irredentism (a nation-state uses force to conquer surrounding areas in other states where ethnically related people live), and colonialism (a nation-state uses force to conquer and exploit a weaker nation or nation-state).

By the time of the French Revolution in 1789, post-Westphalian states had begun to evolve into modern nation-states as we know them today. German and Italian national unification occurred by 1870–1871. The unleashing of independent states in pursuit of their own interests (known as *raison d'état*), largely oblivious to the common European interests (such as stability and peace), produced the dangerous excesses of national chauvinism that led in time to the twentieth-century world wars. Newly centralized powerful states in pursuit of empire building at home and abroad had no interest in the type of international cooperation introduced after 1815, 1919, or 1945. There were no international organizations. International legal norms were limited.

National unification in Italy, Serbia, and Germany put Europe on a trajectory of war because these new nationalistic powers disturbed the territorial status quo on which the 1815 classical balance of power was in part based. Italy unified in the 1860s through a series of wars. For example, in the 1859 Austro–Piedmont War, Austria attacked Piedmont, but Piedmont won with the aid of France and went on to unify all of northern Italy at Austria's expense. Full unification occurred by 1870 with the fall of the papal states. Serbia gained independence from Austria in 1878, but the spread of pan-Slavism (or Slavic nationalism), at the expense of Austria-Hungary, fueled the flames of the Balkan wars leading up to Gavrilo Princip's assassination of Archduke Ferdinand, heir to the throne of Austria-Hungary, which in turn triggered World War I.

At first, German national unity took the approach of economic integration with the establishment of the Zollverein in 1834 (which served as a prototype for the EU and other modern international functional organizations).[6] German political union followed in 1871, but not before three wars of German national unification. In the 1864 Prussian–Danish War, Prussia attacked Denmark and forced it to cede Schleswig-Holstein. In the 1866 Prussian–Austrian War, Prussia eliminated Austrian influence in the German Confederation. In the 1870–1871 Franco–Prussian War, Prussia goaded France into war and, to the surprise of France and Europe, defeated the French. Approximately 162,000 French soldiers were killed. The classical balance of power broke down as a functioning international system because its core principles were ignored by a great power.

The 1871 Treaty of Frankfurt, which ended the Franco–Prussian War, was a French disaster. The French were forced to cede Alsace-Lorraine to Germany, and in the Hall of Mirrors at Versailles—seat of French national culture—the German victors proclaimed the unity of the new German Empire. The loss of these two provinces was the source of the French revenge that would be played out against Germany in 1919 when the roles of victor and vanquished were reversed. The Germans violated the principles of the Vienna system by disturbing the territorial status quo and by extension the classical balance of power overseen by the Great Powers. German unification was orchestrated in a way that hammered the first nail into the coffin of nineteenth-century European unity. The second nail was World War I.

Secret military alliances contravened the classical balance of power system. The Triple Alliance (Germany, Austria, and Italy—the Central Powers) and the Triple Entente (Britain, France, and Russia—the Allies) committed the signatories to the defense of allies should they be attacked. Henry Kissinger argues that it was ironic that the Vienna system, which was so generous to France and which provided it with stability and security after the defeat of Napoleon, would be undermined by his nephew, Louis Napoleon, a few decades later.[7] France undermined its own and European security by aiding Piedmont to weaken Austria. By weakening Austria, France emboldened Prussia to push Austria out of the German Confederation. In turn, an increasingly confident Prussia turned against France. By 1871, German national unification trumped Prussia's earlier adherence to the old classical balance of power.

By the late nineteenth century, the return to economic and political nationalism and interstate rivalries was accompanied by a new increase in trade protectionism even though the Europeans were more economically interdependent in 1914 than they had ever been before. Economic growth began to ebb around 1870, and European governments retreated to new actions of trade protectionism. Germany's victory in the Franco–Prussian War upset not only the balance of political/military power in Europe but the balance of economic power as well. International trade in goods continued, but more slowly after 1870 than before, due to the trade protectionism of economically nationalist states in the late nineteenth century.

The Anglo–German naval arms race, the overall arms race in Europe, and Anglo–French colonial rivalries, exacerbated by an increasingly restless Germany abroad, put further pressure on the unity established at Vienna and brought Europe closer to another pan-continental bloodletting. Tsar Nicholas II called for an international assembly of states in 1899 to respond to the skyrocketing arms race and other international tensions. The Hague Peace Conferences of 1899 and 1907 were the first global peacetime conferences. Twenty-seven states were represented at the 1899 conference, and forty-four at the 1907 conference. Large and small states were present, and small states played an active role. The Hague participants established a Permanent Court of Arbitration to compel (but not require) members to settle interstate conflicts by peaceful means; outlawed what we now recognize as chemical weapons and their means of delivery; and updated and revised customary laws on the rules of war. The Hague signatories banned the use of balloons as a vehicle to project explosives and banned the use of bullets that expand or flatten easily in the human body. Submarine mines that exploded on contact were banned as well. However, little else was achieved in terms of disarmament.

Although the Hague system did not stem the slide toward war, it did establish legal and diplomatic precedents for international cooperation to follow. The notions of conflict prevention, disarmament, peaceful settlement of disputes, and sovereign equality of states are those that would characterize the EU and the UN systems. Even though a third Hague conference was scheduled for 1915, there was too little unity to prevent the outbreak of war in 1914. However, the Hague conferences served as a bridge between Vienna and Versailles and the creation of the world's first permanent global international organization—the League of Nations.

Austria-Hungary held Serbia responsible for the assassination of the Archduke Ferdinand in Sarajevo in 1914. Germany supported Austria, a Triple Alliance ally, in its war against Serbia. Both Germany and Austria failed to take into account the impact of war on Russia's vital interests in the Balkans, where it was considered a protector of its cousins, the southern Slavs. National pride and arrogance, coupled with Austrian and Russian insecurity—at a time when these multinational empires were crumbling—fueled the rush to war. Once Russia mobilized against Austria, and Germany and Russia were at war, Britain and France—Triple Entente partners—were obliged to aid Russia. Triple Alliance members Austria and Italy were obliged to aid Germany. The United States entered the war on the side of the Triple Entente in April 1917, but by late 1917 Russia bowed out because civil war was raging in that country. By 1918, the Western allies defeated Germany. However, since it was not a total defeat, much of the German rightist authoritarian military class remained intact to ally later with Hitler and destroy the Weimar Republic. Instead of keeping a local conflict from boiling over, highly flawed national leaders allowed a local conflict to engulf all of Europe. As in 1815, there were no external threats on which to blame the war. Europe was again at war with itself.

World War I was a common tragedy of more epic proportions than any other that Europe had seen. Approximately 9 million people died and 21 million were wounded. When the war was over and Europe lay in ruins, many wondered why it had started. Four empires collapsed: Germany, Austria-Hungary, Russia, and the Ottoman Empire. France was greatly weakened and, in its weakness and fear of a resurgent Germany, sought to isolate and punish Germany.

World War I proved to the Europeans that in the absence of international cooperation and organization and an international system of security, war can too easily spiral out of control and move from the local level to the European one. Therefore, the Europeans threw their rhetoric behind the League of Nations in 1919 as a panacea for keeping the peace. Sadly, action did not follow rhetoric. World War I should have represented, but did not, a fundamental break with the practice of international relations in Europe.

ELUSIVE UNITY AND WAR AGAIN

The League of Nations was born in the rubble of World War I, much as the Vienna system was born in the rubble of the Napoleonic Wars. In retrospect, and with the benefit of hindsight, the League was doomed from the start. The Versailles Treaty had two conflicting purposes that reflected, on the one hand, Woodrow Wilson's ideal prescription for a new world peace and, on the other, the proclivity of France and Britain to keep Germany down and out. While the treaty created the League of Nations to foster peace, it also imposed a punitive peace on Germany. Therefore, the League was tainted by association with a flawed settlement. In time the terms of the punitive peace eroded, then destroyed, the League of Nations.

Some of the terms of defeat were neither unexpected nor unreasonable relative to other postwar settlements: reparations, the return to France of Alsace-Lorraine, and temporary occupation of parts of Germany. However, the bulk of the terms humiliated and punished Germany beyond reason and sealed the fate of the League of Nations. The punitive peace imposed on France by Germany in 1871 would now come back to haunt Germany in 1919. Germany's new constitutional government, the Weimar Republic, which succeeded the German Empire, was given a diktat—Weimer had to accept the treaty terms or Germany would remain occupied. Unlike France at Vienna, Germany was not allowed to participate at Versailles. The lessons of avoiding a harsh peace were forgotten by the Germans in 1871 and by the French in 1919. The Weimar Republic was forced to sign the treaty in the Hall of Mirrors at the Versailles Palace where it had humiliated the French forty-eight years earlier. French revenge would come back to haunt France during the Nazi invasion and occupation twenty years later.

Germany was compelled to demilitarize: it was to have neither a navy nor an air force and was permitted to retain only a small army, not to exceed 100,000 soldiers. It was forced to cede its overseas colonies in the form of League mandates. More painfully, it was forced to cede easternmost Germany to Poland and the Sudetenland to the new state of Czechoslovakia. Many new states emerged from the collapse of Austria-Hungary, but they were weak and unstable and would remain so, particularly after Hitler gained power and aimed his revenge at the east. It was not until after the collapse of Austria-Hungary that scholars realized what a useful balancing and stabilizing role it had played as a multinational empire in Central Europe and as a buffer

Image 1.1. Signing of the Treaty of Versailles, Hall of Mirrors, Palace of Versailles (1919). Courtesy of U.S. National Archives

between Germany and Russia. Today, the areas once part of Austria-Hungary are either in or associated with the EU.

The Weimar Republic (1919–1933) paid for the excesses of the previous system of government although it bore no responsibility for the war. Weimar was an international pariah: it had neither patrons nor friends. Although a democratic fledgling, the first in German history, it received no special treatment from the other mature European democracies. The Weimar Republic had none of the physical and economic security enjoyed by the Federal Republic of Germany established in 1949. Jean Monnet made the case for reconciliation and integration with Weimar, but his warnings fell on deaf ears in the Government of Georges Clemenceau.

The League of Nations adopted elements of conflict prevention introduced at Vienna and the Hague: collective security, peaceful settlement of disputes, and functional cooperation. The League Covenant eschewed the secret self-defense alliances that had failed to enhance European security. Instead, the new international system was based on collective security: any attack on a League member would be considered an attack on all and would engender collective assistance for the member attacked. The League Council, designed for nine of the Great Powers, each with veto power, was a new variant of the Concert of Europe system but on a permanent legal basis. The Council's responsibility was to maintain international peace and security. It did not succeed. The League Assembly, which was inspired by the precedent of the Hague Peace Conferences, comprised forty-seven members of the League, each with veto power. The Permanent Court of International Justice succeeded the Hague's Permanent Court of Arbitration. The League Secretariat, heir to the nineteenth-century international functional bodies, provided institutional continuity. It consisted of a secretary general and a staff of international civil servants not bound by allegiance to their home governments. In short, the League was in part a process of adaptation of the primitive organizational forms and types of nineteenth-century international organizations and practices.[8]

The League of Nations started off with the rhetoric of peace and disarmament and achieved some functional accomplishments. However, it proved impotent when in the 1930s it had to confront the Italian invasion of Ethiopia, the Japanese invasions of China, and the German invasions of Austria and Czechoslovakia. The League was the world's first global permanent international organization and as such is parent to the EU and other international institutions that have picked up and sought to reconnect the tattered threads of the League's experience. The League addressed multiple functional issues, including postwar reconstruction, collection of economic data, international banking, public health, child welfare, and combating illicit traffic in drugs, pornography, and women and children. The League adopted thirty international conventions, including international regulation of railways, control of manufactured drugs, suppression of counterfeiting, simplification of customs formalities, and protection of industrial property rights.

The early interwar years saw many exercises in the rhetoric of peace, but not much action. The 1925 Locarno Treaties normalized Germany's relations with her neighbors and brought Germany into the League. Germany agreed to the territorial status quo in the west but not in the east, leaving the borders of Poland and Czechoslovakia open to question. The 1928 Kellogg-Briand Pact condemned war as a means of dispute settlement but offered nothing beyond rhetoric. The first Pan-European

Congress to promote European union, held in Vienna in 1926, founded the Pan-European Union. However, this nongovernmental movement had few followers beyond the ardent federalists.

The European economy after World War I was highly fragmented, which surely worsened the political crises that followed in Germany in the 1920s and 1930s. Fragmentation was aggravated by the increased number of new states created by the Versailles settlement in Central and Eastern Europe—each state with its own new set of barriers to trade, each with its own nationalist inclinations to solve economic problems at home by erecting barriers to trade from abroad. The gold standard in the early 1930s collapsed as Britain, followed by others, abandoned the system. Thus, even before the global economic depression of the 1930s, unemployment, balance of payments difficulties, decreasing prices, production, cross-border capital movements, and export markets fueled protectionist sentiment, decreased international cooperation, and set a dangerous tone for the hypernationalism that followed.

The stock market crash in 1929 and passage in the United States of the 1930 Smoot-Hawley Tariff Act raising import tariffs, followed by like actions in other states, introduced a new salvo of trade protectionism as the European states once again retreated to economic and political nationalism in search of solutions to the high level of economic misery resulting from the collapse of the world economy. In the Depression era, League members turned away from one another and from international cooperation to pursue national solutions to international problems. Beggar-thy-neighbor policies like trade protectionism (unilateral increases in import tariffs and the establishment of trade quotas) rose in Europe to historically unprecedented levels. Competitive currency depreciation (a lower currency relative to that of trading partners) was intended to reduce imports and raise exports. Such policies were designed to give unilateral advantage in a Hobbesian world order of zero-sum games, in which the gain of one state comes at the expense of the other.

The Versailles Treaty did not impose unity, and no major power gave its full support to the League of Nations as all major powers had done for the Congress of Vienna and its postwar settlement a hundred and four years earlier. In 1815 the Great Powers were ideologically linked and their number remained constant; in 1919 they had little in common and League Council membership was a revolving door for Germany, Japan, Italy, and Soviet Russia. The United States never joined the League it had helped to create because the U.S. Senate did not ratify the Versailles Treaty. President Wilson's forward-thinking ideas on international cooperation, collective security, disarmament, and national self-determination would have to wait for another day, but the League without the United States was much like a child without its parents. Russia joined late (once the communists gained control after the end of the civil war) and then was expelled for the 1939 invasion of Finland. Germany was not allowed to join until 1926, but Hitler withdrew in 1933 when his Third Reich replaced the Weimar Republic. Japan left in 1933, after its 1931 invasion of Manchuria. Italy left in 1937, following its invasion of Ethiopia in 1935. The leadership of the League was left to the British, who were highly ambivalent about the League to start with, and the French, who grew weaker and less secure vis-à-vis Germany as time passed.

Had Britain or the United States given France the security guarantee (against a future German attack) that it had hoped to receive after World War I, Paris might not have imposed such a harsh peace on Germany. The harshness veiled the insecurity that France felt. The government of Prime Minister Georges Clemenceau did not accept the plea of Jean Monnet to build bridges with Germany. Others in the 1920s proffered the idea of European unity, but few listened and none acted. The window of opportunity closed. Failure of the victorious allies to avoid a punitive treatment of Germany, failure to integrate Germany into the European mainstream, and failure to support German democratization stigmatized the League, weakened Weimar, and sowed the seeds of future instability.

The epitome of European disintegration that presaged World War II came at the infamous 1938 Munich Conference when expediency and appeasement replaced ethics and law. Hitler threatened to invade Czechoslovakia if the Sudetenland was not returned to Germany. Without consulting the Czechoslovak leaders, British and French Heads of Government acquiesced to Hitler's plan by which Germany would retake the Sudetenland and leave the rest of the rump state alone. The Europeans had purchased a bogus peace and the League was again prostrate. Six months later Germany invaded the rump state of Czechoslovakia. A large state again rode roughshod over a small one. Although the League Covenant prohibited collective self-defense arrangements, and instead provided for a system of collective security, by the mid-to-late 1930s Europe was again divided into military alliances: the Axis Powers (Germany, Italy, and Japan) and the Allied Powers (Britain and France).

What does the League of Nations experience say to us about European integration today? Clearly the League was largely a European organization, and France and Britain were the dominant powers. Therefore, what the Europeans decided to make of their

Image 1.2.   The Men at Munich: from left to right, Neville Chamberlain, Edouard Daladier, Adolf Hitler, and Benito Mussolini. Courtesy of German Federal Archives

creation was largely a European exercise in unity or disunity. Certainly the League's mistakes served to improve international organizations after World War II. Unlike the League's system based on unanimity, for example, voting in the EU is based on a majority in a significant number of policy areas. The EU, like the League, serves the interests of both large and small states. Today's European Commission, the EU's coexecutive, draws on the experience of functionalism and in dispute settlement that the League proffered and, like the League, continues the tradition of freeing international civil servants from national instructions so they can pursue collective interests. The League Secretariat employed a new breed of international civil servant expert, which served as a model for the thousands of such individuals who now work at today's Commission, Council Secretariat, and other institutions of the EU. Indeed, the Frenchman Jean Monnet, "who learned the skills of international service and statesmanship in wartime [World War I] coalition machinery, transferred his energy later to the League of Nations" and on to his "outstanding role in the creation and operation of the European institutions."[9] The League, in retrospect, served as a bridge between Vienna and The Hague and the UN and the EU, although it could not stop the march to another world war in 1939.

Pursuant to the Nazi–Soviet Nonaggression Pact, the Germans invaded Poland on September 1, 1939, followed by the Soviet invasion of Poland and the Baltic Republics on September 17. France and Britain declared war against Germany on September 3. In 1940, Germany overran the Low Countries, Denmark, Norway, and France. The fall of France was followed by a four-year German occupation of the north and the creation of a puppet state in the south. Britain stood alone against the scourge of Fascism until the Americans entered the war in December 1941. Most of continental Western and Central Europe came under direct German occupation or influence on a scale of forced unification similar to that of the Napoleonic era, but with more terror and evil. Germany had united most of Europe by force. Map 1.5 depicts the territorial reach of Nazi-occupied or Nazi-dominated Europe at its zenith in 1942, including German allies.

The German invasion of the Soviet Union and the American entry into the war in 1941 was the beginning of the end for the Axis Powers. The vast resources of two continental-size countries, the United States and the Soviet Union, were used together to defeat the greatest menace to humanity, but it would take three more years to achieve victory. The allied invasions of Sicily (1943) and Normandy (1944) and the Soviet offensive in Eastern Europe (1944–1945) together liberated Europe from the Nazis. The cost in lives was staggering. Statistics alone cannot convey the extent of suffering and horror that is almost beyond comprehension: perhaps as many as 50 million military and civilian deaths, including approximately 20 million Soviet citizens, 5.8 million Poles, and 4.2 million Germans, as well as 6 million Jews and 1 million Gypsies systematically murdered in concentration camps. Poland lost one-fifth of its population: 3 million Polish Jews and 3 million other Poles. The dropping of atomic bombs on Japan on August 7 and 9, 1945, ended the Pacific war. Germany and Japan suffered total defeat and were subject to occupation. Europe lay in ruins, and in the vacuum of power left by its weakened condition, power shifted to its peripheries: the United States and the Soviet Union.

World War II was another common European experience of horrific proportions. More than any other European war, it has left an indelible mark, informing and

Map 1.5.   Nazi-Occupied and Nazi-Dominated Europe (1942)

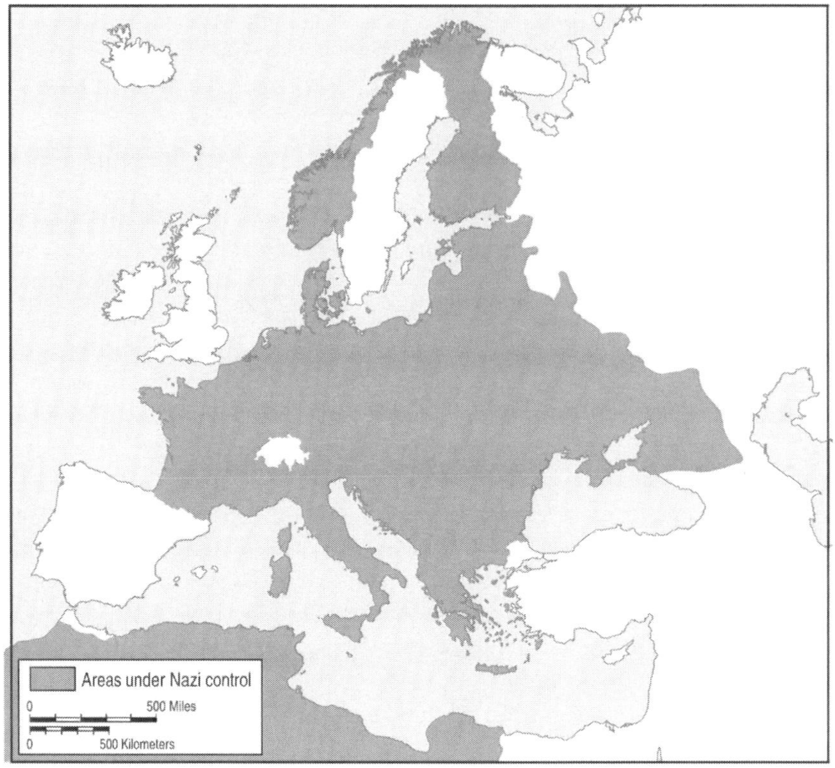

Areas under Nazi control

0   500 Miles

0   500 Kilometers

shaping the early years of postwar European integration. Even now, Europeans feel a strong aversion to war. World War II still influences EU reflexes with regard to conflict prevention and resolution and post-conflict reconstruction. Western Europeans, hearing the echoes of the past, again considered what kind of European order could avoid what had happened. They began to create a unity by voluntary means, first through the economic reconstruction process and then through economic integration. At the same time, the Central and Eastern Europeans, whom the Soviets liberated from the Nazis, were forcibly unified by their liberators into a new bloc of states, a Soviet-dominated communist empire. Just when Europe was freed from one variety of forced unity, it was divided into two unities—one voluntary, the other involuntary. This bifurcation lasted for the next forty-five years. World War II succeeded where World War I had not. It represented a fundamental break with the past. However, as the remainder of this chapter explains, while Europe lay in ruins, a new or renewed concept of peace through unity rose from the dust.

TWO UNITIES AND A COLD WAR

The breakdown of cooperation between the United States and the Soviet Union, the two allied juggernauts who together defeated the great menace posed by the Nazis,

Image 1.3.   Bombing of Cologne (1945). Courtesy of 303rd Bomb Group

meant that the postwar international system would start off with a new confrontation, which had an adverse impact on the newly formed United Nations. The UN, formed in 1945 as the successor to the League of Nations, is based on collective security but allows collective self-defense alliances if consistent with the principles of the UN Charter. The UN, like the League, brought together under one rubric new functionalist bodies designed to eschew the 1930s period of protectionism and give rise to a new era of openness, stability, and multilateralism in the global economy. These bodies included those created as a result of the 1944 Bretton Woods Conference: the International Monetary Fund (IMF), the World Bank, and the General Agreement on Tariffs and Trade (GATT). It was against this backdrop of international cooperation to solve economic and political problems that the European Coal and Steel Community (ECSC) and the European Economic Community (EEC) were established in the 1950s. Unfortunately, the advent of the Cold War—the period of mistrust and competition between the United States and the Soviet Union—stymied the working of the UN system, particularly its Security Council, where the two superpowers often vetoed each other's proposals.

Since neither the Americans nor the Soviets could agree on what to do with Germany after the war, the country was divided into occupation zones. The Soviets occupied East Germany, and the Americans, British, and French, West Germany. The United States and the Soviet Union agreed at their conferences at Yalta and Potsdam that they would occupy the areas they liberated and prepare them for democratic elections. However, rather than hold free elections, the Soviets imposed a harsh single-party communist rule. The Soviets forcibly incorporated the Baltic Republics into the Soviet Union. Yugoslavia was the only state in the Soviet sphere of influence that was able to steer clear of the control of the Soviet Union to establish an independent communist society. Using force, the Soviets established a bogus common market for its satellite states—the Council for Mutual Economic Assistance (1956–1991)—and a bogus collective self-defense organization—the Warsaw Pact (1955–1990). Anti-communist uprisings that occurred in Hungary in 1956 and Czechoslovakia in 1968 were suppressed by Soviet and Warsaw Pact forces. The Soviets cut off land access to West Berlin (1948) and built the Berlin Wall (1961) to keep East Germans from escaping to freedom in West Berlin.

Meanwhile, the countries in the (free) western half of Europe, horrified by the excesses of World War II and the specter of Soviet expansionism, huddled together for safety in numbers. In 1948 the end of parliamentary democracy in Czechoslovakia, the last state to succumb to one-party communist rule, sent shock waves across Western Europe. Once again, an external threat catalyzed European cooperation. Western Europe stood at the confluence of its past, present, and future. It had choices: revert to the politics of disunity and disintegration; do nothing and appease the Soviet Union; or build on an old tradition of unity and integration based on voluntary consent. There was much at stake.

Talk of unity had begun during World War II. In June 1940 an Anglo–French Union was proposed by Jean Monnet to Winston Churchill and Charles de Gaulle, given the desperate situation in Europe and the need to cooperate against the common enemy. The proposal was quickly rendered moot by the fall of France. As early as 1944, the exiled governments of Belgium, the Netherlands, and Luxembourg agreed to form the Benelux Customs Union (1948), a forerunner of the European Union. The ideals of European unity gained momentum in the mid-to-late 1940s. Churchill's thinking in 1946 captured the threat Europe faced from Communism and the vision it needed to meet that threat. In his famous Fulton, Missouri, speech, Churchill warned of an "iron curtain" that was descending across and dividing Europe. In his equally famous Zurich speech, he called for a "kind of United States of Europe."[10] A United States of Europe never materialized, but the free Western European states went on to create new functional institutions, including the Organization for European Economic Cooperation (OEEC, 1948), the Council of Europe (1949), the Western European Union (1955), and the European Economic Community (EEC, 1957)—each discussed in the next section. These institutions served to build up a Western European economy on which today's EU is based. While Western Europe prospered, Central and Eastern Europe stagnated, as did Greece, Portugal, and Spain.

In the late 1980s, failure of the communist system to provide for basic economic needs and freedom of political expression again served to stir unrest and dissatisfaction in the Soviet bloc. As the Soviet Union under Mikhail Gorbachev sought to institute economic and political reforms, new thinking in foreign policy resulted in a key decision in 1988–1989 that led to the collapse of Communism in Central and Eastern Europe. In 1989 the Soviets did not stop the opening of the Hungarian–Austrian border to tourists and refugees and did not put down demonstrations in Poland and Germany. Nor did they prevent the demonstrations in East Berlin that resulted in the tearing down of the Berlin Wall on November 9, 1989. The Soviet bloc countries were free to establish their own political systems. The two Germanies united in November 1990, bringing East Germany into the EU. All-German free democratic elections were held. Subsequently, many of the former Soviet bloc countries joined NATO and the EU between 1995 and 2004.

For the first time in its history Europe was unifying across much of the continent by voluntary means. Europe was largely at peace, although the euphoria of unity was shattered when Yugoslavia unraveled in 1991–1995. Ethnic cleansing was in stark contrast with everything for which the EU stood, and EU diplomacy was not enough to end the conflicts in BiH, Serbia, and Croatia, and later in Kosovo (1999) without NATO air strikes. However, since then, the conflicts have subsided, and the EU is the leading force for reconciliation and reconstruction in BiH and Kosovo. Since the late 1990s, the EU and NATO have been playing an increasingly complementary role, based on cooperation and coordination, in the Western Balkans. To understand how the European Union became the lead player in promoting peace, stability, and reconciliation in Central and Eastern Europe, we go back sixty years to the run up to and early period of modern European integration.

The Reflex to Cooperate: Early Modern European Integration, 1947–1957

The establishment of the European Coal and Steel Community, the ECSC, was such a unique and fortuitous confluence of events and personalities that absent any one of them the EU might not have been born when it was. Once again external threats to and pressures on European security stimulated a collective response—a **reflex to cooperate**. The postwar Soviet threat to Western Europe, the uncertain future of Germany's place in Europe, the Cold War, and the Korean conflict together catalyzed the Western Europeans and the Americans to form collective self-defense alliances. External pressure came from the United States, which advocated Franco–German reconciliation over the opposition or doubts voiced by French and West German public opinion, and supported German rearmament in the wake of the outbreak of the Korean conflict. Military cooperation preceded and in many respects provided a security framework for economic integration.

International systemic change alone did not result in the creation of the ECSC and the EEC. Individual leaders mattered. The vision of individuals, such as Jean Monnet and his collaborators, and the remarkable chemistry that existed between Robert Schuman and Konrad Adenauer—two Catholics from the Franco–German border areas with a common hatred of war—fostered change. Absent any one of these three men, one cannot be certain that the birth of the ECSC would have happened or would have happened when it did. The need to respond to change in Franco–German relations at a time when all of Western Europe faced a common threat triggered an old European reflex to cooperate that predated the 1870–1945 Franco–German cycle of war and revenge. Schuman and Adenauer, and the other leaders of the ECSC, were individuals who put the logic of integration into practice when the ghosts of Europe's past came back to haunt. Had the Western Europeans chosen disunity over unity when faced with common threats and pressures, regional integration might not have taken root, West Germany might have failed the test of democratic transition, the Americans might not have given security guarantees and reconstruction aid, and the Soviets might have successfully expanded their influence or presence deep into countries such as Italy, Greece, and Turkey. An indigenous logic of integration and unity hewn from the collective European memory and experience provided the cornerstone upon which the European Union was constructed. Postwar European integration was born of legacy and of chance. Although the logic of integration appeared intermittently over the course of European history, there was nothing deterministic and linear about postwar regional integration.

COLLECTIVE SELF-DEFENSE AND THE UNITED STATES

Between 1945 and 1946 there was hope that the United States and Soviet Union would carry their wartime cooperation into the postwar period. However, by 1947 it was clear to the United States (as it had been to Churchill a year earlier) that an iron curtain had indeed fallen across Europe, that the United States had to fill the power vacuum left as a result of the collapse of European power in the world, and that an ideological battle, the Cold War, would ensue between the West and the East. The Cold War certainly hastened Western European economic reconstruction and the acceptance by West Germany's neighbors of its place in the postwar regional political economy. One by one, the Soviets snuffed out democratic forces in the countries of Central and Eastern Europe, from the forced merger of the social democratic party with the Soviet-backed communist party in East Germany in 1946 to the end of representative democracy in Czechoslovakia in 1948.

An immediate concern that preceded economic integration was the Western European security situation as the reality of the Cold War settled in by 1947–1948. Western European states were concerned about Soviet expansionism and uncertainty over Germany's future. Collective self-defense was the first area of regional cooperation. The Anglo–French Dunkirk Treaty (1947) was a collective self-defense pact (an attack on one member was considered an attack on all), in which the two states sought double containment of the Soviet Union and Germany. France finally received the security guarantee against a German attack that it had hoped Britain or America would give in 1919. The Dunkirk Treaty was extended to the Benelux states in the Brussels Treaty in 1948.

The British Navy had been the main provider of security in the eastern Mediterranean prior to World War II. Before and after the war, the Greeks and Turks depended on Britain as a barrier against the spread of Russian and then Soviet naval power in the region. In 1947, with Greece engaged in a struggle against Communism and with Turkey resisting Soviet pressures in the Turkish straits, both countries turned to Britain for aid. Weakened by the war and struggling to maintain security in its own region and in its empire, Britain turned to the United States for help. The United States responded on March 12, 1947, with the Truman Doctrine, by which it would provide military aid to countries at risk of Communism. It was thus from Britain that the United States took over as security provider for the region.

When the Western allies unified the currencies used in their occupation zones of Germany into a single currency (the Deutschmark) to fuel economic growth, the

Soviets responded with a land blockade of West Berlin in June 1948. This prompted the United States to begin the Berlin Airlift to bring food and medicine into the beleaguered city, an effort that lasted until the Soviets ended the blockade in May 1949. In the same year, the United States and nine European countries plus Canada established the North Atlantic Treaty Organization (NATO), a collective self-defense pact. Concerned with the security vacuum in Europe and the threat of Soviet expansionism, the United States gave its first ever security guarantee to countries outside the western hemisphere as a central feature in the new U.S. policy of containing Communism. NATO sought "double containment"—that is, containment both of the Soviet Union and Germany, since no one then knew what the future held for Germany. Would it again threaten the peace of Europe?

At first NATO was a piece of paper, a treaty, and its main provision was Article 5—collective self-defense. An attack on one member in the NATO alliance would be considered an attack on all members, who would offer their assistance. When the Korean conflict broke out in 1950, the eastern flank of NATO seemed more exposed to the spread of Communism. The United States and NATO began to station NATO troops in Western Europe in the 1950s, and the U.S. Government called for German rearmament as a bulwark against the spread of Communism. The United States began to envisage the replacement of occupation troops in Germany with NATO troops. It was during this early Cold War period of heightened military insecurity that Western European military cooperation and economic integration became imperative.

REGIONAL ECONOMIC INTEGRATION, THE SCHUMAN PLAN, AND THE UNITED STATES

By 1947 it had become clear to the United States that if it did not act to jump-start the European economy, the communists would gain a political foothold in Western Europe. On June 5, 1947, Secretary of State George C. Marshall delivered a speech at Harvard University that outlined the objectives of a new U.S. policy for European reconstruction. Named after him, the Marshall Plan, known formerly as the European Recovery Program, featured the following political and economic objectives:

- hasten the economic reconstruction of Europe by reviving production, reducing monetary restrictions, and liberalizing trade in order to capture economies of scale;
- situate reconstruction programs, previously based on national plans, on a European scale with joint programs—financed by the United States—across national frontiers, including the occupation zones of western Germany;
- convince the Europeans that German economic revival was not a threat, but rather in the interests of each of the European states;
- foster Franco–German reconciliation and lay the foundations for the acceptance of a future West German state integrated into the European democratic mainstream;
- fill the vacuum of power left as a result of the collapse of Germany and the weakening of the United Kingdom and France;
- sow the seeds of European economic and political cooperation and unity as a bulwark against the spread of communist subversion and Soviet expansionism;
- expand access to European markets for U.S. goods; and

• foster a multilateral liberal world trade order starting with trade liberalization in Europe.

The Marshall Plan was approved by the U.S. Congress as the Economic Recovery Act of 1948. In that legislation, Congress saw in Europe some of the same possibilities for continent-size economic growth and development enjoyed by the United States in its domestic market. Congress recognized that economic cooperation in Europe was essential for lasting peace and prosperity.[11] During the life of the Marshall Plan (1947–1951), the United States transferred approximately $12.5 billion to the countries of Western Europe to hasten economic reconstruction, with one proviso: that the Europeans organize themselves to cooperate in reconstruction projects.[12] Box 1.3 features

Box 1.3. The Marshall Plan and Interstate Reconciliation

The Marshall Plan was both a response to the danger of and a contributor to a divided Europe. The United States conditioned Marshall Plan aid on cooperation among all the European states, including the occupation zones in Germany, to (a) jointly develop reconstruction projects on a cross-border basis; and (b) liberalize intra-European trade. The Marshall Plan was offered to the Soviet bloc but was rejected by Moscow, which concluded that the Americans were trying to dominate Europe. Without access to American economic reconstruction aid, Soviet bloc states would lag behind the prosperity enjoyed by the Western Europeans in the 1950s.

The Marshall Plan recipients formed the Organization for European Economic Cooperation (OEEC) in 1948 to engage in coordination of aid and related projects. Although the United States had hoped the OEEC would become the driving engine of a united Europe, the Europeans established the OEEC as an intergovernmental body, which meant all important decisions were left to the member governments, who acted together on the basis of unanimity.

The Americans were keen to foster a sense of "European interests" in ensuring the success of economic reconstruction on a collective basis. The Europeans, to the contrary, were more interested in focusing reconstruction in the national context. However, the Marshall Plan and the OEEC fostered a new way of thinking in Franco–German relations and in the international relations of Western Europe. The American pressure on France and Germany to reconcile in the context of cross-border reconstruction projects helped to break down ancient habits. From 1947 to 1951, the United States spent approximately $12.5 billion in loans and grants in the European Recovery Program. It was the largest transfer of resources from one region of the world to another in history until German unification in the 1990s.

The Marshall Plan helped lay the basis for the Schuman Plan and the European Coal and Steel Community that followed. It supported indigenous European efforts to foster interstate reconciliation through economic integration. As it turned out, the ECSC, not the OEEC, became the driving engine of regional integration in Western Europe. However, today's European Union is heir to the legacy of cooperation fostered by the ideals and resources of the Marshall Plan.

a brief discussion of the importance of the Marshall Plan for the economic reconstruction of Western Europe. As it turned out, the Marshall Plan was an important instrument to cultivate interstate conciliation among ancient adversaries.

The Council of Europe was established to promote human rights and freedom. Its creation was inspired by the deliberations of the Hague Congress (1948), a meeting of nongovernmental representatives who established the European Movement to promote the ideals of a federal Europe. In its Convention on Human Rights, the council members agreed to prohibit torture and outlaw capital punishment. The members established the European Court of Human Rights (1958) in Strasbourg. In retrospect, neither the OEEC nor the Council of Europe turned out to be the driving engine of postwar European integration as some had thought they would be. Both remained strictly intergovernmental bodies, in which each member retained veto power. As a result, because they lacked decisionmaking flexibility, their scope of action was limited by the unanimity rule. Instead, the ECSC, which provided for majority voting, was to become the stimulus to further regional integration in the 1950s. It offered a wider scope of cooperation based on flexible decisionmaking than did the OEEC and the Council of Europe.

After World War II, the Europeans had lost influence in the world. As Europe lay in ruins, power shifted to the new superpowers, and colonies clamored for independence. Faced with instability at home and threats abroad, Monnet again thought a

Image 1.4.   The Marshall Plan: From left, President Harry S. Truman, Secretary of State George Marshall, Paul G. Hoffman (Head of Economic Recovery Program), Averill Harriman (Head of Economic Cooperation Administration). Courtesy of the Truman Library/The National Archive and Records Administration

collective response was needed. The French, fighting a losing war in Indochina, deal-ing with the Soviet threat in Europe, and concerned by the long shadow of American power in Europe, wanted stability across the Rhineland, given their continuing fears over a resurgent Germany. An occupied Germany wanted to move beyond the humili-ation of defeat and to enjoy the return of state sovereignty. France tried unsuccessfully to get the Western allies to support its efforts to keep Germany in check, a policy that had failed so miserably in 1919. France's fear lay in part in the reemergence of an industrially dominant Germany. Monnet believed that if this fear could be addressed, "the greatest obstacle to a united Europe would be removed." The Franco–German problem, he decided, must become a European problem.[13]

Monnet's solution to the Franco–German dilemma was for victor and vanquished to exercise joint sovereignty over their coal and steel resources, since neither side in the past had felt secure unless it was in command of all the resources along the Franco–German frontier. Others talked of the idea of a Franco–German customs union, but none was as successful as Monnet in putting the idea into practice. Raw materials were located in abundance along or near the Franco–German frontier, and coal and steel were key to economic power in mid-twentieth-century Europe. Monnet argued that integration of these industries would establish "a common basis for eco-nomic development" as a first stage in building a Franco–German union that over time would lend itself to the realization of a federal Europe. For Monnet, there was one solution for France: put French industry on the same footing as that of Germany while freeing Germany from the discrimination born of defeat. The French Govern-ment, he thought, ought to take the lead in proposing the establishment of an interna-tional coal and steel authority.[14] Monnet and his French governmental colleagues—Etienne Hirsch, Pierre Uri, and Paul Reuter—worked on what became the Schuman Declaration (May 9, 1950). The Schuman Declaration reveals the far-reaching ideas the French Government was prepared to put into effect, as the follow-ing excerpts indicate (author's commentary has been added in italics).

> World peace cannot be safeguarded without the making of creative efforts proportionate to the dangers which threaten it. The contribution which an organized and living Europe can bring to civilization is indispensable to the maintenance of peaceful relations. In taking upon herself for more than 20 years the role of champion of a united Europe, France has always had as her essential aim the service of peace. A united Europe was not achieved and we had war.
>
> [*External dangers threaten peace, requiring a European response*]
>
> Europe will not be made all at once, or according to a single plan. It will be built through concrete achievements which first create a de facto solidar-ity. The coming together of the nations of Europe requires the elimination of the age-old opposition of France and Germany. Any action taken must in the first place concern these two countries. With this aim in view, the French Government proposes that action be taken immediately on one limited but decisive point.
>
> [*To end age-old interstate rivalries, cooperation is best pursued one step at a time to build habits of cooperation; this approach is preferred to an overnight grand federal design*]
>
> It proposes that Franco–German production of coal and steel as a whole be placed under a common High Authority, within the framework of an

organization open to the participation of the other countries of Europe. The pooling of coal and steel production should immediately provide for the setting up of common foundations for economic development as a first step in the federation of Europe, and will change the destinies of those regions which have long been devoted to the manufacture of munitions of war, of which they have been the most constant victims.

[*Franco–German cooperation would be open to other European countries and is linked to both economic development and a distant, and intentionally vaguely defined, European federation*]

The solidarity in production thus established will make it plain that any war between France and Germany becomes not merely unthinkable, but materially impossible. The setting up of this powerful productive unit, open to all countries willing to take part and bound ultimately to provide all the member countries with the basic elements of industrial production on the same terms, will lay a true foundation for their economic unification. . . .

[*Pooling of coal and steel production would take out of national hands control over the munitions of war and would be the first concrete step toward more regional integration*]

By pooling basic production and by instituting a new High Authority, whose decisions will bind France, Germany and other member countries, this proposal will lead to the realization of the first concrete foundation of a European federation indispensable to the preservation of peace.[15]

[*Sectoral economic integration is linked to European federation, which is essential to peace*]

Negotiations for the new community lasted a year. On April 18, 1951, the six charter members signed the Treaty of Paris, based on the Schuman Declaration. Coming just six years after World War II, when calamity weighed heavily on the minds of European publics and leaders, the Paris Treaty preamble was very political, and although it remained intentionally vague about the future common destiny, it spelled out a political program to achieve peace and prosperity. According to the preamble, the Heads of Government and State,

CONSIDERING that world peace can be safeguarded only by creative efforts commensurate with the dangers that threaten it,

[*The Cold War threatened another global conflagration just five years after World War II*]

CONVINCED that the contribution which an organized and vital Europe can make to civilization is indispensable to the maintenance of peaceful relations,

RECOGNIZING that Europe can be built only through practical achievements which will first of all create real solidarity, and through the establishment of common bases for economic development,

[*The preference was for a step-by-step approach to economic growth and development at the European level rather than the overnight and radical pursuit of a United States of Europe*]

ANXIOUS to help, by expanding their basic production, to raise the standard of living and further the works of peace,

[*Integration was not only about peace; it was about socioeconomic goals in social democracies*]

RESOLVED to substitute for age old rivalries the merging of their essen-

tial interests; to create, by establishing an economic community, the basis
for a broader and deeper community among peoples long divided by
bloody conflicts; and to lay the foundations for institutions which will give
direction to a destiny henceforward shared,
  [*Collective interests replace old rivalries through economic integration that
  will lay the cornerstone of a vaguely conceived shared destiny*]
  Have decided to create a European Coal and Steel Community.[16]

The Treaty of Paris was ratified by the parliaments of the six charter members (Benelux, France, Italy, and West Germany) during winter 1951 and spring 1952. In
France, the Gaullists and communists voted against the Paris Treaty, but it still passed
by a 377-233 vote. The British declined the invitation to join. Nevertheless, the six
charter states that formed the ECSC transformed the way European interstate relations had been conducted over the past several centuries.

Monnet was named the first President of the High Authority of the ECSC on
August 10, 1952. The High Authority (later called the Commission) and the Court
of Justice were the two supranational bodies of the ECSC. The former initiated and
implemented legislation and managed/regulated the new community, and the latter
interpreted the law binding on the member states. The Council of Ministers was
the intergovernmental body of the ECSC—whose members were ministers from the
member governments—with the power to decide policy. The Common Assembly
(later the European Parliament)—whose representatives were drawn from national
parliaments—had supervisory but not legislative powers. It was, however, the democratic and representative body of the people of the member states.

How did the ECSC happen and what impact did it have? In asking these questions, political scientists draw on levels of analysis (domestic, elite actor, and international system) to identify the most important explanations. The ECSC occurred when
and how it did because of interests, individuals, and the new structure of postwar
international politics. Monnet had the vision of what could and must be done, the
power to convince and compel, and an uncanny sense of timing—of knowing the
right moment to convey his ideas to politicians in a position to put them into practice.
He convinced Schuman to risk reconciliation with Germany as a matter of vital
French interests. Schuman, from Lorraine, understood Germans better than most
French and saw in the narrow window of opportunity in 1950 the chance to end the
cycle of revenge and war. Adenauer, a democrat who had survived Nazi oppression
and came from Cologne, not far from Schuman's birthplace, recognized the offer of
peace and the prospect for sovereign equality as a historic opportunity. Schuman and
Adenauer understood each other and the imperative to change. The Schuman-Ade-
nauer chemistry was a critical element in reconciliation. The ECSC may be seen as an
exercise in West Germany's integration into the economy of Western Europe and as
the critical step in the direction of the EEC that followed just six short years later.
Image 1.5 features four Titans of European integration: Robert Schuman, French
Foreign Minister; Konrad Adenauer, West German Chancellor; Jean Monnet, Presi-
dent of the High Authority of the ECSC; and Paul-Henri Spaak, Belgian Foreign
Affairs Minister and framer of the Spaak Report, which served as the basis of the
Treaty of Rome.

The United States during the Truman and Eisenhower Administrations was quick
to offer diplomatic recognition of and financial aid to the ECSC to demonstrate its

Image 1.5.   Titans of Early European Integration: Clockwise from top left: Robert Schuman, French Foreign Minister; Konrad Adenauer, West German Chancellor; Jean Monnet, President of the High Authority of the ECSC; Paul-Henri Spaak, Belgian Foreign Affairs Minister and framer of the Spaak Report, which served as the basis of the Treaty of Rome. All photos courtesy of the Audiovisual Library of the European Commission

support for integrating West Germany into Western Europe. The American leadership helped grease the axles of a new cooperative spirit between France and Germany. Monnet and his European and American interlocutors, collaborators, and friends—Schuman, Adenauer, John J. McCloy (U.S. High Commissioner to Germany), Truman, and Eisenhower—were the right people at the right place at the right time. Yet the story of the creation of the ECSC must also be contextualized as a solution to an international security dilemma.

The collapse of Europe as a center of world power, the concentration of postwar military power in Moscow and Washington, the Cold War, the threat of nuclear power (which made the struggle over control of coal and steel production pale in comparison), and the Korean conflict made the Franco–German conflict anachronistic. The Schuman Plan succeeded in part "because it gave the nations of Europe an opportunity to surmount historic antagonisms that were fast becoming irrelevant."[17] The ancient warring states of Europe had to get on with creating their space in the new postwar international order. The structure of that order and the threat to the West posed by the Soviets put the Franco–German conflict into a new perspective. There was a sea change in attitudes that broke the barriers of centuries of conflict.

Did the ECSC meet expectations for political reconciliation and economic integration? Scholars differ over the economic impact of the ECSC. Some argue that the ECSC was a success: iron and steel production rose, and coal production did better than expected, given declining market conditions. Others argue that the ECSC failed to establish its authority over the members' industries. Although coal and steel were regulated to avoid crippling shortages or chronic gluts, the overall increase in coal and steel trade had more to do with the economic boom in West Germany than with the policies of the ECSC. Historian John Gillingham maintains that the real significance of the ECSC was that it provided West Germany with a substitute peace treaty and paved the way for wider economic integration later in the decade.[18]

Overall, however, there is a broad consensus among scholars of the period that the lasting impact of the ECSC was not from its accomplishments in setting up a common market for coal, steel, and iron, the results of which were mixed and then overtaken by the EEC, but rather that it began a fundamentally new direction in Franco–German relations. The ECSC was the stepping stone toward much larger projects—the EEC in the late 1950s and the EU in the 1990s. A testimony to the American and European success in putting the Schuman Plan into practice was that by 1957, with the signing of the Treaties of Rome, the Americans were no longer active interlocutors as they had been earlier. The Europeans took ownership of the integration process. Europeans found their collective voice, and their old reflex to cooperate was put to good use. The fledgling was on its own, though still dependent on the American nuclear deterrent through NATO.

EXTENSION OF COLLECTIVE SELF-DEFENSE

In 1950, René Pleven proposed to the French Government the creation of a European army in the form of a European Defense Community (EDC). The Pleven Plan would balance the need for German rearmament (following the Korean conflict), as advocated by the United States, against European sensitivities about the German military. The EDC would allow for German rearmament in the context of a multinational European army acceptable to Germany's western neighbors and to Germans themselves. Adenauer would not permit his country to rearm unless it was on an equal footing with the rest. A European army would also strengthen the security of the fledgling European community represented by the ECSC and would enhance the

European contribution to NATO while empowering the Europeans to accept more responsibility for their own defense needs.

Each of the six ECSC members would supply troops for the European army. Pleven argued that a European army should result not from the grouping of national military units but from a single European political and military authority formed by the different European countries. The contingents furnished by the participating states would be incorporated in the European army at the level of the smallest possible unit. The military forces would serve under a European Defense Minister appointed by member governments and responsible to the ECSC parliamentary assembly and the Council of Ministers. It would have its own common budget. The European Minister of Defense would be responsible for (1) implementation of existing international obligations and the negotiation and implementation of new international engagements on the basis of directives received from the Council of Ministers; and (2) obtaining the contingents, equipment, armaments, and supplies due from each member country to the common army.

Pleven proposed his plan to the French National Assembly on October 24, 1950. Intergovernmental conferences commenced in Paris in February 1951 to sort out the modalities of a European army. The Pleven Plan became the EDC Treaty, signed in Paris on May 27, 1952, by the six ECSC governments. Britain again remained outside. Pleven proposed that within the European army there would be no specific national units larger than a battalion, hoping this would reconcile the French people to German rearmament. He was wrong. On August 30, 1954, the French National Assembly refused to ratify the treaty.

Certainly the plan for a European army was ambitious, especially with the concomitant plans to develop a European Political Community to provide a governmental umbrella for defense and economic integration. Still, five of the six signatories ratified the EDC Treaty, so the problem lay in the French body politic. In France, the EDC was opposed by two political groups: the nationalists, who opposed the supranational elements of a European army and viewed it as too intrusive of French sovereignty, and the communists, who found it unnecessary. In his memoirs, Monnet opined that the collapse of the EDC was a painful parting of the ways. Forces of the past and those of the future tore France apart, he believed, and in the confused debate the former prevailed.[19] The timing of the National Assembly's consideration of the treaty could not have been worse. In the end, Schuman did not pursue immediate ratification, and the delay gave the nationalists and communists time to gather strength when Schuman was out of office.[20]

With the collapse of the EDC and the passage of time, German rearmament became as much a necessity in 1954 as it had been in 1950 when Pleven first proposed the idea of a European army. The French grew more comfortable with the idea or inevitability of German rearmament, so even though the EDC had collapsed, there was still interest in finding a way for Germany to rearm within a Western European framework. British Foreign Minister Anthony Eden proposed in September 1954 that West Germany join the Brussels Treaty. French Prime Minister Pierre Mendes-France accepted the idea and shortly thereafter, following ratification by the French National Assembly and the other parliaments, the Western European Union (WEU) was created out of the Brussels Pact. The WEU was far less ambitious than the EDC, but far more palatable to the French. The WEU allowed for German rearmament in a collective self-defense organization that made rearmament acceptable to West Germany and Western Europe and satisfied the U.S. need for West Germany to serve as a bulwark against the spread of Communism in Europe. The quid pro quo for Bonn's joining the WEU was for all allied occupation troops to be removed from West Germany, thus returning sovereignty to Germany. Along with Italy, the Federal Republic of Germany joined the WEU in 1954 and NATO in 1955. NATO troops replaced occupation troops; thus West Germany put itself at the frontline of the Cold War. It achieved the right to have a conventional army within the WEU/NATO context, but it foreswore nuclear forces.

The most notable provision of the NATO and WEU treaties is Article 5: if any of the contracting parties is attacked, the other contracting parties will provide military and other aid and assistance. The Soviets responded to West Germany's accession to the WEU and NATO with the creation of their own military alliance, the Warsaw Pact (1955–1990). Map 1.6 depicts the extent of the Soviet domination of Eastern Europe in 1955.

NATO played a significant role in the establishment and success of modern European integration. It linked North American and Western European security interests, which in turn made the success of European regional economic integration a priority of the Atlantic Alliance. NATO provided for the security of the ECSC states against a possible Soviet attack and served as a safety valve in the event of a resumption of Franco–German hostilities. NATO was also critical for the success of the ECSC in that it provided West Germany both physical and political security at a time when its fledgling democracy needed to take root.

The collapse of the EDC and its ambitious plan for a European Political Community was viewed as a crisis for those Europeans committed to European integration, and it put Monnet back into action. However, the Europeans made a virtue of necessity. The failure of the EDC helped to launch the admission of West Germany into the Brussels Pact, and this in turn paved the way for the launching of what was to become the European Economic Community. The integration of West Germany into European and transatlantic security structures was no doubt aided by the continuing improvement of Franco–German relations, symbolized in 1955 when the French-occupied Saar was returned to West Germany after a referendum in which a majority of the Saar's citizens favored return to Germany.

THE TREATIES OF ROME

The collapse of the EDC—and limitations of the ECSC as a fulcrum for further European integration—caused Monnet to resign from the Presidency of the High Authority on November 9, 1954, to focus his attention on the next stage of European integration. In the following year, Monnet established the Action Committee for a United States of Europe to garner support in European governments and publics for a renewed commitment to European integration. The participants in the Action Committee during its twenty-year history included political leaders and representatives from major democratic political parties and noncommunist trade union federations from the six member states of the ECSC (and later from Britain).

For Monnet, attention shifted from elusive political unity to new sectors of inte-

Map 1.6. Soviet-Dominated Eastern Europe (1955)

Soviet Bloc States

Soviet Union

gration: transport and energy, particularly the problem of atomic energy for industrial use. As this new form of energy developed—and given Monnet's interest in making nuclear technology as "central to strategies of peace maintenance as it had become to those of war making"—it seemed logical for the Europeans to cooperate to avoid a new round of fresh national rivalries in a new field of armaments.[21] This approach to Europe's atomic future warranted the establishment of a new high authority for peaceful development of atomic energy. Therefore, the Action Committee started with work on atomic energy. Monnet maintained that since the atom could be used to supply energy and produce bombs, its economic and political aspects were inseparable and thus required joint regulation.

Monnet was concerned that a new European community develop atomic energy solely for peaceful purposes. His vision was for the atomic energy community to serve as a spearhead for further economic integration. The Action Committee was unanimous in its support for the atomic energy project. France, already struggling with the hefty costs of developing its nuclear capability, saw it as a guarantee of greater independence of foreign energy supplies. West Germany saw it as a way to enter the atomic age for peaceful purposes.

While the Action Committee was working on atomic energy, the Benelux states proposed a plan for a new integration initiative. The plan was based on the establishment of a customs union for the whole of the ECSC countries. Although economic and business elites were enthusiastic about a new customs union, Monnet and Belgian Foreign Minister Pierre-Henri Spaak were in favor of extending the integration process on a sector-by-sector basis, by targeting individual strategic sectors for collective regulation. The piecemeal approach was sufficiently apolitical, Monnet believed, that it would not encounter frontal political opposition from ECSC member governments.

Monnet called for a meeting of the Foreign Ministers of the ECSC and the United Kingdom to consider the Benelux plan. The meeting was scheduled for June 1, 1955, at Messina. All six ECSC Foreign Ministers met at the historic Messina conference and proclaimed in their collective declaration of June 2 that they were prepared to "take a new step on the road of European construction" by establishing a common market and a community of rules to govern the peaceful use of atomic energy.[22] The Foreign Ministers at Messina charged a committee of government representatives to submit a report on plans for a common market and an atomic energy community to the ECSC by October 1, 1955. The intergovernmental committee chaired by Spaak was charged with making a report on general union, with a focus on the field of nuclear energy. Monnet, the visionary, was also a pragmatist. He eventually relented on the customs union plan and threw his formidable energies into garnering support for the relaunch of the European project after the collapse of the EDC.

Monnet's Action Committee went into high gear to convince governments, parliaments, and public opinion that implementation of the June 2 Messina Declaration was not only desirable but the necessary next step toward a United States of Europe. Meetings of specialists worked on drafts throughout 1955 and 1956. On May 29 and 30, 1956, the Foreign Ministers, who met in Venice, approved the Spaak Report and authorized the start of intergovernmental negotiations for what led to the creation of the European Economic Community (EEC) and the European Atomic Energy Community (Euratom).

The United Kingdom, however, did not take part in the post-Messina talks, preferring instead a free trade area. On February 13, 1957, the Council of the OEEC began negotiations for what became the European Free Trade Association (EFTA) on May 3, 1960. The EFTA signatories were the United Kingdom, Austria, Denmark, Norway, Portugal, Sweden, and Switzerland.

The Spaak Report was adopted without discussion, with the exception of meeting France's demand that a future common market should include colonies and overseas territories. The reflex to cooperate was once again present when the six nations agreed to accept the Spaak Report as the basis for the Treaties of Rome creating the EEC and Euratom. The Treaties were signed on March 25, 1957 (in this book the Treaty of Rome or the Rome Treaty is used to signify the Treaties of Rome; the Rome Treaties may also be referred to as the EEC Treaty or the Euratom Treaty). The EEC Treaty aimed to establish over time a common market that would accomplish the following:

- eliminate internal customs duties and quantitative restrictions on trade among the member states;

Image 1.6.   Signing of the Treaty of Rome (1957). Courtesy of the Audiovisual Library of the European Commission

- establish a common external tariff and a common commercial policy toward third countries;
- adopt common policies in agriculture, transport, and other sectors;
- create a common competition policy;[23]
- abolish obstacles to the free movement of services, capital, and labor; and
- address the economic development needs of the member states to raise the standard of living for their citizens.

Over time, the Treaties of Rome would also establish an atomic energy community to create the conditions for the speedy establishment and growth of nuclear industries. Euratom was very much a response to external threats and pressures concerning Europe's oil dependency following the Suez War.[24] Dependence on imported oil from the Middle East encouraged Western European nations to develop and unite production of atomic energy. The Euratom Treaty aimed to accomplish the following:

- establish uniform safety and health standards;
- facilitate investment;
- make certain through supervision that nuclear materials are not diverted to purposes other than those for which they are intended;
- exercise the right of ownership to special fissile materials;
- create a common market in specialized materials and equipment;
- establish the free movement in capital for investment in nuclear energy; and
- establish relations with other countries in international organizations to foster peaceful uses of nuclear energy.

Unlike the 1951 Treaty of Paris, whose preamble spelled out a vision of a united Europe, the Rome Treaties were far less visionary in that they did not explicitly link economic integration with the goal of political unity. The Rome Treaties were completed twelve years after World War II, when there appeared to be much less urgency regarding institutionalized political cooperation, especially after the collapse of the EDC in 1954. National governments were keen to integrate economically. However, they chose to keep all the important political decisions of Europe's future in their own hands through the Council of Ministers, where they would be directly represented, rather than through what became the Commission, which would remain a largely supranational executive bureaucracy. The EEC Treaty's preamble reveals the primacy placed on economic cooperation over political union, with one exception: in the first clause the Treaty refers implicitly to a political union. However, the rest of the preamble and the Treaty focus on functional issues within a new common market: economic and social progress, improvement in working and living conditions, and economic development of backward regions. The preamble is excerpted below (with author's comments in italics).

Preamble to the EEC Treaty (1957)
DETERMINED to lay the foundations of an ever closer union among the peoples of Europe,
[*The phrase "ever closer union" serves as a catchall to the buildup of the EC/ EU institutions that were to follow*]
RESOLVED to ensure the economic and social progress of their countries by common action to eliminate the barriers which divide Europe,
[*The founders emphasized nonpolitical barriers that divided Europe*]
AFFIRMING as the essential objective of their efforts the constant improvements of the living and working conditions of their peoples,
RECOGNIZING that the removal of existing obstacles calls for concerted action in order to guarantee steady expansion, balanced trade and fair competition,
ANXIOUS to strengthen the unity of their economies and to ensure their harmonious development by reducing the differences existing between the various regions and the backwardness of the less favored regions,
DESIRING to contribute, by means of a common commercial policy, to the progressive abolition of restrictions on international trade,
[*The founders emphasized the need for the new community to have a common commercial policy, including a common external tariff, so that it could pursue with nonmembers freer trade on a global scale; common external tariffs would also protect community producers from cheap imports undermining prices*]
INTENDING to confirm the solidarity which binds Europe and the overseas countries and desiring to ensure the development of their prosperity, in accordance with the principles of the Charter of the United Nations,
RESOLVED by thus pooling their resources to preserve and strengthen peace and liberty, and calling upon the other peoples of Europe who share their ideal to join in their efforts.[25]
[*Subsequent expansions of the EC have more than tripled the size of the original six*]

With the entry into force of the EEC and Euratom Treaties on January 1, 1958, the contours of today's European Union were established and the economy of the six charter members enjoyed sustained growth and development in the 1960s and early 1970s. Walter Hallstein of West Germany became the first President of the European Commission in 1958 and remained in office until 1969. At the same time, West Germany's democracy was consolidated, interstate reconciliation in West Europe flourished, and the Soviets were kept at bay. Although it is impossible to attribute these developments to the EEC, the process of economic integration overall contributed to a more stable, secure, peaceful, and prosperous Western Europe, which in time exposed the weaknesses of the Soviet model of society and likely contributed to the containment of Communism. Although Monnet envisaged that Euratom would stimulate further regional integration in Europe, as it turned out the EEC was to become the driving engine of integration. The EEC offered the member states a scope of economic cooperation in the form of a common market on a continental scale. Such a form of economic cooperation had much broader impact on the interests of national governments than would have been provided by a single-sector enterprise represented first by coal and steel, and then by atomic energy.

The Americans, who played such a large role in the creation of the ECSC, were merely supportive of indigenous European efforts to create the new communities after Messina. The political impetus behind today's European Union started in Paris, but the real thrust behind economic and monetary union began in Rome.

Review

This chapter has demonstrated that the European Union is neither an accident of history nor a result of a deterministic and linear process. There are indeed antecedents of the EU, and the logic of integration has appeared intermittently over the course of European history. However, this does not imply that a dialectic was at play by which one antecedent was followed linearly by another. When the Europeans who occupy this small and exposed peninsula failed to band together to stave off foreign attack—in other words to achieve security in unity—they remained exposed to the perils of disunity, disintegration, and instability within and along their borders. This chapter introduced the themes of unity and disunity, integration and disintegration that have appeared in European history. The reflex to cooperate has often been triggered by external stimuli or by the imperative to create peace orders after pan-European conflagrations.

The fear of disunity and disintegration lingers in the collective European memory, yet external stimuli have not been the only drivers of internal integration. There have been times when Europe was its own worst enemy—when Europe was at war with itself—and periods of disunity and unity occurred independent of foreign threat or attack. Under conditions of internal disunity, Europe was (and still is) vulnerable to external threats. After 1945, Eastern Europe was left with no choice but to acquiesce to the totalitarian rule of Josef Stalin's Soviet Union. Half of the continent suffered from Europe at war with itself. Western Europe, facing the specter of Soviet expansionism, was left with choices about its future.

The ghosts of Europe's past returned. Facing the common threat together, the Western Europeans chose unity in numbers. The external threat again triggered the reflex to cooperate and catalyzed a new era of (Western) European integration. An indigenous logic of integration and unity hewn from the collective European memory provided the cornerstone upon which the European Union was constructed. At the same time, the Cold War provided the glue that helped unify a beleaguered Western Europe. Thus, postwar integration was born of history and of chance. In coping with international systemic change, the communist threat, and the future of Germany, individual leaders mattered very much because they put the logic of integration into practice.

What is present in today's EU was present during other periods of unity: the common denominators of geography, history, religion, economy, and civilization. However, modern European integration in the form of the EU is unlike other constructs of unity. The EU is more likely to manage periods of disunity and disintegration than were its antecedents. The most distinctive quality of European unity in the past fifty years has been that it is an association by voluntary means on a continental scale, unlike any of its previous incarnations. As this chapter demonstrated, for centuries the Europeans struggled without success to balance unity with diversity. Another remarkable feature of today's European Union is that it provides a structure of opportunity within which the balance between national and collective continental interests is determined by negotiation and compromise, not by war. Since it has made war among its member states so unlikely as to be unimaginable, the European Union appears to have finally exorcised the ghosts of Europe's past. However, the specter of disunity and disintegration continues to shape European responses to conflict and conflict resolution, and no one can ever be certain of what the future holds.[26]

With the collapse of Communism and the Soviet Union and the end of the Cold War in the years between 1989 and 1991, the two halves of Europe began to reintegrate. The two halves of Germany unified, and the former Soviet bloc countries applied for membership in the economic and security communities of Western Europe—the EU and NATO. Nearly the whole of Europe was uniting by voluntary means for the first time in its history. The next chapter examines the tectonic shifts in European and international politics unleashed by the end of the Cold War, their implications for the course of European integration, and the theories that help explain the birth and development of the EU.

Key Concepts

acquis communautaire
common denominators of European integration
extreme nationalism
international organization
punitive peace
reflex to cooperate
regional integration

Study Questions

1. In what way is the European Union neither an accident of history nor the result of a deterministic/linear process?

2. How have fears of European disunity and disintegration influenced the EU and its member states?
3. How does the EU as an "association by voluntary means" compare and contrast to the other incarnations of European unity and disunity? Limit your response to four examples and explain each.
4. What were the two major "drivers" of the European reflex to cooperate after World War II, and why?
5. In your opinion, could the ghosts of Europe's past once again threaten its unity and stability? Explain.

Selected Readings

John Gillingham, *Coal, Steel, and the Rebirth of Europe, 1945–1955: The Germans and French from Ruhr Conflict to Economic Community* (Cambridge: Cambridge University Press, 1991).

Michael J. Hogan, *The Marshall Plan: America, Britain, and the Reconstruction of Western Europe, 1947–1952* (Cambridge: Cambridge University Press, 1989).

Charles W. Kegley Jr. and Gregory A. Raymond, *Exorcising the Ghost of Westphalia: Building World Order in the New Millennium* (Upper Saddle River, N.J.: Prentice Hall, 2002).

Jean Monnet, *Memoirs* (Garden City, N.Y.: Doubleday, 1978).

Peter M. R. Stirk, *A History of European Integration since 1914* (London: Pinter, 1996).

CHAPTER 2

Theory and Practice of Modern European Integration

Preview

Chapter 1 situated modern European integration in historical context and concluded that the European Union is not an accident of history. This chapter turns to theory and practice of modern European integration by focusing on four related themes: (a) an overview of major political thinkers in history who called for the unity of Europe in order to conserve the peace; (b) an introduction to conventional political science theories of postwar European integration that drew on earlier political thought; (c) an outline of major developments in modern European integration on which to test the explanatory relevance of conventional theory; and (d) a summary of the main tenets of revisionist theories that help address the inadequacies of the earlier conventional theories based on how the EU actually evolved in recent years.

Where the reader sits theoretically determines how she or he views the EU's progress in meeting its objectives and the needs of its citizens, and how well theories have held up in predicting what the EU has become. The intersection of theory and practice is where the EU is best evaluated against the measures of its own Treaty objectives, the expectations of its citizens, the prescriptions of historical figures, and the explanations of theorists. As theory is not an afterthought of history, readers are encouraged here in Chapter 2 and throughout the volume to build their own bridges between the theory and practice of European integration.

Political Thinkers, Writers, and Statesmen: Seventeenth–Twentieth Centuries

Table 2.1 identifies major political thinkers, writers, and statesmen associated with the idea of European unity.[1] All were haunted by the need for some kind of overarching political unity; some called for federation, others for a looser association. They railed against the incessant interstate rivalries and wars that plagued Europe during and after

Table 2.1: Selected Political Thinkers, Writers, and Statesmen on European Unity, Seventeenth–Twentieth Centuries

Thinker/Statesman	Title/Profession	View/Prescription
17th Century		
Hugo Grotius	Dutch jurist, diplomat	called for society of nations; stressed importance of international law
Maximilien de Bethune	French statesman	called for European Christian federation to promote peace
William Penn	Proprietor of Pennsylvania	called for European union/parliament to keep peace
18th Century		
Charles-Irenée Castel, abbé de Saint-Pierre	French diplomat, cleric, author	conceived a European union of sovereign states to keep peace
Stanislas Leszczynski	King of Poland	called for union of European parliamentary democracies
Immanuel Kant	German philosopher	prescribed a federal Europe to ensure a "perpetual peace"
19th Century		
Friedrich von Gentz	consultant to Metternich	called for union of states under the guidance of the great powers
Henri de Saint-Simon	early socialist thinker	called for united Europe with parliament, common market
Victor Hugo	French novelist	predicted European union/parliament to preserve peace
20th Century		
Richard Coudenhove-Kalergi	federal movement founder	organized federal unity movement with customs union/security pact
Paul Valéry	French author, poet	stressed European civilization as basis for European unity
Aristide Briand	French Foreign Minister	called for European unity at League of Nations
Altiero Spinelli	Italian resistance leader	called for federal Europe while imprisoned by fascists
Winston Churchill	British Prime Minister	called for construction of "a kind of United States of Europe"
Jean Monnet	businessman, economist	inspired the Schuman Plan as first step for uniting Europe
Dwight D. Eisenhower	U.S. President	called for European federation to achieve security

the Thirty Years War and the extreme nationalism that followed. Some stressed the principles of collective security and international law and others economic integration, and some stressed both, in order to curtail the excesses of the European nation-states.

Many wrote during or in the aftermath of war or in response to an external threat that gave impetus for a united approach to common security. In searching for an antidote to war, many thinkers wrote about the need for a voluntary union of states that could draw on the heritage of a common European civilization. Such a union would end cyclical retribution among European states in conflict. Several considered or grappled with the borders of a united Europe, that is, who its members would be, and which states should provide direction for such a union, alliance, or concert.

Political thought on European unity based on voluntary association dates back at least to the fifteenth and sixteenth century, when Christian unity was being shattered and the concept of Europe had begun to replace that of Christendom. The Dutch jurist and diplomat Hugo Grotius, father of international law, called on states to create a society of nations. He argued that it would be advantageous to hold conferences of European Christian powers where disputes between states would be settled by neutral mediators.[2] Maximilien de Bethune, a seventeenth-century French (Protestant) statesman, called for a European federation in the form of a Christian republic consisting of Catholic and Protestant states.

A call for European unity also appeared in the form of an essay written by William Penn, proprietor of the colony of Pennsylvania. Penn wrote that a European parliament was needed in order for states to settle their disputes peacefully. He argued that if deputies of the princely European states met in a general parliament and established rules of justice that all would observe, "Europe would quietly obtain that [which is] so much desired and needed for her harassed inhabitants."[3] Charles-Irenée Castel, abbé de Saint-Pierre, a French diplomat and cleric, called for a permanent European union of Christian sovereign states to keep the peace based on reciprocal commitments to common security.[4] Stanislas Leszczynski, king of Poland and duke of Lorraine, wrote of the need for a union of European states to balance the "unchecked sovereignty" of a state system in conflict.[5]

Writing during the Napoleonic Wars, Immanuel Kant prescribed a federal system of states to ensure a permanent peace based on international law.[6] Henri de Saint-Simon sought to link interstate peace with social justice and economic expansion.[7] He proposed a European parliament and council of states. Friedrich von Gentz, consultant to Metternich, called for a general union of states with federal ties under the guidance of the five great powers: Austria, Britain, France, Prussia, and Russia. In an address to the Paris Peace Congress in 1849, Victor Hugo predicted the creation of a European union of states with a single parliament. It was Hugo who gave currency to the term "United States of Europe."[8]

Following World War I, French author and poet Paul Valéry wrote of the need to rediscover the unity of European civilization and values and the imperative of political unification.[9] During the interwar years, Richard Coudenhove-Kalergi, founder of the Pan-European Union, envisaged a security pact followed by the creation of a customs union. Aristide Briand, French Foreign Minister and President of the Pan-European Union, proposed an intergovernmental association of European states at the League of Nations. However, neither the Pan-European Movement nor the efforts of Briand to foster unity stemmed the tide of war.

Image 2.1.   Supporters of the European Idea: Clockwise from top left: Immanuel Kant, Victor Hugo, Altiero Spinelli, Dwight D. Eisenhower. Spinelli photo courtesy of the Audiovisual Library of the European Commission

During World War II, support for postwar European unity gathered steam in the resistance against the Nazis and in underground organizations across Europe. While imprisoned by the Italian fascists on the island of Ventotene in 1941–1942, Altiero Spinelli, founder of the European Federalist Movement in Italy, and Ernesto Rossi, an anti-fascist journalist, wrote the *Ventotene Manifesto*. Spinelli and Rossi called for a postwar European federation to solve interstate conflict. Their prescription for European unity gathered support after the war.

Speaking at Zurich University on September 19, 1946, Winston Churchill called for "a kind of United States of Europe." Churchill urged an "end of retribution" in Franco–German relations and called on a united Europe "to give a new sense of enlarged patriotism and common citizenship to the distracted peoples of this turbulent and mighty continent."[10] The Zurich speech was not the first time Churchill had spoken on the need for European unity. At Westminster College in Fulton, Missouri, in March 1946, Churchill had warned: "From Stettin in the Baltic to Trieste in the Adriatic, an iron curtain has descended across the Continent. . . . The safety of the world requires a new unity in Europe, from which no nation should be permanently outcast. . . . Surely we should work with conscious purpose for a grand pacification of Europe, within the structure of the United Nations."[11] Churchill's ideas were echoed in the words of President Dwight D. Eisenhower, who in July 1951 called for a "European federation to provide security."

For four centuries, after wars began and in their aftermath, great thinkers called in compelling terms for a united Europe to procure the peace. However, they neither provided detailed plans for putting into effect their ideas nor succeeded in making headway in the corridors of political power at home and abroad. In short, they failed to persuade governments to change the habits of war. What finally changed people's minds in the mid-twentieth century were the horrors of World War II. "It had taken only one generation between 1914 and 1945 for what had been the most prosperous and powerful continent to arrive at a state of complete impotence, brought about by itself."[12]

The purpose of this section was to introduce readers to the rich body of political thought on European unity that predated and ultimately influenced the EU's founding. As discussed in Chapter 1, the ideas of unity entered the realm of political action because Robert Schuman and Konrad Adenauer accepted Monnet's logic that it was in their own national interests to take a gamble for peace, especially at a time when the center of world power had shifted from Europe to the Soviet Union and the United States. Above all others, Monnet's vision of a united Europe has left an indelible mark on today's European Union.[13]

Postwar Political Theories of European Integration

Just as there is a rich body of political thought on European unity, so too is there a rich body of theoretical literature on modern European integration. Theorists have grappled with a core question concerning the practice of integration. Who primarily drives integration—member governments who advance domestic and national interests at European level or common EU institutions that shape and influence what member governments do? Is European integration primarily about member-state governments who delegate powers to common institutions to act on their behalf, or do common institutions have their own scope for agency—such as the influence to shape and drive the integration process? Knowing the right questions to ask is a student's first step in developing a theoretical understanding of European integration. Table 2.2

Table 2.2: Conventional Political Science Theories of European Integration, 1940s–1990s

Theory/Theorist	Key Explanations	Strengths	Shortcomings
Federalism (1940s) — Altiero Spinelli	transfer of sovereignty from state to union, modeled after the United States; preferred to sectoral approach of functionalists	supranationalism seen as cure for hypernationalism; EU is a quasi-federal polity	did not anticipate states would prefer intergovernmentalism over supranationalism
Functionalism (1940s–1950s) — David Mitrany — Jean Monnet	collective interests/actions that enhance human welfare build habits of cooperation among states and spur spillover of cooperation into new/related areas on a sector-by-sector basis	explained functional spillover from ECSC to EEC, and pooling of sovereignty to jointly achieve tasks; Europeanization process drives more integration	failed to anticipate staying power of national interests in EC decisionmaking after the French empty chair crisis
Neofunctionalism (1960s–1970s) — Ernst Haas — Leon Lindberg — Stuart Scheingold — Philippe Schmitter	national interests determine when and in which sectors integration occurs; integration driven by key interest groups organized across borders; functional spillover is neither automatic nor guaranteed; there will be spillback as states cling to national interests and sovereignty, which puts brakes on expansion of integration into high-politics areas	national interests infused into functional logic; spillover occurs not automatically but as result of specific interests; road of integration is rocky; spillback, however, is not the same as institutional immobilism	overemphasized institutions; shortchanged staying power of national interests, import of international politics; underemphasized importance of interstate bargaining/trade-offs that impact integration
Intergovernmentalism (1960s–1980s) — Stanley Hoffmann — Joseph Nye Jr.	governments pursuing national interests drive integration process; functional spillover insufficient to explain/predict EC growth because it underemphasizes diversity of national interests	integration continues in functional areas but states retain sovereignty in foreign policy and defense	too quickly discarded aspects of functionalism that explained EC growth after empty chair crisis ended; discarded impact of Europeanization on states
Liberal Intergovernmentalism (1990s) — Andrew Moravcsik	domestic pressures influence rational governments who bargain at IGCs to maximize advantages; this drives development of EU, as common institutions are needed to implement/enforce new compacts	offers parsimonious explanation of where power to change/influence course of integration in the EU lies	underestimated routine functioning of EU between IGCs and impact of Europeanization on member-state actors

identifies conventional political science theories of European integration from the 1940s to the 1990s by theorists, key explanations, and strengths and weaknesses.

FEDERAL AND FUNCTIONAL LOGICS

Early theorists posited alternative paths to either European or world peace during and in the aftermath of World War II and the excesses of the fascist states. One possibility was a European federal union modeled on the United States; another was international functional cooperation whereby states would build the foundation for peace by cooperating with one another to enhance human welfare in specific sectors.

Altiero Spinelli and other wartime anti-fascists prescribed a postwar peace based on federalism. In this context, **federalism** refers to the creation of a United States of Europe whereby power would be distributed between European and nation-state institutions, with the union having sovereignty in such areas as defense, foreign policy, and fiscal and monetary affairs. As it turned out, few theorists have applied federal theory as a cogent explanation of the early period of European integration. A more enduring theory of European integration inspired by functional logic attracted interest among scholars in the early postwar era, and still does today, albeit in different theoretical constructs. The nation-state survived World War II, there was to be no postwar federal union, and early theories of integration did not focus on federalism. Federal thinking in the 1940s was more a prescription for change than a theory of integration. That said, in recent years, federalism has proven to be a useful framework for shaping the debates over the relationship of EU institutions and member states and for comparing and contrasting the EU's federal features with those of other federal unions (e.g., the United States), a topic taken up in chapter 5.

David Mitrany's 1943 study *A Working Peace System* introduced the theory of functionalism, proposing that world peace would be achieved through institutionalized international cooperation. The theory of **functionalism** posits that pragmatic cooperation among states raises human welfare and enhances world peace. National divisions become less important relative to international functional bodies. Mitrany did not prescribe a scheme of world government but proffered a peace system in which routine cooperation to solve global problems might in time lead to a global political authority. Writing during World War II about the postwar order, Mitrany surmised: "Peace will not be secure if we organize the world by what divides it. But in the measure in which such peace-building activities develop and succeed, one might hope that the mere prevention of conflict, crucial as that may be, would in time fall to a subordinate place in the scheme of international things, while we would turn to what are the real tasks of our common society—the conquest of poverty and of disease and of ignorance."[14]

Mitrany's work was later applied to the European Community setting by the neofunctionalist school of thought led by Ernst Haas in the 1950s and 1960s. Haas recognized that Mitrany's functional alternative was at work in the creation and development of the ECSC.[15] Haas argued in his theory of **neofunctionalism** that what drove functional cooperation was the work of important political groups whose interests favored integration. If they perceived that their interests were advanced in one area of cooperation, they would be inclined to attempt more of the same but in other related areas. This is referred to as neofunctional spillover.

In *The Political Dynamics of European Economic Integration*, Leon Lindberg, a student of Haas, defined political integration as a process by which states jointly decide key policies and delegate decisionmaking power to new central bodies.[16] Political, economic, and other elites across the polities of the member states are persuaded to shift political activities and expectations to a new center—a new locus of decisionmaking. Lindberg identified prerequisites for political integration to occur: the creation of new central bodies (which represent the common interest) and the development and expansion of significant policies and tasks supported by the member states, who view their interests as consistent with the new undertaking.

The explanatory limitations of the expansive logic of functionalism were exposed in 1965 when French President Charles de Gaulle boycotted the EC Council of Ministers. In the case of the French empty chair crisis, theory—which should presage reality if it has good predictive capability—trailed reality. Scholars such as Lindberg, Stuart Scheingold, and Philippe Schmitter put forward a revised neofunctionalism.[17] The revisionists recognized that spillover would be neither automatic nor guaranteed. Spillback—or even periods of retrenchment or stagnation—would characterize the integration process. The EC would not wither; it would exist alongside the nation-state, but there would not likely be a United States of Europe.

Whereas Lindberg and others sought to revise functionalism after the resolution of the French empty chair crisis, Stanley Hoffmann introduced a new theory of integration that took into account the importance of the state in European integration, thus eschewing the functionalist logic even in its revised incarnation.[18] Hoffmann's new theory of intergovernmentalism is introduced below. Suffice it to say, theorists of this era were adjusting their explanatory concepts in response to changes in the direction of European integration. Their legacy is a rich explanation of European integration in the 1960s. Neofunctionalism has not ceased to exist as a theory of integration because scholars still subscribe to many of its key elements, while others have borrowed those key elements as they developed new theories of integration. Theorists continue to grapple with how to predict accurately the course of integration.

INTERGOVERNMENTALISM AND ITS VARIANTS

De Gaulle's aggressive action in defense of French national interests vis-à-vis the EC precipitated Hoffmann to advance a new theory. Rather than advocate for a united Europe along federal lines, de Gaulle argued for a Europe where intergovernmental (i.e., interstate) cooperation and negotiation would occur, rather than functionalist-inspired supranationalism. De Gaulle was not advocating the end of European integration; rather, he favored the ascendancy of the member governments relative to the common institutions.

Thus, the new theory of **intergovernmentalism** stresses the importance of national interests inside the EU. In an intergovernmental Europe, the member states would retain control over such bastions of their sovereignty as fiscal policy, foreign policy, and defense, but they would continue to engage in economic integration. Hoffmann argued that the scope of integration was largely determined by member-state governments who, in pursuit of their national interests, agreed to negotiate compacts that could advance the common policies and institutions of the EC. The emphasis of intergovernmentalism was on the member governments as drivers of the integration process, not the supranational institutions.

Whereas Hoffmann turned to intergovernmentalism, other scholars, more inclined to a liberal approach to international affairs, sought to embed European integration in global interdependence. Although proffering not a theory of integration but a descriptive concept of the global political economy, scholars in the 1970s sought to anchor the phenomenon of European integration in the phenomemon of international interdependence. They attempted to explain EC integration as a subset of global systemic patterns of behavior among states and transnational influences. Led by Ernst Haas in 1975, when he finally discarded neofunctionalism as a theory of EC integration, and by Robert Keohane and Joseph Nye Jr., interdependence scholars focused on the mutual dependence among states and the increasing importance of transnational organizations, such as multinational corporations, in the workings of the International Political Economy (IPE).[19] Although useful to anchor EC integration in global phenomena, the concept of interdependence never evolved into a theory of regional integration but instead fed into other perspectives, including revised intergovernmentalism (introduced below).

In the late 1990s, Andrew Moravcsik, a Hoffmann student, further refined and expanded upon early intergovernmentalism, christening his revisionist thought "liberal intergovernmentalism." Moravcsik's **liberal intergovernmentalism** focused on major periodic Intergovernmental Conferences, or IGCs, where the EC/EU would embark on a new treaty or Treaty revision (e.g., Rome Treaty, Single European Act [SEA], Treaty on European Union [TEU]) as the most important catalyst to growth of the EU.[20] Bundles of interstate bargains that might result from IGCs would propel the EU into new directions of growth. Whereas neofunctionalists emphasize welfare-enhancing common institutions and players as drivers of the integration process, Moravcsik emphasized as the most important drivers of integration those governments that make rational choices and represent powerful domestic commercial and other interests. He concluded that "European integration was a series of rational adaptations by national leaders to constraints and opportunities stemming from the evolution of an interdependent world economy, the relative power of states in the international system, and the potential for international institutions to bolster the credibility of interstate bargains."[21]

Whereas the revised neofunctionalists attempted, quite appropriately, to bridge a theory of integration with a theory of politics, Moravcsik makes a cleaner break with neofunctionalism. He does not adequately consider the long-term shaping influences on the member governments of the *acquis communautaire*, the role of the central institutions and players, and the very real processes of Europeanization that occur between and across episodic IGCs. As a result, it may be that Moravcsik misses the forest of integration for the trees of intergovernmentalism. Without the influence of the EU on the member states—to advance the common good with new initiatives and put into practice, enforce, and interpret intergovernmental compacts—one wonders how the EU would have grown into what it is today.

In retrospect, the abandonment of neofunctionalism by leading scholars, including Ernst Haas by the mid-1970s, was premature. Out of the trough of 1965, the EC and its member states entered a period of growth in institutional power and legitimacy in the 1970s, particularly after British accession. Hoffmann was too pessimistic about the growth prospects of the EC. Intergovernmentalism was too preoccupied with state preferences at the expense of the richly textured interaction of states and common institutions that individually and jointly pursue their interests and act with regard to their preferences.

In response to the relaunch of the EC project as a result of the SEA and to the dissatisfaction with intergovernmentalism, other streams of thought have been developed in the past few years that refocus on the importance of EU institutions as autonomous players in decisionmaking and on how these and other EU players form preferences. These more recent revisionist theoretical insights focus on alternative and provocative perspectives: e.g., the important role of EU institutions as agents of national governments with varying scope for autonomous actions, who help drive the integration process. These so-called institutionalists posit that both member governments and EU bodies matter, but how they matter depends on different sectors of regional integration and different decisionmaking processes. For now, we turn to the evolution of European integration from 1957 to the present; we will then end the chapter with a critique of the relative explanatory power of the conventional theories of integration and introduce the more recent revisionist ones.

Peaks and Troughs of Modern European Integration

This survey of the development of the EC indicates that modern European integration has been by no means a linear process.[22] As the reader will note, there have been peaks and troughs. At times, the troughs resulted eventually in improvements in the integration process that allowed new peaks of growth and development. There are also times in the history of the EU when there are neither peaks nor troughs but periods of uncertainty, when the pendulum that swings between the two extremes is still.

GROWTH, TURMOIL, AND COMPROMISE: 1958–1969

The early period began and ended on high notes: the entering into operation of the EEC and Euratom in 1958 and the stunning growth and development of the EEC that followed; and the Hague Summit in 1969, which paved the way for the extension of cooperation among the member states into new areas, particularly foreign policy cooperation. In between the high notes, however, turmoil and compromise characterized developments as France recoiled from the growing supranationalism of the nascent EC polity.

Britain was deeply troubled by the supranational features of the EEC yet wanted the benefits of free industrial trade without the submission of state sovereignty to central authorities. Britain, Austria, Denmark, Norway, Portugal, Sweden, and Switzerland established an industrial free trade area—the European Free Trade Association (EFTA)—in 1959. Time proved that the EEC was to be the more economically dynamic of the two rival blocs.

The EC economy boomed in the 1960s as all internal tariffs and quotas were removed and the Common External Tariff (CET) was established in July 1968, a year and a half ahead of schedule. The Common Agricultural Policy (CAP), the most supranational of EC policies, came into force in 1963, and the EC negotiated as a single trading bloc at the opening of the Kennedy Round of multilateral trade negotiations for the GATT in 1964. The brakes on this period of growth and development in the EC's early history were applied by the French Government with its decisions to block British entry into the EC and boycott the EC Council of Ministers. The bid for French hegemony in Western Europe was due in large part to the explicitly nationalist policies of Charles de Gaulle, President of the Fifth Republic (1958–1969). Indeed, as the following discussion indicates, it was no accident that the birth and early growth of the EEC coincided with the beginning and end of de Gaulle's Administration.

The French Fourth Republic (1946–1958), which was a bastion of support for European integration, collapsed over the Algerian crisis, which reached a head in 1958 when the French army in Algeria threatened a coup if Paris gave independence to Algeria. De Gaulle, ardent proponent of French grandeur and of the robust pursuit of national interests at the EC level, was called out of retirement to form the Fifth Republic. Its new constitution gave the Presidency enormous power in foreign policy and defense. The Gaullist Government's vision of the EC in the 1960s was to situate France as a leader of a unified (European) force in the world, independent of either Washington or Moscow. In 1961 the French proposed the Fouchet Plan to create a French-dominated common defense and foreign policy of the six ECSC member states. Decisionmaking would be based on unanimity, in contrast to the majority voting that occurred in the EC. The plan collapsed in 1963 when the Dutch and others recoiled at the idea of French domination. More divisive for Western Europe was de Gaulle's veto of the British membership bid in 1963 and again in 1967.

In 1961 the United Kingdom, followed by Denmark, Ireland, and Norway, first applied for membership. The Nordic states, dependent on the British market for exports, tied their future in or outside the EC on Britain's decision regarding accession. It was a difficult decision for Britain. It had chosen not to join the ECSC and EEC in the 1950s for a variety of reasons. As an island state with a vast empire overseas, Britain tended to eschew long-term involvement in continental affairs, except when its security was threatened by a hegemon such as Napoleon or Hitler. For a time it had stood alone against the Nazis in World War II, until the Americans entered the war. Britain had not suffered the horrific effects of the ground war that had engulfed the continental Europeans, and because it did not lose its sovereignty as did France in 1940 and Germany in 1945, Britain did not view the ECSC in the same immediate terms as the continental powers. Britain's special relationship with the United States and its commitments to and preoccupation with empire gave the British the sense that they had choices, and they were not willing to choose Europe over America or over the Commonwealth.

In retrospect, the British suffered from a cognitive lag—a lag in time between the decline of empire and the cognition of this decline in the minds of the British people. Thus, British aloofness vis-à-vis Europe helps explain the British choice. This changed after the 1956 Suez War, when British, French, and Israeli forces invaded Egypt, and the Americans pressed for an immediate end to the invasion. That event, coupled with Britain's decision to begin to decolonize, catalyzed a reassessment of British foreign policy in general and British relations with the EC in particular. The British decided to make a bid to join the EC. However, geopolitical reasons alone do not explain Britain's reassessment of the EC. The EC economy grew far faster than the British economy in the 1960s, just when British trade with Europe was growing more important relative to that with the Commonwealth countries. Why then did the French veto Britain's application bid?

Distrustful of the Americans and their special relationship with Britain, de Gaulle suggested that Britain was not committed to Europe. More importantly, France was not interested in sharing with Britain a leadership position in Europe, especially with regard to West Germany. The 1963 Franco–German Treaty of Friendship (Elysée Treaty) was another reminder of the importance to Gaullist France of its bilateral relationship with Bonn relative to its relationships with London and Washington.

Whereas the French veto of British membership strained relations across the Channel as well as between France and her European partners, a far more serious crisis was unleashed in 1965. The so-called **French empty chair crisis** refers to the seven-month period between June 1965 and January 1966 when the French Government withdrew its representative to the European Community and did not participate in meetings of the Council of Ministers. French President Charles de Gaulle sought to arrest the growing supranational powers of the EC and particularly of the Commission, which he thought was gaining too much influence relative to that of the member states.

The short-term catalyst to the crisis was the issue of whether the EC ought to have ownership of the revenues generated by EC farm import levies and customs duties.[23] However, the long-term catalyst was the tension between supranational (majority voting) and intergovernmental (decisionmaking based on unanimity) trends in the EC. With majority voting, a member state with a vital national interest at stake can be forced to accept the will of the majority and thus suffer a loss of sovereignty. With decisionmaking by unanimity, each member government retains the power to vote against a piece of proposed legislation and thus retains sovereignty.

The **Luxembourg Compromise**—a January 29, 1966, statement among the six member governments—brought the French back into the fold and ended their boycott. To end the crisis, member states focused attention on the need for the vital national interests of member states to be taken into consideration when EC legislation is being reviewed by the Council. Box 2.1 features a brief discussion of the key elements and effects of the Luxembourg Compromise.

The Merger Treaty—which brought the ECSC, EEC, and Euratom under a single Commission, Council of Ministers, Parliamentary Assembly, and Court of Justice—entered into force in 1967. In that year the British again applied for membership, as did the Danes, Irish, and Norwegians. Again the French opposed the British bid. However, when de Gaulle resigned in 1969, his successor, President Georges Pompidou, lifted opposition to British membership. The 1969 **Hague Summit** of the EC Heads of Government and State (HOGS) reached three path-breaking agreements: the leaders approved in principle the opening of accession negotiations with the British and other applicants (which commenced in 1970), committed to the establishment of economic and monetary union by 1980, and established the means to cooperate in foreign policy. By 1970, with the trough period behind, the EC

Image 2.2   Charles de Gaulle. Courtesy of the U.S. Library of Congress

entered a new period of growth and expansion before a period of stagnation set in a decade later.

EXPANSION AND SCLEROSIS: 1970–1985

After the stresses of the 1960s over British membership and the French boycott, the EC expanded horizontally (in membership) and vertically (in new policy arenas) in the 1970s. In 1979 the EC took a major step toward representative democracy when it held the first direct elections for members of the EP. However, beginning in the 1970s and continuing into the early 1980s, the EC economy stagnated and the Euro-

Box 2.1.   The Luxembourg Compromise

Having encountered domestic opposition to his boycott of the EC—and recognizing that the EC market, including the Common Agricultural Policy, was of vital importance to core French interests—de Gaulle agreed to French participation at a special meeting of the EC Foreign Ministers in January 1966 in Luxembourg. The purpose of the meeting was to seek an end to the crisis. No Commission representative was invited. Drafted by Belgian statesman Paul-Henri Spaak, the compromise focused on how to balance the need for the member governments to adopt EC decisions while protecting their vital national interests should an EC proposal for action threaten those interests.

Five member governments, excluding France, agreed that they would seek consensus on a legislative proposal subject to majority voting when vital interests of any member state were declared to be at stake. If a consensus could not be reached, the five would move to a vote. The French Government stated that when vital interests of a member state were at stake, discussion in the Council must continue until unanimity is reached. Thus France implicitly reserved the right to exercise its veto of a legislative proposal subject to majority voting if consensus could not be reached.

In retrospect, the Luxembourg Compromise was an agreement to disagree because it reflected a split between France and the others over voting rights. It also reflected an agreement among all six members that they had a stake in the future of European integration. As it turned out, majority voting was allowed from 1967 on, as provided for in the Rome Treaty. Member governments in the Council often prefer to resort to consensus when adopting legislative proposals, but since the 1980s, majority voting has been used with more frequency. Furthermore, since the 1990s, member governments have resorted to "opting out" of certain new EU agreements in order not to block adoption of new initiatives. Although member governments very rarely invoke the Luxembourg Compromise, the possibility that it may be invoked is always present in Council deliberations.

The Luxembourg Compromise was important to the growth and development of the EU since it helped fasten the member states more closely to their own union without threatening their national sovereignties. The EU became less supranational and more intergovernmental in its tone, but not in its substance. The Commission was compelled to play a more modest and cautious role in the integration in the 1960s and 1970s, careful to respect the sovereign proclivities of the national governments, which was a direct outcome of the French boycott. Some of the Commission's influence was lost when the Committee of Permanent Representatives was created in 1965 and each of the member governments posted an ambassador to the EC to assist decisionmaking in the Council. However, the Commission's central role as the EU's policy initiator, executor, manager, and champion has not receded, as demonstrated by its lead role in the 1992 Project and the establishment of the economic and monetary union (EMU). The tension between supranational and intergovernmental approaches to integration continues to this day to define the scope for new areas of EU cooperation and action.

peans needed a new political impetus to rekindle the integration process. The re-launching of the EC began in 1985 as the EC entered a new period of dynamism.

With the promise of British accession and the growing pressures on the EC to respond to international political and security developments, a new intergovernmental forum for foreign policy cooperation was launched in 1970: European Political Cooperation (EPC). EPC remained outside the EC Treaty framework until 1987. However, since its membership was limited to the EC member states, and none of them opted out of EPC, this forum became over time closely associated with the work of the EC's own external economic, aid, and diplomatic programs. The promise of the EC's first **enlargement** was realized in 1973. Britain, Denmark, and Ireland joined, but the Norwegians voted to stay outside. The Greeks joined in 1981. Each enlargement of the EC caused a metamorphosis of the EC into something new and different. The accession of Britain expanded the EC's global dimension; Ireland gave the EC a focus on third world development issues; Denmark brought a Nordic perspective on humanitarianism; Greece brought Western Europe east to the Balkans and the Middle East—areas of risk and of opportunity.

In 1970, the EC members adopted the Werner Plan, which called for the establishment of an economic and monetary union by 1980. However, EC plans were scuttled as a result of two shocks to the international monetary system between 1971 and 1974. The first was the U.S. decision to suspend dollar convertibility and break with fixed exchange rates (which ended the Bretton Woods–era international monetary system). EC members responded to the new era of floating exchange rates by instituting a "snake-in-the-tunnel" monetary grid in which they limited their exchange rate fluctuations in order to provide more financial stability for trade markets. The second shock to the monetary system came from oil price hikes and an embargo, but the EC member states' response was hardly evocative of the spirit of a European community.

With the outbreak of the 1973 Yom Kippur War between Israel and its neighbors, the Organization of Arab Petroleum Exporting Countries (OAPEC), an oil cartel, embargoed oil sales to the Netherlands (for its support of Israel) and tripled the world market price for oil, throwing the EC and the rest of the West and Japan into recession. The EC members provided oil to the Netherlands but failed to forge a common approach to the cartel, notwithstanding the efforts of the Commission to do so. Individual member states negotiated bilateral oil deals with cartel members, thus putting national interests over a common EC approach. This cavernous trough in EC history made many question the value of the EC as a political community if it could not negotiate as a bloc with a cartel that engaged in economic warfare against one of its members. How relevant was European integration in a crisis that affected the economic security of the member states? The recession of the mid-1970s that followed the oil embargo and price hikes further divided the EC as member states pursued national—rather than common EC—fixes to the ravages of the recession and unemployment.

Out of the trough came two reassessments by the EC and its member states of the EC role in international politics in the 1970s and in international economics in the 1980s.

In the 1970s, EPC was strengthened, and the EC strengthened its Mediterranean Policy by offering better terms of trade and political dialogue with the states around the Mediterranean Basin. The EC also commenced the Euro–Arab Dialogue and took steps to curry favor in the Arab world, which Israel saw as a major shift in European relations with the Jewish state.

In a popular referendum in 1975, a majority of British voters opted to remain in the EC—putting to rest the threat of withdrawal, yet not ending British ambivalence about being in Europe. The EC also expanded vertically in the 1970s as new institutions and policies were created. In 1974 the European Council was instituted as the forum for summits of the HOGS, and the European Court of Auditors (ECA) was established to review the expenditures of the EC institutions. The year 1979 was momentous for deepening and democratizing the EC with the institution of the European Monetary System (EMS) and direct elections to the European Parliament. The EMS, a voluntary accord of member states, established exchange-rate fluctuation bands in order to avoid monetary shocks that would adversely affect trade among the member states. EMS was the EC's response to the end of the Bretton Woods monetary system earlier in the decade. The Common Fisheries Policy was established in 1983. After years of demands launched by British Prime Ministers to reduce Britain's budgetary contributions to the EC, accord was reached in 1984. The EC members agreed to raise the ceiling of national VAT (value added tax) contributions to the EC from 1 percent to 1.4 percent.

In the late 1970s and early 1980s, in what became known as the era of **Eurosclerosis**, European economic competitiveness languished (particularly in light of the meteoric rise of Japanese and East Asian economic competitiveness). France was promoting mergers of firms to create national champions lavished with state subsidies. However, all of its Keynesian policies of jump-starting the economy not only failed but were out of sync with most of the other EC members, especially Britain, which had already begun to denationalize industry and move toward a policy of economic liberalism.

Moreover, the common market was divided and weakened by thousands of non-tariff barriers (NTBs), and the EC was stagnating, politically and economically. NTBs, such as customs formalities and health standards, government subsidies, and standards of production tailored to domestic industry over outside competition, were expanded by member governments to protect domestic production from competition from other member states. NTBs precluded firms from enjoying economies of scale just when inward foreign investment and imported goods competed with domestic producers.

A coalition of European industries and the EC Commission responded in 1985 with the *White Paper on Completing the Internal Market*, which was adopted by the European Council that same year. (By the 1980s–1990s, the Europeans began using the term "internal market" rather than common market.) In the *White Paper*, the Commission proposed eliminating NTBs by the end of 1992. Also in 1985 a cadre of EC members agreed to abolish border controls among themselves and to strengthen the external borders of their territories. The charter members of what came to be known as the Schengen Accord included France, Germany, and the Benelux countries. The Schengen Accord is a prime example of a **multiple-speed approach** to European integration. As the EU grows in membership and expands into new sectors of cooperation, member governments may choose to board the train at different speeds, but in the same direction. Today, twenty-two of the twenty-seven member states have acceded to the Schengen Accord.

The EC held an intergovernmental conference (IGC) in September–December

1985, out of which the member governments agreed to bring the Commission's ideas on "completing the internal market" into the Treaty framework. Once again, the EC entered a deep trough before it dug itself out. It helped that the right EC and national political and economic leaders were in the right place at the right time. They were led by Commission President Jacques Delors (the Jean Monnet of the 1980s), with support from an unexpected source: British Prime Minister Margaret Thatcher, Europe's intergovernmentalist without equal at the time. She recognized the value of a more open European economy, less dependent on government subsidies and NTBs and more enlivened by the rigor of economic liberalization on a continental scale.

REVITALIZATION, ENLARGEMENT, AND NEW COMPACTS: 1986–2004

At the start of this period of renewal, as the EC was evolving into the EU, it was engaged in a process of enlargement: Spain and Portugal in 1986 and Austria, Finland, and Sweden in 1995. At the same time that the EC was growing in membership, it was also seeking to "deepen" the union by improving and strengthening its decision-making institutions and policies. It did so with the signing of the SEA in February 1986, following the completion of the IGC, and with the entry into force of the SEA on July 1, 1987.

The first major revision of the EC Treaty in thirty years, the SEA's most important attribute was to set the deadline of January 1, 1993, to eliminate NTBs and to harmonize national production standards for goods into mutually acceptable EC-wide production standards. The SEA increased the influence of the EP in some areas of legislation; gave the EP a veto over accession of new member states and ratification of association accords with third countries; and subjected some new areas of legislative activity to qualified majority voting (member states assigned weighted votes based on population). Critically important to the emergence of the EC as a foreign policy actor, the SEA codified and institutionalized EPC (1970) and the European Council (1974), although neither was brought under the purview of the EC Treaty at the time.

The SEA rekindled the integration process after a decade or so of stagnation and fragmentation. It also rekindled interest in EMU. Supporters of EMU maintained that the internal market, even after the SEA, would still be weakened and divided by currency fluctuations that adversely affected trade and investment flows. In 1988, the EC Council of Ministers asked Commission President Jacques Delors to head a committee to consider how the EC might evolve into an EMU. In 1989, President Delors outlined a plan for the establishment of an EMU over three phases: fixing exchange rates; establishing an EC central bank to set interest rates; and introducing a new EC currency that would replace the currencies of the member states.

The end of the Cold War between 1989 and 1991 witnessed sea changes that catapulted the EC into a new phase of development. Once again, the EC responded to external stimuli as a catalyst for change. New democracies in Central and Eastern Europe (CEE), the unification of Germany resulting in the absorption of the former East Germany into the EC, and the collapse of the Soviet Union forced the EC to consider issues of **widening and deepening**. Widening refers to the expansion of the EC to include new members from CEE. The EC was expected to help these states solidify their democratic and market transitions and to stabilize post–Cold War Europe. Deepening of the EC to make it work better and more efficiently had to precede widening; otherwise the EC risked paralysis. Deepening was critically important for the French, especially in the area of economic and monetary union, because Paris sought to strengthen its ties with a unified, larger, and more powerful Germany and anchor it more deeply in European integration.

In three treaties the EC member states addressed change in and around Europe: Maastricht (1993); Amsterdam (1998); and Nice (2003). Table 2.3 lists the changes to EU governmental decisionmaking brought about by these three treaties.

The Treaty on European Union (TEU), or Maastricht Treaty, was the result of two IGCs on EMU and political union in 1991. The TEU was signed by the member governments on February 7, 1992, and entered into force on November 1, 1993. Ratification by the member states of the TEU was messy. In its referendum, the French electorate just barely voted to accept the TEU. The Germans had to wait to October 1993 before their Constitutional Court ruled that the TEU did not infringe on the German constitution. The Danes, in a paper-thin majority, initially voted against ratification. To obtain a yes vote, Copenhagen negotiated opt-outs for Denmark, making clear to the Danish electorate that the country would not participate in monetary union and future military missions if its government chose not to do so. The second Danish vote resulted in the ratification of the TEU with the requisite opt-outs.

The TEU established the three-pillar EU: Pillar One (Rome Treaties) was the EEC, which the TEU renamed the "European Community," and EMU; Pillar Two was the Common Foreign and Security Policy (CFSP), which succeeded the old EPC; and Pillar Three was Justice and Home Affairs (JHA), established to foster cooperation among member state judiciaries and police forces. The TEU created the economic and monetary union over three progressive stages and established the rights of all member-state citizens to enjoy EU citizenship—to vote in EP elections anywhere in the EU, stand as a candidate in local and EP elections, work and live anywhere in the EU, and seek consular aid in any embassy/consulate of a member state government.

The TEU called for an IGC to deal more carefully with institutional reform ahead of eastern enlargement. In March 1996, the new IGC was convened to prepare for what became the Amsterdam Treaty, signed by the member governments on June 17, 1997, and entered into force on May 1, 1999. The Amsterdam Treaty set the threshold required to achieve a qualified majority vote (QMV) at 71 percent. It also provided for enhanced cooperation among member states who could muster a QMV and who wished to act in all areas of Pillar One and in criminal and police matters. The Treaty instituted an obligation by the EU to take into account environmental protection requirements, including sustainable development in defining and implementing all policies.

The Amsterdam Treaty set a five-year transition period in which to transfer certain policies from Pillar Three (JHA) to Pillar One (EC). These policies affected the areas of immigration, visas, residence permits, asylum, refugees, and juridical cooperation in certain civil matters (with opt-outs for Britain, Denmark, and Ireland). The Social Charter was incorporated into the Treaty framework (with Britain no longer having an opt-out), as was the Schengen Accord (elimination of border controls, with opt-outs for Britain, Denmark, and Ireland).

The Amsterdam Treaty streamlined the functioning of CFSP by making more

Table 2.3: Evolution of the Powers of EU Institutions by Treaty, 1993-2003

Treaty / Institution	Maastricht (1993)	Amsterdam (1998)	Nice (2003)
European Commission	expanded Commission's term from four to five years (to complement five-year term of office for EP members)	limited size of Commission to 20 members and provided for large member states to relinquish one of their two commissioners	stipulated that after EU reaches 27 members, there will be fewer Commissioners than member states; Commissioners will rotate in/out on an equal basis
	extended Commisson's right of legislative initiative	provided that national governments' nominations of Commissioners made in common accord with Commission President	authorized Commission President to allocate portfolios among Commissioners and to call for a Commissioner's resignation
European Parliament	introduced codecision: right of EP to veto limited number of legislative proposals in Pillar One	extended codecision to 50 percent of legislative proposals in Pillar One	extended codecision to most legislative proposals in pillar one
	authorized EP to approve appointment of a new Commission	authorized EP to approve Council nominee for Commission President	capped number of MEPs at 732
	authorized EP to appoint EU Ombudsman to investigate / mediate citizen complaints	required EP to consult European Economic and Social Committee	
Council of the EU	extended use of qualified majority voting (QMV)	established the Office of the High Representative for CFSP and policy planning/early warning units; expanded use of QMV	authorized European Council to decide unanimously on number of Commissioners not to exceed 27
European Court of Justice	empowered ECJ to levy fines on member governments failing to implement EC laws or comply with ECJ judgements in Pillar One	authorized ECJ to rule on areas of freedom, security and justice based on references by national courts/tribunals of last instance	established specialized chambers to address workload issues; CFI gained more tasks; ECJ may sit in a Grand Chamber of 13 judges
Other Bodies	established the Committee of Regions	authorized European Court of Auditors to bring actions before ECJ; expanded ECA audit powers to cover all recipients of EU funds	

use of QMV when adopting or implementing joint actions; introduced the use of constructive abstention, which allows a member government to abstain with regard to (but not veto) a joint action; established a High Representative for CFSP and specialized units to monitor and analyze international developments and their consequences; and incorporated the Petersberg Tasks of peacekeeping, humanitarian relief, and other soft security tasks into the Treaty framework.

However, efforts to negotiate the size of the Council and Commission and to reform the weights in QMV in advance of the EU's anticipated eastern enlargement failed. Therefore, yet another IGC had to be planned for 1999. In contrast to these internal institutional divisions, the member states were prepared to take new and significant steps to increase cooperation in international security affairs. Indeed at the Helsinki EU Council in 1999, the EU agreed to establish the European Security and Defense Policy (ESDP) and a rapid reaction force to allow member states to support multilateral peacekeeping and humanitarian relief functions. At last, the IGC for the new treaty got under way in 2000 and the Nice Treaty was signed by member states in February 2001.

Once again skittish about Ireland's place in a more political Europe, Irish voters failed to give sufficient support for the Nice Treaty in a June 2001 referendum (53 percent against, 46 percent for, based on a voter turnout of under 35 percent). However, a second referendum passed (62 percent for, 37 percent against, based on a voter turnout of 49 percent). The holding of the second referendum was preceded by Ireland's recommitment to a policy of neutrality and the acknowledgment of this policy by Ireland's EU partners. Having entered into force in February 2003, the Nice Treaty was a modest outcome of institutional deepening. The Treaty introduced democratic reforms and changes in voting and other procedures designed to make the EU run more efficiently and democratically as it enlarges to include new members.

The Treaty authorized a reweighing of votes in the formula for achieving a qualified majority (used to pass legislation) that results in an increase in weighted votes for the most populated member states. The larger member states had long complained that the lesser populated smaller states were overrepresented in the QMV equation relative to the more heavily populated states. The Treaty also increased the number of areas subject to qualified majority voting in order to ease decisionmaking in an enlarged union. However, the Treaty provided that a member state in the Council could request verification that a qualified majority actually represented at least 62 percent of the total EU population. The qualified majority threshold was increased to 73.91 percent of the votes, based on an enlarged union of 27 member states.

A few months after the Nice Treaty was signed, the EU faced three major developments. Terrorists attacked the United States (September 11, 2001), the European Council called for a constitutional convention to draft a new treaty (December 2001), and the new euro notes and coins were introduced (January 1, 2002), with national currencies withdrawn by February 2003. The EU responded speedily and vigorously to the attacks on the United States by beefing up its own measures to combat international terrorism, including the introduction of an EU-wide arrest warrant. Amidst these developments in early 2002, a quiet ending came to the fifty-year-old Paris Treaty that had created the ECSC. The EU took over the responsibilities of the ECSC, and its officials viewed the end of the ECSC as historically significant.

We now turn to a brief discussion of the intense interplay between issues of widening and deepening of the European Union between 2002 and 2004. The December 2001 European Council declared the need to bring EU citizens closer to their union, to further prepare the EU for an enlarged membership, and to develop the EU as a more credible player in world affairs. These leaders understood that the Nice Treaty did not provide adequately for the reforms in EU governmental decisionmaking needed for an enlarged union to act efficiently and effectively. This challenge prompted the European Council to call for a constitutional convention to convene in 2002 (which it did in February) to draft a new treaty to be considered by a new IGC in 2003. The European Council hoped that, by bringing the myriad EC/EU Treaties under one constitutional rubric, a newly streamlined EU governmental decisionmaking system would make for a more competent union in its actions at home and abroad. Under the chairmanship of former French President Valery Giscard d'Estaing, the convention consisted of 105 representatives from the EU bodies and national parliaments and representatives from the Heads of Government or State of each of the EU member states and the candidate countries.

The prospect of enlargement hovered over and gave stimulus to the constitutional convention. In December 2002, following the Commission's favorable progress reports on each of the applicants in October, the European Council agreed to conclude negotiations with ten aspirants—Malta, Cyprus, Poland, Latvia, Lithuania, Estonia, Hungary, Czech Republic, Slovakia, and Slovenia. Six months later, the convention presented a draft constitutional treaty to the European Council. The European Council called for the new IGC to begin considering the draft treaty in October 2003. The treaty would reform, streamline, and democratize the EU to prepare it for a membership of twenty-seven or more. The European Council agreed to the new Constitutional Treaty in June 2004 and the HOGS signed the Treaty in Rome in October.

Just as the EU was embarking on its new constitutional journey, treaties of accession were signed and ratified in 2003, and ten new member states acceded to the EU in May 2004. Map 2.1 depicts the newly enlarged EU, which more than quadrupled the size of the charter membership of six. Soon thereafter, the EU made historic decisions about further eastern enlargement. The EU granted "candidate status" for three states: Turkey in 1999, Croatia in 2004, and Macedonia in 2005, and it made commitments to the possibility of future membership for the remaining Western Balkan states.

The EU declared Turkey a candidate country in 1999. However, accession negotiations, which did not commence until 2005, have not developed smoothly, either because the Turks themselves are divided on EU membership and/or because EU member governments (e.g., France and Germany) have stated their opposition to Turkish membership despite prior commitments. Although the EU and Turkey have opened twelve of the thirty-five chapters of the future accession treaty, only one chapter (science and research) has been provisionally closed. Cyprus, now an EU member, has blocked closure of two chapters (energy and culture/education) that had been negotiated. Accession negotiations are also stalled over problems related to the nonrecognition by Turkey and Cyprus of each other.

Accession negotiations with Croatia opened in 2006. Croatia and the EU have opened twenty-eight of thirty-five chapters of the future treaty, of which thirteen chapters are provisionally closed. However, the maritime and land border dispute

Map 2.1.   The European Union and Candidate Countries (2009)

Member States   Candidate Countries

Country Abbreviations: ⊛   Capitals (selected)
                                         City Abbreviations:
Belg. = Belgium   Mont. = Montenegro
Cr. = Croatia   Neth. = Netherlands   Br. = Bratislava   Sa. = Sarajevo
L. = Lichtenstein   Sl. = Slovenia   L. = Ljubljana   T. = Tirana
Lux. = Luxembourg   Slov. = Slovak Republic P.= Podgorica   Z. = Zagreb
Mac. = Macedonia   S.M. = San Marino   S. = Skojpe
Mon. = Monoco   Switz. = Switzerland

between Slovenia and Croatia will need to be settled before Croatia joins the EU. The start of Macedonia's accession negotiations has been delayed due to disagreement between Macedonia and Greece on a mutually acceptable name for the Macedonian state. Greece opposes the name Macedonia since it has a province by that name. As a result, the EU refers to Macedonia as the Former Yugoslav Republic of Macedonia

(FYROM). Negotiations have also been delayed over EU concerns regarding needed reforms to address corruption in Macedonia.

RETURN OF UNCERTAINTY: 2005–PRESENT

The process of ratification of the EU Constitutional Treaty among the member governments began in 2005. The EP recommended ratification of the Treaty in January 2005 (500 for, 137 against, 40 abstentions), and by the time of the French and Dutch referenda in May/June 2005, ten member states had ratified the Treaty. However, the French and Dutch voted no in popular referenda, forcing the June European Council to postpone the ratification process for a period of reflection. The HOGS decided in 2006 to extend the reflection period through 2008 with the goal of considering Treaty ratification in 2009. Some French and Dutch voters rejected the Constitutional Treaty because they feared the impact of an ever-growing EU on their own economic and political interests. As a result, in 2006 the European Council emphasized that the EU needed to be able to absorb new members before further expansion. The "absorption capacity" of the EU could become "code" for putting the brakes on further enlargement.

Against the sobering uncertainty surrounding the future of the Constitutional Treaty, the Presidents of the European Council, Commission, and EP signed the Declaration of Berlin on March 25, 2007, on the occasion of the fiftieth anniversary of the signing of the Treaties of Rome. The three Presidents stressed the significance of the EU's contribution to the unification and peace of Europe and called on the renewal of the European commitment to protect the accomplishments of the past while addressing the common European future. As it turned out, the HOGs decided in June 2007 to replace the troubled Constitutional Treaty with a less politically charged "reform treaty." Provisions in the Constitutional Treaty for such state-like emblems as a European anthem and foreign minister raised concerns from Europeans who, while wanting institutional reform, preferred to keep the word "constitutional" out of the EU treaty language. Thus the new reform treaty would amend, not replace, existing EU treaties, yet still institute needed innovations. A new IGC commenced during the Portuguese EU Presidency in July and concluded in December 2007, when all twenty-seven member states agreed to the reform treaty, now named the Lisbon Treaty, and commenced their ratification processes.

Among the most significant changes brought about by the Lisbon Treaty is the replacement of the Maastricht Treaty's three pillars with a "pillarless" single European Union, established as a bona fide entity in international law and thus able to enter into international treaty commitments and become a member of an international organization. Previously, only Pillar One had international legal personality. The Lisbon Treaty renames the old Rome Treaty, now called the Treaty on the Functioning of the European Union, and moves into it most of the functions of the old third pillar, JHA. The TEU remains much the same, including the CFSP, with the exception that the union now has international legal standing. EURATOM remains a separate treaty.

The Treaty extends codecision (right of the EP to join the Council in voting on legislation) and qualified majority voting to most areas of the union, including agriculture and most JHA areas; [24] replaces the term "codecision" with the term "ordinary legislative procedure"; permits EU citizens to sign a petition (based on one million signatures) to call on the Commission to propose new policies; introduces into EU law the Charter of Fundamental Rights, which codifies and guarantees the binding rights of union law for all member citizens, governments, and EU institutions; increases the involvement of national parliaments in EU decisionmaking by empowering them to monitor the legal bases for EU policies; establishes the basis among the member states for mutual support in the event of a terrorist attack or an energy supply crisis; and provides procedures for member states to withdraw from the union.

The Lisbon Treaty creates two new posts: the High Representative for the Union in Foreign Affairs and Security Policy (High Representative) and the President of the European Council. The High Representative, who double-hats as the Commission Vice President for External Relations, ensures consistency across the EU's diverse, diffuse, and multifaceted foreign affairs agencies, policies, programs, and procedures. The Treaty of Lisbon also creates a new European External Action Service. The Service will feature EU missions around the world, comprising officials from the European Commissions, the Council, and the member states. The new President of the European Council, appointed for a two-and-a-half-year term, chairs the meetings of the HOGs and represents the EU abroad.

Ratification of the Lisbon Treaty went awry, before it finally entered into force in late 2009. The EP approved the Lisbon Treaty in 2009 by a margin of 525 votes for to 115 against and all member state parliaments approved the Treaty by 2009. In ways reminiscent of the no vote concerning the Nice Treaty in 2001, the Irish electorate voted 53.4 percent against and 46.6 percent for the Lisbon Treaty, based on a voter turnout of 53 percent. Irish voters were concerned with issues having little or no specific reference to the Treaty. They were worried about safeguarding Irish identity and neutrality, the Irish tax system, and the loss of the Irish Commissioner. Many voting no felt they did not know enough about the Lisbon Treaty to affirm it. The paradox of the Irish no vote was that while a majority voted against the Treaty, a majority of Irish people felt their membership in the EU was a good thing and most indicated that they wanted to remain in the union.

In December 2008, the HOGs addressed Irish concerns over the Lisbon Treaty and assured the Irish Government that in no way does the Treaty extend to Irish concerns about taxation, neutrality and such other issues/concerns as the right to life and education. To assuage Irish concerns, the HOGS agreed that each member state will retain a Commissioner under the Lisbon Treaty, a decision that would require ratification by the member states after Lisbon entered into force. In May 2009, the HOGS approved the legal guarantees requested by Ireland in protocols to the Lisbon Treaty. As a result, Ireland agreed to hold a second referendum in October 2009. With a voter turnout of 59 percent, 67.13 voted in the affirmative and 32.9 percent in the negative.

Just when the EU was about to celebrate the Irish referendum results, the Czech President held back his signature on the ratification bill that had been enacted by the two houses of the Czech parliament. President Klaus pressed the HOGs to accept a protocol to be annexed to the Lisbon Treaty that would exempt the Czech Republic from the Charter of Fundamental Rights (Poland and the UK had already negotiated their own opt-outs from the Charter). An ardent critic of the Lisbon Treaty, the Czech President, at this late moment in the ratification process, sought to exempt the Czechs from any Sudeten German claims on land confiscated by the Czech government after World War II. In November, the European Council agreed to the Czech opt-out to the Charter on Fundamental Rights in order to ensure that the Lisbon Treaty would enter into force on December 1, 2009, which it did.

As the EU enters the second decade of the twenty-first century, it still grapples with widening and deepening, striking the "right" balance between national sovereignty and identity and what the EU should do. Indeed the pressure for further membership expansion continued unabated when Montenegro applied for membership in 2008, followed by Iceland and Albania in 2009. The tension between the EU as the agent of the member states and the principals, the member governments themselves, continues to be fraught with possibility and limitation. In 2008 and 2009, the worse recession to hit Europe and the world since the Great Depression put enormous pressure on the union and its member states to act in coordinated fashion, a topic addressed in Chapter 6. Despite its aches and pains, and the ever-present need to maintain and protect the accomplishments of the *acquis communitaire*, the EU continues to rest on a solid legal, economic, and political foundation. The Treaty of Lisbon, which is fully covered in Chapter 5 (Inside EU Governmental Decisionmaking), promises to allow the union and the member states to consolidate both the effects of enlargement and the newly introduced rules and procedures.

Political Theory of European Integration Revisited

This chapter began with an overview of the political thought associated with the idea of European unity dating back several centuries. It then introduced readers to the postwar theory of regional integration before outlining the major political, economic, and institutional developments of the EU since the signing of the Treaties of Rome. How well did political theory explain and anticipate the course of integration? The quest to create a peace order in Europe is as old as the state of warfare that brought ruin to Europeans from the Thirty Years War and Napoleonic conflicts to the First and Second World Wars. The political thinkers, writers, and statesmen identified in table 2.1 prescribed a voluntary association of European states to temper the adverse impacts of extreme forms of nationalism and to reduce the likelihood of war. Although these individuals offered little guidance on how to put their ideals into political action, they each contributed to a body of thought that presaged and contextualized the birth of modern European integration when it finally did take shape in the mid-twentieth century.

Whereas leading thinkers and political leaders from as early as the seventeenth century offered rhetoric and prescription with regard to European unity, they provided neither a theory of integration nor a blueprint for unity. Conversely, post–World War II political theorists have sought to create a more systematic, even scientific, theoretical approach to examining the ideas of European integration, drawing on the work of earlier thinkers. Their definitions, descriptions, explanations, and predictions of European integration, summarized in table 2.2, shaped generations of students seeking to understand why and how warring states make, keep, and build on peace.

It comes as no surprise that systematic theoretical work on regional integration increased after World War II—the worst human disaster in modern times. This war more than any other demarcated the European politics of the past—the cycle of conflict between France and Germany, extreme nationalism, and genocide—from those of the present—interstate reconciliation, economic and political integration, and respect for the rule of law and the rights of individuals. It also comes as no surprise that some of those who responded to the pernicious effects of hypernationalism in 1914 prescribed a federal solution to Europe's woes after World War I. Their calls were ignored, or came too late, with the Japanese invasions of China and German invasion of Czechoslovakia that preceded the outbreak of World War II. Others followed the clarion call for a United States of Europe while incarcerated by the fascists during World War II because the ancient states of Europe had again brought war on themselves. However, federalism was less a theory of regional integration than a political objective. Indeed federalism in the form of a United States of Europe was rejected as a course of action by functionalists and intergovernmentalists. As it turned out, the nation-state and the EU have come to exist concomitantly. The EU has indeed developed some federal features, but the EU would not become a United States of Europe. Nevertheless, federalist theories help us better understand those federal features of the EU in comparison to other federal systems, such as the United States and Canada.

CONVENTIONAL POLITICAL THEORIES OF MODERN EUROPEAN INTEGRATION

The first theorist of regional integration was Mitrany, whose functional logic was subsequently applied to the creation of the ECSC and EEC. He offered insights into the logic of integration based on functional and welfare-raising interests of states who needed each other to solve common problems with combined resources. Mitrany picked up on the success of nineteenth- and twentieth-century international functional bodies (discussed in Chapter 1). Although Monnet was interested in the eventual establishment of a federal Europe, he viewed Mitrany's functionalist approach as a practical means to achieve an ambitious long-term end. Functionalism as a theory of functional spillover reached its limits by the 1960s, first because it failed to incorporate the politics of enduring and distinctive national interests and second because it was all about process with no clarity about the final outcome of functional spillover. Would functionalism remain an end in itself, a process without a terminus? Would it end in federal union, or would the member states and the EU exist concomitantly without forming a federal unity? Functionalists were silent about the endgame.

Monnet relied on the attractive power of international institutions with their civil servants, and on the civil servants of member governments, to work for the good of Europe to drive the integration process. He did not understand that integration would reach limits if it did not garner the support and engagement of European publics and meet the national interests of the member governments. For example, when Kurt Schumacher—leader of the West German social democrats and trade unionists—opposed the creation of the ECSC, Monnet said: "We were not prepared to negotiate with private interest groups about a venture of such great public importance."[25] Functionalist theory did not predict the French empty chair crisis in 1965 and the growing renationalization of big decisions related to the future of the EC. The gulf between Monnet's passion to create "Europe" through practical (and bureaucratic) first steps and the role of public opinion in making that happen grew in time. This continued until the Danes voted against the TEU in the 1990s and EU leaders and supporters finally began to pay attention to what was always missing in Monnet's equation for the development of Europe: the people. In defense of his own bias, Monnet argued, "We believed in starting with limited achievements, the establishment of a de facto solidarity from which a federal state would gradually emerge. I have never believed that one fine day Europe would be created by some great political mutation and I thought it wrong to consult the peoples of Europe about the structure of a community of which they had no practical experience."[26]

The French empty chair crisis caused the neofunctionalists, led by Ernst Haas, to reconsider, then abandon, the logic of functional spillover in favor of new approaches. It is thus not surprising that as the member governments reasserted their primacy over the EC's big questions after 1965 through negotiated compacts at IGCs, intergovernmental perspectives on European integration began to gain traction over older logics. Intergovernmentalism inserted into integration theory what was missing in neofunctionalism: the pursuit of rational (goal-enhancing) national interests and interstate bargaining without which the integration process would grind to a halt. However, the intergovernmentalists rushed to throw the baby out with the bath water. Intergovernmentalists rightly focused on the outcomes of periodic IGCs that shaped the next generation of integration. Yet they ignored at their peril the synergy between national and regional interests played out every day within the member states and at the EU level in a process that became known as "Europeanization." They also ignored the shaping influences of what had already been agreed—the *acquis communautaire*.

In truth, the key to unlocking the mystery of European integration from a theoretical perspective is to recognize that neofunctionalism and intergovernmentalism are two sides of the same coin. A rounded, robust, and nuanced conceptualization requires an understanding of both logics at work, emphasizing different important elements of European integration. Still, revisionist theorists in the 1980s and 1990s remained dissatisfied with neofunctionalism and intergovernmentalism because these older theories did not explain why and how institutions form their own preferences and identities and develop their own scope for influence—or agency. What revisionist theorists most found missing in the older streams of thought was the interplay between institutions with agency and governments who grant, and try to take back, authority.

REVISIONIST THEORIES OF MODERN EUROPEAN INTEGRATION

Scholars since the 1990s focused on three nagging questions left unanswered by neofunctionalism and liberal intergovernmentalism:

1. How and why do EU institutions grow and develop over time based on the original delegation of authority granted to them by national governments (**historical institutionalism**)?

2. How and why do EU bodies retain significant influence, or agency, to advance their own institutional interests (**rational choice institutionalism**)?
3. How and why do individual citizens, leaders, societies, and institutions of the EU and its member states form their preferences, attitudes, perceptions, and identities regarding European integration (**social constructivism**)?[27]

Historical and rational choice institutionalism are variants of institutional theory of EU governmental decisionmaking. Historical institutionalists—who help us to explain the politics of regional integration as a process—feature the core concepts of path dependency and unintended consequences featured in figure II.1 (see p. 126). **Path dependency** refers to the effect of EU institutions over time, and the effect they have on the behavior of the member governments who initially created them. Historical institutionalists predict that EU bodies will pursue their own preferences and take actions that may diverge from the intention of member governments who granted them the original authority to act on their behalf, most often at periodic IGCs.

Unintended consequences refer to the effects of choices made long ago about institutions by member governments. Today's governments feel the weight of past decisions, especially if they are bound to rules they no longer wish to honor. However, historical institutionalists suggest that such governments would like to overcome the long shadow of historical legacy, but find that to do so would be too costly to make the effort worthwhile. Theorists of rational choice institutionalism explain why the costs, overall, outweigh the gains.

Rational choice institutionalists are interested in learning (1) why governments delegate authority to EU bodies; and (2) why and how EU bodies seek to widen their scope of autonomous agency (or influence).[28] This theory posits that EU member governments (1) together delegate authority to EU bodies as their agents to reduce the costs of running the EU on a day-to-day basis (these costs are known as transaction costs); and (2) generally honor their commitments to the law of the EU because it is in their own interests to make sure all EU members abide by the common rules—rules designed to keep violators and free riders from seeking advantage at the expense of others. The EU reduces the transaction costs of member governments by policing/enforcing EU decisions made by the member governments and adjudicating disputes between member governments and firms.

The central concept of rational choice institutionalism is **principal–agent analysis**, which focuses theoretical attention on the creative tension between EU member governments and EU bodies. Member governments rationally seek to maximize the benefits and limit the costs of membership in the EU, and they depend on the EU to conduct their collective business fairly and cost effectively. EU bodies rationally seek to widen their scope of agency autonomously from member governments because they have their own individual institutional interests. They do so because this is what they determine to be the appropriate behavior for the environment in which they perform their roles as actors in EU governmental decisionmaking.

Social constructivists, who claim that the EU does not just consist of EU bodies in pursuit of rational interests, help us to understand how EU and national institutions, societies, and individuals within them construct their own identities and preferences with regard to the process of European integration.[29] How are preferences about European integration formed and how do these preferences affect EU institutional learning and behavior? The constructivist is interested in understanding and explaining what it means to be a member of a union and how a union based on collective identities develops. There cannot be a European Union without a European identity. What membership in the union means is separate from yet linked to the rational pursuit by member governments of collective policies through collective institutions.

A central focus of social constructivism is Europeanization—the process of how European integration is internalized by individuals, societies, and governments of the member countries and how a collective European identity is created. Echoing earlier neofunctional thought, constructivists remind us to focus on the existential nature of the EU. After all, the member governments and their citizens voluntarily join, remain in, and abide by the laws of the union they have created. The motivation to engage in European integration is more than just a rational choice.

Perspectives from both variants of institutionalism, particularly principal–agent analysis, combined with constructivism promise to better frame theoretically the course of European integration. Neofunctionalists did not focus sufficiently on the relationship between EU principals and agents as a continuing dynamic and focused too much on the power of EU institutions and special interest groups at the expense of member governments. Intergovernmentalists did not focus sufficiently on the scope for EU institutional agency and on the importance of how preferences and identities are formed at the European level that affect the integration process. Principal–agent analysis provides a helpful conceptual framework for studying European integration. It takes into account the interplay and tension between principals and agents in the EU. Both member governments and EU bodies are important in accurately describing and explaining the overall development of European integration and of the EU as a polity. Social constructivists round out and help complete our understanding of institutional behavior. This is because constructivists focus on a process of interaction or Europeanization that over time shapes identities, preferences, values, and interests of Europeans and European institutions.

Part II of this book will thus draw extensively on principal–agent analysis. Such a conceptual framework nicely captures the complex interactions of EU governmental decisionmakers and takes into account the relative weight of member governments and EU bodies across different sectors of policy integration and with regard to different decisionmaking procedures. Principal–agent analysis is a helpful bridge between institutionalism and constructivism and incorporates what is important to know of neofunctionalism and intergovernmentalism. However, readers are encouraged to critique older and new theoretical concepts and develop their own theoretical explanations of European integration. So far, scholars have yet to develop and prove a theory that explains everything about EU governmental decisionmaking.

Review

This chapter introduced students to conventional and revisionist theory in relation to the development of the EU over the past half-century. There can be no more interesting and exciting place to examine and evaluate European integration than at the intersection of theory and practice, where ideals and ideas rub up against hard-nosed realities. Just as the EU has widened and deepened over time, so have theories of integration. Ideally, the better the theory, the more likely it will presage, not trail, real-world developments. The state of theory of European integration is vibrant, as newer streams of thought challenge older ones. A balance must be found between the time-tested explanatory concepts of older theories and newer hypotheses that are subjected to the same rigorous testing. However, it is unwise to pile one theory on top of another and to conclude that all theories explain all things, since the purpose of theory is to be selective. Without selectivity we will only create mirror images of reality, and in reality's infinite complexity we will miss the forest for the trees.

This chapter sought to reveal an enduring logic of European integration, despite the fits and starts of the past fifty years. The overview of major developments by four discernible time periods provided in this chapter suggests a nonlinear process of breakthroughs and setbacks and periods of crisis and stagnation. Nonetheless, there has been evolution overall—a form of functional spillover—from the early common market to monetary union; from foreign policy, police, juridical, and other areas of cooperation to the granting of European citizenship and a charter of fundamental rights; and from a weak and tangential EP to a democratically elected one with increasingly important legislative powers. In time, it matters little if the functional spillover was driven by member-state compacts, supranational institutions, or a combination of both, since the overall effects are the same: more peace, prosperity, and stability.

The EU endures because it is in the interests of its member states to do so and because it encompasses a collective European heritage hewn from common civilization and memory. The EU also endures because of the strong reflex to cooperate felt by its member states and peoples, no doubt in response to past and current conflicts and challenges that require combined solutions. In Chapter 3 on economic and legal foundations of European integration—and indeed throughout the rest of the book—we revisit theory to test its explanatory power and relevance. Theory remains important to students of European integration as it filters and shapes our understanding of what the EU is and does, and why. We want to make sure we have the best filter to gain the most accurate understanding.

Key Concepts

enlargement
Eurosclerosis
federalism
French empty chair crisis
functionalism
Hague Summit
historical institutionalism
intergovernmentalism
liberal intergovernmentalism
Luxembourg Compromise
multiple-speed approach
neofunctionalism
path dependency
principal–agent analysis

rational choice institutionalism
social constructivism
unintended consequences
widening and deepening

Study Questions

1. What has most shaped political thought on European unity from the seventeenth through twentieth centuries, and why?
2. Why and how did World War II represent such a fundamental break in European politics and history? Why is this break important to the study of the origins of postwar European integration?
3. What three major events other than World War II do you think most shaped the evolution of the EC/EU, and why?
4. What theory or theories of European integration do you find most compelling in explaining the evolution of the EU over the past half-century, and why?

Selected Readings

Walter Lipgens, *A History of European Integration* (Oxford: Clarendon, 1982).

Andrew Moravcsik, *The Choice for Europe: Social Purpose and State Power from Messina to Maastricht* (Ithaca, N.Y.: Cornell University Press, 1998).

Brent F. Nelsen and Alexander Stubb, eds., *The European Union: Readings on the Theory and Practice of European Integration*, 3rd ed. (Boulder, Colo.: Lynne Rienner, 2003).

Mark A. Pollack, *The Engines of European Integration: Delegation, Agency, and Agenda Setting in the EU* (Oxford: Oxford University Press, 2003).

———, "Theorizing EU Policy-Making," in *Policy-Making in the European Union*, ed. Helen Wallace, William Wallace, and Mark A. Pollack (Oxford: Oxford University Press, 2005).

Antje Wiener and Thomas Diez, *European Integration Theory*, 2nd ed. (Oxford: Oxford University Press, 2009).

CHAPTER 3

The Economic and Legal Foundations of the European Community

Preview

This chapter completes Part I of the book—foundations of modern European integration. Chapter 1 established that modern European integration did not develop in an historical vacuum. Chapter 2 linked political thought and theory to modern European integration and posted the main policy landmarks in EU history. The chronological review of key developments enabled us to begin to critique the relative explanatory power of theories at the end of the last chapter. Students continue to test the relevance of different theoretical explanations as they examine the economics and law of European integration, the subject of our attention in Chapter 3.

The core of the EU remains the establishment of the internal market and monetary union. However, the EU would not exist as we know it today in the absence of the rule of law. The interpretation of Treaty law by the EC courts, the European Court of Justice (ECJ) and the Court of First Instance (CFI), has had a profound influence on the (1) growth and development of the EU as a market and monetary union; and (2) rights and responsibilities of all the players in that union—states, institutions, firms, individuals, and groups.

Up until the entry into force of the Lisbon Treaty, the acronym EC—rather than EU—was used for good reason when examining economic and legal aspects of European integration. The legal framework for the EC itself, the functioning of the internal market and monetary union, and the competence of the ECJ to pass judgment in these areas, had remained in the Treaty of Rome as amended (referred to hereafter as the Treaty). Following passage of the Treaty of European Union (TEU), the EC was placed in Pillar One of the three-pillared EU. However, Pillar Two (CFSP) and Pillar Three (JHA) were designed to be intergovernmental in nature, and thus fell outside the legal-supranational framework of the EC. Strictly speaking, the EC, not the EU, had legal standing to enter into and be subject to international agreements. However, the Lisbon Treaty abandons the pillar structure and establishes the EU, and not just the EC, as an international legal personality. Although the EU as a whole may now enter into international treaty obligations and join international institutions, the ECJ will not have legal purview over defense and security policy. The Lisbon Treaty changes the name of the ECJ to the Court of Justice of the EU and that of the CFI to the General Court. Since this chapter covers EC law and the role of EC courts in it over the past fifty years, our study of law will not use the new lexicon.

The logic of regional economic integration, the process by which barriers to trade are removed among member states to enhance economic welfare, was embraced by the founders of the ECSC and EEC in the 1950s as the primary means to achieve economic and political objectives. The first half of this chapter examines the economic principles, theories, and concepts of European integration. Although imperfect and incomplete, the internal market and monetary union testify to the remarkable achievement of a group of states previously embroiled in war for centuries. Key to success of the development of European economic integration was the early establishment of an EC legal system to interpret and enforce Treaty law and to ensure the law's uniform application.

The second half of the chapter examines the ECJ's structure, function, key legal principles, procedures for legal redress, and cases that have shaped the course of EC legal integration. The juridical basis of the EC starts with the founding and subsequent treaties and the impact the EC courts have had in (1) interpreting what the founders meant by what they created; (2) compelling national courts and governments to respect the supremacy of EC law; and (3) providing legal recourse to individuals directly affected by Treaty law and EC actions. The ECJ's impact in these three areas is similar to that of the U.S. Supreme Court, which interprets the intent of the U.S. Constitution, determines when federal law supercedes state law, and decides when a citizen may bring a case to federal court.

The ECJ has left an indelible mark on the constitutional development and character of the EC during its first half-century. No other EC body has had as much scope for autonomous influence, or agency. The chapter grapples with the question of what the future holds for the continued influence and activism of the ECJ. Insights from liberal intergovernmentalism—and historical and rational choice institutionalism—offer different emphases worth closer scrutiny by student readers.

The Economics of the European Community

Economic integration was chosen by the EC founders as the preferred policy mechanism to rebuild peace, hasten reconstruction, foster and cement reconciliation, respond to external security threats, and enhance human welfare. The failed beggar-thy-neighbor policies of the interwar era were rejected by the West European political and economic elites. Instead they embraced liberal policies of openness and functional cooperation associated with regional economic integration. In time, these elites won over many of those unsure about or opposed to economic integration in their domestic polities, such as French trade unionists and West German social democrats. There was a powerful logic to regional integration that met the economic, political, and security needs of the time. A chief difference between 1950 and, say, 1919 or 1871 was that European interests were incorporated into the scope of national interests, and the two sets of interests reinforced each other. As a result, the nation-state was strengthened and the idea of European unity was given substance after four centuries of chronic warfare.

Regional economic integration refers to a group of nation-states in a region who embark on a gradual process by which they eliminate barriers to trade among one another. The purposes of regional economic integration are both economic (increase human welfare by achieving higher levels of growth) and political (cultivate peace, stability, and cooperation). There are four types of regional economic integration: free trade area, customs union, common market, and economic and monetary union.

In a **free trade area (FTA)**, states in a region eliminate tariffs and other restrictions, such as quantitative restrictions (quotas), among themselves but retain their own external tariffs with the outside world. The European Free Trade Association (EFTA) and the North American Free Trade Agreement (NAFTA) are two examples. Although FTA members eliminate internal tariffs and thus relinquish one element of state sovereignty, no other transfer of sovereignty is involved—in contrast to higher forms of regional economic integration.

In a **customs union**, states not only eliminate tariffs and other trade barriers among themselves but establish a Common External Tariff (CET) with the rest of the world and common institutions that manage the union. The CET is the main feature of a customs union. Without it, a nonmember exporter who enters a union at its least taxed entry point could re-export products anywhere within the union duty free. Such action would undermine the purpose of a customs union—that is, to give internal producers preferential access to union markets. Producers within the union would be disadvantaged if their goods were to be underpriced by unwanted imported competition. A customs union represents a major leap in economic integration for its member states. They cede sovereignty to the union to set external tariffs and establish common regulatory, legal, and political bodies. Examples of customs unions include the Zollverein of Germanic states in the nineteenth century and the Belgium–Luxembourg Economic Union of 1921.

A **common market**, such as the EEC, is a customs union that establishes and regulates an internal market that has free internal movement of goods, services, labor, and capital/investment (production factors). A common market provides for monetary cooperation and the creation of competition, industrial, regional, environmental, and other common policies. The EEC established a common market for all sectors of the member states' economies by the 1970s, with the exception of the defense industry, which falls outside the Treaty purview. However, the EU continues to struggle to ensure free movement of labor and trade in services (see Chapter 6). Since the 1990s, the EU refers to its common market as the internal market.

An **economic and monetary union (EMU)** is the highest form of regional economic integration. In the EU's case, EMU is a common market and a currency union of 16 of the 27 member states. Some have elected to remain outside, such as Britain, Sweden, and Denmark (Copenhagen is reconsidering); others, such as the Baltic Republics, may wish to join in the future if they meet the Maastricht convergence criteria. It is important to note that the EU is a monetary union, but not a fiscal union; therefore, it is a partially completed economic and monetary union. The EU has a single currency for members of the so-called Eurozone, but the power to tax (fiscal policy) remains in the hands of the member states. In an economic and monetary union, there is extensive simultaneous integration of both macroeconomic and monetary policy, including the establishment of a single currency and a central bank that sets interest rates. When the EEC became the EU through the TEU in 1993, the EU set as a goal the economic and monetary union. Over time, exchange rates were fixed, the European Central Bank (ECB) was established, and the common currency, the euro, was introduced.

Having identified the major stages of regional economic integration, we now turn to three important theoretical approaches to the study of regional economic integration: customs union theory, Optimum Currency Area (OCA) theory, and International Political Economy (IPE). Together, these approaches help explain why sovereign states form and remain in regional integration schemes.

CUSTOMS UNION THEORY

The European initiative to form a customs union represents a case of regional economic integration. Traditionally, regional integration is thought to give rise to both winners and losers. Who wins and who loses depends on which firms can compete once internal barriers to trade among union members are eliminated. By raising the price of imported goods, national tariffs are designed to protect domestic firms from cheap imports. For example, the EU has high import levies on agricultural products to protect farmers from low-priced imports. EU import levies on agricultural products have resulted in the much higher price Europeans pay for food than, say, Americans.

We know that forming a customs union means eliminating tariffs on imports from member states while establishing a common tariff on imports from nonmembers. Once a union's member states eliminate tariffs and other barriers to trade vis-à-vis one another, previously protected domestic firms are subject to new competitive rigors from efficient producers elsewhere in the union. Producers outside the union too are generally affected by such a move. Their competitive position relative to producers of member states has changed with the formation of the customs union because members' producers receive preferential treatment. Scholars have debated whether or not the EU represents a threat to the multilateral global trading system based on the idea of most-favored-nation treatment (nondiscrimination among trade partners).

Many, but not all, scholars of regional economic integration theory have concluded that the EU has generated more welfare gains for internal producers and consumers when compared to preunion times. Many of the EU's major trading partners have also witnessed an increase in their exports to the union, but not in all sectors (e.g., agriculture and textiles). However, intra-EU trade (trade among union members) has grown considerably faster than extra-EU trade (trade between union and nonunion members), which is held to be a consequence of the formation of a customs union and common market.[1] Assessing the welfare effects on members and nonmembers is a complex affair. Customs union theory provides a useful starting point.

Customs union theory, a branch of free trade theory, focuses on welfare gains and losses associated with the creation of a customs union. Free trade is viewed by customs union theorists as desirable as it increases production and consumption and contributes to increases in real income. If states eliminate internal barriers to trade and create a customs union, they can gain from an overall increase in welfare for both producer and consumer. This theory also compares trade created and trade diverted as a result of the establishment of the union, which in turn allows economists to evaluate welfare gains and losses that result from the customs union. States considering whether to join a customs union try to ascertain what their expected benefits and costs will be, and those already inside the union may evaluate how they have fared. Customs union theory generally posits that welfare gains would include:

- an increase in production, consumption, and competition as a result of removing barriers to trade;
- a more efficient allocation of resources across markets;
- inward investment in the union by foreign firms who set up production capability to get around the CET;
- an increase in the supply of less expensive goods for consumers, which occurs when one member firm is substituted for another as a source of supply because it offers lower costs;
- the stimulation of modernization, technological advances, and economic growth; and
- improved competitiveness for leaner, more efficient union producers who increase market share not only in the union but abroad.

Welfare losses associated with the creation of a custom union may include loss of jobs as a result of new waves of competition that occur in a borderless market. However, economists maintain that such job losses will be only temporary. The reallocation of resources requires workers to find new jobs. Customs union theory generally features five key concepts that account for the welfare gains and losses that result from the establishment of a customs union: comparative advantage, economies of scale, preferential treatment for internal producers, and trade creation and diversion.

Comparative advantage refers to the specialization of production based on which firms can produce goods most efficiently and provide consumers with the lowest prices. Comparative advantage in a large single market refers to a process of adjustment whereby the most competitive firms are rewarded with new markets and consumers. Less efficient, high-cost firms either learn to compete, go out of business, or enter new areas of production where they can enjoy comparative advantage. Increasing welfare gains for producers and consumers is the ultimate benefit expected by member states who engage in regional economic integration.

Economies of scale refer to the gains achieved by creating a larger single market for goods and services. Economies of scale allow an optimum scale for the production of goods and services not possible in the context of the home market. As economic barriers to trade are eliminated, nationally-scaled firms enjoy duty-free access to a much larger market. As these union producers increase the scale of their production, they may be able to increase efficiencies, that is, decrease average production costs, and offer lower prices to consumers to stay competitive or gain competitiveness. Economies of scale tend to increase trade and thus prosperity and increase consumer choice for better-priced goods overall. Economies of scale also encourage a more efficient (optimum) allocation of resources such as capital and labor from less to more profitable areas of the union. The customs union allows more cost-effective production as a result of economies of scale, and the CET gives domestic producers preferential access to the internal market over cheaper goods imported from outside the market.

Preferential treatment refers to the benefits that accrue to internal producers who enjoy duty-free trade within the union in contrast to external producers who must pay the duty. For example, most U.S. agricultural exports to the EU face import duties, but EU producers enjoy duty-free or preferential access to the customs union.

The balance between new trade created and trade diverted as a result of a customs union is the key focus of customs union theory. It is on this basis that welfare gains and losses are measured. The concepts of trade creation and trade diversion were introduced by Jacob Viner and further developed by others.[2] The theory predicts that trade created and trade diverted result when member firms and individual consumers seek to procure the lowest-cost source of supply. If this source of supply is found in the union, there is **trade creation** and welfare is gained within the union. Trade creation is thought by customs union theorists to make production more efficient. Higher domestic production occurs in member countries since it is cheaper for a union member to import from another union member. With the lifting of tariffs, customs unions give incentives to producers to become more competitive. Union producers who are efficient and offer consumers low-cost products will gain more market shares than those who are less competitive. Expanded trade brings gains in welfare for both the producer, who gains new market shares and earns profits, and the consumer, whose preferences are satisfied. Trade creation and expansion has occurred in the EU market more in the industrial sector than in others, such as agriculture and textiles.

If the source of supply is found outside the union, there is **trade diversion** as trade is shifted away from the lowest-cost producer outside the union to a less efficient and more expensive producer inside the union. There is a welfare loss as gains from trade (comparative advantages) are not maximized.[3] For example, there has been serious loss of EU market shares in agriculture for New Zealand as a result of the EU's use of variable import levies, price supports, and export subsidies to support farm income and hold down cheaper farm imports. However, since the EU is a large and fairly open market vis-à-vis the rest of the world, and because its share of world trade is large, the risks of trade diversion are reduced. Furthermore, EU trade with nonmembers expanded because of the spur in domestic EU demand for foreign imports as a result of an increase in growth and income, and as a result of the GATT and WTO tariff-cutting rounds of multilateral trade negotiations.

The value of customs union theory is that it offers a framework for considering welfare gains and losses. Since trade diversion alone reduces welfare, the ideal scenario in a customs union is that more trade has been created than diverted. However, the answer will not be known for certain until after a customs union has been in operation for some time.[4] We know that, as a result of the establishment of the EU, trade was created, expanded, and diverted. Many scholars conclude that intra-EU trade rose at a much faster rate than extra-EU trade. Extra-EU trade also rose, but not as fast.[5] EU members trade more with one another than they do with the outside world. Thus in the EU, trade creation has generally been greater than trade diversion, and the customs union has led to welfare gains overall.

The EU is the world's largest and richest economic entity, largest single importer and exporter, and largest governmental donor of foreign aid. The EU is an economic magnet for European states. The economic risks/costs of remaining outside appear greater than the risks/costs of joining. What this means is that the member states decided when they joined the union that the prospect of gain would outweigh cost. By virtue of remaining in the union, they have determined that gains continue to outweigh costs. Customs union theory helps explain the economic benefits and costs to members who join a customs union or common market. But why do states join a monetary union? The section that follows offers insights into that very question by introducing Optimum Currency Area theory.

OPTIMUM CURRENCY AREA THEORY

Customs union theory predicts the growth of intra-union trade. As internal EU trade grew, the member states found that currency fluctuations after the collapse of the Bretton Woods fixed exchange-rate system had adverse effects on the operations of the common market. The more intra-EU trade grew, the more the member states were subject to exchange rate risks. Fluctuating exchange rates made trade and investment less reliable and predictable because they introduced new costs and more uncertainty, detracting from the benefits of a large and free internal market. The EU members responded to the adverse effects of floating exchange rates by creating mechanisms to reduce the scope of exchange-rate fluctuations. This section introduces a theory of regional monetary integration before turning to the establishment of the EMU in the 1990s.

Optimum Currency Area (OCA) theory defines and explains the economic conditions necessary for a monetary union to be created and sustained. Each prospective member needs to evaluate whether it makes sense to join a currency union. OCA theory suggests that countries that have already engaged in extensive institutionalized regional economic integration are likely to form a monetary union. Such states have economies that are open to international trade in goods and services and thus already exposed to the risks associated with international monetary flows. Economic and monetary union advantages open economy states because it offers increased stability of income and employment.[6]

OCA theory emphasizes the optimum or "right" size for achieving monetary union—neither too small nor too large. A monetary union has to have enough countries to ensure comparative advantage, product differentiation, and economies of scale.[7] The larger a common market grows in membership, the harder it will be to establish a monetary union. If the currency union enlarges beyond the point "where the marginal cost and marginal benefit curve intersect for the group," the union will exceed its optimum size, which reduces the marginal benefits.[8]

OCA theory anticipates that union members will have similar public and private policy preferences with regard to acceptable levels of unemployment and inflation. OCA theory also predicts that states will forfeit sovereignty to set exchange rates if they calculate that the benefits of joining the union will outweigh the costs of remaining outside. The benefits of joining the union will include the elimination of exchange-rate volatility and of the transaction costs associated with converting currencies with other union members. This in turn will stimulate trade and investment within the union and the flow of capital from outside the union into the union. The more the members of a currency union trade with one another, the more they benefit from membership in the union. In time, a currency union will more efficiently allocate resources. Economic cycles will become more synchronized.

According to OCA theory, the costs of joining the union will include the loss of sovereignty during a period of national or local recession when states may not resort to monetary policy by lowering interest rates. Member states also cannot raise interest rates to temper inflation in a period of overheated growth. The cost of union membership may be a problem if countries differ in socially and politically acceptable rates of inflation and unemployment.[9] To address unemployment and economic development, the EU expends considerable resources through its regional policy programs, e.g., EU subsidies, grants, and loans for disadvantaged areas of the member states. As will be discussed in Chapter 6, EU regional development aid aims to help redistribute wealth and provide support for new infrastructures and labor retraining. However, many economists argue that EU regional spending is neither as efficient nor as effective a means of addressing local economic difficulties as national use of monetary policy to help a region in distress.

The Rome Treaty did not envisage EMU as an explicit objective, but it provided for close consultation and coordination of monetary and exchange-rate policies. In the 1970 Werner Report, the member states aimed to create a monetary union by 1980. However, the collapse of the fixed exchange-rate system and the economic effects of the oil crisis in the early 1970s dashed those hopes. In order to address the adverse impact of fluctuating exchange rates on the common market, some of the member states entered into what was known as the **snake-in-the-tunnel** between 1973 and 1979. The snake was a set of voluntary agreements to reduce exchange-rate volatility. Participants agreed to a series of fixed rates allowing for a 2.25 percent deviation between the strongest and weakest currencies.

In 1979, the European Monetary System (EMS), a more formal but still voluntary intergovernmental monetary system, was put into place to enhance monetary stability. EMS was not part of the EC treaty system, but only members of the EC could join the EMS. EMS exchange rates were fixed but left enough flexibility to allow for periodic adjustments. Currencies could diverge by 2.25 percent from the other member currencies (6 percent for Italy). When currencies either strengthened or weakened beyond the ceiling or floor, the member states' central banks would buy or sell reserve currency to bring the errant currency back into the accepted band. Britain remained outside, joined later, and left again. The currency fluctuation ban for EMS was widened to 15 percent in 1992. The concept behind the EMS was to pressure member governments not to allow their currencies to get too far out of line with other rates and to enact policies to bring them back into line before realignment was the only recourse. EMS members were expected to exercise discipline and bring about coordination and convergence of policies. The European Currency Unit introduced an average basket of the member currencies and served as an actual asset.

EMS provided some elements of monetary stability during its lifetime until the EMU was introduced following enactment of the TEU in 1993. This was the first time the objective of monetary union was brought inside the Treaty framework. The TEU provided for the progressive introduction of EMU in phases.

The European Central Bank (ECB) was established in 1998. In the following year, a single monetary policy was established, the euro was launched, the ECB set interest rates, and exchange rates were irrevocably locked. In 2002 the euro replaced the member currencies, at which time monetary policy became fully integrated. The criteria for joining, besides the political will, are that members must (a) have independent central banks; (b) have inflation rates not higher than 1.5 percent above the average of the inflation rates of the three lowest inflation EMU countries; (c) not devalue their currency within two years before joining the Exchange Rate Mechanism (ERM); and (d) not allow their total budget deficits to exceed 60 percent of GDP or their annual budget deficit to exceed 3 percent of GDP. The optimal size of the union was determined by the number of countries that were eligible and could meet the convergence criteria for joining and remaining in the EMU. These criteria and a study of EU monetary institutions, policies, and practices may be found in Chapter 6.

Whether or not EMU today constitutes an Optimum Currency Area is open to debate. There is insufficient labor mobility across the Eurozone members; workers cannot move with relative ease from a depressed economic area to one with more employment. The economic cycles of the members are not sufficiently synchronized, and member governments facing a national or regional economic downturn feel the need to resort to monetary policy, but cannot. That said, an Optimum Currency Area may well exist among the Eurozone "Rhineland" countries where economic cycles are linked even though labor markets are rigid: Germany, France, Belgium, the Netherlands, and Luxembourg.[10]

Image 3.1.   Euro Notes. Courtesy of the Audiovisual Library of the European Commission

INTERNATIONAL POLITICAL ECONOMY

Customs union and OCA theories help explain the economic logic behind regional economic integration. However, the study of the economic foundations of the EU would be incomplete without an examination of the politics behind the decision of the EC states to integrate economically in the 1950s and monetarily in the 1990s. **International Political Economy (IPE)**, a conceptual approach to the study of international affairs, emphasizes the interplay between economic and political forces in the creation and subsequent growth of the EU. An IPE approach helps to explain how the logic of regional economic integration was achieved as a political reality. Politics in the form of national/domestic interests, the role of key individual players, the regional economic and political situation, and the currents of change in the international arena that necessitated national and European responses gave impetus to the creation of the EU. Without the political catalysts, economic theory would remain merely abstract.

The governments that formed the ECSC and EEC were not starry-eyed European federalists bent on replacing the antique nation-states with a United States of Europe. Instead they pursued their national security, political, and economic interests at a European level when it suited them. The EU's founding was largely due to a confluence of national economic, political, and security interests advanced by elites who all supported the establishment of a new peace order. All had on their minds the imperative not only to cooperate in the face of the Soviet threat but to put into place a customs union in relation to the enormous economic and political power of the United States. The member-state governments—all anticommunist—embraced social democracy to varying degrees, so it was not a stretch for them to envisage the EC as a means to enhance the welfare of their citizens at the regional collective level. Functionalism is in many respects an extension of social democracy at an international level. Each of the players found something in the ECSC/EEC that met national interests. National interests refer to vital economic and security interests of a nation-state over time, shaped by political culture and political development. However, what was different in European international relations was that European interests—peace, stability, and prosperity on a continental scale—were incorporated into the national interests. The interplay between European and national interests has been the necessary dynamic, and created the friction, that has allowed the Europeans to develop their union while retaining the nation-state.

The role of individual national elites who sit at the intersection of national and European interests has been instrumental in forging new areas of cooperation at EC/EU levels. It took political elites to make economic and monetary integration happen. French and German national interests and elites provide multiple examples of the interplay between national and European interests. The ECSC happened in large part because France (Robert Schuman) wanted to keep West Germany from reestablishing economic and political hegemony, and West Germany (Konrad Adenauer) wanted legitimacy and the return to sovereignty. The EEC happened in large part because France wanted duty-free access to the West German agricultural market, and West Germany wanted access to the French industrial market. Years later, in 1979, it was France (Valéry Giscard d'Estaing) and West Germany (Helmut Schmidt) who in their common interest created the EMS. With the unification of Germany in 1990, France again feared the resurgence of German hegemony and responded by seeking to anchor the enlarged unified Germany more deeply in a new European Union (1993) and in an economic and monetary union that followed. For France, EMU was about politics, but for Germany, it was about economics—the spread of fiscal restraint, low inflation, and currency strength and stability from the Deutschmark to the new euro. It was France (François Mitterand), Germany (Helmut Kohl), and the Commission (Jacques Delors) who were the critical interlocutors involved in the launch of the common market and its development into the economic and monetary union.

National interests and elites were not operating in a vacuum of international politics. When faced with the choice of locking West Germany into regional security and economic institutions in the face of Soviet expansionism or returning to the failed policies that had followed World War I, the Western European states chose reconciliation and integration. The pressure from the United States to reconcile and integrate was also an important catalyst in 1950. The bipolarity of the postwar international system reminded the Europeans that if they were ever to regain the influence they had once had over their own affairs and those of the world, they would need a collective basis for cooperation in order to lessen dependence on the two-bloc system.

RECAP

Theory is as good as its ability to define, describe, explain, and predict outcomes. The value of customs union theory is that it stresses the reasons for states to join a union. If the union incurs more economic and political costs than gains, it will be a non-starter. It will either not get off the ground or fail once started. Neither has happened to the EU. The EU is founded on the logic of regional economic integration, which has endured over time. Optimum Currency Area theory is useful in explaining the difficulties associated with finding the right formula for monetary integration and predicting the conditions for an economic and monetary union to work. How long the EU's monetary union will remain an Optimum Currency Area remains to be seen with the large increase in membership and the enormous difficulties member states are having in meeting the criteria required to retain membership in the EMU. The IPE approach picks up where economic theory leaves off. It stresses the interplay of economic and political conditions and individuals that together made possible the EU's founding and development. The union that developed after the founding depended on holding the member states accountable to EC law. This is why we now turn our attention to the role of the EC courts in enforcing the economic and political decisions to integrate.

The Law of the European Community

For over fifty years, the Treaty—interpreted and transformed by the European Court of Justice in its jurisprudence—formed an imperfect and incomplete constitution of the EC.[11] The ECJ has created a new legal order autonomous from, yet having primacy over, the legal orders of the member states. This section introduces readers to the sources of EC law, describes the jurisdiction, structure, and function of the EC courts, explores the avenues of legal redress, and identifies major EC legal principles and landmark cases. It ends with a theoretical analysis of the course of EC legal integration.

The **sources of EC law** include the Treaty as amended; laws enacted by EU bodies; policies and actions taken by the EU and transposed into national enacting legislation; principles developed by the ECJ; rulings and opinions taken by the ECJ; legal and constitutional values, traditions, and practices of the member states; and international treaties enacted by the EC. The scope of EC law, and the **jurisdiction of the EC Courts**, is limited to those areas where the Treaty grants competence to the EC, such as trade and antitrust policies. The Lisbon Treaty grants legal purview to the ECJ over most JHA areas with the exception of judicial cooperation in criminal matters and police cooperation. Member states retain sovereignty in all areas not covered by the Treaty, such as defense and fiscal policy. However, there are areas where the EC and the member states share competence, such as most aspects of trade in services and intellectual property rights. Moreover, although the ECJ does not have purview over CFSP, it does have the authority to rule on the legality of restrictive measures, such as EU economic sanctions against foreign firms, individuals or countries. The ECJ ensures that the proper boundary between CFSP and other elements of EU foreign policy are respected.

Since the EC is not a nation-state like the United States, the scope of EC law is not nearly as broad as that of the federal law of the United States. The competence of the ECJ is not as broad as that of the U.S. Supreme Court. However, in the EU, the Treaty, like the U.S. Constitution, leaves to the states all areas of jurisdiction not specifically granted to the union (in the EU case, the common institutions, and in the U.S., the federal government).

The EC's two Courts, the ECJ and the CFI, are located in Luxembourg. Each in its own jurisdiction is empowered to interpret and apply the Treaty to ensure that the law of the EC is observed. National law and EC law exist concomitantly. The ECJ, which is responsible for constitutional and political issues of high importance, is the senior of the two courts. It gives legal judgments in cases brought before it and ensures the uniform interpretation of EC law and the legality of acts of the EC bodies. Uniformity refers to the Treaty's charge to the ECJ to ensure that EC laws are interpreted and applied in the same way in each of the member states. The ECJ—charged by the Treaty to enforce Treaty rules—has exclusive, unlimited, and obligatory competence to hear and rule on disputes over EC law brought before it

- between member states;
- between member states and EC bodies;
- between individuals and member states; and
- between individuals and EC bodies.

The most common cases include requests to overturn acts of EC bodies or member states; claims that an EC body has failed to fulfill Treaty obligations; and requests by national courts for an ECJ opinion or interpretation in cases involving EC law (preliminary reference). In the United States, in contrast, a federal or state court may not render an opinion in the absence of a case or controversy before that court. When

Image 3.2. European Court of Justice in Luxembourg. Courtesy of the Audiovisual Library of the European Commission

the ECJ makes a ruling in the context of the national judiciary, it has impact on all national courts, just as in federal judicial systems.

To reduce the ECJ's caseload, the Single European Act provided for what became the CFI, which the Council established in 1988. The CFI is attached to the ECJ, but it is not a new institution per se. The U.S. Congress, like the Council, may establish specialized courts to reduce the burden on state and federal courts. However, the CFI has no equivalent in the United States. Its mandate is much broader than that of any specialized court established by Congress to alleviate some of the caseload burden on state and federal courts. The CFI has jurisdiction to hear

- certain preliminary references not heard by the ECJ;
- most direct actions brought by individuals against EC bodies;
- most administrative and staff disputes until December 2005, when the EU Civil Service Tribunal, established by the Nice Treaty and attached to the CFI, began operations to handle such cases;
- certain appeals following Commission rulings on competition cases or rulings of specialized judicial panels created by the Nice Treaty (CFI decisions may be appealed to the ECJ on points of law; however, most CFI decisions are not appealed); and
- other categories of proceedings entrusted to the CFI by the ECJ.

STRUCTURE AND FUNCTION

To help focus and clarify our study of the EC Courts, we compare their features to those of another, older, and more sophisticated federal judiciary—the U.S. Supreme

Court. The EC Courts are **hybrid courts** that act in four different capacities: international, administrative, constitutional, and tribunal.[12] As an international court, the ECJ rules on disputes between states concerning the application of the Treaty. As an administrative court, the CFI determines if member states infringe EC law.[13] As a constitutional court, the ECJ ensures the legality of the acts of EC bodies and ensures that EC law is observed uniformly by the member states. As a tribunal, the EC Courts are responsible for technical areas of law (e.g., intellectual property). Here the ECJ and the U.S. Supreme Court are not at all governmental equals. EC law is supreme over conflicting member-state law, and ECJ rulings are imposed on and accepted by sovereign states. Thus, the Treaty empowers the ECJ to act as a supranational court where it has the competence. Conversely, the Supreme Court is neither a supranational nor an international court, but a national one. Its rulings are supreme vis-à-vis constituent, but not sovereign, states.

Each member government appoints its own ECJ Judge, subject to the unanimous agreement (common accord) of the Council. The ECJ Judges are assisted by eight Advocates General, who offer reasoned opinions on cases for the Judges' consideration.[14] Judges and Advocates General are former members of the highest courts of their home states or are well-known lawyers. The six-year appointments of Judges and Advocates General are renewable on a staggered basis to ensure institutional continuity. However, some EC legal scholars express concern that renewable appointments by national governments of ECJ Justices subject those individuals to political influences.[15] In the United States, opportunity exists for political consideration at the time of appointment of Supreme Court Justices and of the Chief Justice. The American President has enormous political influence over Supreme Court appointments, including that of the Chief Justice, subject to Senate confirmation. The Senate confirms Justices based on a simple majority vote after a recommendation of the Senate Judiciary Committee. In contrast, EC member governments neither nominate nor confirm the President of the ECJ. The ECJ Judges select their own President for a renewable three-year term.

Not all Judges of the ECJ hear every case. The ECJ sits as a full court, a grand chamber (thirteen Judges), or in chambers of three or five Judges, depending on the nature of the case to be heard. The ECJ sits as a full court in very exceptional cases provided for in the Treaty.[16]

Like the ECJ Judges, the CFI Judges, who come from each of the member states, elect their President for a renewable three-year term. The European Council may increase the number of Judges and determines the rotation of their appointment. CFI Judges have six-year terms renewable on a staggered basis.[17] The CFI Judges sit in chambers of three or five Judges. In certain cases, a chamber may consist of just one Judge. To reduce the backlog of cases in the CFI and thus avoid delays in justice, the Treaty of Nice empowered the Council to create specialized judicial panels to hear certain kinds of cases, such as those involving patents, civil service, and intellectual property. To establish such panels, the Council acts unanimously on a Commission proposal or at the request of the ECJ, in consultation with the EP and the ECJ. The Council appoints the Judges on these panels on the basis of unanimity. Decisions of these specialized panels are appealable to the CFI under certain conditions. The power of the European Council to establish specialized judicial panels and courts is similar to the power of the U.S. Congress, which has established such specialized courts as the Bankruptcy Court and the Foreign Intelligence Surveillance Court.

The EC Courts are assisted by legal secretaries, rapporteurs, translators, and a registrar, who perform important research, reporting, and administrative tasks.[18] French is the working language of the ECJ, but ECJ documents are translated into the EU's official languages. The EC Court system—namely the ECJ and CFI plus the national judiciaries—is less complex than that of the U.S. court system. The U.S. court system features the Supreme Court, thirteen federal courts of appeal, ninety-four federal district courts, and fifty state court judiciaries. The voting method in the ECJ is based on consensus or simple majority. However, unlike the U.S. Supreme Court, the ECJ does not publish separate and dissenting opinions. This practice may deny EC individuals the reasoned judgment that went into a collective decision, but it helps enhance ECJ independence of member governments, especially at the time of the Justices' reappointment.

In the U.S. Supreme Court, five Justices constitute a majority. An individual Justice who is part of the majority opinion writes an opinion on behalf of the majority. Individual Justices in the minority may choose to write a dissenting opinion. There are also concurring opinions written by individual Justices who are part of the majority and agree with the outcome of the case, but who disagree with the reasoning of the majority. Thus, a key distinction between the ECJ and the U.S. Supreme Court is that the ECJ speaks as an institution and the Supreme Court is much more individualistic. Apart from the one majority opinion (issued by an individual Supreme Court Justice), all other opinions represent the voice of an individual Justice.

The Treaty empowers the EC Courts to enforce Treaty rules. Long-standing, time-tested constitutions are not static and anachronistic documents. The Treaty, like the U.S. Constitution, is broadly and necessarily subject to juridical interpretation regarding the rights and responsibilities of the constituent players. The EC Courts have wide latitude to interpret what the founders wanted when they wrote the Treaty; for example, their rulings and opinions have substantially influenced both the formulation and implementation of EC rules governing the free movement of goods and services.

AVENUES OF LEGAL REDRESS

In EC law, only the member-state judiciaries interpret state law as it relates to EC law. Through preliminary reference, the ECJ engages national courts in dialogue, and it depends on national judiciaries to interpret and enforce its interpretations of EC law within their own states. This has proven to be a win-win situation for the ECJ and the member-state judiciaries. National courts arrive at their own interpretation of the relationship between national and EC law *after* having received the ECJ opinion. This in turn enhances the relationship between national and EC courts, makes EC law and ECJ interpretations more acceptable domestically, and advances European integration overall. Conversely, the U.S. Constitution prohibits the Supreme Court from rendering advisory opinions and engaging formally in dialogue with the lower courts. Federal courts may order state courts to uphold federal law. When the Supreme Court renders an opinion, the lower courts are obliged to follow that ruling.

The difference between the EC and United States over the relationship between higher and lower courts may explain why there was much more acceptance of the jurisdiction of the ECJ by the member states in the EC's early decades than there was of the Supreme Court's jurisdiction by the U.S. states in the early decades of the United States.

The Treaty provides three major avenues for legal redress: annulment, infringement, and preliminary reference. **Annulment** refers to the decision of the ECJ to overturn a decision of an EC body. **Infringement** refers to the ECJ's determination that an EC body or member state has violated EC rules or laws. **Preliminary reference** refers to the response of the EC Courts to queries from national judiciaries about points of EC law. Together, these avenues of legal redress hold the EC bodies and member states responsible to the EC's rule of law and guarantee individuals their Treaty rights. The legal principles and landmark cases that have arisen from the pursuit of these avenues of legal redress have strengthened the **uniform application of EC law**. The uniform application of EC law refers to the principle that EC law must be applied uniformly in all the member states. In this way, the EC has become not only a community based on a unified market and currency but one based on the rule of law.

Annulment: The ECJ has the right to review the legality of the actions of the EC bodies in annulment proceedings brought by (a) member states; (b) the Commission and Council; (c) the EP, the ECB, and the Court of Auditors when they are protecting their prerogatives; and—under more restricted terms—(d) private applicants or natural and legal persons (individuals, firms, and certain associations) when decisions are of either individual or direct concern to them. Under the Lisbon Treaty, an individual may bring a proceeding to the EC courts in relation to legal actions of the EU that do not require implementing action by the member states where those actions directly affect the individual. Grounds for annulment include lack of competence, infringement of Treaty law and its application, and misuse of power. Annulment is similar to the power of judicial review exercised by American courts. American courts are empowered to declare any piece of federal or state legislation invalid when it conflicts with the Constitution.

Two landmark annulment cases, *Les Verts* (1983) and *Chernobyl* (1988), deserve attention for their impacts regarding the EC legal order and for their roles in the development of the European Parliament as a major EC body. In these decisions, the ECJ included the EP in the list of EC bodies that could bring an annulment proceeding or be subject to one. The ECJ rulings in these landmark cases were codified in the TEU in 1993.

The ECJ determined in *Les Verts* that the French Green Party could bring an annulment proceeding against a decision of the EP concerning financing of party electoral campaigns. The French Greens in the EP sought annulment of measures adopted by the EP concerning reimbursement of party expenses in the 1984 EC parliamentary elections even though the French Green Party was not represented in the EP at the time the measures were adopted. The Greens, however, intended to challenge the parliamentary elections. The party alleged that the EP's measures for financing political party electoral campaigns were discriminatory because they favored political groups that were already represented in the EP. The Greens argued that the ECJ's jurisdiction in the area of annulment could not be restricted to measures taken by the Commission and Council "without giving rise to a denial of justice."[19] The Green Party had to establish two things: (a) that it had the legal right to challenge the EP under Treaty rules on annulment; and (b) that it was concerned individually by the measures it was contesting. The ECJ ruled that the EP actions were subject to judicial review by the ECJ to determine if such actions conformed to the Treaty. The ECJ concluded that the Green Party was individually concerned: public funds were not distributed equally in the context of the preparation for the 1984 EP elections.

In *Chernobyl*, the EP sought annulment of a Council regulation (a piece of EC legislation) concerning the Chernobyl nuclear power station accident in 1986. The Euratom Treaty empowered the Council to vote on the regulation after consulting the EP. The SEA enhanced the role of the EP in EC governmental decisionmaking. On that basis the EP requested that the Commission interpret the Treaty to give it recourse to annulment proceedings. The Commission did not meet this request, and the Council argued that the Treaty does not grant the authority to the EP to bring annulment proceedings forward. The EP countered that it could not rely on the Commission to defend its prerogatives, given that the other two EC bodies disagreed with it over the correct legal basis of the disputed regulation. Even though the Commission had the duty to ensure respect for those prerogatives, it could not be expected to bring annulment proceedings that it believed to be unfounded.

The ECJ concluded that the EP has the right to bring proceedings for annulment of an act adopted by the Council or Commission if the EP thereby seeks to safeguard its prerogatives and alleges infringement. Thus, in *Chernobyl* the ECJ created a new right of action to preserve the balance among institutions created in the Treaty.[20]

Two other annulment cases demonstrate the authority of the EC courts. In October 2001 the Commission banned a merger between Tetra Laval and Sidel and in January 2002 ordered the separation of the two companies. Tetra Laval is a Swiss-based manufacturer of carton drinks packaging and Sidel is a French designer/manufacturer of packaging equipment and bottles of polyethylene terephthalate—PET. The Commission argued that the merger would allow Tetra Laval and Sidel to further dominate the packaging market. The companies appealed the decision to the CFI. The CFI annulled the decision of the Commission to prohibit the merger and annulled the decision to order the "demerger" of the two companies. The ECJ confirmed the annulment decisions of the CFI, arguing that the CFI correctly exercised its power of judicial review granted by the Treaty to the EC Courts. The ECJ determined that the Commission's economic analysis of the effects of the merger was based on errors in the assessment and that the Commission did not take into account commitments offered by the company to change its practices. The case demonstrates that even though the Commission has Treaty authority to rule on anticompetitive behavior of firms alleged to abuse a dominant position in a market, it does not have the final word, since companies may appeal decisions of both the Commission and the CFI.

In another case concerning the balance between institutions, the ECJ annulled a Council decision approving Portugal's grant of state aid to pork producers (2004). These farmers had benefited by state aid granted in 1994 and 1995, and the Commission had declared the aid incompatible with state aid rules associated with the common market organization for pork production. In arguing that the Treaty empowers the Commission to monitor state aids and determine which aids are and are not compatible with the Common Agricultural Policy, the Court ruled that the Council cannot authorize either a state aid that the Commission has already declared illegal or a new state aid that allocates to the beneficiaries of that aid an amount intended to compensate for repayments they have had to make following a Commission decision.

Infringement. The ECJ ensures that the law of the EC is respected by member states and EC bodies. Neither the member states nor the EC bodies can avoid a review ensuring that their adopted measures conform to the Treaty. The Commission—guardian of and watchdog for the Treaty—initiates infringement proceedings when it determines that a member state has breached or failed to fulfill its Treaty obligations. Any individual, under certain conditions, may complain to the ECJ that an EC body has failed to act with regard to its Treaty obligations. Member states and EC bodies may be challenged not only for infringing Treaty rules or the rule of law related to the Treaty's application but for infringement of an essential procedural requirement, misuse of powers, or failure to act. Here there are parallels with the U.S. federal court system, which can hear complaints that governmental bodies have acted in violation of the U.S. Constitution or federal law.

As early as 1972, the ECJ declared in *Commission v Italy* that the Treaty imposes an obligation on member states to respect EC rules. The ECJ reasoned that two consequences ensue when a member state unilaterally breaks the balance between advantages and obligations derived from adherence to the EC. That state throws into question the equality of the member states before the law of the EC. It also causes discrimination at the expense of its nationals "and of the member state itself, which places itself outside EC rules."[21] The ECJ has determined that the member states must remove from their domestic legal order any provisions incompatible with EC law. As a result of the enactment of the TEU in 1993, member states who fail to take steps that bring them into compliance with an ECJ judgment may be subject to financial sanctions.

With regard to infringement cases, the Commission invites the member government in question to explain the allegation. If the Commission considers the explanation to be insufficient, it adopts a "reasoned opinion," which sets a deadline by which the member government must take measures to comply with Treaty obligations. If the member government does not comply with the Commission's opinion, the Commission may bring the matter to the ECJ. The case may be brought to the ECJ following the issuance of a Commission's reasoned opinion or a delay of three months. The Commission has the burden to prove existence of an alleged infringement.

The Commission has made only sporadic use of its infringement powers, preferring instead to guide member governments in bilateral negotiations. Member governments may introduce infringement proceedings against one another, but this procedure is rarely used because they are reluctant to turn to the EC to resolve disputes with one another. Examples of infringement cases brought by the Commission include the actions of Greece in 1989 and France in 2004.

In *Commission v Greece* (1989), the ECJ found that Greece had infringed the Treaty. Athens failed to impose EC import duties on corn from Yugoslavia and to pay these duties to the EC as required by the common market organization for cereals. Since the Treaty requires member governments to take all measures necessary to ensure the effective application of EC law, the ECJ also determined that Greece infringed the Treaty by not pursuing disciplinary or criminal proceedings against those who engaged in fraudulent practices. In *Commission v France* (2004) the ECJ found France had failed to implement a 1995 Council Directive that required member governments to inspect at least 25 percent of the number of individual vessels entering their ports during each calendar year. The Commission argued that this infringement increased the risk of maritime accidents that could endanger human lives or result in water pollution.

Preliminary Reference: A national court with a pending case in which a question arises related to EC law may ask either the ECJ or the CFI, depending on the subject of the query, to interpret the relevant EC law. The Treaty grants the ECJ jurisdiction to give preliminary rulings with regard to the interpretation of (a) the Treaty as amended; (b) acts of EC bodies and the validity of those acts; and (c) international agreements entered into by the EC. In interpreting the spirit of the Treaty, the ECJ allows national courts to query not just the meaning of EC laws but the direct effect of those laws on individuals. If the EC Courts decide to respond to the preliminary reference, they do not render a judgment but provide a clarification or interpretation of EC law that the highest national courts apply. For instance, the ECJ reasoned in *Costa v ENEL* (1963) that the Treaty does not give it jurisdiction to apply EC law to specific cases in national courts or to decide on the validity of domestic law in relation to EC law. However, the ECJ did conclude that it has the jurisdiction to extract from questions posed by the national courts those questions that alone pertain to the interpretation of the Treaty. What makes the ECJ ruling "preliminary" is that the ruling is "interlocutory": the ruling is a step in the national courts' proceedings.[22] The national courts apply preliminary rulings to the facts of the pending case.

Preliminary references were first used, sparingly, in the 1960s, in such areas as free movement of goods and agricultural support. However, once internal tariffs were removed by 1968 and the free movement of goods, services, capital, and labor increased, so too did the frequency of preliminary references. By the 1990s, such references extended to areas related to market integration, including taxation, competition, environmental protection, and gender equality. Although the Treaty founders established the procedure of preliminary reference to ensure a uniform interpretation of EC law, the procedure has turned out to be a fulcrum of legal integration, especially since the 1970s. Moreover, preliminary reference has had a positive impact on the legitimacy of the ECJ in relation to the national courts. Preliminary reference has been a win-win game for the ECJ and national courts. It has

- facilitated a direct dialogue between national and EC judges, something eschewed by the U.S. Supreme Court in its relationship with lower courts;
- acquainted national courts with EC law and acquainted the ECJ with the particular implications of its rulings, which, at times, have influenced the evolution of the ECJ's own jurisprudence;[23]
- enhanced the uniform application of EC law consonant with Treaty objectives by involving the ECJ in cases pending before the national courts;
- strengthened the hand of national courts in enforcing EC law; all sanctions available in national law may be applied by national authorities in enforcing EC law;
- met with widespread compliance at the national level, more so than in infringement decisions; and
- contributed to the EC legal system's legitimacy by leaving with the national courts final decisions in cases in which the EC Courts have made preliminary rulings. As a

consequence, a cooperative (rather than hierarchical) relationship has developed be-tween the ECJ and national courts.[24]

This chapter thus far has outlined the avenues of legal redress for the players in the EC legal system. It now turns to the main EC legal principles and how they have been implemented in practice. Legal principle and practice together have produced a body of EC law that has left indelible marks on the member governments and on the community to which they have given life.

PRINCIPLES AND LANDMARKS

The study of EC law requires us to understand both legal principles and major rulings. The former—unwritten and implied—give rise to and influence the latter. A legal principle is a judicial interpretation of the Treaty—when the Treaty itself is not clear or is silent—that has far-reaching implications. A major ruling puts into practice a legal principle. The two major doctrinal principles established by the ECJ in its rulings and interpretations are **direct effect** (only individuals directly affected by a breach of EC law have standing to appeal to the ECJ or to a national court) and **supremacy** (EC law takes precedence over national law when the latter is inconsistent with the former). These two principles, not explicit in the Treaty, are related yet important to distinguish. Put into practice by ECJ opinions and rulings, these principles have most contributed to the reach of EC law into the life of individuals and their member states.

Principle of Direct Effect: Direct effect refers to the Treaty and parts of EC legislation, or secondary law, that confer rights and duties on the member states, individuals, and other legal persons within these states. The EC does not yet have a bill of rights like that of the U.S. Constitution (although the Lisbon Treaty features a charter of fundamental rights). The Treaty does not explicitly grant individuals standing to challenge breaches of EC law before the ECJ. Whether the EC conferred rights on individuals thar national courts had to protect was also not made explicit in the Treaty. In contrast, EC bodies and member states have avenues of legal redress that are explicit in the Treaty. At first, the only avenue of legal redress for individuals was to complain to the Commission, which in turn could open legal proceedings. How-ever, in the EC's early years, the ECJ interpreted the Treaty as a source of rights that may be invoked by private individuals before the Court. For example, as discussed below, the ECJ in *Van Gend en Loos* (1962) recognized that Treaty provisions have direct effect on individuals, who are thus able to use the preliminary reference proce-dure.

There are two ways in which an individual who maintains that he or she is directly affected can bring a case before the ECJ: (a) an individual who maintains that the passage of a national law that directly affects him or her violates the Treaty may appeal to the national court, which then may ask the ECJ for a preliminary ruling; or (b) an individual who maintains that an EC action that directly affects him or her violates the EC Treaty may complain to his or her national court. In such cases, the national courts rule on the complaint whether or not the ECJ is asked for a preliminary ruling.

Only provisions of the Treaty that enjoy direct effect may be invoked directly by individuals before domestic courts.[25]

In *Van Gend en Loos*, a Dutch firm challenged before a Dutch administrative tribunal (the Tariff Commission) a decision of the state to apply a higher customs duty for an imported good (West German urea-formaldehyde) than that applicable before the Rome Treaty had entered into force. The importer charged that the Dutch Government infringed Treaty rules prohibiting the introduction of new tariffs on intra-EC trade, and argued that it was directly affected by the infringement. The Dutch tribunal made a preliminary reference to the ECJ to ask if the provision had direct application in the domestic court (if nationals of a member state, on the basis of a Treaty article, may lay claim to a right that the national court must protect),[26] and if the Court wished to rule on the legality of an increase in duties.

Early on, the ECJ decided not to rule directly against member governments who are accused of violating the Treaty in order to avoid intruding too deeply into the sovereignty of the member states. Instead, the ECJ stated that in *Van Gend en Loos* the real issue was whether an increase in customs duties charged on a given product as a result of a new classification of the product (rather than as a result of an increase in the rate) contravened the Treaty.[27] The ECJ referred to Treaty objectives laid out in the preambular language. It deduced from the existence of EC bodies and procedures, according to Raymond Dehouse, "a desire on the part of the authors of the treaty to create a new legal order where the subjects are member states and their nationals."[28] The ECJ determined the following:

- The Dutch authorities acted illegally when creating a new product classification that had the effect of raising the duty rate, which contravened the Treaty.
- The Treaty—which created a customs union—confers rights on individuals that the ECJ enforces. These rights arise not only when they are expressly granted by the Treaty, but also by reason of obligations that the Treaty imposes on individuals, member states, and EC bodies.[29]
- Effective functioning of the customs union required the prohibition of duties on imports from inside the union. If member states attempted to infringe on individual rights under the Treaty, those individuals would lose the direct legal protection afforded them by the Treaty.[30]

Since the Dutch case was initiated in the national court by an individual, the use of the preliminary reference procedure underlined the importance attached to the vigilance of individuals who wish to protect their legal rights under EC law. The ECJ established individuals as agents of a centralized implementation of EC law and thus "gave EC law to the people" by introducing the principle of direct effect.[31] The case continues to be viewed by EC legal scholars as the cornerstone of the ECJ's jurisprudential edifice.[32] Indeed, as a result of *Van Gend en Loos* the ECJ went on to establish the doctrine of direct effect in later cases.

In *Costa v ENEL* (1964), shareholders in a nationalized electric company challenged Italy's nationalization laws on grounds that Treaty laws were breached. Mr. Costa disputed his electric bill. The Italian court asked the ECJ if the nationalization of the company was legal under EC law. The Italian Government claimed that its judges should apply national law with no reference to EC law, thus challenging the validity of the principle of preliminary reference. The ECJ concluded that since the Treaty created its own legal system, which has become an integral part of the member states' legal systems, the national courts are bound to apply EC law. Thus member states have limited their sovereign rights in specific areas. The ECJ accepted the Italian Government's claim that the Treaty gives no jurisdiction to the Court either to apply the Treaty to a specific case or to decide on the validity of a provision of domestic law in relation to the Treaty. However, the ECJ stressed that it has the power to extract from a question, even if imperfectly formed by the national courts, those issues which alone pertain to the interpretation of the Treaty (as it articulated in *Van Gend en Loos*).

Costa v ENEL is significant to both the principle of EC legal sovereignty vis-à-vis member states and the rights of individuals to legal redress at EC level. By allowing private individuals to claim direct effect, the ECJ granted individuals rights under EC law that individuals do not have in international law. The ECJ introduced the notion of a transfer of competence from national to EC legal systems, opened the door to individuals, and encouraged a dialogue with national judiciaries.[33] The ECJ views as advantageous the use of national courts to implement EC law. For example, when national courts implement ECJ preliminary rulings at home, both the courts and their rulings carry more authority than when national courts are compelled to implement more intrusive ECJ rulings (e.g., infringement or annulment).

Supremacy. Direct effect is not itself sufficient to guarantee the application of EC law.[34] When national laws are thought to conflict with EC laws and the contention is brought to the ECJ, the ECJ has frequently upheld the supremacy of EC law. While the Treaty is silent when a national law conflicts with an EC law, the ECJ has ruled that member states must take measures necessary to ensure the fulfillment of their Treaty obligations. Would the ECJ's interpretation of the supremacy of EC law convince national courts to play a crucial role in ensuring the effectiveness of EC law? The question was answered in *Costa v ENEL*. The ECJ, in establishing the supremacy principle, concluded that the Treaty created an EC legal system that has become an integral part of the member states' legal systems, and that member states have limited their sovereign rights in certain fields.[35]

In *Simmenthal* (1977), an Italian court referred a dispute over the compatibility with EC law of Italian veterinary regulations and public health fees levied on Italian beef and veal imports. The Italian court held that the fees were incompatible with EC law and ordered the Italian Government to repay them with interest. The Italian Government argued that the court could not refuse to apply a national law even if in conflict with EC law and that only the Italian Constitutional Court had the authority to declare the Italian regulations or fees unconstitutional. The ECJ ruled that the primacy doctrine renders national law provisions unlawful when they are in conflict with those of EC law. The ECJ also ruled that the primacy doctrine precludes the valid adoption of new national laws incompatible with EC law.[36]

In the following year, the Italian Constitutional Court ruled that a national law in conflict with EC law must be regarded as a breach of the Italian constitution. In *Publico Ministero v Ratti* (1978), a producer of solvents and varnishes faced criminal proceedings for having met the requirements of EC directives on labeling of dangerous products before the directives had been implemented in the Italian legal system. A directive is a binding set of principles, objectives, and requirements in a specific area to which member governments give effect by passing individual national implementation measures (see Chapter 6). The ECJ concluded that member states are not liable for failing to implement EC directives before the deadline for national implementation has expired. However, it also held that Ratti could not be penalized by the national government for complying with EC directives before national implementation. The case is a landmark in the evolution and practice of the principles of supremacy and direct effect.

The ECJ established that EC directives, like EC law, confer rights on individuals that the national courts are bound to uphold, and that EC directives and law take precedence when national legislation is incompatible with them. By agreeing to hear *Publico Ministero v Ratti*, the ECJ used the opportunity, once again, to establish the right of individuals who are directly affected by EC law to bring alleged infringements to the attention of the ECJ. Had member governments been allowed to delay implementation of EC directives by the required due dates, the uniform and effective implementation of the Treaty would be undermined. Raymond Dehouse wrote:

> By virtue of this audacious reasoning, EC law enjoys absolute supremacy over all national provisions, even those of a constitutional nature. With one stroke of the pen, the ECJ conferred on the treaty an autonomy similar to that of a constitution in a federal system.[37]

In *Foto-Frost v Hauptzollamt Lubeck-Ost* (1985), the German court asked the ECJ for a preliminary reference as to the validity of a Commission action that was being challenged in the main proceedings. The ECJ concurred with the national court that the national court did not have jurisdiction to rule. Thus, in *Foto-Frost*, the ECJ denied national courts the power to declare EC acts invalid. The ECJ held that the Treaty empowers the Court to ensure EC law is uniformly applied by national courts. The requirement of uniformity is imperative when the validity of EC actions is in question and when differences exist between EC and national law. Without the legal certainty that comes with uniformity, the unity of the EC legal system and its application would be imperiled. In this case, the ECJ established that it alone can invalidate acts of EC bodies that do not conform to Treaty law. The ECJ also made it clear that national court decisions cannot be appealed before the ECJ.

The ECJ has gone on to hold states liable for damages caused by their failure to fulfill Treaty obligations. For example, in *Francovich and Others* (1990), the Italian Government was considered liable for damage caused by failure to fulfill its EC obligations when it did not implement a 1980 EC directive that established guarantees to protect employees in the event of employer insolvency. In *Francovich*, the ECJ concluded that the full effect of EC rules would be impaired and the protection of rights that they granted would be weakened if individuals were not able to obtain compensation when their rights were infringed when member states breached EC laws.[38] The ECJ declared the principle of state liability for breach of EC law "to be inherent in the system of the treaty."[39] The ECJ ruled that implied in the Treaty is the principle that member states in breach of their Treaty obligations are (a) accountable for such a breach, and (b) obliged to pay compensation to individuals who were harmed as a result of the breach.[40] Francovich was codified in the TEU.

A preliminary reference requested of the ECJ by the British House of Lords speaks volumes to the far-reaching effects of the supremacy of EC over national law. The reference had to do with the proposed reform in 1988 of the British Merchant Shipping Act of 1894. In proceedings before the British courts, shipping companies argued that proposed reforms to increase the requirements for registration of UK fishing vessels infringed the Treaty. The Commission agreed and began infringement proceedings against the United Kingdom. The Commission and the Lords were faced with an interesting question. Does EC law empower national courts to order "interim relief" to suspend the application of a disputed national law, even if under national law such interim relief is not available? British law does not allow interim measures to be granted against the government to suspend the application of an act of Parliament.[41]

The ECJ determined that any national legal system or law is incompatible with EC law if it withholds from national courts the power to do everything necessary to set aside national legal provisions that may prevent EC rules from having full effect. The ECJ held that the Treaty would be impaired if a national court, having stayed proceedings pending a request for a preliminary ruling by the ECJ, were not able to grant interim relief until it delivered its judgment following a reply given by the ECJ. The ECJ implied that under such circumstances interim relief must be available.

A study of the supremacy of EC law would not be complete without the inclusion of a case where the ECJ ruled in favor of a national law that many, especially the Commission, thought clearly breached Treaty law. In 1994 the Commission referred to the ECJ the Greek trade embargo on the Former Yugoslav Republic of Macedonia instituted on February 16, 1994. The Commission argued that the Greek action breached the Common Commercial Policy of the EC, which prohibits unilateral external trade actions of the member states. The European Parliament adopted a resolution on March 10, 1994, condemning the Greek embargo and called on Greece to resume its dialogue with Macedonia for a negotiated settlement. The Greek Government, which railed against the name of the new republic (proclaimed in 1991), argued that the embargo was necessary since Greece felt threatened by the independence of the new Macedonian state and by its use of Macedonian symbols that challenged Greek sovereignty over a northern Greek province also named Macedonia. The Commission in turn doubted that the Greek argument based on a security threat was well founded. However, the Treaty does provide a safeguard clause that allows a member state under exceptional circumstances to take action it deems necessary to address a situation in which its internal and external security is threatened. In the end, the ECJ ruled in favor of Greece, for it did not wish to directly challenge the sovereignty of Greece in determining its own internal and external security needs, even though the embargo violated the supremacy of EC law.

As the preceding analyses of the principles of direct effect and supremacy indicate, the EC could not have developed a supranational body of law and practice—and an effective common market—had national laws that did not conform with Treaty laws been left unchallenged. The two principles are interrelated. There is no point in establishing a doctrine of the direct effect of EC law that national courts are bound to uphold if those rights are overridden by a contrary rule of national law.[42]

CASES BY AREA OF EC COMPETENCE

The preceding section introducing the principles and practice of EC law offered depth of analysis. This section, which explores a handful of landmark cases by areas of EC competence, offers breadth of analysis. For every area of EC competence under the Treaty, the ECJ has rendered opinions and judgments. What follows is an examination of important ECJ rulings in three areas of EC competence: the internal market (free movement); the rights of individuals (including equal treatment for women and men); and external relations (the scope of the EC's international activities related to the functioning of the common market).

Internal Market: Without ECJ rulings that interpret and uphold the spirit and letter of the Treaty, the EC as the world's single largest internal market would not exist. Legal integration affirmed, then consolidated, economic integration. For example, without each of the member states recognizing one another's standards for production of goods and their free movement across borders, there would be no basis for uniform law governing commercial relations among the member states. Indeed in *Cassis de Dijon* (1978), the ECJ affirmed the principle of mutual recognition of national legislation and the rights of individuals to enjoy the free movement of goods.

Cassis involved a French importer of spirits who sought access to the German market for his product, Cassis de Dijon, and argued that member states should not use technical rules to protect trade. German law forbade the sale of spirits whose alcohol content was less than 25 percent, thus preventing the sale of Cassis de Dijon, whose alcoholic content was about 20 percent. The German claim was based on consumer health concerns, but the fact that Cassis de Dijon has alcohol content less than the German requirement mocked the German health claim! The ECJ implied in its ruling that if a product satisfies the regulations of one EC member state, those regulations ought to be accepted by the other member states as functional equivalents.

On the basis of this ECJ ruling, the Commission would go on to write the *White Paper on Completing the Internal Market* (1985) that served as the basis for the Single European Act. The SEA required the member states to recognize one another's regulatory requirements, such as product standards, in order to open the internal market to freer trade by the end of 1992. Put simply, the Commission—emboldened by the ECJ's expansive interpretation of the Treaty on the issue of mutual recognition of national standards of production in *Cassis de Dijon*—went on to initiate legislation that overcame decades of NTBs, such as national product standards that discriminated against free trade. The ECJ through the Commission drove market integration that compelled change from recalcitrant member governments who were using NTBs to favor domestic over European producers. Neofunctionalists cite the import of the *Cassis* ruling as an example of the "zone of discretion" in which the EC Courts interpret the law of the Treaty, independently of governments, to drive market integration beyond where governments wish to take it.[43]

Perhaps one of the most interesting cases involving the clash of national culinary tastes and EC competition law came in 1987, when the ECJ ruled that the 1516 Bavarian law banning the use of beer additives could not be used as a nontariff barrier blocking imports of beer from elsewhere in the EU. Although the Germans argued that the law allowing only beer with no additives to be sold was based on health concerns, the Commission argued and the ECJ agreed that the additives ban was disproportionate to the health risk involved. The case dated back to 1982, when the Commission brought it forward on the basis of a complaint by an Alsatian brewer that the German beer requirement was in effect a nontariff barrier. Germans still purchase their own additives-free beer but must allow beer from elsewhere in the EU to "flow freely" into Germany. The ECJ ruling reconfirmed the principle of mutual recognition in standards of production for trade articulated in the *Cassis* decision.

A more recent infringement case was concluded in 2005 after the Commission charged the Spanish region of Valencia with permitting the use of lime twigs or snares to trap thrushes. Spain argued that the hunting of thrushes was a long-established tradition in Valencia and that ending it would cause social unrest. The ECJ determined that the practice violated a 1979 Directive on conservation of wild birds. The member states are held responsible for the actions of their own regions and local authorities under EC law.

Trademark registration was at issue over a CFI ruling in 2009. The CFI confirmed a ruling of the EC Office for Harmonization of the Internal Market not to register the name "Budweiser" as an EC trademark as requested by the U.S. brewer, Anheuser-Busch. The application for trademark registration was rejected since the name "Budweiser" was already an EC trademark of the Czech brewer Budejovich Budvar.

Individuals: The ECJ has ruled on the rights of individuals conferred by the Treaty and in particular on the rights of individuals with regard to equality in the workplace, equal treatment, and nondiscrimination. Over time, the ECJ has "transformed basic principles which were to guide the actions of member states and EC bodies into 'basic freedoms' which private parties can invoke before courts."[44] For example, in *Respondent v Chief Constable of West Yorkshire Police* (2004), the respondent, a male-to-female transsexual, was denied employment as a constable on grounds that as a woman she could not search male suspects and as a man she could not search female suspects.[45] The Chief Constable argued that under British law he could not hire a constable who could not conduct a full search of a criminal suspect. The respondent relied on an EC law prohibiting discrimination on the grounds of sex. In its opinion, the House of Lords determined that EC law requires the respondent to be recognized in her reassigned gender. The case is important because it vests individual citizens of EU member states with legal rights based on EC law; it is also another example of the supremacy of EC over national law when the latter conflicts with the former. The ECJ itself has upheld the rights of individuals in a variety of cases, including:

- *Stauder v Ulm* (1969): The ECJ ruled that names of social welfare recipients of subsidized butter cannot be released to retailers. The fundamental right of the privacy of individuals must be protected as a general principle of EC law.
- *Defrenne v Sabena* (1976): The ECJ ruled that an individual (in this case a female Belgian airline flight attendant) had a right to equal pay for equal work (for men and women), recognized under Treaty law, although not under Belgian law. The case barred discrimination in the workplace.
- *Rinner Kuhn v FWW Spezial Gebau Dereinigung GrabH and Co. KFG* (1989): The ECJ determined that national rules enabling employers to exclude part-time employees from the benefit of continued salary during illness are contrary to the Treaty as the exclusion affected a large number of women workers. However, an exception to this rule is permitted if employers can show that the exclusion is not based on sex discrimination.
- *Cowan v Le Tresor Public* (1989): The ECJ held that the French authorities had to pay damages to a British tourist who was mugged outside a Parisian metro station.

French criminal law requires payment of damages to victims of crime. The Treaty prohibits discrimination based on nationality among EU citizens. The ECJ was able to extend Treaty law to this case because Cowan was a recipient of a service provided within the EU and thus protected from discriminatory practices.

- *Marshall II* (1991): The ECJ invalidated a statutory limitation on damages in a gender discrimination case. Member states could not cap compensation payable to the victims of discrimination.
- *Bonafaci v Italy* (1991): The ECJ established that a member state is obliged to pay compensation for harm caused to individuals by a breach of EC law for which the member state can be held accountable.
- *Bosman v Royal Club Liegeois* (1993): The ECJ recognized the rights of football (soccer) players to transfer to another team with no financial penalty at the end of their contracts.
- *Brasserie du Percheur v Germany* (1993) and *Factoratme* (1993): The ECJ laid down conditions permitting the invocation of the principle of state liability. The ECJ established the right of individuals to reparations when the rule of EC law has been infringed by a state.

External Relations: In its rulings and interpretations over the years, the ECJ has expanded the competence of the EC in international affairs where the EC has exclusive competence or **shared competence** with the member states. Shared competence refers to instances in the Treaty as interpreted by the ECJ when the EC institutions and the member governments share sovereignty in selected areas (see below).

The Treaty grants jurisdiction to the ECJ to respond to preliminary references from national courts with regard to interpretation of international agreements concluded by the EC. Thus the ECJ is different from other international courts. For example, the UN's International Court of Justice only considers actions between states who accept the Court's compulsory jurisdiction, while the ECJ can address agreements between member and nonmember states. The ECJ has also expanded the competence of the EC in the area of international agreements. The Treaty lays out procedures for concluding international agreements.

In *ERTA* (1970), the ECJ ruled on a dispute between the Commission and Council over an international road transport agreement. The Commission sought annulment of the negotiating position that had been articulated by the Council (and adopted by the member states). The issue was whether the absence of explicit treaty provisions empowering the Commission to reach international transport accords barred the Commission from doing so. The Council argued that the Commission was so barred, and the member states agreed, a position that would leave such accords up to them. The Commission, however, maintained the issue fell within the EC competence on transport policy, arguing that the competence to define a common transport policy necessitated the right to conclude agreements with third countries. Without the right to execute third-country agreements, the Commission argued, EC transport policy would be compromised.

The ECJ agreed with the Commission's argument, declaring that the EC had been endowed with an international legal personality. The ECJ determined that member states no longer have the right, acting individually or even collectively, to undertake obligations with third countries that affect common policies envisaged by the

Treaty.[46] The Court stated that in international law, the Treaty is binding on contracting parties, but the effect of EC law on domestic legal orders is largely determined by the constitutional law of each contracting party.

ERTA was important to the development of the EC's exclusive competence to act externally. However, in recent years the ECJ has begun to articulate a new principle in EC law—that of shared or parallel competences in which both the EC and member states have competence for external relations in certain areas of the Treaty. For example, in a 1994 opinion on the World Trade Organization (WTO), the ECJ held that the EC and member governments each had competence to negotiate WTO agreements on services and trade-related aspects of intellectual property, since these areas did not fall entirely under Treaty competence as part of the Common Commercial Policy. This has had a significant effect on the EC because the WTO agreements had to be jointly concluded by the Commission and the member states. The ECJ has clearly retreated from granting the Commission exclusive competence to act for the member states in all areas of international commerce. The Court has become more mindful of the sensitivity of certain issues related to the sovereignty of the member states.[47]

An infringement case relevant to EC competition in international trade and the *ERTA* case began in 2002 over "open skies" agreements between individual EC countries and the United States. These agreements regulate the access of airlines to international airports. The Commission brought infringement proceedings against member states who had concluded open skies agreements with the United States (Austria, Belgium, Denmark, Finland, Germany, Luxembourg, Sweden) on the grounds that such agreements infringed the EC's exclusive competence. The Commission also charged that these seven member states and the United Kingdom (a party to the 1977 Bermuda II agreement) infringed on Treaty rules concerning the right of establishment, by which the Treaty guarantees the right of individuals and firms to establish a firm in the territory of any member state.[48] The ECJ agreed with the Commission that open skies agreements were discriminatory under the Treaty's right of establishment rules because they excluded EC airlines whose governments did not negotiate agreements with the United States. Invoking the precedent of *ERTA*, the ECJ warned that the member states can no longer negotiate on matters within the exclusive external competence of the EC and must rectify any incompatibilities that arise out of these agreements, even if it is necessary to renounce these agreements.[49]

LOOKING BACK, LOOKING AHEAD

Law is where the study of the EU as an evolving supranational entity ought to start. In the absence of treaty law, there would be no framework of certainty, uniformity in the application of the law, and rights, obligations, and responsibilities made clear to all the EU's players—member states, common bodies, and individuals. The chapter started with a question about the impact that the EC Courts have had on the development of the union over the past half-century. The impact has been monumental, although theorists of institutionalism and intergovernmentalism differ over the independence of the ECJ in recent years. Are the EC Courts actors free to influence the integration process independently of member governments, or are they servants of member governments who drive the integration process? The answer to the question is important to the future of European integration, which this chapter has argued depends on the uniformity and supremacy of treaty law.

From the perspective of historical institutionalism, the member governments delegated authority to the EC Courts to interpret the meaning of law so that the untried Treaty of the 1950s could be put into practice as the founders intended. In so doing, the ECJ compelled national judiciaries to respect the supremacy of EC law, and provided legal recourse to individuals directly affected by Treaty law and EC actions. Had the ECJ not moved expeditiously early on to establish the principles of supremacy and direct effect, it would have been a matter of time before the member states would have reasserted their national prerogatives, undermining the spirit and letter of the founding Treaty. What gave life to these principles were ECJ landmark cases. These landmarks together established a fifty-year-old body of supranational law that governed first the economic and later the monetary union and the myriad policies that flowed from them.

One scholar of comparative judicial systems has been struck by what she calls the paradox of the experience of the U.S. Supreme Court during the first seventy years of the American federal union and that of the ECJ during the first fifty years of the EC.[50] During the early decades of the United States, some state courts defied the authority of the Supreme Court. In particular, they challenged the authority of the Supreme Court to oversee the interpretation by state courts of federal law in cases alleging a clash between state and federal law. During the first two decades of the European Community, there was minimal defiance (e.g., in France) by national courts of the ECJ's jurisdiction and the supremacy of EC over national law. The U.S. Constitution specified the supremacy of federal over state law. The Treaty did not specify the supremacy of EC law, but the ECJ established the principles of supremacy and direct effect of EC law as binding on the member states in 1963.

What is so paradoxical is that the U.S. states had sparse—and the EC states long—experience with sovereignty. The EC states had been nation-states with separate, rich cultures for centuries. The thirteen original U.S. states were only sovereign for a short period between the American Revolution and Confederation and the Federation under the U.S. Constitution. One would think the U.S. states would have been more accepting of national judicial supremacy than the EC states. This suggests that even though the EC was created by mature sovereign states, the postwar reflex and will to cooperate were strong, and the constituent member governments realized they had to delegate juridical powers to the ECJ if the union were to endure.

Historical institutionalism provides a useful framework for analyzing the growth and development of the EC Courts from the original and subsequent delegations of authority granted to them in the Treaty. The EC founders knew that the ECJ was needed to make intergovernmental compacts work, but they and member governments could not know in the 1950s how far the EC Courts would expand their authority. In other words, some member governments, particularly those, like Italy, threatened by the supremacy of the ECJ, could not foresee these unintended consequences of the early grants of authority to the ECJ.

Rational choice institutionalists recognize that the ECJ through its rulings has exerted enormous influence over the EC and its member states. Principal–agent analysis nicely frames the scope for agency that the EC Courts have, independent of the original delegations of authority granted to them by national governments in the Treaties. The Courts have enjoyed a large discretionary scope to interpret the law independently of member governments. No EU body has had such a wide latitude to exercise its influence, or agency. The member governments understood early on, even with some reservations or opposition, that the EC could not work without a uniform interpretation of the law and without the supremacy of EC law. Without the ECJ to uphold the rule of law, the EC—and now the EU—would not exist.

Although governments appoint Judges, and Judges cannot be ignorant of or insensitive to politics at home, they are still largely independent of national pressures. Indeed, as this section has demonstrated, the EC Courts are sensitive to the effects of their jurisprudence on national governments. They want to avoid unnecessary infringements on national juridical sovereignty for fear that a national court or government might reject an ECJ ruling, which would throw the union into a constitutional crisis.

That said, the ECJ has far more protection than the Commission from those national governments who may wish to take back authority delegated to the ECJ but find that they cannot escape their dependence on the Courts and still expect the union to function. It would be very difficult and time consuming to overturn the decisions of the EC Courts through legislative change or Treaty amendment. Since member governments find that the EU offers more benefits than costs, they are resigned to accept the independent scope for agency of the Courts.

Intergovernmentalists focus on the EC Courts as agents of member governments who influence the EC Courts through such means as appointment of Judges, passage of EC legislation, and intergovernmental compacts that categorically drive integration in one direction or the other. Intergovernmentalists signal a concern about the Courts' scope for agency in the union's second half-century. The ECJ's early activism quickly strengthened the EC's legitimacy and purpose as well as the rule of EC law and its uniform and effective application. We cannot be certain, however, that the activism of the ECJ in the first fifty years, which upholds the spirit and letter of the EC Treaties, will continue in the next fifty years. From the perspective of intergovernmentalism, the EC Courts have begun to take a more conservative and cautious approach to their caseloads, especially since the 1990s, in response to member governments who, like the Gaullists in the mid-1960s, seek to retain or retake national prerogatives vis-à-vis the EU. The EC Courts have preferred to strike a careful balance between upholding the Treaty law and respecting member states' legal traditions and procedures. A restrained ECJ is focusing more on its role as Treaty guardian rather than motor of integration.[51]

This self-restraint parallels a broader shift in European integration in the 1990s to a partial renationalization of EU public policy initiatives based on the principle of subsidiarity first codified in the Amsterdam Treaty. Subsidiarity requires that decisions that do not fall under the scope of the EC's exclusive competences should be kept closest to the member governments and only "bumped up" to the EU level when collective action is necessary. The reawakening of national prerogatives and interests, political and juridical, relative to the growth of the EU was thrown into relief by the Danish voters' rejection of the TEU (1992), Irish voters' rejection of the Treaty of Nice (2001) and the Lisbon Treaty (2008), and the French and Dutch voters' rejection of the EU Constitutional Treaty (2005). (Danish and Irish voters did accept these

Treaties in second referenda after modifications.) The EC Courts are not insensitive to declining support for more European integration, as demonstrated in public opinion polls (see Chapter 8).

An undercurrent of juridical sovereignty in the member states came when the German Constitutional Court reserved to itself the right to decide if a conflict between German and EC law exists, endorsing a theoretical base for a future defiance of EC law. In the *Maastricht II* decision (October 12, 1993), the German high court reasoned that a fundamental right enshrined in the German Basic Law (German Constitution)—the right to vote—implied the right to elect the Bundestag (the lower house of the German parliament) with its own sovereign powers to legislate. This right to operate legislatively could in the future restrict the powers that the EU may one day claim.[52]

In its first fifty years, the ECJ was no shrinking violet as interpreter and protector of EC law, even as some member governments took a more hard-line approach to European integration. Regardless of which theory best explains legal integration, many scholars agree that the ECJ has become a "judicial giant" that has successfully positioned itself "at the constitutional center of Europe, a Europe in which national legal orders suddenly feel under threat."[53]

One of the leading scholars of EC law, Joseph Weiler, laments the unchanged architecture of the EC Courts, and the gap between what the EU and the EC Courts have become and the existing Treaty framework. The Treaties of Nice and Lisbon introduced no profound changes to the EC legal system.[54] "The original EC system received its nth coat of new paint, but it is still the old Commission-Council-Parliament engine creaking beneath the [hood]. . . . The EC continues to drive in its rusty and trusted 1950 model with the steering wheel firmly in the hands of the Court of Justice."[55]

Critics of the EC Courts have pointed to their inefficiencies in addressing the backlog of cases to be heard and the lengthy period that proceedings take, leading these critics to voice the old adage, "Justice delayed is justice denied." However, the ECJ reported that in 2008 the number of cases brought to closure increased by 15 percent over 2003.[56] In 2008 the ECJ brought to closure 567 cases, up from 494 in 2003. In 2008, 592 new cases were brought to the EC Courts, up from 561 in 2003. The number of cases pending before the Courts in 2008 was 767, down from 974 in 2003. In 2008 the length of preliminary reference proceedings fell to18 months from 25 months in 2003. Direct effect cases were handled within 17 months in 2008, down from 25 in 2003. Appeals took 18 months to resolve in 2008, down from 28 months in 2003. The ECJ claims that greater efficiencies have improved its performance in expediting cases. It has prioritized cases and simplified procedures. The Court appears to be cognizant of and responsive to its critics even as it experiences an upward trend in the volume of litigation.

Before we move to our conclusion, students of the ECJ ought to note that it remains, like many other EU bodies, male-dominated. As of 2009, there were just three women ECJ judges among the 27 Judges. There were no women Judges from 1952 to 1999. As member governments appoint their own ECJ Judges, the problem of gender equality depends on appointment decisions made in the national capitals. On the U.S. Supreme Court as of 2009, there were just two women among the nine

Justices, suggesting that the ECJ is not unique among other supreme courts for having many more men than women Judges.

Although it is impossible to predict the future course of EU legal integration, three things are clear from the preceding analysis:

1. Without uniform application of the law, what the Europeans have accomplished to date in their union will not last.
2. A pendulum swings between the sovereignty of the state and the agency of the union. At times it tilts toward the prerogatives of the national governments and at other times toward those of the EU. The EC Courts have an important role in helping to strike the right balance between respect for national law and respect for EC law.
3. The jurisdiction of the EC Courts depends on the willingness of national courts to accept it.[57]

The two-way trust and cooperation that existed over the past half-century between the EC and national courts cannot be taken for granted in the EU's second half-century. Theorists and scholars will continue to debate whether the EC courts are structures independent of member states or merely agents of them.

Review

This chapter concludes Part I—the study of the historical, economic, and legal foundations of the EU. Chapter 1 demonstrated that the EU is neither an historical anomaly nor an accident of history. Chapter 2 posited that the context for regional economic integration in the 1950s was the dire need to reverse the warlike trends of the preceding centuries. The Europeans could draw on the lessons of wars past, particularly those of the twentieth century, and the periodic experiences they had with past attempts at unity—most of them involuntary.

The first half of Chapter 3 examined the economic principles, theories, and concepts that explain the logic of European integration. Although imperfect and incomplete, the creation of the economic and monetary union in just fifty years is one of the great interstate accomplishments of the twentieth century. The second half of the chapter demonstrated that the EU today would not exist as we know it in the absence of the rule of law. We examined the EC Courts' structure, function, key legal principles, procedures for legal redress, and cases that have shaped the course of EC legal integration. No other EU body has enjoyed as much scope for autonomous agency as the ECJ. The logic of regional economic integration buttressed by the rule of law has most shaped the contours of the EU as a supranational entity. The logic of integration is economic, but it is also political. The political will to sustain the EU in the next fifty years will be no less important than it was in the first fifty years.

The foundation bloc of regional economic integration was joined by the foundation bloc of legal integration. Without a common body, understanding, and implementation of the law of the internal market, the Europeans would have failed to maintain the cohesion necessary for regional economic integration to commence, sustain itself, and evolve into new and more sophisticated forms of integration and cooperation.

Key Concepts

Economic Concepts
common market
comparative advantage
customs union
customs union theory
economic and monetary union (EMU)
economies of scale
free trade area (FTA)
International Political Economy (IPE)
Optimum Currency Area (OCA) theory
preferential treatment
regional economic integration
snake-in-the-tunnel
trade creation
trade diversion

Legal Concepts
annulment
direct effect
hybrid courts
infringement
jurisdiction of the EC Courts
preliminary reference
shared competence
sources of EC law
supremacy of EC law
uniform application of EC law

Study Questions

1. How do economics and law together constitute the foundations of modern European integration?
2. How well have customs union theory and Optimum Currency Area theory explained and predicted the development of the EC first as a common market and then as an EMU?
3. What does an IPE perspective lend to an explanation of how the EC got started as a customs union?
4. What are the legal principles that most contribute to the reach of EC law into the member states and the lives of individuals?
5. What three cases of the ECJ do you think had the most profound impact on the development of the EC in relation to its member states and its citizens? Why?
6. In what ways do the U.S. Supreme Court and the ECJ compare and contrast?
7. What contributed to the success of the ECJ's judicial activism in the EC's first few decades, and what appears to contribute to the ECJ's more recent judicial restraint?

Selected Readings

Anthony Arnull, *The European Union and Its Court of Justice* (Oxford: Oxford University Press, 1999).

Grainne de Burca and J. H. H. Weiler, eds., *The European Court of Justice* (Oxford: Oxford University Press, 2001).

Renaud Dehouse, *The European Court of Justice* (New York: St. Martin's, 1994).

European Commission Legal Service, http://ec.europa.eu/dgs/legal_service/arrets/index_en.htm

European Court of Justice, Court of First Instance, and European Civil Service Tribunal, http://curia.europa.eu/

Leslie Friedman Goldstein, *Constituting Federal Sovereignty: The European Union in Comparative Context* (Baltimore: Johns Hopkins University Press, 2001).

Willem Molle, *The Economics of European Integration: Theory, Practice, Policy* (Aldershot: Ashgate, 2001).

Part II

THE EUROPEAN UNION IN PRACTICE

Part I of this book constructed our understanding of the European Union on the foundation blocks of history, theory, and law. Part II turns to hardscrabble reality. How does the EU function as a polity where national and European interests are articulated and aggregated? The EU does not have a government like that of a nation-state. It has neither a Prime Minister organically linked to a parliament as in Britain nor a popularly elected President responsible for the defense of the union as in the United States. Yet it is a polity in practice and in fact—albeit one that is a work in progress. In the powers and functions of the EU bodies, there are counterparts comparable to those of nation-states and features not unfamiliar to citizens who have a basic understanding of how their own parliaments, governments, and judiciaries work. Therefore, Part II, like Part I, offers insights from comparative government to distinguish decisionmaking in the EU from decisionmaking in another union of states across the Atlantic—the United States. Part II deconstructs the EU into its essential parts to understand their function in relation to one another. Figure II.1 depicts EU governance as a decisionmaking continuum of

- inputs—internal and external political actors who seek to influence policymaking;
- process—conversion of inputs into policy outputs as the result of making choices inside the EU polity;
- outputs—policy decisions that result from the interaction of competing actors at national and EU levels and from the deliberations of the EC courts; and
- outcomes and feedback—the effects of outputs on intended constituencies, on the functioning of the EU political system, and on new sources of inputs, and the perceptions of how well the EU works in general.

Figure II.1. EU Governmental Decisionmaking Model

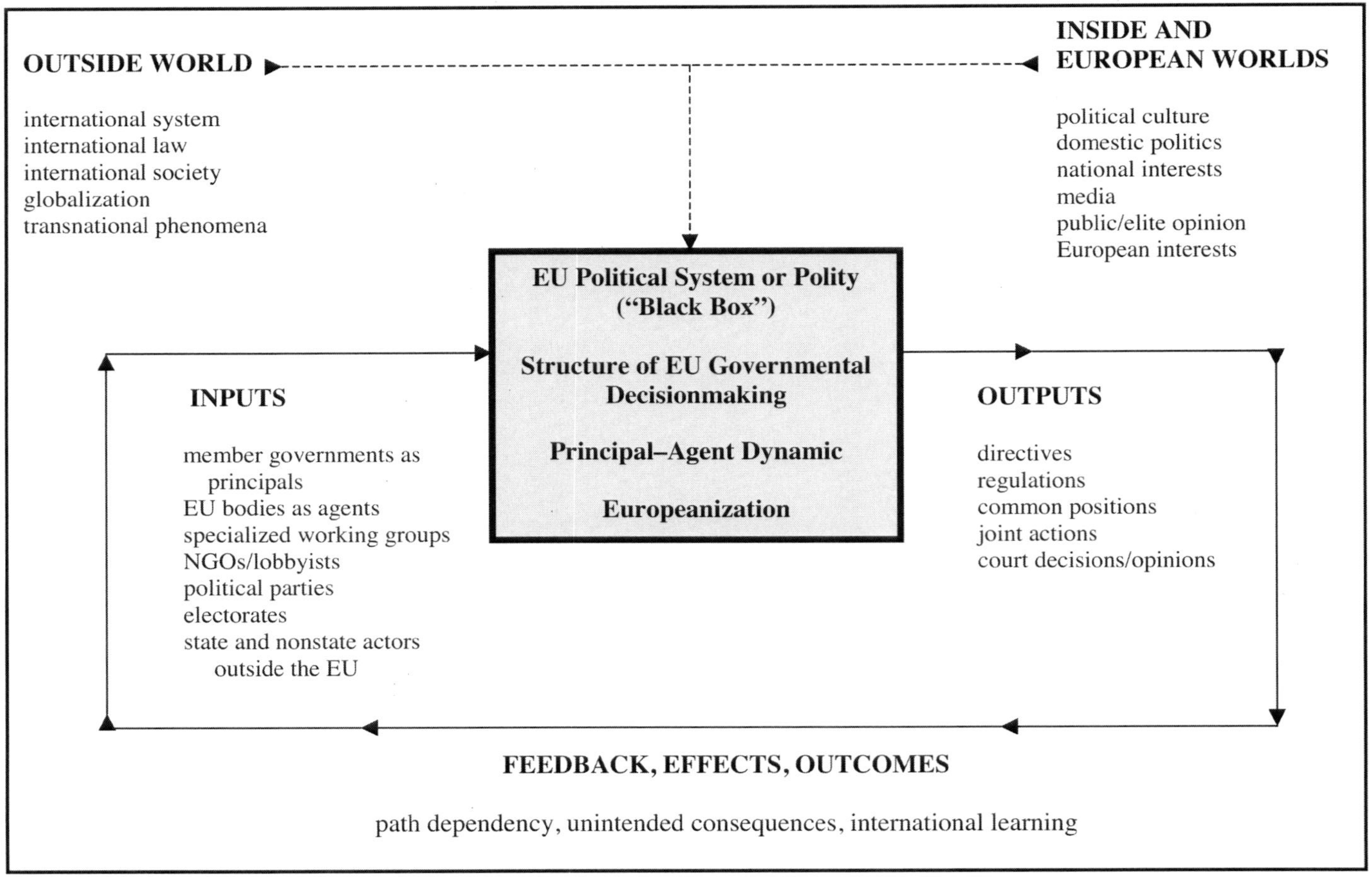

OUTSIDE WORLD

international system
international law
international society
globalization
transnational phenomena

**INSIDE AND
EUROPEAN WORLDS**

political culture
domestic politics
national interests
media
public/elite opinion
European interests

**EU Political System or Polity
("Black Box")**

**Structure of EU Governmental
Decisionmaking**

Principal–Agent Dynamic

Europeanization

OUTPUTS

directives
regulations
common positions
joint actions
court decisions/opinions

INPUTS

member governments as
    principals
EU bodies as agents
specialized working groups
NGOs/lobbyists
political parties
electorates
state and nonstate actors
    outside the EU

FEEDBACK, EFFECTS, OUTCOMES

path dependency, unintended consequences, international learning

Figure II.1, an adaptation of David Easton's classic model of how governments make decisions, helps explain how the EU polity works.[1] The Eastonian model identifies elements of legislative action along a governmental decisionmaking continuum and throws into relief the relationship of the parts to the whole of the EU polity. The inputs and outputs of EU governmental decisionmaking depicted in the model are generic to pluralistic political systems, such as Canada and the United States, with one key exception. The polity depicted has an added layer of governance—the European Union, with its intergovernmental and supranational institutions, working groups, committees, lobbyists, and other vested players. Each has influence over the EU decisionmaking process.

Easton employs the metaphor of a black box to refer to the process in any functioning government by which inputs are turned into outputs. Understanding this complex process of actors and procedures in governmental decisionmaking at the national level eludes many citizens. Since the EU adds another layer of governance onto that of the member states, Europeans find their union exceedingly mystifying. So do students of European integration who are challenged to probe the workings of the EU political system—in the union's mysterious black box. Political scientists who specialize in comparative government spend careers examining how inputs are converted into outputs in different political systems.

Of particular interest to students of EU politics is the interplay between the EU bodies and the member governments and other actors—and between the EU bodies themselves—inside the black box. We know that only together do these governmental and nongovernmental bodies make policy. To help demystify the inner workings of the EU political system, we incorporate into our model insights from the work of Mark Pollack and others on principal–agent analysis.[2] Our model identifies member governments who, as principals, delegate powers and tasks to EU bodies—or agents. EU agents manage the union (Commission), enforce common agreements of the union (ECJ), audit the union (ECA), enhance security inside the union (European Police Agency) and democratize the union (EP). Together these and other EU bodies constitute a new and unique structure of governmental decisionmaking. The effective interplay of principals and agents inside the black box—influenced by national and EU actors—results in outputs depicted in Figure II.1. What the EU as a polity produces in terms of outputs, or policy goods, matters to how the EU is perceived by its member-state elites and publics.

When EU bodies have the scope to act autonomously and purposively in the pursuit of the common (European) good or in defense of their institutional interests, they are said to have "agency." The more scope for agency an EU body has, the more autonomous it is of member governments. EU agency is a required ingredient for the conversion of inputs into outputs in an effective and timely fashion. This is particularly noteworthy in Europe, since member governments generally have not had a successful history of making international organizations work well to their own and collective advantage. The scope for agency of EU bodies depends on their willingness, creativity, entrepreneurial leadership, and effectiveness to advance European interests as well as their own institutional interests by forging compromises among national interests. EU bodies over the past fifty years have enjoyed, overall, a permissive consensus among member governments whereby elites pursued the work of integration in the absence of opposition from publics. Overall, the member governments have perceived that European integration has been advantageous for national interests.

EU bodies do not blithely turn inputs into outputs as agents of states. They have an ethos of advancing EU interests and pressing member governments to do so as well. Once EU bodies are delegated authority by member states, they often develop along a path that, while dependent on the initial delegation of power, takes them in directions far different from the original intent of the member states. For example, the member states in the Council delegated competition (antitrust) powers to the Commission, which in turn challenged powerful firms charged with abuse of a dominant position in the internal market. Over time, some member states began to regret the delegation of this power as the Commission became bolder in its pursuit of anticompetitive practices. The Council tried to take some of those delegated powers back, but found that it still needed the Commission to be the union policeman, overseeing that competition in the internal market remains on a level playing field.

Member governments delegate tasks to EU bodies (e.g., the Commission, the ECA, the European Central Bank, or the ECJ) that reduce the transaction costs of doing business in the EU. Transaction costs include overseeing the functioning of the EU and its policies; interpreting the Treaty; monitoring the completion of, compliance with, and enforcement of agreements to make them credible and to avoid free riders; and regulating money supply by setting interest rates. Delegation also occurs so that EU bodies may (1) advocate for, set the agenda of, and drive through legislative proposals that might otherwise not reach fruition if the EU had to rely on individual national interests and governments; (2) hasten the implementation of and improve efficiency in common EU policies; and (3) lend more weight and influence to the member states as a collective in international negotiations and conferences.[3]

The same member governments who delegated powers to EU bodies have also sought to limit the scope for autonomous agency of those bodies. For example, as explained and predicted by theorists of rational choice institutionalism, the Council has set up committees of national representatives (called comitology) to advise, manage, and otherwise oversee how the Commission implements EU law, given the political powers and scope for agency involved in decisions regarding how policies are put into practice. However, as will be demonstrated in Part 2, it is not likely the member governments would or could eliminate the scope for agency of the EU bodies, lest the EU they created to serve their interests becomes unglued. The EU could not function without the uniform interpretation of the rule of law determined by the ECJ—the body most independent of the member governments. The Commission performs tasks that cannot be replicated by governments, and its paucity of human and capital resources makes it dependent on national administrations to help formulate and implement EU legislation. The EP is not so much the recipient of delegated powers from the member governments as it is the beneficiary of pressures on the member governments to increase the democratic legitimacy of the EU by making it more representative.[4]

Liberal intergovernmentalist theorists place relatively heavy attention on the member governments, who, during episodes of interstate bargaining for Treaty changes at EU level, decide if and when to empower EU bodies with agency beyond the existing *acquis*. Institutionalists and their forerunners, the neofunctionalists, emphasize the autonomous scope for agency that EU bodies acquire vis-à-vis the member governments between history-making intergovernmental conferences. Both theoretical perspectives help to explain (1) the power of member governments to make (and unmake) EU decisions and to delegate and take back tasks assigned to EU agents; and (2) "the range of choice open to EU member states that is constrained in important ways by the logic of the project they themselves have created."[5] EU bodies with their enormous staying power are a source of continuity.

A principal–agent model whose insights are incorporated into our model of EU governmental decisionmaking nicely bridges the relationship between member governments (as principals), who delegate authority to EU bodies to run the union, and EU bodies (as agents), who promote their own institutional interests as well as European interests. The scope for autonomous agency is the tension between grantors and recipients of delegated authority inside the EU polity. What the author most likes about this perspective is that it steers clear of old debates over which theory, intergovernmentalism or neofunctionalism, best explains what drives European integration.

The object of decisionmaking is the production of outputs: decisions that enhance welfare, or laws to ensure compliance. The decisionmaking model depicted in figure II.1 gets more interesting when it focuses on the relationship of outputs (generic to political systems) to outcomes (intended effects). Feedback on EU policy outputs comes from elite and public opinion and from election results: that is, what people perceive of what the EU does. Outcomes are critical to the functioning and future of the EU. They determine if the EU has an impact on member governments and citizens and if EU bodies have the scope for effective agency so that they may again grease the axles of the decisionmaking system for the next policy initiative. Without agency, the EU would be a much more conventional international organization. It would certainly not be what it is today. Effective agency is the critical ingredient for policy outcomes that matter to member citizens, governments, and groups.

Part II features four chapters that build on the model of EU governmental decisionmaking depicted in figure II.1. Chapter 4 introduces the model and focuses on the contexts and actors of EU governmental decisionmaking as a segue to Chapter 5, which examines the structure, function, and powers of the major institutions in relation to the EU as a single political system. Chapter 5 also features an analysis of the EU political system in comparison to that of the federal government of the United States. Chapters 6 and 7 turn to the major outputs of EU governmental decisionmaking with regard to internal and external policies. Part II therefore rivets attention on the core relevance of the union to Europeans. Part III reconstructs our knowledge of the elements of the EU in order to analyze their overall effects on member governments and citizens.

CHAPTER 4

The Contexts and Actors of EU Governmental Decisionmaking

Preview

Contexts shape the preferences and interests of actors in the EU political system. Actors are those who have input into the EU political system. The model depicted in figure II.1 situates EU governmental decisionmaking in three critically important contexts: the inside world, the European world, and the external world. In the inside world, the member states' distinctive political cultures and histories, domestic politics, and public/elite opinion influence policy preferences and interests of national and subnational political actors in EU governmental decisionmaking. In the European world, regional or **European interests** based on uniquely common experiences, preferences, and reflexes shape the EU as a new sui generis actor in world politics. In the outside world, the EU polity is influenced by great power rivalries, international legal, societal, and other norms, and the growing importance of transnational phenomena that challenge the EU to respond diplomatically.

The Contexts of EU Governmental Decisionmaking

INSIDE WORLD

EU member states have distinct political cultures and national interests that shape and influence national policy at EU level. **Political culture** reflects the impact of the memory of national history and experience on citizen views of government, politics, and national interests played out at EU level. **National interests** refer to the existence of enduring state preferences in the pursuit of foreign economic, political, and security policy played out at EU level. Some EU members are broadly supportive of European integration; others less so. In either instance, the political culture that shapes national interests in turn influences the EU policy of national governments.

Belgium, for example, has a national interest in European integration. Memories of invasion and occupation twice in the twentieth century, Belgium's central place in the creation, development, and location of the EU institutions, and its weak sense of national unity give reason for many Belgians to be comfortable in a united Europe. Similarly, Germans generally accept their membership in the EU as something good for Germany. Memories of national socialism make Germans comfortable in framing German identity in a larger collective. German democratic transition and consolidation in the 1950s were influenced and stabilized by the country's membership in the EC and NATO. Germany and the EC in a sense evolved in a symbiotic relationship. Although in recent years Germans are inclined to pursue national interests within the EU more assertively than before 1990, the Federal Republic has a long-term national interest in the success of European integration.

For its part, France has its own enduring national interest in the success of the European project. After all, the Fourth Republic took the lead role in the EU's founding, not just to anchor Germany in a union of peace and stability but to provide leadership in Europe, and through Europe in the world. There is much in the EU that resembles French preferences, for example, support for the allocation of EU resources to protect farmers and subsidize aircraft production. Unlike Belgium, France has a strong sense of national identity, which results in an approach to European integration based more on the intergovernmental than supranational variety. Despite their differing political cultures and approaches to integration, public opinion toward European integration in general in France and Belgium has been historically favorable.

Conversely, Sweden shares no such strong national interest in European integration. There is no plurality of support for the EU among Swedes. National experience and history shape Swedish perceptions of and policy in the EU. Unlike Belgium, Sweden was not invaded in the twentieth century, so there was no urgency for EU integration. The country has a long history of independence and was a great power at its zenith in the eighteenth century. Its location, far from the geographical core of the EU, and its regional Nordic perspective help explain why Sweden joined the EU late, why many Swedes are skeptical of integration, and why Sweden has not adopted the euro. Although Austria is a Eurozone country, it shares with Sweden much of the discomfort and ambivalence found in Sweden. Austria's ambivalence owes much to concerns not only over the place of Austria—a country that was once the center of a great empire—within the EU, but concerns about free movement of labor from the new Eastern European members into Austria.

Domestic politics and public opinion matter enormously to what member governments can and cannot achieve at EU level. There are times when the EU is perceived by elites and publics as the epicenter of innovative ideas and policies, such as the 1992 Project and the introduction of the euro. The pendulum swings to the EU institutions. There are other times when the EU is perceived as less advantageous to the member states and the pendulum swings back to the member states, for example, when many member governments ignored the Commission's call for a unified approach and negotiated open skies agreements with the United States. Such agreements regulated use of airspace and airports by airlines companies in signatory countries; today an EU–U.S. accord replaces the old bilateral agreements.

Domestic politics have subsumed EU politics. Domestic politics and public opinion are also a source of common EU policies. For example, German support for the

EU dialogue with Iran, which in the 1980s and 1990s ran counter to U.S. policy, and EU efforts to use diplomacy to compel Iran to cease development of a nuclear weapons program drew on a broad public consensus in Germany favoring diplomacy, dialogue, and engagement over isolation, confrontation, and trade embargoes.

Domestic politics can also constrain the constitutional development of the EU even after member governments negotiate, conclude, and attain parliamentary ratification of new treaty provisions. For example, various plans for Treaty revisions or changes have been rejected in popular referenda. In Chapter 2 we learned that such "no votes" occurred in popular referenda by electorates of Denmark on the TEU (1992), Ireland on the Nice Treaty (2001), the Netherlands and France on the EU Constitutional Treaty (2005), and Ireland on the Lisbon Treaty (2008).

Public opinion matters when European integration, driven by political and economic elites, gets ahead of public preferences. At the same time, the EU is, for better or for worse, the creation of elites. The creation and development of the EC in its early decades was a top-down phenomenon driven by elites in the charter members. For examples, German Chancellor Brandt's policy in the 1970s of improving West German relations with East Germany—*ostpolitik*—resulted in a reappraisal of the EC's own Eastern policy that led to the adoption of an EC *ostpolitik* as well. The SEA and the EMU were driven by elites (Valéry Giscard d'Estaing, Helmut Schmidt, and Jacques Delors) to complete the internal market and give it a common currency. Lastly, in response to the Kosovo crisis and a need for the British Labor Government to regain a place at the core of the EU, Prime Minister Tony Blair caused a sea change in British policy in 1998. He lifted British opposition to the EU's undertaking certain kinds of security operations in support of humanitarian relief, conflict prevention and resolution, and peacekeeping. His shift in policy triggered a chain of new EU security policy developments beginning with the Franco–British St. Malo summit in 1998, which paved the way for the EU's adoption of the European Security and Defense Policy beginning in 1999.

Political elites were not always champions of European integration. French Presidents François Mitterand and Jacques Chirac took unilateral actions that undermined or sidestepped the EU. In the early 1990s, Mitterand initiated a peace initiative in the Balkans without consulting his EU partners; Chirac undertook nuclear testing despite strong protests from many EU partners. In 1991 the government of Chancellor Helmut Kohl granted diplomatic recognition to Slovenia and Croatia ahead of Germany's EU partners. The German recognition may have helped fan the flames of war in neighboring Bosnia-Herzegovina (BiH), where the Bosnian Serb minority, which feared the future of its status in an independent BiH, opposed independence from the rump Yugoslav state.

Part of the perception and reality of the EU as an elitist organization has to do with the fact that pro-integration political parties, whether at national or European levels, never captured public imagination and sustained support. The EU was more a creation of a movement of European idealists than it was a popular endeavor. Although the EP, discussed in Chapter 5, is the democratically elected representative body of the EU, voter turnout in the parliamentary elections is declining. The gap between elite and popular support for the EU is one of the biggest problems of European integration. As a result, when we examine the context of EU governmental decisionmaking, both elite and popular opinion must be taken into account. Elites are paying more attention to public opinion than before.

EUROPEAN WORLD

EU policies at home and abroad are based not just on national interests but on broadly similar and complementary European values (beliefs), norms (habits of behavior), and interests (pursuit of needs) rooted in

- a common civilization and geography;
- the memory of wartime misery and postwar interstate reconciliation;
- the establishment of a democratic peace (mature democracies do not go to war against each other);
- a penchant for conflict prevention and resolution;
- a preference for a social market approach to capitalism;
- adherence to common bodies of law and practice; and
- a world where environmental concerns, economic and social development, social justice, and the rule of law are part and parcel of political rhetoric, discourse, and at times government action.

A process of socialization—**Europeanization**—shapes how the member governments and EU bodies interact with one another to make policy. The process refers to the custom and habit of cooperation, the rules of the game that are socialized by the players of the game, the give-and-take of negotiation and compromise, the built-in proclivity to achieve consensus, and the development over time of a sense of European identity. Europeanization occurs within the EU institutions where the member governments and their representatives and the EU civil servants work in Brussels, Luxembourg, and Strasbourg. It also occurs in the growing interactions among bureaucrats in different national governments engaged with EU issues in EU committees and working groups. They too experience a convergence of common interests, an ethos that is brought back to the home administrations. Europeanization also occurs among expert groups and nongovernmental organizations involved who influence the inputs and outputs of EU governmental decisionmaking. Public and elite opinion on EU matters is influenced by public and private media in Brussels, location of one of the world's largest press corps.

Europeanization often, but not always, shapes, conditions, and tempers national interests. Many national officials posted in or seconded to Brussels become socialized in the ethos of EU governmental decisionmaking. Europeanization is also prevalent in the EU's external policies. The foreign policy actions of the EU reflect a unique European brand of diplomacy and foreign policy. The EU has its own self-styled foreign policy interests, missions, and initiatives in the world independent of any one member state or of any one external stimulus. Often, but not always, the EU member states find that when they act together abroad, they derive benefits from a politics of scale.[1] This notion refers to the benefits of collective EU action over unilateral national action. When the EU speaks and acts with one voice internationally, the EU resonates far more than when the members speak and act individually. Members may take joint foreign policy actions at lower transaction costs and risks—but with more scale—than when they act on their own. Foreign policy actions that reflect an indigenous and uniquely European quality include special partnerships with many of the world's leading and middle-size states, former colonies, and other regional blocs; and the pursuit of policies that advance human rights, counter proliferation, crime, terrorism, and environmental degradation, and support regional integration movements around the world. Chapter 7 focuses exclusively on EU foreign and security policy.

No discussion of the context of the European world is complete without mention of the considerable amount of time, effort, and other resources Europeans place in the *process* of solving problems. To Americans, with their "can do" risk-taking spirit, the EU can appear engaged more in process than outcomes. For Europeans, process is often outcome. Many in the EU share an ethos of compromise and cooperation to achieve settlement on a common objective even if the process takes a long time before all are on board. Often the lowest common denominator is the result.

OUTSIDE WORLD

As figure II.1 indicates, the outside world affects EU governmental decisionmaking. The EU is influenced by international politics, law, and society; globalization in all its variants; and transnational phenomena. The EU is as exposed to international systemic change as are its member governments. Here neorealist theory focuses correctly on the impact of the structure of world politics on international actors. For example, the post–World War II bipolar international system and the ensuing Cold War hastened Franco–German reconciliation and the creation of the ECSC as bulwarks in the face of the common enemy. They shaped but also limited what the Europeans could do in international affairs given the dominance of and their dependence on the United States.

However, the international system of the 1950s began to give way to a more fluid and plural distribution of world power by the 1970s. Given increasing global interdependence combined with superpower détente, the EU found that new areas of international activity independent of the United States opened up to it, especially in Eastern Europe, the Soviet bloc, Latin America, and the Middle East and with regard to such international issue areas as human rights and economic development. With the end to the rigidities of the Cold War in 1989–1990, the shift in world politics catapulted the European Community into a European Union with enormous international responsibilities. The EU found itself in a position of leadership, assisting the democratic transitions and market reforms in the Central and Eastern European and former Soviet bloc states. The EU was responsible for the peaceful transition of Europe.

International systemic change forced the EU, for the first time in its history, to start "exporting" security to a needy world. It had been a consumer of security from the United States and NATO for forty years. In demonstrating to itself and the outside world that it could act in areas that reflect its interests, it moved out from the shadow of the United States. Moreover, in the 1990s and now the 2000s, the EU has demonstrated its ability both to oppose the United States on key international issues (climate change, International Criminal Court, capital punishment) and to work with the

United States on other issues where there is agreement (combating HIV/AIDS, supporting the resumption of Israeli–Palestinian peace talks, and, now, opposing Iran's efforts to enrich uranium).[2] In other words, since the end of the Cold War, the United States and the European Union have become competitors and partners in international politics, as they have always been in international economics.

The EU is affected by international society as well, and here constructivist perspectives on regional integration are useful.[3] International society differs from international system. International society refers to values (human and minority rights), norms (sustainable development), and rules (respect for the rule of law, constitutional and representative government, multilateral agreements) that are universally held and practiced. International society magnifies the values the EU practices at home, (e.g., in such areas as conflict prevention, postwar stabilization and reconstruction, humanitarian relief, and democratization). International society also makes itself felt in the context of EU governmental decisionmaking when the outside world demands and expects that the EU act in defense of victims of human and minority rights abuses, in response to global warming, and in opposition to capital punishment.

The norms and values of international society that help to contextualize EU governmental decisionmaking are not the only drivers of global change that transcend interstate relations. Globalization and other transnational phenomena influence EU policymaking. **Globalization** broadly refers to the impact certain global transnational phenomena are having on a world of nation-states whose increasingly porous borders cannot stop the intrusion of such phenomena on their societies. The EU, like state actors, responds to economic globalization by endeavoring to become more competitive in European and global markets and entering into agreements with nonmember states that help to manage and improve the terms of international trade. The EU, like state actors, is forced to respond to the pernicious effects of political globalization—the scourges of transnational terrorism and crime, particularly trafficking in women and children, drug trafficking, and money laundering, and the problem of the proliferation of weapons of mass destruction. The EU cooperates closely with national partners like the U.S. and Canada and organizational partners like the UN to address these threats.

The Inputs into EU Governmental Decisionmaking

The object of political actors who wish to influence decisionmaking is the EU political system, or black box. The political system requires an understanding of the interplay of influential actors at the subnational, national, and European levels. This is a tall but necessary order. This section surveys the most important sources of political influence on EU governmental decisionmaking. Figure II.1 identifies these political actors:

- member governments who in the Council advance national positions on EU issues;
- EU bodies who have their own institutional interests to advance as well as those of the common European good;

- European NGOs, such as special interest groups and their lobbyists, both at the national and EU levels;
- national and European electorates, whose votes determine the composition of the Council, the European Council, and the EP; and
- state and nonstate actors outside the EU—nonmember governments, international organizations, and nongovernmental organizations outside the EU who make demands on the EU to act, often before the EU is ready to do so.

EU MEMBER GOVERNMENTS, INSTITUTIONS, AND NGOs

Whether in the European Council or the Council of the EU, member governments have the most important input into EU governmental decisionmaking. Outside the European Council and the Council, no other EU body has complete decisionmaking authority over *all* aspects of EU activity. The European Council is the only EU body that has the power to delegate authority to other bodies and then set limits on those agents so that they have just enough agency to manage and regulate the union without eroding the member states' core sovereign interests. Each member government has permanent representation in Brussels, where the member-state officials serve as the watchdogs of national interests. However powerful member governments are at the fulcrum of the EU polity, **subnational governments** of the EU—regions, states such as the German Länder—are gaining influence. Regions and subnational governments of the EU

- are economically powerful magnets for employment with trained workforces and centers of technology, production, services, and trade regionally and globally (areas of Belgium, Germany, and France adjacent to and centered on Luxembourg City, a leading banking capital);
- have cultural, linguistic, or regional identities and economic interests that are distinct from their nation-state (Spanish Catalonia and its capital, Barcelona);
- are centers of advanced learning whose universities cooperate with industry at a regional level (the Rhone-Alps and its capital, Lyon);
- deal better with global problems that have infiltrated the EU—transnational crime and terrorism, money laundering, drug trafficking, and illegal immigration (Barcelona);
- make cultural, trade, and other agreements with other subnational entities in the EU (Saxony);
- adroitly use access to the EU to influence decisionmaking (see Committee of Regions, below) and, in some cases, skirt national governments to advance their own interests (Scotland); and
- receive significant aid spending from the European Regional Development Fund (ERDF) and, with encouragement from the Commission, participate in the management of the ERDF (Spanish Basque region, southern Italy).

National and subnational governmental bodies are key coadministrators with the Commission of EU spending. Eighty percent of the EU budget (agriculture and regional development aid) consists of subsidies paid out by national and subnational bodies, who in turn lobby the EU to maintain spending levels desirable to their constituents. In its implementation powers, the Commission depends on and monitors these governments to the extent its resources allow, similar to the ways federal systems of government, like the United States, depend on state and local governments to implement federal policies. When the Commission turns to national and subnational governments to implement EU legislation, there is a kind of reverse agency. The Commission and other EU bodies to whom the member governments delegated powers to run the union do not have the scale of resources to implement what the Council or Council and EP have legislated. The Commission delegates agency back to national and subnational governments, who implement EU legislation in order to lower its transaction costs.

Subnational governments are represented in the Committee of the Regions (CoR), an advisory body of 344 elected local and regional officials. Members are appointed by the Council on the basis of nominations made by their member governments. However, once appointed, they act independently of national governments during their terms. The CoR is consulted by the Commission, Council, or EP on proposed legislation for regional perspectives with regard to combating social exclusion; communications; economic and social cohesion; education, training, and youth; energy infrastructure; enlargement of the EU; environment; transport networks and policy; and other areas of concern to local and regional governments. The CoR may initiate its own reports and offer opinions in areas where regional interests are involved.[4] The Lisbon Treaty extends the term of the CoR members from four to five years.

Over two hundred subnational governments (regional and local authorities) have their own offices in Brussels in order to influence EU decisionmaking with regard to regional development aid. For example, many of the German Länder have missions in Brussels. The Länder, due to their position in German federalism, are among the most powerful regions in the EU because they are directly represented in the Bundesrat, where they have constitutional powers to vote on EU legislation that affects them.

Interest groups are represented in the Brussels-based European Economic and Social Committee (EESC) with its 344 members from across the union. Interests represented in the EESC include employers, trade unions, and others, such as consumers, farmers, and those engaged in white-collar professions. The EESC advises the Council, Commission, and EP and issues reports on its own initiative in economic and social areas. The Treaty mandates that the Commission or Council consult the EESC in such areas as the internal market, regional and social policy, the environment, agriculture, free movement of labor, and research and development. The Commission and Council may also consult the EESC when they wish to in areas not required by the Treaty. The Commission is obliged to consider the views of the EESC as it proposes legislation in these areas.[5] The Lisbon Treaty extends the length of term of members of the EESC from four to five years.

Thousands of interest groups organized on a European level are also represented by their associations and lobbyists in Brussels and Strasbourg. For example, business is represented by the Union of Industrial and Employers' Confederation of Europe; industrialists by the European Round Table of Industrialists; labor by the European Trade Union Confederation; farmers by the Confederation of Professional Agricultural Organizations; consumers by the European Bureau of Consumers' Associations and the European Consumers Organization; women by the European Women's

Lobby; and the environment by the European Environmental Bureau. The European banking industry has a presence in and influence at the EP as well.[6] Although no one knows with certainty how many lobbyists there are in Brussels, some suggest as many as fifteen thousand.

In addition to these interest groups, the Commission cultivates its ties with NGOs. The scope of their presence in Brussels and utility to the Commission depends on the expertise and information they provide, given the limited human and capital resources available to the Commission. An example of the impact of NGOs on EU policy came in the 1980s when German and European NGO activities on behalf of human rights had much to do with German support for the EU's human rights policies in Central America.[7] In the 1990s, the French Human Rights League, joined by thirty socialist, communist, and Green legislators, warned France and the EU not to resume normal diplomatic relations with Iran until the Iranian Government officially revoked its support for terrorism, refrained from killing dissidents, and ended the death sentence placed on Salman Rushdie.[8] Some NGOs help drive transatlantic trade liberalization. Business, labor, environmental, and other groups participate in transatlantic dialogues that in turn influence policy choices of the EU and United States.

POLITICAL PARTIES AND ELECTORATES

National and European political parties/groups and electorates influence the composition and preferences of national governments and EU bodies. The national and EU parliaments are representative democracies whose deputies are usually members of political parties. A political party is a nongovernmental organization of individuals who share a common set of political beliefs (or ideology) that they wish to put into action at local, regional, national, and European levels. The chief objective of a political party is to get its candidates elected to public office so that it can influence governmental decisionmaking in ways consistent with its ideological preferences. In parliamentary democracies, voters elect those who run for seats in national parliaments. The successful candidates in turn determine which political party or parties form a government and select a Head of Government, or Prime Minister. The Heads of Government (and Cypriot, Finnish, French, and Romanian Heads of State) sit in the European Council, where broad policy guidelines for the EU are made. Governmental ministers from the member states sit in the Council, where they vote on Commission policy initiatives.

Voters also elect MEPs, who with the Council legislate in most areas of EU activity. National political parties help get their candidates elected to the EP. Once elected to the EP, MEPs sit in transnational European political party groupings that have links to like-minded political parties back home. EP party groups help structure the work of the EP and provide incentives for MEPs to remain attached to them (where they sit, to what committees they are assigned).

Voters make their voices heard. In states that hold popular referenda on Treaty changes for the EU, voters again have an opportunity to speak. For example, we already know that Irish voters in their referendum rejected the Lisbon Treaty in 2008. That said, European electorates' overall input into EU governmental decisionmaking is frustratingly limited when compared to the political influence that the specialized working groups of the Commission and Council, and the policy networks that influence both, have in EU policy formulation and execution. For example, the Council has established working groups that are designed to oversee, shape, and in some cases veto the way in which the Commission implements legislation, yet these groups are not linked back to the EP and escape the scrutiny of publics, except those interested in or affected by a specific piece of legislation, such as agricultural support or regional aid. In truth, though, even at the level of national governments in the EU and elsewhere among advanced representative democracies, specialized working groups that are not publicly transparent influence the formulation and execution of governmental policy (see Chapter 5 for further examination).

ACTORS OUTSIDE THE EUROPEAN UNION

The EU is influenced by actors that are governments (nation-states), subnational entities (provinces within nation-states), intergovernmental organizations or IGOs (international governmental institutions), and nongovernmental organizations or NGOs (groups that are neither states nor IGOs). The Commission has 130 diplomatic missions abroad and receives 160 diplomatic missions from other countries. In both instances, the EU is the object of foreign influence. The Council has its own representative posted to the United Nations in New York. The EP is opening an office in Washington, D.C. The Lisbon Treaty establishes the legal basis for the creation of a new external action service of EU diplomatic personnel and missions abroad. Even subnational governments, including U.S. states and Canadian provinces, have official representations in Brussels where they promote their interests. U.S. states have roughly 190 offices abroad, many in the EU.[9] In many respects, nonmember states who press the EU to act in response to external stimuli (demands for trade preferences, support for a diplomatic cause) force the EU to act in response even if the EU is not yet ready or does not wish to do so. This process of "externalization," a feature in the neofunctional integration theoretical literature in the 1970s, helps to explain the impact of external demands on the EU that generate new EU responses.[10]

The EU is increasingly pressed by intergovernmental organizations, especially the UN, to engage in international security and humanitarian operations. For examples, the EU and the Secretary-General of the UN have cooperated in the EU peacekeeping mission in the Democratic Republic of Congo (DRC) and the EU works closely in Palestine with the UN Relief Works Agency (UNRWA). The EU and NATO cooperate very closely regarding security in BiH and Kosovo as they have done previously in Macedonia. The EU and the African Union cooperate to assist African Union peacekeepers in Darfur, Sudan.

NGOs influence EU governmental decisionmaking because they too press the EU to act in ways consistent with their interests and needs. NGOs, which are represented in Brussels, interact and cooperate extensively with the EU in many areas of international affairs. IGOs and NGOs (e.g., Amnesty International, Euro–Mediterranean Human Rights Network, Friends of the Earth, Human Rights Watch) seek EU support for their causes, and the EU depends on these organizations (e.g., the International Red Cross) as subcontractors of EU foreign and humanitarian aid.

NGOs also make demands on the EU. Friends of the Earth Europe, for example, which has a trade coordinator posted to Brussels, has criticized the EU for accepting a WTO report concluding that the EU's previous ban on the release of genetically modified organisms violated multilateral trade rules. Friends of the Earth Europe urged the EU to challenge the WTO report and called on the EU to "protect people and the environment from industrial excesses."[11] In 2006 Human Rights Watch published a report critical of the EU and its member governments, claiming that the EU minimized human rights violations in such states as Russia, Saudi Arabia, and China—states needed by the EU in the fight against transnational terrorism. In the same report, Human Rights Watch suggested that the EU policy of firmness was correct and important in its dealings with the Uzbek Government following the May 2005 massacre.[12]

Review

Chapter 4 identified the contexts and actors of EU governmental decisionmaking. The politics and economics of the EU now deeply affect the member states. Elections, referenda, and changing political and economic fortunes within the member states affect what happens at the EU level. External pressures on the EU have often prompted the EU to act in response to or in defense of its interests. Economic globalization and the continuing dependence of the EU on export and import trade and on outside energy sources will mean that the outside world will continue to contextualize what the EU does at home and abroad. Political globalization catalyzes the EU to respond to transnational security threats to the European homeland and border areas.

Actors are the players who have input into decisionmaking. This chapter has demonstrated the expected input of member governments and EU bodies in EU governmental decisionmaking, but it has also identified the importance of other governmental and nongovernmental actors. How legislative proposals are shaped is as important as how they become law. Having examined the shaping contexts of the EU polity and identified those who have influence on it, we can now move to Chapter 5, which probes the black box to help demystify when and how inputs, shaped by context, become outputs or decisions.

Key Concepts

European interests
Europeanization
globalization
national interests
political culture
subnational governments

Study Questions

1. Why do governments delegate tasks to EU bodies? Offer three examples of such delegation and explain each.

2. What is agency and why is it important in EU governmental decisionmaking? Offer three examples and explain.
3. Why is the scope for agency of EU bodies subject to limitations imposed by the member governments? Offer three examples of how member governments constrain agency and explain each.

Selected Readings

Neill Nugent, *The Government and Politics of the European Union* (Durham, N.C.: Duke University Press, 2003).

Mark A. Pollack, *The Engines of European Integration: Delegation, Agency, and Agenda Setting in the EU* (Oxford: Oxford University Press, 2003).

Helen Wallace, William Wallace, and Mark A Pollack, *Policy-Making in the European Union* (Oxford: Oxford University Press, 2005).

CHAPTER 5

Inside EU Governmental Decisionmaking

Preview

The process of governmental decisionmaking is located inside the black box. As discussed in Chapter 4, the **black box** is a metaphor for the process of converting inputs into outputs. This core function of government receives much attention in political science, particularly among students of comparative politics. Chapter 5 aims to demystify the EU's black box by examining how the EU bodies work together with the member states and other actors who influence governmental decisionmaking.

Readers are not expected to learn every vein and artery of the EU body, but rather to gain enough of a basic understanding of its biology to examine how the parts relate to the whole. As depicted in figure II.1, the black box, or EU political system, is influenced by those inside and outside the EU. To know how decisions are made goes to the heart of government and politics at national or EU levels. For average European citizens, and more so for those outside the union, it matters little how the EU makes decisions—that is, whether the primary decisionmaking procedure is intergovernmental, supranational, or a hybrid. What matters most to Europeans who are generally cognizant of the EU is that their union works efficiently, effectively, and transparently and that it does not needlessly tread on what national and subnational governments can do better themselves.

The European Union's measure of which policy decisions should be made at EU level and which ought to remain at national and local levels is awkwardly referred to as **subsidiarity**. Codified in the Treaty of Amsterdam, the subsidiarity principle mandates that in areas, such as health care and education, that do not fall under the scope of the EU's exclusive competences, decisionmaking should remain at national level. Decisionmaking is only to be bumped up to EU level when collective action is necessary and is more efficient and effective, such as running the monetary union and the internal market. This principle of EU governance is designed to ensure that action at EU level is justified. The principle allows the member states to avoid unnecessary delegation of authority to EU bodies, but it also justifies when the EU needs to act.

When the EU does act, it ought to leave maximum and flexible room for each member government to implement the joint action. Thus, when the EU takes action under the prerequisite of subsidiarity, it is guided by another treaty principle: proportionality. Proportionality refers to the content or form of EU action that must not exceed what is necessary to achieve the objective of the treaty in the areas where the union has competence.

This chapter focuses on the relationships among the decisionmaking actors in the EU political system. It concerns itself with demystifying the process of who does what with whom, when, and with what effect. Table 5.1, a good place to start, depicts the structure, function, and powers of the major EU bodies. Inside the black box, EU institutions do not act merely as impartial arbiters in the process of translating national preferences into European policies.[1] They also tend to cultivate compromises among member governments to advance European interests.

The student of EU governmental decisionmaking "must be concerned with explaining a range of different decisions taken at different levels in a multilevel system of governance."[2] By examining the EU as a polity, however imperfect and incomplete, we focus on the different layers of decisionmaking that produce outputs. By deconstructing the EU polity into its individual parts and reassembling them into a single governmental decisionmaking system, we learn best how the EU works. Theory helps. Insights from principal–agent analysis best capture the creative tension between the member governments and the EU bodies. The pendulum of European integration swings between member states, who retain and delegate sovereignty, and EU bodies, who cultivate their scope for agency. It is in this spirit of investigation—of demystifying the elements of the EU polity—that we now turn to the study of the main players inside the black box.

Conscience of the European Union: The Commission

The Commission is the supranational coexecutive and bureaucracy that advocates for and upholds the interests of the EU based on Treaty law. Table 5.1 depicts the Commission's structure, functions, and major powers. Together with the Council, the Commission is the main agenda-setter in the EU, except in such areas as security and defense. It provides for institutional memory and continuity and cultivates consensus-building in the European interest. Thus, the Commission is the EU's conscience because it is designed to look after the good of the whole, which no one government or group of governments could do alone. Its mandate, delegated to it by the member governments, is to do the right thing to advance the common interest—in other words, to do what the governmental principals themselves have found so elusive in their relations with one another since the Thirty Years War. The Commission embodies the hopes of many for the transformation of the European nation-states from neighbors in war to neighbors in peace.

European integration scholars generally agree that they know more what the Commission is not than what it is. It is neither the government of a state nor merely a secretariat of an international institution, such as the permanent staff of the WTO. The Commission combines executive and bureaucratic governmental functions. It cooperates closely with and depends on national and subnational governments as it proposes policy; and it enforces policy with the ECJ. There is no other international body in the world like the Commission, which makes it challenging for scholars to categorize and explain.

APPOINTMENT AND DELEGATION

What makes the Commission supranational is that once appointed and confirmed, Commissioners neither report to nor seek instructions from member governments. Instead, they are charged by the Treaty to advance the common European interest. Commission staff, known as EU civil servants or *fonctionnaires*, work for the European Union, not its member governments. Commissioners are political appointees who come and go. However, most officials of the Commission are lifetime European civil servants. They have institutional memory and expertise and discretionary influence in the way policy is crafted and implemented. For example, the Commission has some scope for discretion, or agency, when ruling on antitrust cases, negotiating with non-members in the area of trade policy, and working with countries who have applied for EU membership.

The Commissioners and their President are appointed in a complex process that involves the member governments and the European Parliament (EP). The nomination and appointment of a Commission President and the College of Commissioners (the collective body of Commissioners) for five-year terms occur in the following order of steps, according to the Treaty and the procedures laid down by the EU bodies involved:

1. The member governments in the European Council nominate the Commission President on the basis of a qualified majority vote. The Heads of Government and State (HOGS) nominated Portuguese Prime Minister José Manuel Barroso for a first term in June 2004 and a second term in June 2009. Under the Lisbon Treaty, the European Council is required to take into account the results of the EP elections and to consult with the EP before nominating the Commission President.
2. The nominee for Commission President is approved by the EP. Barroso was confirmed in July 2004 by a vote of 413 for and 251 against. In September 2009, he was again confirmed by a vote of 382 for and 219 against. Under the Lisbon Treaty, if the EP chooses not to vote to support a European Council nominee for Commission President, the European Council will propose a new candidate.
3. Each member government nominates a Commissioner.
4. The proposed slate of Commissioners nominated by the member governments is subject to QMV by the European Council and the consent of the Commission President-Nominee.
5. Relevant committees of the EP hold hearings to query each Commissioner-Nominee. In October 2004, EP opposition to the candidate for Commissioner from Italy was so great, and the threat of an EP no vote on the investiture of the Barroso Commission so real, that the Italian government was forced to bring forward a different, more acceptable nominee.
6. The plenary session of the EP votes to confirm the composition of the new Com-

Table 5.1: Powers of Major EU Institutions

Institution/ Date of Origin	Size/ Secretariat	Term	Leader	Major Functions/Powers	Voting	Example of Competence
Commission (1952) –supranational executive and bureaucracy	27 members; 33,000 staff; Brussels, Luxembourg	appointed by member states subject to confirmation of EP for 5-year term	José Manuel Barroso, President, 5-year term	guards/enforces Treaty; initiates/executes legislation and budget; issues reports, studies, regulations, and directives; rules on competition cases; oversees daily EU functioning; represents/ negotiates abroad; receives diplomatic envoys	simple majority	fined Microsoft in 2004; ordered it to take action to correct Microsoft's dominant market position for operating systems of personal computers
Council (1952) –intergovernmental executive and legislator	27 Cabinet Ministers of member governments; 3,500 staff; Brussels, Luxembourg	no term	presidency held by member states on a rotating basis, except for Foreign Affairs Council chaired by the High Representative	colegislates with EP; decides policy in areas of security and defense; approves budget with EP; asks Commission to conduct studies/submit proposals	unanimity, consensus, qualified majority, constructive abstention, enhanced cooperation	signed an agreement with the United States in 2003 permitting aircraft carriers to transfer air passenger data for U.S. customs authorities
European Parliament (1952) –transnational colegislator	736 MEPs;* 5,000 staff; Strasbourg, Brussels, Luxembourg *751 in 2014	elected for 5-year term	Jerzy Buzek, President, 2.5-year term	colegislates with Council; oversees EU bodies; approves budget with Council; approves enlargement/ associations; confirms/ censures Commission; asks Commission to conduct studies/submit proposals; adopts reports	simple or absolute majority	put pressure on Santer Commission to resign in 1999 under a threat to pass a motion of censure over charges of financial mismanagement in Commission

Table 5.1: Powers of Major EU Institutions (continued)

Institution/ Date of Origin	Size/ Secretariat	Term	Leader	Major Functions/Powers	Voting	Example of Competence
Court of Justice of the EU (1952) –supranational court	27 Judges; Luxembourg	appointed for 6-year renewable terms by member governments	Vassilios Skouris, President, 3-year term	interprets Treaty; rules on treaty law; ensures uniformity of EC law	simple majority	ruled in 1964 that national courts are bound to apply EC law
European Council (1975) –intergovernmental Summit of Heads of Government/ State plus European Council President, Commission President, and High Representative	27 members; Brussels	no term	Herman Van Rompuy, President, 2.5-year term	sets broad guidelines; makes overarching decisions; offers strategic direction and impetus; breaks logjams; delegates powers to EU bodies to reduce transaction costs; nominates/ appoints Commission and Commission President, Council Secretary-General, High Representative, and Executive Board/President of the ECB; convenes IGCs	consensus; QMV on selection of European Council and Commission Presidents and on appointment of new Commission	approved in 2004 the opening of membership negotiations with Turkey in 2005; invited Commission and Council to prepare regulations framework
European Court of Auditors (1977) –independent auditor	27 members; 800 staff; Luxembourg	appointed for 6-year renewable terms	Vítor Manuel da Silva Caldeira, President, 3-year term	audits implementation of EU budget and financial status of EU bodies	simple majority	twice in the 1990s exposed financial mismanagement of programs by Commission

mission, which it did, for example, in November, 2004, with a vote of 449 in favor, 149 against, and 82 abstentions. The Commission may not take office until the EP votes to approve it.

7. The European Council makes the appointment of the new Commission based on QMV.

8. The ECJ President administers the oath of office for the Commission President-Designate and the new Commissioners-Designate.

A new Commission is appointed every five years (in years ending in 4 and 9), soon after the results of the EP elections. This close alignment of the five-year terms of the EP and Commission brings EU governmental decisionmaking closer to a parliamentary system. Legislators hold accountable the political appointees in the executive. Each new parliament has time to get up to speed on the needs of the union and the front-burner issues before the Commission is appointed. Moreover, the member governments are able to gauge EU public opinion from the results of the EP elections as they choose the new Commission leadership.

Once appointed, individual Commissioners and the Commission President are free for five years from the specter of being removed from office by member governments. In this way, a Commissioner is independent of the home government, although a government may choose not to reappoint the Commissioner at the end of his or her term. For example, British Prime Minister Margaret Thatcher, who nominated Lord Cockfield as Commissioner in 1985, chose not to reappoint him in 1989 for what she thought were his pro-integrationist views. The degree to which individual Commissioners allow their work in Brussels to be affected by their prospective reappointments depends on each individual. During their terms, however, Commissioners are strongly influenced both by the process of Europeanization in the College of the Commissioners and by the strong ethos of working together for the common good.

The Commission is answerable to the EP, which has a supervisory role vis-à-vis the Commission. By subjecting a supranational executive to an elected parliament, the EU has established a constitutional system of checks and balances. Commissioners attend EP plenary sessions where they reply to queries by MEPs and seek to justify chosen policies. Commissioners also respond to written queries from MEPs. The EP retains the right to oblige the Commission as a whole to resign. It does so by passing a motion of MEPs by a double majority: 50 percent plus one, and a majority of votes cast. The EP has never censured the Commission, but the specter of this blunt political object is nonetheless potent. For example, in 1999, the Santer Commission resigned under pressure when faced with a damning report addressing allegations of fraud, financial mismanagement, and nepotism in the Commission.[3]

The EP votes to confirm the Commission as a whole, not individual Commissioners; similarly, it has the authority to censure the Commission as a whole (on the basis of a majority of the votes cast), but not individual Commissioners. The logic of the EP's confirmation of the Commission as a whole is that it enhances the influence and authority of the Commission President over his or her fellow Commissioners (whom the President can dismiss or reassign). This in turn lends more coherence to the Commission as a whole and contributes to its autonomy from the EP once investiture occurs. It also contributes to the collective responsibility of the College of Commissioners.

Image 5.1. The Barroso Commission (2009). Courtesy of the Audiovisual Library of the European Commission

The EP does not have the authority to censure an individual Commissioner, with good reason. The College of Commissioners functions on the basis of "collective responsibility." All Commissioners share responsibility for Commission proposals and for the actions of one another.

Commissioners-Designate pledge to carry out their duties in the general interest of the EU, fully independent of any other government or body. However, the Commissioners are often well-known politicians with close ties to national politics. Many have served as government ministers (Jacques Delors of France) and some as Prime Ministers (Gaston Thorn and Jacques Santer of Luxembourg; Romano Prodi of Italy). Therefore, it would be a mistake to assume that Commissioners are not influenced by national interests. That said, two caveats are noteworthy. First, the Commission President, nominated by the European Council, is the only Commissioner not nominated by a member government. He or she is more independent of member governments than the other members of the College. Second, despite the links between Commissioners and their national governments, the Commissioners generally work well as a collegial body once they are appointed, confirmed, and assume duties in Brussels. If individual Commissioners are known to blatantly advance their country's national interests, they lose influence, credibility, and effectiveness within the College.[4]

STRUCTURE

The President not only is the chief executive of the Commission but, given his or her functions, serves as a coexecutive of the EU with the European Council President. He or she is expected to ensure consistency, efficiency, and collegiality of purpose for the Commission. With his or her fellow Commissioners, the Commission President is first among equals in many respects, but because the President has the power to assign and reassign portfolios to Commissioners, and some portfolios carry more prestige (external relations) than others (maritime affairs and fisheries), the President has the most political power in the College. President Barroso not only distributes the portfolios of the new Commissioners but may change those assignments at a later date or require a Commissioner to resign. Since ambitious Commissioners who plan to seek reappointment will want reassignment from less to more important assignments, they will want to keep the Commission President on their side.

President Barroso represents the Commission abroad and with other EU bodies. He oversees the Commission's Secretariat-General, which assists him in coordinating the work of the Commission, and he provides a political direction for the Commission as a whole. Each Commissioner is assisted by a cabinet headed by a *chef de cabinet*. The **cabinet** consists of a select group of aides who keep their Commissioner briefed, seek support from other cabinets for the policies initiated by their Commissioner, and work with other cabinets to reach and implement agreements.[5] The cabinets provide important access to the Commissioner for member governments, other EU bodies, lobbyists, interest groups, and others who seek to influence policies before they are enacted. The growing importance of cabinets in the work of the Commission is one of the ways the member governments limit the Commission's scope for agency. Cabinet officials are often seconded (posted) to the Commission from the member govern-

Image 5.2.   The European Commission 2009 (Berlaymont Building, Brussels). Courtesy of the Audiovisual Library of the European Commission

ments. They remain in close contact with the administration back home, where they will return once their time in Brussels comes to an end.

Up until recently, large EU member states had two Commissioners, and the smaller states had one. However, to avoid the ever growing number of Commissioners when there are only so many portfolios to go around, the Nice Treaty limited each member state to just one Commissioner. Moreover, the Lisbon Treaty would have limited the number of Commissioners to two-thirds of the EU member states in 2014 (unless the European Council unanimously decided to alter this number). Member states would have rotated on and off the Commission. However, following the Irish rejection of the Lisbon Treaty, the European Council was forced to make a concession on the issue of the number of Commissioners in order to meet the Irish Government's preconditions for holding a second referendum. In June 2009, the European Council agreed that it would enact legislation once Lisbon is ratified to retain the one member state/one Commissioner rule. It will likely do so as an addendum to the accession treaty between the EU and Croatia.

The Commission consists of 33,000 staff members and translators—who come from all of the member states and conduct the day-to-day work of the Commission. They are organized into twenty-seven Directorates-General (DGs), some of which include Agriculture; Budget; Competition; Development; Economic and Financial Affairs; Energy and Transport; Enlargement; Environment; Internal Market; Justice, Freedom and Security; and Regional Policy. Each Commissioner is assigned to one or more DGs. Directors-General, who are responsible for the directorates, or divisions, within each DG, report to their assigned Commissioners. In addition, a number of agencies and services cover the gamut of policy areas of the EU associated with the Commission (see section on Agencies of the EU).[6]

Although French and English are the Commission's working languages for internal business, the Commission translates all EU documents into the twenty-three official languages of the EU. Most of the Commission staff is located in Brussels, but some offices, such as the Statistical and Publications Offices, are located in Luxembourg. Translators, administrative assistants, and expert professionals of the Commission staff are knowledgeable in their assigned fields, draw on institutional memory, and work regularly with national civil servants, member state and NGO representatives, and networks of policy advisors in Brussels to facilitate the Commission's work.[7] Networks of government representatives, EU officials, lobbyists, and private-sector interests congregate around different DGs (and EP committees) based on the policy sector where legislation is being considered.

FUNCTION AND AGENCY

The Commission is the guardian, overseer, and enforcer of the Treaty and the formulator, executor, and manager of policies under its remit. It drafts and implements the budget and appropriates funds. The Commission depends on member governments to manage and control funds, and it is subject to the audits of the European Court of Auditors (ECA).

Of all the major functions of the Commission listed in table 5.1, the Commission's role as guardian of the Treaty and the *acquis communautaire* is perhaps the most essential. The EU founders had the foresight to recognize that nation-states do not think naturally of the common interest before their own (or equate the two as mutually inclusive and reinforcing). They realized that if the EU were to survive where the League of Nations had failed, it would require not only majority voting but common bodies to police the agreements made by member governments to one another and to their union.

Closely related to its role as guardian is the Commission's role as overseer of the day-to-day functioning of the EU. The Commission is charged by the Treaty to enforce EU law. The Commission and the ECJ are responsible for ascertaining if EU law is properly applied by member firms, states, and EU bodies. As discussed in Chapter 3, if the Commission finds that a member government appears to have breached treaty law, it commences an infringement procedure. The Commission explains to the member government why it believes the Treaty has been infringed and establishes a deadline by which the government must respond to the Commission. If the Commission and the member government cannot reach an agreement on how to address the alleged infringement, the Commission refers the case to the ECJ. ECJ rulings are binding on the member states.

For example, in 2003 the Commission recommended to the Council that Germany and France be cited for running budget deficits in excess of the rules established by the member governments in the Stability and Growth Pact (SGP). The pact is designed to maintain the fiscal stability of the Eurozone countries. The Commission is required to undertake surveillance of members' budgetary deficits and report on those who are close to or in breach of the ceiling of 3 percent of GDP. As a result of efforts by Germany and France to overturn the Commission's recommendation, a qualified majority in support of the Commission could not be achieved in the Council. Many smaller member states, which had complied with the rules of the SGP (e.g., the Netherlands, Austria, Finland), supported the Commission, while larger ones, particularly Britain and Italy, supported France and Germany. The Commission took France and Germany to the ECJ in 2004. The ECJ found both countries in breach of their commitments under the SGP.

The Commission is also charged by the Treaty to bring to the ECJ any member government that has failed to comply with Treaty law—for example, by not transposing EU agreements into national legislation within a reasonable amount of time, or failing in other ways to adhere to the *acquis*.[8] Member governments have a mixed record with regard to the transposition of EU law into national laws. An example of noncompliance came in 2005 when the Commission commenced infringement proceedings against Luxembourg for failure to implement a 2002 Council Directive that required member governments to put energy-efficient use and consumption labels on household air conditioners to encourage consumers to purchase more energy-efficient appliances. Member governments are legally obligated to report to the Commission on the progress made in transposing or incorporating EU law into national law. Luxembourg was the only EU member state in 2005 that failed to notify the Commission of the measures it was taking to transpose the Council Directive into national legislation.

The Commission manages the EU's competition policy. It monitors mergers and cartels to keep any one firm from establishing a dominant position on the EU market and thus eroding free competition. It monitors EU member governments that seek to subsidize industries (through state aid) to make them more competitive. Such state aid may distort competition in the EU market. Cases are brought to the attention of the Commission for investigation by its own modestly-sized staff and by member governments, firms, and individuals.

In some cases, the Commission prohibits a merger, cartel, or state aid; in other instances, it approves such actions but attaches strings to limit the anticompetitive effects of a dominant position or of state aid. For example, in 2002 the Commission imposed fines of €124 million on Austrian banks for their participation in a price cartel. The Commission found that the CEOs of eight Austrian banks met regularly with the objective of fixing rates on deposits and loans "to the detriment of business and consumers."[9] A far more important case occurred in 2004 when the Commission imposed a large fine on Microsoft Corporation and ordered it to take corrective measures (see chapter 6).

ROLE IN EU GOVERNMENTAL DECISIONMAKING

Beyond its role as Treaty guardian, the Commission's most important functions are to initiate, execute, and oversee policy. Although the Commission is the sole policy initiator in the internal market and the monetary union, the EP and the Council may ask the Commission to initiate a policy proposal for action. In addition, the Lisbon Treaty empowers EU citizens who sign a one-million-strong petition to ask the Commission to initiate a proposal. In each of these instances, the Commission's power is enhanced, since the initiator has scope for influencing the final draft. In most areas of CFSP and JHA, pursuant to the Lisbon Treaty, the Commission shares the powers of legislative initiative with the Council where it has competence to act. However, the Lisbon Treaty also stipulates that in the area of police and judicial cooperation in criminal matters, one-quarter of member governments may initiate legislative proposals as well as the Commission (see Chapter 6 for more information).

Among the most important instruments for legislative action are proposals, directives and regulations, and White and Green Papers, all examined in Chapter 6. The bulk of EU governmental decisionmaking starts with the Commission as policy initiator and ends with the Commission as policy implementer and overseer. The policies proposed by the Commission take the forms of programs, budgets, and legislation.

A policy proposal originates in the DG where it is drafted. For example, if the proposal has to do with agricultural price supports, the DG for Agriculture drafts and eventually presents the proposed legislation to the College of Commissioners. When drafting legislation, the DG is influenced by the *acquis* and by the guidelines received from the European Council, the Council, and the Commission. The Commission depends on technical advice and expertise from "expert committees" (specialists and officials from national governments) and from "consultative committees" (technical experts organized and financed by the Commission). The advice of experts, interest groups (e.g., industry), national officials, and other interested parties is solicited at this stage. The Commission is known for the care it takes in consulting outside groups to achieve two purposes: (1) to ensure that the proposal meets the subsidiarity principle; and (2) to ensure that technical advice is solicited to improve the proposal before it is sent on to the EP and Council. The Commission depends on outside feedback, given its limited resources and personnel with needed specialized expertise.

The proposal is revised and then reviewed by the Commission's Legal Service and by the cabinets in the context of their weekly meetings. As the Commission's agency designed to facilitate and ensure coordination across the institution, the Secretariat-General reviews the proposed legislation to ensure that the units and interests of the Commission have been taken into account. Only then will the Secretariat-General place the proposal on the agenda of the meeting of the full Commission. The responsible DG then presents the proposed legislation to the Commissioners.

There are four possibilities once the proposal is considered by the College: (1) the proposal is adopted by consensus (without a formal vote) and sent to the EP, the Council, and the national parliaments; (2) a vote occurs and the measure passes if a simple majority of Commissioners votes affirmatively, at which time the measure is sent to the EP and Council; (3) the measure may be sent back to the sponsoring DG for a redraft; or (4) a decision is deferred. The Commission sends its legislative proposals to the EU affairs committees of the national parliaments for their examination and input.[10] Through this procedure, national parliamentarians may ask questions and make comments. The practice before the Lisbon Treaty was informal.

The Lisbon Treaty requires the Commission to send its Green and White Papers, annual legislative program, and draft legislative proposals to the national parliaments at the same time it does so to the EP and Council. National parliaments have eight weeks to send the EU institutions their opinions/concerns should the proposal not conform to the principle of subsidiarity. If one third of national parliaments consider the proposal not to conform with subsidiarity, the Commission is obliged to review its draft. If the proposal covers judicial cooperation in criminal matters and police cooperation, the threshold is one-quarter. The Commission has three choices: maintain, amend, or withdraw. If it maintains, the Commission sends the Council and the EP its opinion.

As the proposal makes its way through the EP and Council, the Commission continues to consult national governments and parliaments, including the members' representatives in Brussels, working groups of the Council, nongovernmental organizations such as interest groups, and EU advisory bodies—for example, the EESC and CoR. The Commission may be called on by the EP or Council to amend its proposal in order to gain the support needed for passage. Professor Neill Nugent explains: "The Commission must concern itself not only with what it believes to be desirable but also with what is possible. The policy preferences of others must be recognized and, where necessary and appropriate, be accommodated."[11]

The Commission monitors the movement of its proposed legislation. As the proposed legislation works its way through the EP and Council, the Commission attempts to mediate differences needed to foster agreement. At the same time, it keeps an eye on its own institutional and European interests. For example, the Commission drafters of the proposed legislation make themselves available to relevant EP committees and plenaries, working groups of the Council, and the Committee of Permanent Representatives.

The Commission is responsible for implementing legislation once the EP and Council have finished the legislative process. Often legislation passed by the EP and Council takes the form of broad policy guidelines. Thus it falls to the Commission working with the bureaucracies of national governments to find common ground on how to implement legislation. This implementation may take the form of regulations or directives issued by the Commission. The Commission also depends on member governments and on individuals, firms, and interest groups to report alleged infringement of or failure to implement EU law. It also tries to compel enforcement by publishing the status of implementation of EU laws by each of the member governments. The member states delegate tasks to the Commission to initiate and execute legislation, but the Commission in turn delegates tasks back to the member governments to implement what has been legislated.

Although the member governments delegated implementation powers to the Commission, they were unwilling to give the Commission a blank check. Since implementation of legislation is as much a political act as it is a legal one, and given the wide scope for discretionary power (or agency) in the way laws are put into effect and interpreted, the member governments through the Council established a mechanism to keep a watchful eye on the Commission as policy implementer. The Treaty provides for the Council to delegate implementation authority to the Commission, but with strings attached.

In order to take back some of the power delegated to the Commission to implement legislation once enacted—to reduce the scope for autonomous agency enjoyed by the Commission—the Council constructed a system of committees, known awkwardly as **comitology**. Comitology, as discussed earlier, is a system of committees composed of member government representatives who advise the Commission on issues arising from the implementation of Council (and EP) decisions. They benignly advise the Commission in some areas and impose national wishes on the Commission in others.[12] Well over two hundred committees have either advisory, management, or regulatory functions with regard to the powers delegated to the Commission in the

Treaty to implement legislation enacted by the Council or the Council and the EP. The Commission chairs the committees, whose members include national civil servants and technical experts. Each committee has its own voting and operating procedures. The management committees deal with large EU expenditure areas such as agriculture and regional aid. The regulatory committees deal with such areas as environmental protection and food safety. The advisory committees (e.g., Competition Policy) render advice that the Commission is obliged to consider.

Although far removed from the scrutiny of the public, these committees that advise or direct the Commission in its powers to implement legislation provide a useful mechanism for bringing national perspectives to bear on Commission implementation decisionmaking. After all, national and subnational governments administer EU laws, so it is wise to have their input in advance. However, the MEPs had good reason to oppose comitology, since originally only Council committees had the power to influence implementation of those laws enacted by the EP and Council. Without input from the EP, a piece of legislation could be implemented in a way that did not conform to the EP's understanding of the law it had passed. In other words, the Council got to oversee the Commission's implementation of legislation, but the EP did not. As a result, the EP argued for and in the late 1990s attained a role in comitology.

The Commission sends the EP all relevant committee information and informs the EP when a piece of legislation is referred back to the Council because a committee could not agree on the modalities of implementation. The EP renders an opinion on the implementation aspects of that legislation. The Commission can ignore the EP opinion, offer a new draft implementation measure, or submit a new legislative proposal to the Council and EP.

Comitology is part and parcel of EU governmental decisionmaking inside the black box, but it is not widely understood by European publics and only cursorily understood by scholars of European integration. However, even though the comitology system is far removed from public cognizance in Europe, the same kinds of implementation issues arise in the national settings of the member states after domestic legislation is enacted.

Although the bulk of the work of the Commission is consumed by the internal functioning of the EU, external relations are also an important part of its function (see Chapter 7). The Commission President represents the Commission at international summits and conferences and at the European Council Summits of Heads of Government and State. The Commission is represented abroad by delegations, and it also receives missions from many of the world's countries. The Treaty of Lisbon provides for the establishment of an external action service that will comprise Commission representatives, seconded national diplomats, and Council Secretariat staff posted at EU delegations around the world. Under the Lisbon Treaty, it will be necessary to sort out who will do what in representing the EU abroad among the following positions: the Commission President, the new High Representative of the Union for Foreign Affairs and Security Policy (High Representative)—who double hats as the Commission Vice President—and the President of the European Council.

TAKING STOCK

The Commission is guardian and enforcer of the Treaty, the initiator and executor of policy, and the conscience of the EU. It is impossible to envisage the EU without the Commission because of the unique functions it performs and its Treaty mandate to advance the common interest.

It is often charged by some in the member states for being too powerful, but one ought not exaggerate its size. First, its staff size is no bloated bureaucracy relative to the powers delegated to it and when compared to large metropolitan city administrations in Europe and around the world. Second, what limits the Commission's power relative to that of the member governments is that as an organization it is divided sectorally. This makes it difficult for the Commission to operate cohesively. The sectoralization of the Commission mirrors the same problem in the Council. Since the EU is governed on a sector-by-sector basis, it very difficult to balance different interests while achieving overall EU objectives. Third, the Commission's scope for autonomous agency is checked by the member governments through such means as comitology and the appointment of the Commission President. Fourth, the Commission works as a partner with national and subnational governments to implement legislation. At the same time, it is open to influence and information from sectoral interests when proposing legislation.

The Commission could do a better job advancing gender equality in its own house. As is the case with the EC judiciary, women are much less represented than men in the College of Commissioners. There were no women Commissioners until 1989, when two were appointed. There were five women among the twenty Commissioners in the Santer Commission, seven among thirty in the Prodi Commission, and eight among twenty-five in the first Barroso Commission. The second Barroso Commission is expected to have nine women Commissioners.

In sum, the Commission is the repository of the union's supranational and functional powers. The Commission has no governmental equal anywhere in the world. No other group of sovereign states has granted a common body such far-reaching powers usually reserved for the sovereign state. What makes the EU distinct in the annals of international organization is that while national and European interests often converge, when they do not there is a need for a body, like the Commission, to serve a police function. The Commission plays the role of bad cop in order for the member governments to be the good cop. This allows the member governments to blame Brussels in order to avoid losing support for an unpopular policy. The "good cop/bad cop" approach succeeds to a point, but bashing the Commission can work for only so long. Whereas the Commission fuses executive and bureaucratic powers, the Council fuses executive powers with legislative ones. Both are subject to the growing influence of the EP. It is to the Council that we now turn.

Fulcrum of Political Power in the European Union: The Council

The Council (formerly known as Council of Ministers) is the fulcrum of political power in the EU. Its member governments have the power to delegate tasks to other

EU bodies and the power to veto many important decisions. Like the Commission, it is unique in the world. However, its executive and legislative functions are features recognizable in national governments. Nevertheless, the Council cannot be likened to a national government, since it cannot initiate legislation in most areas of EU activity. That said, the Council has executive responsibilities in areas of foreign and security policy and police cooperation, where, in many instances, it has the shared right of initiative with the Commission. The Council is a step closer in democratic legitimacy to the European electorates than is the Commission. Its ministerial representatives come from governments that have formed majorities in their national parliaments as the result of democratic elections; however, what ministers in the Council do seems worlds away from publics back home.

Table 5.1 depicts the political powers of the Council. Governmental ministers from each of the member states assemble in different Councils established to handle all of the EU policy areas. Following entry into force of the Lisbon Treaty, the ten Councils are Agriculture and Fisheries; Competitiveness; General Affairs; Economic and Financial Affairs; Education, Youth, and Culture; Employment, Social Policy, Health, and Consumer Affairs; Environment; Foreign Affairs; Justice and Home Affairs; and Transport, Telecommunications, and Energy. The Lisbon Treaty provides for the chair of the Council meetings to rotate among the member governments on a six-monthly basis, with the exception of the Foreign Affairs Council, which is chaired by the High Representative. In 2010, Spain, followed by Belgium, holds the presidency chair of the Council. As stated, ministers are members of cabinets of national governments back home. They are appointed by their Head of Government (e.g., the Prime Minister) whose political party forms either a majority of seats in the national

Image 5.3. The Council of the European Union (Justus Lipsius Building, Brussels).
Courtesy of the Council of the European Union

parliament or a coalition of political parties to have a parliamentary majority. These political appointees answer to their Head of Government and are expected to represent the national interest in the EU institutions. The ministers in Council are subject to oversight by the EU affairs committees of their national parliaments, but the quality and potency of that oversight vary among the national parliaments.

At the same time that government ministers fight for their national interests in EU legislation, once in Brussels, they engage in a process of negotiation and compromise in the Council, shaped by habits and customs of cooperation and by the *acquis*. This process of Europeanization means that there is ample give-and-take among government ministers in the Council.

STRUCTURE AND FUNCTION

Among the various Councils, four are the most powerful and influential. They are the General Affairs Council (GAC), which prepares meetings of the European Council in liaison with the President of the European Council; the Foreign Affairs Council (FAC), responsible for CFSP and CSDP; the Justice and Home Affairs (JHA) Council, responsible for judicial and police cooperation; and the Economic and Financial Affairs Council (Ecofin), responsible for EMU. As mentioned, the High Representative, who chairs the FAC, also serves as the Commission Vice President, thus creating a link in foreign policy between the Commission and the Council. The High Representative will be assisted by the creation of the future European External Action Service.

The Council has legislative and executive powers. It decides (with the EP in most areas) on proposed legislation sent to it by the Commission. Since the Treaty charges the Commission with sole power of legislative initiative in areas related to the functioning of the internal market and the monetary union, the Council asks the Commission to conduct studies and initiate proposals from which may spring legislative proposals that interest the Council. The Council also adopts opinions, resolutions, and recommendations that influence what the Commission proposes.

The member government holding the rotating chair of the Council (1) presides over meetings of, and sets agendas for, the ministers in the Council, the Permanent Representatives, and the high-level committees and working groups; (2) prioritizes initiatives and seeks support for those that can be completed if possible during the chair's term; and (3) balances national interests with European ones. Two Council bodies—the Council Secretariat and the Committee of Permanent Representatives (COREPER)—offer continuity between chairs of the Council, provide expertise needed on which to base policy decisions, and coordinate advisory working groups and committees. It is to these two bodies we now turn our attention.

The Council as an intergovernmental body relies on the Council Secretariat, a supranational body. Founded in 1952 (and given formal legal status in the TEU), the Secretariat's 3,500 permanent EU civil servants provide institutional memory and continuity and offer policy coordination, a European perspective, and in-house expertise. The Secretariat not only provides logistical assistance to and advice for the chair of the Council but is known to offer assistance in order to reach compromises. The Secretariat staff gives momentum to complete the review of proposed legislation. It thus has elements of agency that assist governmental decisionmaking inside the Council. An appointee of the European Council, the Secretary-General presides over the Council Secretariat. Pierre de Boisseau succeeded Javier Solana in that position in late 2009. In addition to its dependence on the Secretariat, the Council depends on COREPER to represent the interests of each member's Foreign Ministry and other government ministries back home, as well as those of the government in power.

COREPER, whose roots also go back to the origins of the EC, was formally brought under the Treaty rubric in 1967 with the entry into force of the Merger Treaty. Charged with reaching agreements on policy initiatives so that the Ministers need only address those issues that cannot otherwise be resolved, COREPER is one of the most influential EU entities. Each member government has a Permanent Representation (embassy) in Brussels and a Permanent Representative (ambassador), aided by a Deputy Permanent Representative. Permanent Representations consist of diplomats and other officials seconded by each member's Foreign Ministry or other national governmental bodies. The work of COREPER is so vast that it requires a division of labor between the Deputy Permanent Representatives and the Permanent Representatives—COREPER I and COREPER II, respectively. Under the Lisbon Treaty, the chair of COREPER is the member government chairing the GAC.

The Deputy Permanent Representatives in COREPER I handle conciliation when the Council and the EP differ over legislative proposals. The Permanent Representatives in COREPER II handle more politically sensitive and difficult issues, such as association accords, enlargement, institutional questions, multiannual budget negotiations, Structural and Cohesion Funds, and Treaty change. The Permanent Representatives report to their Foreign Ministers and Ecofin Ministers, and through them to the European Council. COREPER I and II meet weekly in Brussels.

Although the Permanent Representatives work for their national governments, which give them instructions, they are engaged in a process of Europeanization by which compromises are negotiated in a largely cooperative spirit. Standing at the intersection of national and European interests, the Permanent Representatives at times have recourse only to the lowest common denominator. At other times, the common good is advanced to a higher common denominator.

Given the voluminous and complex workload of several EU policy sectors, and their political importance to the member governments, the Council is assisted by Special Council Committees that provide advice. These committees are not the same as those that advise the Commission on implementation of legislation (comitology). Each is staffed by officials of the Permanent Representations and by officials seconded by the relevant national ministry and assisted by the Council Secretariat. Some of these advisory bodies are: Article 113 Committee (Common Commercial Policy); Special Committee on Agriculture or SCA (Common Agricultural Policy); Economic and Financial Committee (EMU); Article 36 Committee (JHA); and Political and Security Committee (PSC), which covers CFSP and CSDP, including the European Union Military Committee (EUMC) and the European Union Military Staff (EUMS).

In addition to standing committees, the Council makes use of ad hoc committees (also known as High Level Groups) to develop new ideas for policy initiatives. There are also working groups or parties, many ad hoc, that analyze, negotiate, and often reach agreement on proposed legislation sent by the Commission.

ROLE IN EU GOVERNMENTAL DECISIONMAKING

Council voting on major pieces of legislation may take five forms: (1) unanimity; (2) consensus; (3) constructive abstention; (4) qualified majority vote (QMV); or (5) enhanced cooperation. In voting based on **unanimity**, all member governments formally vote on a piece of legislation. If a member government vetoes a legislative proposal, the initiative fails. The Treaty requires unanimity when the Council votes on the multiannual financial framework, Treaty changes, enlargement, CFSP and CSDP (deployment of forces), taxation, finance issues and certain aspects of JHA. Unanimity is also required when the Council seeks to amend a Commission proposal over Commission opposition.

In **consensus**, the member governments agree to a piece of legislation without a formal vote. Member state representatives often prefer to issue their concerns about (or oppose) legislation at lower levels, such as working groups and COREPER, rather than voting against a proposal in the Council. The chair will continue negotiations until he or she knows that all Ministers are in agreement. This way no member government is forced to vote no. The problem, of course, is that the quest for consensus often results in accord based on the lowest common denominator. In CFSP and CSDP, a member government may also elect to abstain on a vote. This abstention is referred to as "constructive abstention." A government accepts that the measure commits the EU to action, but as an abstainer it is not obliged to carry out the measure.

Under the Lisbon Treaty, decisionmaking in the Council is normally subject to QMV, again with such notable exceptions as taxation and defense. However, in CSDP, there are certain areas of decisionmaking where QMV may be used to implement a decision already taken on a new position or action. The use of QMV most distinguishes the EU from other international organizations since it allows a majority of members to move forward with a proposal even though some have voted in the negative.

In **qualified majority** voting, the EU member states apportion a number of weighted votes to each member, based on size of population. The more populous member states have more of these weighted votes, but the relationship of population size to weighted votes actually favors the smaller states, who might otherwise be dominated by the larger ones in EU governmental decisionmaking. As the EU has grown to include a large number of small states, weights were recalculated in the Nice Treaty to give the heavily populated states more weights in the QMV calculation than before; however, the less populated states still enjoy higher relative weights. For example, Poland's population is nearly ten times larger than Luxembourg's, but Poland does not receive ten times more votes than Luxembourg. The Nice Treaty was a hard-won compromise over new weights in the qualified majority to accommodate EU enlargement. The number of votes was raised to make it appear that all member states were given an increase, but the larger (more populous) states received larger increases in their weighted votes relative to the smaller (less populous) states.

The breakdown in weighted votes is as follows: France, Germany, Italy, and the United Kingdom have 29 votes; Poland and Spain, 27; Romania, 14; Netherlands, 13; Belgium, Czech Republic, Greece, Hungary, and Portugal, 12; Austria, Sweden, and Bulgaria, 10; Denmark, Ireland, Lithuania, Slovakia, and Finland, 7; Cyprus, Estonia, Latvia, Luxembourg, and Slovenia, 4; and Malta, 3.

There is a total of 345 votes, of which a qualified majority is 258 votes (75 percent); 258 votes are required to pass a law. A **blocking minority** is 88 votes (25.5 percent); 88 votes block enactment. The Nice Treaty introduced a new triple majority requirement when the Council uses QMV: a qualified majority (258 of 345 votes); a majority of member states; and a population that is 62 percent of the EU population if a member state requests such a confirmation. If confirmation is requested and the vote does not meet the threshold, the measure is not adopted.[13]

An abstention in QMV registers the same as a vote against a proposal, since 258 votes are required to enact legislation. However, when unanimity is used, an abstention is the same as a vote to support the proposal. It is odd that a proposal can be enacted based on unanimity when it would fail using QMV. The member governments prefer this oddity because they can abstain if they do not wish to vote in support of a proposal (perhaps because of domestic politics) without preventing the passage of the proposal, as explained below.

Although the Nice Treaty negotiations to reweigh qualified majority votes were divisive, the truth is that in Council the chair rarely calls for a QMV (even when the Treaty provides for it), but rather determines if there is a consensus on a piece of proposed legislation. If a consensus does not exist, negotiations continue. The chair normally brings up the motion for adoption only when there is a consensus. Government Ministers prefer not to vote formally because (1) there is a record of the vote, and the Minister may face hostility if the action is unpopular back home; and (2) if Ministers are in a minority, they would prefer not to be spoilers by voting in the negative. That said, there may be times when member governments that are not in favor of a legislative proposal, but know it will pass by a QMV vote, prefer a qualified majority. That way, they can vote no, which may be important in the context of domestic politics, without blocking legislation.

Under the Treaty of Lisbon, effective 2014, decisionmaking in the Council will change. Up until 2014, the Council will continue to vote on the basis of QMV as described above. In 2014, weighted majority voting will be replaced by a double majority system, whereby for a successful piece of legislation to pass, 55 percent of member states representing 65 percent of the EU population will be required. A proposal can be rejected by a blocking minority of four member states, representing 35 percent of the EU population. However, between 2014 and 2017, a member government can request a vote on a legislative proposal on the basis of QMV.

The 2014 change in EU decisionmaking marks a major shift in the way the EU works. The intent of the Lisbon Treaty is to make it easier for EU member states to form majorities to pass legislation (in contrast to the Nice Treaty), especially as the union continues to grow in membership. The new method gives added voting power to the more populous states at the expense of the less populous states, who in the past enjoyed a composition of weighted votes that magnified their power relative to population size. However, in the event that four large states together do not agree to block a piece of proposed legislation, large states will still need to collaborate with the smaller ones to form a blocking minority.

Enhanced cooperation is used as a last resort when some member governments choose to work more closely in selected areas in the absence of the full and active support of all member governments. Before the Lisbon Treaty, enhanced cooperation, which required the participation of one-third of the member states, was limited to security and defense areas. Under the Lisbon Treaty, such cooperation is no longer limited to security and defense, but extends to all areas where the EU is competent to act under the Treaty. Enhanced cooperation under the Lisbon Treaty is triggered by a minimum of nine member governments who wish to collaborate. In internal EU matters, external economic relations and humanitarian aid, such cooperation requires the Commission's support and the approval of the Council and EP. In the area of CFSP, the Council's unanimous approval is required.

Upon the arrival of a Commission legislative proposal, the Council begins its examination at the level of the working groups, whose focus is on the technical details. Working group members attempt to iron out differences and seek agreement before passing the proposal up to COREPER or the SCA (which comprises senior national officials from the agricultural ministries), where the focus is on the political and policy effects of the proposal. Governmental representatives in these bodies have two tasks, not always complementary: to defend national interests and to find common ground with others to reach agreement. The proposal may be bumped up to the Council or sent back to the working groups for further refinement.

In the Council, Ministers either adopt without discussion what has already been decided at the level of COREPER or SCA or, failing accord at that level, seek agreement among themselves. As mentioned, most differences over legislative proposals are ironed out before they get to the Council. Formal approval of a legislative proposal occurs at Council level, where members decide either by consensus or qualified majority. If there is no accord in the Council, the proposal may be referred back to the Council and Commission for further work and returned to the Council for a final decision. When the Council cannot reach agreement, the final arbiter is the European Council.

Sometimes the Council wishes to maintain a momentum in a policy area where its members have an interest, but in which the Council is not yet ready to engage in a formal legislative process. It then issues agreements, declarations, and resolutions. By these means the Council makes policy statements that, although not legally binding, influence policymaking in a more general, less formal way.

Most legislative proposals are subject to the codecision procedure, which gives the EP veto power. Prior to the Lisbon Treaty, in certain areas of EMU and JHA, fiscal harmonization, agriculture, and commercial policy, the Council had full legislative enactment authority and the EP was only consulted. However, the Treaty of Lisbon renames codecision the ordinary legislative procedure and extends it to nearly all sectors of integration and to all areas of the EU budget, including the Common Agricultural Policy and many policies related to the areas of Justice and Home Affairs.

TAKING STOCK

Whereas the Commission is a supranational organization, the Council is generally an intergovernmental forum because its members are government ministers who come together to defend and pursue national interests. Voting on the most sensitive political issues (enlargement, constitutional changes) is subject to unanimity, which means the veto power lurks in the background but is rarely invoked. That said, the Council also has some supranational features in at least three respects: (1) when voting is based on a qualified majority, there is a surrender of sovereignty, as the state that is in the minority or abstains has to accept the will of the majority; (2) a process of Europeanization tends to encourage COREPER to find compromises between what can be achieved together and vital national interests; and (3) the Council Secretariat consists of permanent staff who take an oath to the EU and thus provide institutional memory and expertise that is more supranational than intergovernmental.

Where the Commission and Council most contrast is in the Council's closer proximity to electorates. The Council's ministerial representatives come from governments that have formed majorities in national parliaments as the result of democratic elections. However, the Council's work is often shrouded in secrecy, far removed from the public's eye.

A final word on theory. An intergovernmental perspective suggests that the pursuit of national interests is what chiefly drives decisionmaking in the Council. Indeed, there are times when national interests are entrenched and compromise elusive. Yet, as this section has demonstrated, the Council is both an intergovernmental and supranational body. If its members focused only on the narrow pursuit of national interests, Council decisionmaking would stall.

The Sovereigns of the European Union: The European Council

The Council reports and is responsive to the European Council, which was not established until 1974. At first the European Council existed outside the Treaty framework, but in 1987 the SEA brought it into the Treaty's legal system. The Lisbon Treaty established the European Council as a full and formal EU institution. The Heads of Government and State (HOGS) assemble in the European Council as the sovereign leaders of the EU. They are joined by the Commission President and the High Representative. The European Council meets at least twice during each Presidency, but often more frequently. Table 5.1 depicts the structure, functions, and powers of the European Council. As sovereigns, the HOGS can and do decide the most important issues of the EU, especially its future direction. After all, the European Council commands a panorama view of the entire union.

The European Council has the power to make three major appointments: (1) the Commission President, based on the recommendation of the Council and a vote of approval from the EP; (2) the members of the Executive Board of the European Central Bank (ECB)—the Board President, Vice President, and four other members—based on a recommendation from the Council after it has consulted the EP and the Governing Council of the ECB; and (3) the President of the ECB, based on a recommendation from the Committee of Central Bank Governors, after it has consulted the EP and Council.

© Council of the EU

Image 5.4.   The European Council Summit during the French Presidency, October 2008. Courtesy of the Council of the European Union

The European Council also decides on the multiannual financial framework that sets out budgetary parameters within which, each year, the EP and Council decide the budget based on a Commission proposal. Prior to the entry into force of the Lisbon Treaty, each member government waited its turn to preside over the European Council, and the rotation was in January and July. The Presidency rotated among the member states in such a way that one out of every three successive Presidencies came from a large member state (defined by population). For example, the French EU Presidency during the second half of 2008 was followed in 2009 by the Presidencies of two smaller states, the Czech Republic and Sweden. There were good arguments for and against retaining the six-month rotating Presidency. Each member government had a chance to help lead the EU, and smaller states got a chance to perform on the global stage. However, with a twenty-seven member union, the opportunity would come infrequently. The Lisbon Treaty replaces the rotating Presidency of the European Council with one elected by the European Council, using QMV, for a term of two-and-a-half years, once renewable. In November 2009, Belgian Prime Minister Herman Van Rompuy was elected the first President of the European Council under the Lisbon Treaty's new provisions for that office.

Voice of the European Union: The European Parliament

The EP is the voice of the citizens of the EU. It is the EU's only directly elected and thus representative body. At times, the EP functions well. It engages with the Council to enact legislation that affects the lives of EU citizens, and its budgetary and other Treaty powers are essential to the functioning of the union. At other times, it seems as if the EP punches below its weight. It does not have the same powers as a national parliament. Its members are often more loyal to their domestic political party bases than to their European party group—with which they sit and deliberate in EP plenary sessions. EP decisionmaking procedures are as labyrinthine as comitology. The story of the three host cities of the EP—Strasbourg, Brussels, and Luxembourg—mirrors the complicated, messy, and expensive compromises necessary to make a union of states and its parliament work.

Strasbourg hosts the twelve yearly plenary sessions, although some mini-plenaries are held in Brussels. Roughly half of the 5,000 employees of the EP work either in Brussels, which is the location of committee meetings, or in Luxembourg, location of the EP Secretariat. Belgium, Luxembourg, and France all have claims to locate the work of the EP in their territories for reasons of national pride and economic benefit. As a result, even though it would be economical for all EP activities to be centered in Brussels where most EU bodies are located, this may not happen soon. The cost to the EU taxpayer for the commute of MEPs and their staffers between Brussels and Strasbourg exceeds €200 million annually.

This section of the chapter introduces the reader to how MEPs become members; the structure, function, and powers of the EP; and the EP's role in EU governmental decisionmaking, before taking stock at the end.

Image 5.5.   The European Parliament (top: Louise Weiss Building, Strasbourg; bottom: Espace Léopold Building, Brussels). Courtesy of the European Parliament

MEMBERSHIP AND COMPOSITION

The EP is a unicameral legislature whose 736 members are elected to five-year terms (in years ending in 4 and 9, e.g., 2009 and 2014) on the basis of proportional representation in each of the member states. MEPs generally have the support of their political party back home but sit in transnational European political groups at the EP. Any citizen of the EU may run as a candidate and vote (minimum age is twenty-one) in her or his EU country of residence. Table 5.2 illustrates the number of seats allotted to each member state based on population and the number of constituents per MEP.[14]

The allocation of seats to member states is negotiated by governments at IGCs and codified in the Treaty. Germany has the largest number of seats (99) and Malta, the smallest (5). However, smaller states have more representation relative to larger ones. For example, in the parliamentary session following the 2009 EP elections, Spain with a population of 44 million has 50 seats, whereas Ireland with a population of 4.4 million has 12. The Spanish population is ten times larger than Ireland's, but the number of seats Spain has is about four times larger. If Spain were to receive ten times more seats than Ireland, Spain would have 132 seats. If Ireland were to receive ten times fewer seats than Spain (with Spain remaining at 54 seats), Ireland would have just 5. In the former instance, the EP would have to enlarge beyond its already unwieldy number, and in the latter the Irish electorate would suffer an enormous cut.

For states with populations smaller than Ireland's, for example, Luxembourg, the situation would be more precarious. In the parliamentary session beginning in 2009, Sweden, with a population of 9.3 million, has 18 seats, while Luxembourg, with a population just under 500,000, has 6. Sweden has a population nineteen times larger than that of Luxembourg, but the number of seats it has in the EP is three times more than Luxembourg's. If Sweden were to receive nineteen times more seats than Luxembourg, Sweden would receive 114 seats, and again the EP would have to expand the number of seats beyond its already huge number. If Luxembourg were to receive nineteen times fewer seats than Sweden (with Sweden remaining at 18 seats), Luxembourg would have no seats. The EU has a large ratio of small to large states, and EU member governments have veto power over any changes in seat allotment. Historically the EU has put a premium on sovereign equality among all its member states. We know from Chapter 2 that smaller states have played important roles in the origins and subsequent development of the EU.

Most candidates for EP elections and all of those elected are chosen by national political parties. When candidates for the EP run in national elections, they do so on a national, not European, political party manifesto. Since political loyalty is much stronger at national than EP level and MEPs owe their seats to their national political parties, not their EP party groups, MEPs are responsive to cues from the leadership of the national political party and to domestic issues for which that party has positions. Therefore, although there is some increase in cohesion among EP party groups, most MEPs, when torn between a position taken by the European party group and the national political party, will err on the side of the national political party. Part of the problem is that recent EP elections appear more like referenda on sitting governments in the member states than genuine European elections.

As in the case of the ECJ and other EU bodies, women are underrepresented. Women constituted approximately one-third of MEPs in the 2004–2009 and 2009–

Table 5.2: MEPs by Member State and Voter Turnout (2009)

	No. of MEPs	No. of constituents per MEP	% Voter Turnout 1994/1999/2004/2009
Large States			
Germany	99	829,000	60 / 45 / 43 / 43
France	72	904,000	53 / 47 / 43 / 40
United Kingdom	72	856,000	36 / 24 / 39 / 34
Italy	72	835,000	75 / 70 / 73 / 65
Spain	50	917,000	59 / 64 / 45 / 46
Poland	50	763,000	21 / 25
Middle-Size States			
Romania	33	651,000	29 / 28[a]
Netherlands	25	661,000	36 / 30 / 39 / 37
Greece	22	512,000	71 / 70 / 63 / 53
Portugal	22	483,000	35 / 40 / 39 / 37
Belgium	22	488,000	91 / 90 / 91 / 91
Czech Republic	22	476,000	28 / 28
Hungary	22	456,000	38 / 36
Sweden	18	515,000	42 / 38 / 38 / 46
Austria	17	492,000	68 / 49 / 42 / 46
Bulgaria	17	447,000	27 / 37[a]
Small States			
Denmark	13	424,000	53 / 50 / 48 / 60
Slovakia	13	416,000	17 / 20
Finland	13	411,000	60 / 30 / 39 / 40
Ireland	12	376,000	44 / 50 / 59 / 58
Lithuania	12	279,000	48 / 21
Latvia	8	282,000	41 / 53
Slovenia	7	293,000	28 / 28
Estonia	6	223,000	27 / 44
Cyprus	6	134,000	71 / 59
Luxembourg	6	82,000	89 / 86 / 89 / 91
Malta	5	83,000	82 / 79
EU	736[c]	679,000	57 / 50 / 46 / 43[b]

[a] Romania and Bulgaria had off-year elections in 2007.

[b] Voter turnout on average for the EU in the EP elections of 1989 was 59 percent; in 1984, 61 percent; in 1979, 63 percent. In some EU countries (e.g., Italy and Belgium), there is a constitutional requirement to vote.

[c] The Nice Treaty laid down the EP membership at 736. The Lisbon Treaty increases the number of MEPs to 751.

2014 parliamentary sessions. Finnish and Swedish women MEPs constituted 62 and 56 percent, respectively, of their countries' allocated seats in the EP in 2009. In contrast, Polish and Czech women MEPs constituted just 22 and 18 percent, respectively, of their countries' allotted seats in the EP in 2009. Malta had no women MEPs in 2009.

When MEPs arrive at the EP, they assemble in seven transnational European political party groups. Based on the June 2009 parliamentary elections, in which 736 seats were contested, the political groups (and number of MEPs) are:

- center-right and generally pro-EU European People's Party (265 members)—the only EP group with members from all 27 member states;
- left-of-center Group of the Progressive Alliance of Socialists and Democrats (184);
- center/center-right and pro-EU Alliance of Liberals and Democrats (84);
- left-of-center Greens/European Free Alliance (55);
- anti-federalist European Conservatives and Reformists Group (54);
- leftist Confederal Group of the United European Left/Nordic Green Left (35);
- far-right anti-EU Europe of Freedom and Democracy (32);
- non-affiliated groups (27).

The two dominant party groups following the 2009 elections constituted 61 percent of the seats in the EP: the European People's Party and the Group of the Progressive Alliance of Socialists and Democrats. These two groups are the only two truly European political parties, in that they have members from each of the member states.

The largest groups are coalitions of diverse interests centered on broad ideologies that range from left to center to right, so what each group stands for is not always clear. Since European political party groups have diverse members, they have trouble maintaining cohesion. European political party groups offer fewer rewards and benefits to their members than national ones. Still, these groups, which have their own secretariats and leaderships, offer enough incentives for MEPs to remain loyal to them and to provide some cohesion, especially among the larger, older, and more recognized political groups.

Party groups structure and direct the political work and activities of the EP. They have financial resources, participate in the selection of the EP leadership, allocate committee assignments and positions, assist in coalition formation, structure debate, articulate party positions, and influence the agenda of EP plenary sessions. They also foster cooperation among their members to increase influence in EP decisionmaking (e.g., selection of the EP President and appointment of members to EP bodies and committees). Party groups also agree to common positions on Commission legislative proposals in advance of plenary sessions.

STRUCTURE

In the past half-century, no other EU body has seen its powers increase in EU governmental decisionmaking as much as the EP.[15] To demonstrate this exponential growth, we begin with the EP's origins in the original Treaty framework before examining its increase in powers from the SEA and the TEU to the present. The EP's ancestor was created in 1952, when the Paris Treaty established the Common Assembly of the ECSC to oversee the High Authority. MEPs were appointed by national legislatures. The Common Assembly changed its name in 1962 to the European Parliament. The Treaty granted the EP advisory powers and provided for the possibility of direct elections—held for the first time in 1979. The holding of elections contributed to the EU's democratic credentials but ended an important "organic link" between national parliaments and the EU.[16] Discussions about the establishment of a second chamber of the EP comprising national parliamentarians have not yet gained traction because of the insurmountable opposition from national parliamentarians and governments.[17]

The SEA introduced the cooperation procedure (the EP was granted the right to offer amendments on certain legislation) and granted the EP the power to offer or deny assent over the admission of new EU members and association accords. The cooperation procedure essentially allows the EP to have a second reading on proposed legislation. The Council considers the EP's opinion and sends its position on the legislative proposal back to the EP. The EP has three months to either accept or reject the Council's position. Should the EP reject the Council's position, its rejection can, within a three-month period, be overridden by a unanimous decision of the Council.

The TEU granted the EP the (1) power to be consulted on the nominations for the Presidents of the Commission and the ECB; (2) power to confirm the Commission (the right to vote confidence in the Commission as a whole for its nomination) before the Commissioners took the oath of office; (3) right to be consulted on the board appointments of the ECB; (4) power of codecision whereby the EP and Council began to colegislate in fifteen Treaty articles; and (5) right to be consulted by the Council on CFSP and JHA issues.

The Amsterdam Treaty extended codecision to thirty-seven Treaty articles and made legally binding the EP's confirmation of the European Council's nominee for Commission President. The Nice Treaty extended codecision to forty-five Treaty articles, and gave the EP the right to take other EU institutions to court. As earlier mentioned, the Treaty of Lisbon would extend codecision to all sectors of integration, including agriculture, and to all budgetary areas.

The parliamentary leadership, party groups, and political committees lend structure to the work of the EP. The MEPs and these organizational structures are assisted by the staff of the EP, whether in Brussels, Luxembourg, or Strasbourg. The parliamentary leadership consists of a President and fourteen Vice Presidents, all elected for two-and-a-half-year terms. The President directs the activities of the EP, oversees the functioning of the administrative structure, presides over the assembly chamber and plenary sessions, refers matters to committees, and represents the EP in and outside the EU. The President and political-group chairs determine the seating arrangements in the chamber, arrange the work programs of the EP, and approve EP initiative reports.

The President also chairs the Conference of Presidents which consists of the chairs of the political groups and the EP President and the EP Bureau. The EP Bureau consists of the President and the fourteen Vice Presidents. The Bureau handles routine administration and finances, drafts the preliminary EP budget, appoints the Secretary-General and other officials to EP administrative positions, and performs other tasks.

As in other parliaments, the work of the EP is divided into and carried out by committees. MEPs are assigned to one of twenty committees that receive and examine legislative proposals from the plenary sessions and report back to those sessions with committee positions, including proposed amendments, in advance of voting. Committee-appointed rapporteurs act as committee spokespersons and explain committee positions on legislative proposals at plenary sessions. The most active of the EP committees are Economic and Monetary Affairs; Environment, Public Health, and Consumer Policy; Regional Policy, Transport, and Tourism; Industry, External Trade, Research, and Energy; Foreign Affairs, Human Rights, and Common Foreign and Defense Policy; Legal Affairs and Internal Market; Agriculture and Rural Development; Research and Energy; Fisheries; Budgets; Employment and Social Affairs; Citizens' Freedoms and Rights and Justice and Home Affairs; and Budgetary Control.

POWERS AND ROLE IN EU GOVERNMENTAL DECISIONMAKING

The EP plays an important role in many, but not all, areas of the EU. It has major nonlegislative powers (censure, appointment, confirmation, oversight, budget, enlargement, association accords with third countries), as well as legislative powers in most areas of the Treaty. The Treaty provides for the EP's role in passage of the annual EU budget, and the procedures used for the annual budget cycle are governed by interinstitutional accords among the EP, Commission, and Council. Their roles in the budgetary process are examined later in the chapter.

The EP most often votes by simple and absolute majorities. As a general rule, a simple majority in the EP requires 50 percent plus one of those MEPs present and voting. For example, the EP uses a simple majority when it adopts its own initiative reports. When voting in the second reading of codecision (see the discussion of codecision later in the chapter), the EP is required to vote on the proposed amendment by an absolute majority of all MEPs, not just those who vote. For EP votes on the accession of new EU members, an absolute majority is required. A motion of censure of the European Commission must command a double majority—50 percent plus one of MEPs, and two-thirds of the votes cast. For passage of the final annual EU budget, an absolute majority of MEPs and three-fifths of votes cast are required; for rejection, an absolute majority and two-thirds of votes cast are required.

Censure, Oversight, and Appointment. Prior to the TEU, the only leverage the EP had over the Commission was to threaten to pass a motion of censure, which would force the resignation of the entire College. To date, the EP has never carried out a motion of censure, although it has threatened to do so. The EP scrutinizes the work of the Council and Commission in ways familiar to EU member states' national parliaments and the U.S. Congress, who oversee their own executives. By asking both written and oral questions of officials of the Council Presidency, the Council, and the Commission, MEPs gather the information they need to fulfill their duties and represent constituent interests. For example, in 2008, the EP presented over 7,300 questions to the Commission and over 1,000 questions to the Council. Council and Commission responses to MEP queries are published in the *Official Journal*. The EP receives the annual work program from the Commission and, before the Lisbon Treaty, received the six-monthly work program of the Council Presidency. Commissioners and other DG officials give testimony before EP committees. The Presidents of the ECB and heads of EU agencies also make reports and respond to queries. The EP appoints the EU Ombudsman, who responds to citizen complaints regarding EU bodies, officials, and policies, as well as some members of EU agencies, such as the European Center for Disease Prevention and Control and the European Environmental Agency, among other agencies.

Although the Treaty does not grant the EP any oversight powers vis-à-vis the European Council, the President of the EP does address the HOGS at the start of each European Council Summit. The Presidential address gives the EP an opportunity to explain its own work program and offer feedback on the work before the European Council. The EP has no explicit oversight powers in CFSP and in areas of JHA not subject to codecision. It is informed of developments in these areas by the Council, but it is not always consulted. However, the EP does have purview in these areas if their costs are paid by the EU budget.

Confirmation: Although the Treaty grants no authority to the EP in the confirmation of candidates for the EU Courts, it does provide for the Council to consult the EP on appointments to the ECA and to the Executive Board and Presidency of the ECB. The EP also holds hearings on the nomination of the Director of the European Anti-Fraud Office. The right to be consulted gives the EP an opportunity to press the member governments when it thinks a poor choice has been made.

The TEU provided that the member governments nominate the Commission President by common accord, after having consulted the EP. In practice, as described below, it became difficult if not impossible for the Council to appoint a Commission President over serious opposition in the EP. The Amsterdam Treaty codified the practice by which the EP approved the European Council nominee for Commission President. However, it is important to note that the EP can only exercise a veto over the Commission President-Nominee. It cannot nominate its own choice for Commission President.

There is also an important role for the EP in selecting a new Commission. In the TEU, the member states delegated authority to the EP to approve the appointment of a new Commission as a whole. The member governments nominate the other candidates for Commissioners in consultation with the Commission President-Nominee. The nominees for Commissioners are then appointed by the member governments by common accord and, with the Commission President-Designate, are together subject to a vote of approval by the EP.

The EP seized the opportunity of delegated authority to decisively expand its agency by establishing its own working procedures governing the confirmation process. The EP procedures called for the Commission President-Nominee to make a statement to the EP followed by a debate before the EP would approve or reject the nomination. In the event of a negative vote, the EP President would request the member government that made the nomination to withdraw it and submit a new one. These procedures established by the EP maximized its impact on the confirmation process in ways the member governments did not anticipate and did not welcome.[18] The EP also

- called for the Commission President to be a public figure experienced in European affairs in the home country or at the EU level;
- called for the names of nominees for Commissioners to be submitted to it two

months before the confirmation vote (November after June EP elections) to allow sufficient time to conduct hearings of the nominees, to allow the Commission President-Designate to present the new Commission program, and to hold the EP's vote in time for the new Commission to take office in January; and

• warned governments not to nominate a candidate for Commission President whom the EP has previously rejected.[19]

The first Commission President-Nominee to be subjected to these new EP confirmation procedures was Luxembourg Prime Minister Jacques Santer, a compromise candidate after the Germans rejected Dutch Prime Minister Ruud Lubbers and the British rejected Belgian Prime Minister Jean-Luc Dehaene. After what some MEPs felt was Santer's lackluster performance at his confirmation hearings in July 1994, the EP voted to approve his nomination by a small margin (260 votes for and 238 against, with 23 abstentions).

After it had approved Santer's nomination as Commission President, the EP then moved to put into effect the timetable and procedures for the confirmation of the nominated Commission as a whole. The TEU did not specify the EP procedures for the confirmation of the Commission. The Santer Commission was the first to be subject to the EP's new confirmation powers. The EP decided to hold hearings for individual nominees. Such hearings risked singling out nominees for what is supposed to be a collegiate body, but the hearings also advanced the powers of the EP and enhanced checks and balances within the union's black box. Santer assigned portfolios to the member governments' nominees by November, which gave MEPs sufficient time to prepare for confirmation hearings scheduled for January 1995. Each nominee was asked by the EP to make a statement and respond to questions before the appropriate EP committee. The committee reported its conclusions to the EP President. The nominee for Commission President then presented the program of the new Commission to the plenary session of the EP. The EP then voted on the new Commission by roll call (a majority of the votes cast is required for confirmation).

The EP President decided to publish the committee papers that detailed both the qualities of the individual nominees and criticisms leveled against them. Five nominees were targeted for criticism by some MEPs over poor performance at the hearings, less than candid testimony, or the lack of a good fit between the portfolio assigned and the nominee chosen.[20] Santer presented the Commission's program after the individual hearings were over and, in the course of the debate that followed, attempted to address concerns expressed by MEPs while reasserting the Commission's autonomy and collegiality. MEPs were generally satisfied with his response and with the way the new EP confirmation procedures were put into operation. They voted to support the investiture of the new Commission on January 18 with 417 for, 104 against, and 59 abstentions.

Thus, by taking ownership of its own procedures, the EP lent more weight to its role in the confirmation process. The will not to act as a rubber stamp for the Council was again demonstrated in November 2004 during the confirmation hearings for the Barroso Commission. EP political groups forced a change in the Italian nominee for Commissioner, Rocco Buttiglione, on the basis of his testimony before the EP's Justice and Home Affairs Committee and his unsympathetic views on women's and gay issues. These views were especially problematic since Commission President-Designate

Barroso had given portfolios related to these areas to the Italian nominee. Facing the specter of a no vote by the EP on the investiture of the new Commission because of significant opposition to the Italian nomination, Italy renominated a Commissioner who was acceptable to the EP and Barroso.

Assent: **Assent** is one of the major decisionmaking powers that the member governments delegate to the EP. The Treaty authorizes the EP to offer or withhold assent to approval of admission of new EU member states, enlargement of the EU, and association accords with privileged third countries. Other examples of the use of the assent procedure include framework agreements on the EU budget, as well as certain issues related to the ECB and ESCB and to Cohesion and Structural Funds. In the assent procedure, the Council adopts a position on the basis of unanimity on a Commission legislative proposal. The EP approves or rejects the Council position. The Council adopts the legislation if the EP offers its approval. The Treaty does not empower the EP to offer amendments in areas where the Treaty empowers the EP to offer or deny assent. However, the assent procedure compels the Council to take EP concerns into account. Two other main forms of EU governmental decisionmaking involving the EP are consultation and codecision; a third procedure, cooperation, is rarely used.[21]

Consultation: In the **consultation procedure**, the EP has one reading on a legislative proposal from the Commission. Using a simple majority, the EP either accepts, amends, or rejects the proposals and forwards its opinion to the Commission. The Commission either revises the legislative proposal, taking into account the EP amendments, or it rejects the EP amendments. In its opinion, the Commission offers reasons why it has accepted or rejected the amendments. The newly revised proposal is forwarded to the Council. Using QMV, the Council may accept the revised or amended proposal. In either case the bill is enacted. The Council may reject the revised proposal by unanimity, in which case the proposal without the EP amendments becomes law. The consultation procedure puts pressure on the Commission to consider the preferences of the EP, but here the EP has advisory or consultative power—not legislative power.

The consultation procedure applies to such decisions as appointment of ECA members, certain aspects of EMU, JHA, and environmental policies, and nuclear energy. Consultation also extends to amendments to the statute of the European Investment Bank and adoption of measures not covered in the Treaty.[22] In 2007, the EP was involved in 152 consultation procedures. In 66 of the legislative proposals, the EP proposed amendments and in two instances the EP rejected the proposals.

Codecision (renamed ordinary legislative procedure under the Lisbon Treaty): Although the EP may ask the Commission to initiate legislative action, the EP does not enjoy the power of legislative initiative. However, the bulk of legislation is decided by the EP and Council in the **codecision** procedure, which gives each body a veto over passage of legislation. Under the Nice Treaty, codecision was required for over one-half of legislation enacted by the EU. The Lisbon Treaty extends codecision to nearly all areas, including agriculture and fisheries, but not to fiscal measures.[23] In codecision, there are two readings of proposed legislation. If there the EP and Council are in accord after the first reading, the bill becomes law. If there is no accord at the end of the second reading, the two bodies join the Commission in a conciliation process to see if a joint text can be negotiated. For example, in 2008, 170 legislative proposals were decided by codecision. Of these, 140 (or 82 percent) were decided in the first reading and 29 (or 17 percent) were decided at the second reading. Only one proposal entered the conciliation process.[24] Thus, it is clear how well the EP and Council work together to enact legislation. Much time is invested in interinstitutional communication to ease the completion of the legislative process.

The first reading. The Commission publishes and sends a legislative proposal to the EP and Council for the first reading. It consults the CoR and the EESC. The EP either adopts an opinion on the proposal that accepts the text unchanged or it offers amendments using an absolute majority of all MEPs. The Commission offers its opinion to the Council that either accepts or rejects EP amendments with explanations. If at the first reading the EP and Council are in accord over the legislative proposal, and if the Council lends unanimous support to EP amendments, the bill is enacted. If the Council accepts EP amendments using QMV (with some exceptions, e.g., in the area of social security), the bill becomes law. If there are no EP or Council amendments, the Council may vote to adopt the proposal using QMV, and the bill becomes law. If none of the above transpires, the Council may adopt a "common position" by QMV that amends the Commission proposal if it does not accept all of the EP amendments. The Council's common position, which explains why the Council has proffered amendments to the Commission's text, is then forwarded to the EP by the Commission as a communication for a second reading.[25]

The second reading. The EP has four possible responses when the Council adopts a common position. Within three months the EP can either

- not act at all on the Council's common position—at which time the Council, within three months, adopts the proposal using QMV and the bill is enacted;
- approve the Council's common position using an absolute majority—at which time the Council, within three months, adopts the proposal using QMV and the bill is enacted;
- reject the Council's common position using absolute majority of its members, in which case the legislative proposal is not enacted; or
- amend the Council's common position using absolute majority of its members.

The Commission offers its view on the EP's amendments in the second reading. The Council must respond within three months. The legislative proposal is enacted at this stage of the codecision procedure if (1) the Council accepts all EP amendments (using QMV) that the Commission accepted; or (2) the Council accepts all EP amendments (by unanimity) that the Commission rejected. If the Council accepts all of the EP's amendments, the legislation is enacted. Given interinstitutional efforts to see through the passage of legislation, it is rare when the Council vetoes the EP or rejects its amendments. Indeed, the lion's share of legislation makes it through the first or second reading. Thus, rarely do the EP and Council go to the final phase of the codecision procedure: conciliation.

Conciliation: When the Council informs the EP it does not accept the second reading amendments, the contested proposal is referred to a conciliation committee convened by the President of the Council in conjunction with the President of the EP. However, efforts are made by the Commission, Council, and EP (trialogue) to reach accord, called a joint text, in advance of the convening of the Conciliation

Committee.[26] In the EP, adoption of a joint text requires a majority. The **Conciliation Committee** consists of an equal number of representatives drawn from the EP and Council (usually COREPER senior officials) who have voting rights, and one nonvoting representative from the Commission. In this final stage of codecision, one of two things transpires (usually within six weeks). Either no joint text is agreed upon and the legislative proposal is not enacted, or a joint text is agreed upon and then forwarded to the EP and Council. If both adopt the text within six weeks, the bill is enacted. The text is signed by the EP and Council Presidents and the legislation is published in the *Official Journal*. In the EP, an absolute majority is required. In the Council, QMV suffices. If either the EP or the Council does not consent to the joint text within six weeks, the bill is not enacted.

TAKING STOCK

The EP, like the other EU bodies, is sui generis among governmental bodies in the world not least because it is neither the legislature of a state nor merely the general assembly of an international organization. It is the world's only democratic and transnational legislative body. The EP is particularly unique for its transnational and supranational features. In many respects, the EP is the EU's most paradoxical institution. As the voice of the people of the EU, it is gaining powers and confidence—and it is impossible to imagine the EU without the EP. It enjoys the status of legitimacy associated with the distinction of being the only directly elected body of the EU citizens. However, while gaining confidence, its voice has not yet matured to full resonance: it lacks sufficient cohesion and popular support and it still cannot initiate legislation. Despite its limits, if you were to imagine the EU without its parliament, you would find a political system

> dominated by bureaucrats and diplomats loosely supervised by ministers flying periodically to Brussels. The existence of a body of full-time representatives to the heart of decisionmaking in Brussels, asking questions, knocking on doors, bringing the spotlight to shine on dark corners, in dialogue with their constituents back home, makes the EU system more open, transparent, and democratic than would otherwise be the case.[27]

No other EU body has changed as much as the EP over the past fifty years, especially since the introduction of codecision. The member governments have increasingly delegated decisionmaking authority to the EP in response to criticisms about the EU's democratic deficit—or gap between the citizens and the governing bodies of the union perceived by those citizens as far removed and not sufficiently representative of their interests.[28] In some of its rulings, the ECJ secured EP powers. For example, in the Isoglucose case in 1980, the ECJ annulled legislation adopted by the Council because the Council had not waited to receive the EP opinion under the Treaty provisions for the consultation procedure.

In its turn, the EP has proven astute, adroit, and opportunistic in developing the powers delegated to it by the member states in order to maximize its impact inside the black box. The more authority the member governments have delegated to the

EP, the more the EP has expanded its scope for autonomous agency (as expected by theorists of historical and rational choice institutionalism).

The EP has the authority to ask the Commission to initiate legislative proposals of interest to it. The EP can publish reports that put pressure on the Commission to respond. An example of the power of the EP to initiate influential self-studies came in 1987. The EP released a report calling on the EC to ban the import of baby seal pelts on humanitarian grounds. In response, a Commission legislative proposal adopted by the Council banned baby seal imports into the EC even though the Council and the Commission had demonstrated some reluctance to pursue the issue.

The EP and Council have authority over the annual budget of the EU. The EP's oversight and confirmation of the executive and its legislative veto are powers familiar to the parliaments of nation-states. However, the EP has a wider scope of autonomy than do national parliaments. It cannot be terminated by a Prime Minister or Chancellor who calls for early elections. Conversely, the EP has the power to dismiss the Commission, a threat that has given it significant leverage and authority.

Notwithstanding the influence the EP has as described above, its powers are still constrained by member governments and their national parliaments, who are willing to enhance representative democracy at the EU level only so far. The EP has no formal relationship with or explicit influence over the European Council, the apex of EU governmental decisionmaking. Unlike national parliaments, it cannot vote "no confidence" in a Head of Government, which would force the executive to resign, and it cannot force new parliamentary elections. The EU coexecutives, the Commission and Council, do not require a governing majority from the EP in order to gain and remain in power. The EP does not control the legislative agenda as does the Commission, and it does not have full legislative enactment powers as does the Council. The EP has no legislative role in CFSP and some areas of JHA unless there are EU budgetary implications. It exercises less political control than national parliaments over the national Ministers in the Council.[29] Although the EP's authority is enhanced by its powers of censure and to veto the budget, these are blunt tools of influence rarely if ever used.

Just as the EP is positioned by the Lisbon Treaty to gain more powers in EU governmental decisionmaking, it faces a rather damning reality: the lack of voter interest in what it does. As illustrated in table 5.2, voter turnout for EP elections among the 27 member states dropped from 57 percent in 1994 to 43 percent in 2009. It is quite low among several of the Central and Eastern European states (CEE), especially in the Czech Republic, Poland, Romania, Slovakia, and Slovenia; and it has declined in Germany, France, Greece, Austria, and Finland. Higher voter turnouts occur in Belgium, Italy, Greece, and Luxembourg where voting is compulsory. The drop in voter turnout for EP elections is not unique among the Western democracies. Voter turnout for presidential elections in the United States, for example, was down in the 1990s to around 50 percent. Nevertheless, the EP needs to have a higher voter turnout to demonstrate its legitimacy to speak and act for the citizens of the union.

The problem of voter turnout has many roots. The large constituencies per MEP make it hard for MEPs and electorates to connect in meaningful ways. Here the more populous states are at a disadvantage compared with smaller ones because their MEPs have many more constituents to tend to. For example, as depicted in table 5.2, MEPs from the large and middle-size states have constituencies between 700,000 and 900,000, while those from the smaller states have constituencies that range from 83,000 to 424,000. Part of the problem may be that citizens fail to understand the importance of the EP in their lives. EU citizens themselves need to understand that the EP is an increasingly important body in EU governmental decisionmaking and that their vote in the election of their MEP matters. It would help if Europeans had a clear idea of what the EP does. Voter apathy toward the EP may reflect in general the distance between Europeans and the EU itself. The EU's purview does not extend to many areas of domestic policy where the national governments remain sovereign and where voter interest remains strongest: social welfare, taxation, city crime, health, and education, to name a few.[30] If the EP cannot command sufficient voter turnout to leverage its legitimacy as *the* EU's representative body, it cannot take a more equal place among—or "punch above its weight" with—the other EU bodies.

In sum, the EP is the union's imperfect yet indispensable assembly. Its members and leaders should cultivate more loyalty to party groups to lend more cohesion to the EP vis-à-vis the other EU bodies. The EP can redouble efforts to educate EU citizens about the importance of their voting rights—after all, it is the EU's colegislator and the Treaty of Lisbon extends codecision to most EU legislative areas. However, an increase in EP powers in EU governmental decisionmaking continues to appear incongruent when just 43 percent of EU citizens bother to vote in EP elections

The Budgetary Process: A Thumbnail Sketch

We briefly take a pause from our study of institutions to focus on the basic steps in the annual budgetary process. Historically, the EU budget has comprised just 2 percent of public expenditures of the EU member states; 98 percent constituted public expenditures of national and subnational governments. The EU has three of its own revenues to pay for the costs of its programs: import levies, a percentage of value-added tax (VAT) not to exceed 1 percent of the combined GNP of the member states, and a percentage of GNP calculated each year to cover the difference between EU expenditures and the amount the EU receives from import levies and VAT. The EU budget is shaped or rather limited by these parameters.

The Commission collects the revenues of the EU. It proposes and implements the budget; the Council and the EP have the power to modify the Commission's proposal; and the EP has the power to accept or reject the budget. The EP exercises oversight of the budget once approved, and the ECA (European Court of Auditors, introduced in the next section) conducts an annual audit of the budget. The Council decides by unanimity on a multiannual financial framework every seven years that lays down the ceiling for expenditures during that period. The current framework covers the period between 2007 and 2013. The EU has capped spending in this period at €862 billion, or 1.045 percent of the GNP of the EU member states.[31] The Lisbon Treaty retains the requirement that the Council act unanimously when adopting the multiannual financial framework rather than use QMV. Some argue that use of unanimity makes decisionmaking not only very difficult but conducive to reaching decisions at the lowest common denominator.

Prior to the Lisbon Treaty, the EU budget was divided into two types of spending: compulsory and noncompulsory. Compulsory spending was required by the Treaty and was largely consumed by agricultural price supports and subsidies. The Council was the final decisionmaker on compulsory spending. Thus, it could accept or reject proposed EP amendments. The EP has rejected the Council's proposed budget only three times (in 1979, 1982, and 1984). Noncompulsory spending was primarily consumed by economic and social cohesion, other internal policies, EU institutions, and foreign aid. The EP and the Council engaged in decisionmaking on all noncompulsory areas of the budget. The Lisbon Treaty abolishes distinctions between compulsory and noncompulsory expenditures. The EP will thus have decisionmaking authority alongside the Council in all budget areas of the EU.

Every spring, the EU begins its annual budgetary decisionmaking process that usually ends by the following winter. At the start of the budget process, the Commission forwards to the Council a preliminary draft budget proposal for the Council's first reading. The working groups of national officials are first to read the draft in the Council. Their job is to seek accord on as many issues as possible before delivering the draft to COREPER, which in turn prepares the draft and irons out differences before submitting the revised proposal to the Budget Ministers in the Council. The Commission, Council, and EP seek a final budget agreement—on the basis of interinstitutional accords—by cooperating and negotiating in trialogues between the various readings of the budget proposal. After having modified the Commission's draft, the Council forwards the draft preliminary budget to the EP by July for its first reading. The EP has forty-five days to act, after which the draft is considered adopted.

Before the plenary session receives the draft, the EP Committee on Budgets and other EP committees review it, and either accept the Council draft or propose amendments.[32] The EP may modify or amend spending items. After the EP plenary votes on amendments and other changes, it votes on a resolution that incorporates its version of the draft budget proposal. The EP's version of the draft budget proposal is returned to the Council for its second reading, usually in the fall. The Council has just fifteen days to respond to the EP's proposed amendments and modifications as well as to information provided by the Commission. Once the Budget Ministers adopt the Council's second reading, the budget proposal returns to the EP for its second reading, normally in December. At the EP's second reading, it may amend modifications to expenditure items in the Council's proposal within fifteen days. The EP then votes to accept or reject the budget in its entirety. The EP uses a two-thirds majority to reject the draft budget as a whole. Should this rejection occur, the entire budget process is restarted. In the meantime, EU expenditures would remain at the level of the previous year's spending.

The EP receives annual reports from the Council and Commission on the implementation of the budget and audit reports from the ECA. The Treaty mandates that the EP vote (in the form of resolution) to give or not give discharge to the implementation of the budget for the past year. Discharge allows accounts to be closed for that year. The power to give or deny discharge has proven to be an instrument of EP influence over the Commission, a subject discussed below. Given the scale of spending in the EU, the member states had the foresight to establish an independent auditor. It is to that auditor, the ECA, that we now turn.

The Auditor of the European Union:
The European Court of Auditors

Table 5.1 depicts the powers of the independent, Luxembourg-based ECA, created in 1975 (replacing existing audit bodies), made operational in 1977, recognized as an official EC institution by the TEU in 1993, and recognized as an official EU institution by the Amsterdam Treaty in 1998. As the ECA was a designated EU institution, its purview was extended to all areas of the EU. The Amsterdam Treaty also confirmed the right of the ECA to bring an action to the ECJ to protect its prerogatives with regard to the other EU bodies. The member governments have thus delegated audit powers to the ECA, for only an independent external auditor could provide an objective examination of EU revenues and expenditures. The closest but not exact equivalent to the ECA in the United States is the Government Accountability Office.

Each member government nominates its auditor for a six-year renewable term. The nominee is subject to appointment by the Council (by QMV) after consultation with the EP (the EP Budgetary Control Committee holds hearings for ECA nominees). Once appointed, the auditors act independently of the member states. ECA members elect their own President for a three-year renewable term. The staff of approximately eight hundred auditors, support staff, and translators, like other EU civil servants, is charged with performing duties in the EU interest. The Treaty charges the ECA to audit the implementation of the EU's general budget and EU development funds and the financial status of EU bodies and agencies. The ECA reports on the soundness of EU financial management. It may also be asked to give formal opinions on legislative proposals with financial impacts.

The ECA delivers an annual report to the EP on the EU's financial management. If the EP is satisfied with the report, it directs the Commission to implement the budget. The ECA publishes audit reports and opinions in the *Official Journal* and online at www.eca.eu.int. In its annual report, the ECA includes a "statement of assurance" and other observations on the EU's general budget and funds for the year in retrospect. The ECA examines whether all EU revenues and expenditures have been received or incurred in a regular and lawful manner and whether sound financial management is the norm.

The ECA may audit any EU body or person, including national, regional, and local authorities who receive EU aid. It may make on-the-spot visits to these recipients, and it has right of access to any information it needs to perform its audit. It cannot enforce its findings, but if it discovers any financial irregularities, it communicates them to the EU bodies in a position to take corrective action. In 1992 and 1997, the EP took serious offense at ECA reports critical of Commission management and spending.

In its 1992 annual report, the ECA criticized the Commission for certain expenditures over which the Commission had insufficient control. It cited member states for inadequate controls in the use of EU agricultural and cotton credits and in Structural Fund payments. Some cotton farmers had divided up their production to be eligible for aid designed to assist small producers. Regional aid to CEE states was given without sufficient preparation, and useless or inappropriate food aid was supplied to Russia.[33]

In its 1997 annual report, the ECA criticized the Commission for mismanagement of EU aid programs for CEE states, the former Soviet Union, and the non-EU Mediterranean states. As earlier mentioned, in March 1998 the EP deferred discharge on the 1996 budget. Disturbed by what it thought to be an "insufficiently robust" Commission response to its concerns about the ECA report on financial mismanagement, the EP again voted against giving discharge on December 17, 1998.[34] Commission President Santer called on the EP to either back or censure the College of Commissioners. The Santer Commission resigned hours before a motion of censure failed to pass in the EP. As these examples show, the ECA has the power of information and the EP the power of agency to enforce a system of checks and balances between the legislature and executive of the EU.

The ECA also publishes special reports on each EU body or agency (unless otherwise specified) and on detailed financial management audits of special budget areas. As mentioned, it presents its annual report to the EP at plenary sessions after having presented it to the EP Committee of Budgetary Control. The report is also presented to the Ecofin Council. The ECA also assists the EP in the exercise of its power of control over the implementation of the EC budget through the publication of audit reports and opinions.

The ECA's influence on EU governmental decisionmaking is used to improve the financial management and administration of EU finances and programs. The ECA ensures accountability of the use of public funds. The ECA brings its features as a supranational institution to all areas of the EU. The work of the ECA is an institutional bridge that connects the different parts of the EU, and its audits, which are made public. Finally, the ECA has scope for autonomous agency. It decides how to organize itself and when to schedule audits. If the Commission is the conscience and the EP the voice of the EU, then the ECA is the EU's financial conscience. It helps to guarantee the citizens of the EU member states that their money is spent effectively.

The Banks of the European Union

Two banks associated with the EU are established by Treaty law: the Frankfurt-based European Central Bank (ECB), established in 1998, and the Luxembourg-based European Investment Bank (EIB), established in 1958. The ECB, with its staff of 550 employees, is charged with maintaining price stability in the Eurozone by controlling the money supply (e.g., setting interest rates) and by monitoring price trends and assessing the risks they pose to price stability. The ECB manages the euro, conducts foreign exchange operations, ensures the smooth operation of payments systems, formulates and implements EU economic and monetary policy, and, with the aid of national central banks, collects, develops, compiles, and distributes interest rate and other monetary and economic statistics. Three of the old EU member states, Sweden, Denmark, and Britain, have not adopted the euro. Three of the new EU member states who joined in 2005 have adopted it: Slovenia, Cyprus, and Malta. The national central banks of the members and nonmembers of the Eurozone comprise, with the ECB, the European System of Central Banks (ESCB). The Treaty charges the ESCB with the task of maintaining price stability while defining and implementing monetary policy, conducting foreign exchange operations, and managing the official foreign reserves of the member states. Under the Lisbon Treaty, the Euro Group, which comprises the Eurozone members, may adopt a recommendation on whether a new member state may join the Eurozone.

One of the defining features of the ECB and the national central banks in the euro area is that they must be politically independent of any other body, including the member governments. The ECB Governing Council (six Executive Board members and the national central bank governors of the Eurozone countries) defines monetary policy for the Eurozone and fixes interest rates. The ECB Executive Board consists of the ECB President, the Vice President, and four others appointed by Eurozone members for nonrenewable eight-year terms. All are individuals distinguished by their professional experience in banking or monetary affairs. The Executive Board implements monetary policy defined by the Governing Council. It instructs national central banks, prepares for Governing Council meetings, and manages the day-to-day work of the ECB. The General Council (ECB President and Vice President and the twenty-seven national central bank governors) assists the ECB in its work and undertakes advisory, technical, and administrative responsibilities, including the supervision of the Exchange Rate Mechanism (ERM). In 2004, the Estonian, Lithuanian, and Slovakian currencies joined the ERM as the first step toward joining EMU.

The EIB finances investment projects (at very competitive interest rates) that promote European integration and balance economic development with social cohesion. The EIB, which does not use EU funds, finances its loans through borrowing on financial markets and through the member states who are the EIB's shareholders. The EIB has a staff of 850 employees. The Board of Governors (usually the Finance Ministers from each of the EU member states) makes decisions with regard to bank activities; the twenty-seven-member Board of Directors decides on loans, fixes interest rates, and raises funds; and the Management Committee implements decisions of the Board of Directors. Some of the projects financed by the EIB include new road and rail links that improve EU transport networks. In 2007, the EIB granted loans of €48 billion, of which €41 billion were for EU and EFTA states and €7 billion were for nonmember states.

The Agencies of the European Union

The agencies of the EU are each established by a legislative act to perform specific scientific, managerial, or technical tasks. These agencies are referred to as agencies, institutes, foundations, centers, or authorities. Three agencies are related to CFSP: the European Institute for Security Studies, which publishes security analyses; the European Union Satellite Center, which gathers data from space; and the European Defense Agency, which assists the EU members in reaching the defense procurement requirements of the CSDP. Two agencies are associated with the JHA: the European Police Office (Europol) and the European Judicial Cooperation Unit (Eurojust). However, in 2010, Europol ceases to exist as an EU agency and becomes an EU institution. Unlike an agency, an institution is subject to the budgetary and financial regulations of the Commission and the EP.

Established in 1992, the Hague-based Europol aims to assist the member states in cooperating to prevent and combat organized global transnational crime in such areas as drug trafficking, money laundering, trade in nuclear and radioactive sub-stances, and terrorism. Europol consists of representatives from each of the national law enforcement agencies of the member states. Europol is accountable to the JHA Ministers of the member governments. Its management board consists of one repre-sentative from each of the member states.

Established in 2002, the Hague-based Eurojust aims to assist the prosecuting authorities of the EU member states to cooperate in combating cross-border crime in such areas as fraud and corruption, money laundering, and environmental crime. It facilitates the exchange of information, mutual legal assistance, and extradition of criminal suspects. Each member state is represented in Eurojust by either a judge, a prosecutor, or a police officer, who together form the managing board of Eurojust and elect its President for a three-year term.

Other agencies associated with the internal market of the EU include, in order of the year established:

1975 European Center for the Development of Vocational Training
1975 European Foundation for the Improvement of Living and Working Conditions
1990 European Environment Agency
1990 European Training Foundation
1993 European Monitoring Center for Drugs and Drug Addiction
1993 European Agency for the Evaluation of Medicinal Products
1994 Office for Harmonization in the Internal Market
1994 European Agency for Safety and Health at Work
1994 Community Plant Variety Office
1994 Translation Center
1994 European Agency for Reconstruction
1995 European Medicines Agency
2003 European Food Safety Authority
2003 European Maritime Safety Agency
2003 European Aviation Safety Agency
2004 European Network and Information Security Agency
2004 European Center for Disease Prevention and Control
2004 European Railway Agency
2004 European Global Navigation Satellite System Supervisory Authority
2005 European Agency for the Management of Operational Cooperation at the Exter-nal Borders
2005 Community Fisheries Control Agency
2007 European Chemical Agency
2007 European Institute for Gender Equality
2007 European Union Agency for Fundamental Rights
2008 European Institute of Innovation and Technology

The European Union and the United States: Insights from Comparative Government

This last section of the chapter affords the opportunity to learn about EU governmen-tal decisionmaking by comparison. The framework of comparative analysis lends itself ideally to the study of EU governmental decisionmaking. What makes the EU particularly interesting to students of government is that it is situated at the intersection of comparative government and international politics, two subfields of political science. The EU is at the same time a group of states with similar and different governmental features subject to comparison and contrast and a regional peace system among previously warring nation-states. We learn more about EU governance when we compare it to other forms of government.

The EU and its member governments are constitutional democratic representative polities, like the United States. Although the EU and the United States are not governmental equals, they do share many common federal features. Their executives, legislatures, and judiciaries share many common powers. Both are voluntary unions comprising groups of states who emerged in an era of turmoil and change. Each responded at its creation to an external security threat. For the former American colonists, the external threats were the British and the Native Americans. For the Western Europeans, the external threat (and catalyst of change) was the Soviet Union and the expansion of Communism from east to west. Each union collectively responded to the abuse of political power—British colonialism in America and totalitarianism in Europe (Nazism, Fascism, and Communism). No one or two of their number could have created a new union without the critical mass of the rest. Thirteen U.S. states and six EC states collectively exploited the economies and politics of scale needed to break free of the old order and create a new one. Each created a new plural order of political and economic openness and freedom, prosperity, stability, and representative democracy. Each did so by creating a form of government that was not in existence before.

A key difference between the EU and United States is that the former is a regional system of international relations among sovereign states to stop the cycle of war that had plagued the member states, whereas the latter had neither this kind of history nor a need to adopt a new peace system. However, although the American colonies, while competitors, did not formally engage in war against one another, the U.S. states did in fact do so. The 1860–1865 Civil War had a brutality, loss of life and limb, and technological awfulness that presaged what was to come during World War I. The difference between the U.S. Civil War and the European wars from 1618 to 1945 was that the former was a civil conflict and the latter were international. The effect of both, however, was to solidify the need for central government, first in the form of a stronger federal government in the United States, and later in a central administration in the form of the EU.

The EU is a system of international relations among sovereign states with a central form of governance that regulates areas of competence in which the EU has its own sovereignty or shares sovereignty with the member states. In foreign and security policy, the EU states retain their sovereignty—but engage in extensive cooperation and coordination. The United States is not a system of international relations among sovereign states. Each of its constituent states has sovereignty unless otherwise specified in the Constitution, but this is an internal sovereignty. The U.S. states are prohibited by the Constitution from engaging in the practice of foreign policy—an area of sovereignty reserved to the federal government.

The United States is a federal system with no higher governmental authority above it. Most of the EU states are unitary systems (no separation of powers as in the

United States), with the exceptions of Germany, Austria, and Belgium, which are federal and are comfortable with federalism. Many of the unitary EU states wish to keep a federal Europe at bay. They fear it would undermine the sovereignty of their centralized governments.

This section compares and contrasts governmental features common to the EU and U.S. political systems—constitutionalism and federalism; separation of powers, and checks and balances—before ending with a comparative analysis of executive and legislative functions.

CONSTITUTIONALISM AND FEDERALISM

The U.S. Constitution is the constitution of a nation-state. The EU Treaty provides the constitutional basis of a union of states. The constituent states of each union are subject to an additional layer of government and an additional body of law that—following high court rulings—is generally supreme over individual state law when conflicts arise. Both have jurisdiction limited to what their respective constitutions grant them. In other words, neither the EU nor the U.S. governments may act outside the powers delegated to them by their respective constitutions. Amendments and other changes to the U.S. Constitution require ratification. In the United States, ratification requires the assent of two-thirds of both houses of Congress and three-quarters of the U.S. states. However, in the EU, Treaty ratification does not require the EP's assent. In the EU, ratification requires unanimity among the member states' legislatures (and in some members, passage of a popular referendum).

The United States is a sovereign entity constituted in law. The U.S. Constitution grants the sovereignty of the American people to their elected government—the United States of America. In contrast, the sovereignty of the EU does not rest with the people of the EU member states but with the member governments. The Treaty grants no sovereignty of the people of the member states to the European Union. The EU is not a sovereign entity constituted in law, although the Lisbon Treaty now establishes the EU as an international legal personality.

The tenth amendment of the U.S. Constitution states that all powers not given to the federal government belong to the people and the states. Similarly, the Treaty stipulates the areas where the EU has sovereignty or shared sovereignty. The member states remain sovereign in all other areas. However, the ECJ was more successful in expanding EU sovereign powers during the first fifty years of the EU than was the U.S. Supreme Court in the first fifty years of the United States.

National law and EU law exist concomitantly, just as the EU exists concomitantly with each nation-state that is a member of the EU. The scope of EU law and the jurisdiction of the EU Courts are limited to those areas where the Treaty grants competence to the EU, such as setting and negotiating external tariffs and administering regional development, environmental, agricultural, and antitrust policies. Member states retain sovereignty in all areas not covered by the Treaty, such as defense and fiscal policy. However, there are areas where the EU and the member states share competence and thus have overlapping sovereignties, such as international agreements in trade in services.

The scope of EU law and the competence of the ECJ are not nearly as broad as those of the U.S. Constitution and the U.S. Supreme Court, but neither is the EU a nation-state like the United States. Again, even in the United States, as in the EU, the Constitution (or the Treaty) leaves to the states all areas of jurisdiction not specifically granted to the federal government. The U.S. Constitution is more explicit than the Treaty about where power lies. The supremacy clause of the Constitution makes clear that federal laws are the supreme law of the land. It was expected that the federal judiciary would uphold the supremacy clause, which it did over some opposition from state governments and judiciaries from the start of the Republic through the Civil War. As Leslie Friedman Goldstein points out, the Treaty, which at first seemed "a more or less run of the mill multilateral Treaty," had nothing resembling the supremacy clause of the U.S. Constitution; however, the ECJ began in the early 1960s to take a multilateral Treaty and turn it into a "judicially enforceable, higher law that takes precedence within each of the member states, even over subsequent national legislation or constitutional provisions to the contrary."[35]

SEPARATION OF POWERS AND CHECKS AND BALANCES

In response to the abuse of centralized power by the British crown that led to the American Revolution, the United States established a governmental decisionmaking system whereby power would never again be concentrated in a single branch of government. The U.S. Constitution was designed to empower, and limit, governmental authority, just as the Treaty was designed to empower, but also limit, the governmental authority of the EU bodies. In the United States, power is limited in at least two ways: (1) the establishment of a federal republic, whereby governmental power is distributed vertically among federal (national), state, and local governments; and (2) the establishment of twin systems of separation of powers and checks and balances. The Constitution separates the powers of the three organs of the national government, the executive, legislature, and judiciary, and delegates to each its own tasks. The separation of powers is achieved and cemented by a system of checks and balances whereby no one branch can usurp the authority of the others. Each has its role to play in governmental decisionmaking, without which the government could not function.[36]

The EU member states are all parliamentary systems in which there is no separation of powers because the executive has a symbiotic relationship with the legislature. France, Finland, and Cyprus have mixed parliamentary-presidential systems in which there is executive-legislative symbiosis, but their Presidents are directly elected and have more political power than the other EU Heads of State. Perhaps one explanation why the EU achieved significant advances in regional integration and cooperation, while other international organizations across time have not, is that parliamentary systems of government have heads of government who overall have an easier time in making international agreements than do presidential systems like the United States. In the EU member governments, the head of government commands (or nearly always commands) a majority of support in the legislature. This means that, barring a loss of that majority, she or he can expect legislative support, given the fairly high degree of party loyalty and cohesion in Europe. In the United States, the executive and legislature share foreign policy powers, and without Congress there is little the President can do that costs money and requires congressional confirmation.

In each of the EU member states, parliaments have sovereignty (in Cyprus, Finland, and France, parliaments cede some sovereignty to popularly elected Presidents). As mentioned above, in parliamentary systems, the Prime Minister and her or his government command a majority of seats in parliament, which selects them to govern. The government relies on its parliamentary majority to pass legislation, but it can be removed from office by a vote of no confidence. This is not possible in the U.S. system, given the aversion to fusion and concentration of government powers, although a U.S. President can be impeached and, if convicted, removed from office. No U.S. President has ever been so removed, although two have been impeached: Andrew Johnson and William J. Clinton Jr. Similarly, in the EU the EP may censure the entire Commission and force it into resignation, but as in the United States, this is a blunt instrument to be used sparingly.

The U.S. federal executive and the Commission are subject to constitutional checks imposed by Congress and the Supreme Court in the case of the United States, and by the Council, the EP, and the ECJ in the case of the EU. In both governmental systems, the passage of laws and the powers of institutions are subject to the review of the highest courts: the Supreme Court and the ECJ. The checks on the Commission include (1) appointment/reappointment of Commissioners (Council and the EP); (2) censure and oversight (EP); (3) budget control (Council and EP); (4) financial audit (ECA); and (5) judicial review (ECJ). The checks on the executive branch of the U.S. federal government include (1) Senate confirmation of the President's nominees for cabinet and top federal posts; (2) impeachment (House of Representatives) and conviction (U.S. Senate) of the President; (3) oversight (Congress); (4) budget control (Congress); (5) financial audit (Congress); and (6) judicial review (U.S. Supreme Court).

Thus the EP and Congress scrutinize their respective executives. However, a key difference is that the EP has two powers Congress does not have: the Commission as a whole has to be approved by the EP, and the entire Commission can be dismissed by the EP. Although the EP and Congress are independent of governmental executives, the EP is not sovereign like the British House of Commons. However, unlike the House of Commons, the EP is independent of the EU executive, which cannot dismiss it.

Since both the EU and U.S. constitutions apply checks and balances, the passage and review of legislation require the involvement of different branches of government. In the U.S. federal government, powers are divided among the three branches—the executive, the legislative, and the judicial. Although in the EU governmental power is distributed among the same three branches, the member governments through the Council and European Council have a preponderance of power.

In both the EU and the U.S. systems, regulatory authority is delegated by governments and legislatures (principals) to governmental bodies or agents to manage, regulate, audit, and oversee the functioning of government. These agents—regulatory bodies such as the Food and Drug Administration and Environmental Protection Agency in the United States and the antitrust DG of the Commission and the independent ECA—are given the scope for agency as a result of the powers delegated to them by their governmental principals. In the EU, many powers of the executive/ bureaucracy and the legislature are delegated by the Council to help make the EU run better (Commission) or to make it more democratic (EP). In contrast, in the United

States, many powers of the executive/bureaucracy are delegated by Congress to run the executive branch of the federal government.

The key difference between American and European checks and balances is that in Europe (1) the Council has a preponderance of power with no equal in the United States; and (2) the member states are parliamentary systems that fuse legislative and executive powers, unlike the United States, which prohibits fusion. In the United States, the executive cannot legislate. Like the Commission, it initiates and executes. In the EU, the Council as coexecutive legislates but does not initiate in areas related to the internal market and monetary union and shares competence to initiate with the Commission in the area of CFSP (but not in areas of defense).

Although the EU member governments fuse legislative and executive powers at EU level, the Commission President, once appointed, is not symbiotically linked to the EP, and the Council President does not owe his or her existence to a majority support in the EP. Further, as no government forms as a result of the election of a majority in the EP, the EU and U.S. (federal) legislatures are more alike than are the EP and the national legislatures of the EU member states. This is because elections to Congress and the EP have nothing to do with the selection of the Head of Government. In contrast, there is a symbiotic link between government and parliament in the EU member states. Governments form when they garner a majority in their national parliaments. Thus, the EU level of governance comes closer to the U.S. system of national government, where the three branches retain powers independent of yet linked to one another.

THE EU AND U.S. EXECUTIVES

The U.S. and EU each have constitutional documents in which governments delegate authority to central institutions to do the public's work. As head of the executive branch, the U.S. President is the chief of the entire federal bureaucracy and thus draws on its vast knowledge base and resources to propose and execute budgets, legislation, and policies. Conversely, executive power in the EU is divided between the European Commission and Council Presidents, neither of whom has recourse to the resources of their U.S. counterpart. Indeed, the Commission President draws on resources and staff similar in size to single ministries in some of the EU member governments or large city administrations in Europe and America. The European Council President draws on an even smaller Secretariat-bureaucracy. The Commission President has a five-year, once renewable term; the European Council President has a two-and-a-half-year once renewable term; and the U.S. President has a four-year, once-renewable term. The U.S. and two EU Presidencies have representative powers in dealings with other governmental bodies in their unions and with the outside world. The U.S. President initiates legislation, which the European Council President cannot do in the area of the internal market and monetary union unless he or she asks the Commission to do so.

Whereas the head of the Commission's civil servants is the Commission President, a political appointee of the member governments, the head of the U.S. federal bureaucracy is the President of the United States, a popularly elected official via the Electoral College. Herein lies a problem of democratic legitimacy for the Commission.

Its President is appointed by the HOGS, who are either popularly elected (France) or who enjoy a majority support in their national parliaments (Britain). Thus the Commission President is subject to democratic legitimacy and to public scrutiny only because the member governments make the appointment on behalf of their electorates, and because MEPs have the power to confirm or deny appointment and to remove a Commission from office on behalf of their electorates. However, the Commission President and the Commissioners, and those who report to them, are further removed from the source of political legitimacy, the electorates, than is the U.S. President, who has a popular mandate. In addition the Commission and American Presidencies differ greatly in stature. According to Professor John McCormick,

> the Commission President has the same stature as early nineteenth-century U.S. Presidents, who had less of a role in government than either Congress or the states and were seen more as executives than as leaders. However, just as Franklin Roosevelt gave the job a newly powerful and assertive role in government in the 1930s, so the presidency of the Commission took on a new and more forceful character under Delors.[37]

The U.S. President appoints his cabinet members subject to Senate confirmation. Conversely, the Commission President does not have the power to nominate the Commissioners. Although this power is held by the member governments, the Commission President influences the HOGS to nominate the most competent individuals with whom he or she can work well. Whereas the U.S. President's cabinet members (most of whom are called Secretaries) are individually subject to Senate confirmation, this is not the case with the Commissioners, who are not individually subject to confirmation. Only the Commission President and Commissioners as a whole body are subject to confirmation and to a motion of censure, at which time the entire College would have to resign.

Once a Commissioner is appointed and confirmed, a member government cannot recall or remove its Commissioner for the length of the five-year term. The EP, which can remove a Commission by a vote of censure, cannot remove individual Commissioners. Thus, in this respect, the independence of Commissioners is greater than that of government ministers in the member states and department Secretaries in the United States. In the United States it is the President, not Congress, who may terminate governmental political appointees.

Further comparison reveals that the EU and U.S. executives—the Commission and U.S. Presidents—and their respective administrations and bureaucracies

- function as governmental bodies with departments (U.S.) or Directorates-General (EU) whose work feeds into and off other governmental bodies as part of a single political system;
- have political appointees (1) who are nominated by governments, subject to parliamentary consent, and are subject to oversight by and funding from parliaments (U.S. Senate and the EP); (2) who serve fixed terms; (3) who are responsible to one another and to a President; and (4) to whom civil servants ultimately report;
- include lifelong civil servants who, with their institutional memory and expertise, run the day-to-day work of government and have discretionary power—or agency—in the way policy is implemented;

- do not take orders from and do not work for the constituent states;
- have executive functions such as providing overall political direction for their administrations, distributing government posts and portfolios, overseeing cabinet meetings, requiring their cabinet officers to resign, and representing the interests of their branch of government before other governmental bodies (Congress, EP) and to foreign governments and international bodies;
- have a chief of staff (Commission Secretary-General, White House Chief of Staff), who ensures coordination and efficiency for the President;
- prepare, submit, and implement the budgets of their respective unions and are engaged in the initiation and implementation of legislative proposals;
- depend on and monitor national (EU states) and subnational governments (EU regions, U.S. states and localities) to implement the policies of the union (EU, U.S. federal government); and
- have legislatures that may remove the executives from office (if the U.S. President is impeached and voted out of office by Congress, and if the EP votes a motion of censure to remove the entire Commission).

THE EU AND U.S. LEGISLATURES

The EP, like Congress, is independent of the executive. The EP is unicameral and the U.S. Congress is bicameral. Indeed, Konrad Adenauer, first President of the ECSC Council in 1952, compared the Council and European Parliament together to a bicameral legislature. It took fifty years for the EP to gain the powers of a colegislator.[38] However, if one views the Council, given its legislative duties, as the upper house of the EP, the EU looks more like a bicameral than a unicameral legislature.

In the United States, members of Congress are elected in winner-take-all, single-member districts. MEPs are elected in single-member districts based on proportional representation or variants thereof. The EP, like Congress and other parliaments, is divided into committees and political parties.

In the U.S. House of Representatives, seats are distributed among state congressional districts by population, and in the U.S. Senate, among states evenly, with two per state. In the EP, seats are distributed among member states by population, although, as earlier mentioned, the equation favors the number of MEPs from small over large states. Unlike the U.S. Senate, there is no fixed number that is equal for all states. In the "other" EU legislature, the Council, small states are equal to large when votes are determined by unanimity, but when voting is determined by a qualified majority, large states have more weight than small ones. However, here again the weights of small states are higher relative to those of larger ones. The EU has gone to great lengths to avoid the domination of the small by the large states, that is, to ensure as much sovereign equality among the members as possible. This too is unprecedented in the history of international organizations.

In Congress, political party cohesion is a function of party leadership, but in the EP, party group cohesion is weak and leadership has limited leverage over members. MEPs and members of Congress each are closely affiliated with and influenced by interest groups.

Whereas the U.S. Congress and President need each other to enact legislation

(Congress must pass the legislation and the President must sign it) and run the government, the EP has no Treaty powers related to the European Council and has limited access to it. The EP may censure and force the Commission to resign, but the U.S. Congress does not have this power over the U.S. executive short of impeachment and removal from office.

Whereas the Council has both legislative and executive functions, which are fused, the Congress has no executive functions. The U.S. President has the power of veto, as does the EP (in codecision and assent). A U.S. Presidential veto may be overturned by a two-thirds majority of both houses of Congress. The EP has the power to veto legislation promoted by the Council, but only in areas of codecision, assent, and the budget. The problem with codecision is that the EP does not have the technical expertise enjoyed by other parliaments, including Congress, which has access to expert knowledge from the Congressional Research Service and the Congressional Budget Office, not to mention the enormous capacity of the federal bureaucracy.

Whereas the U.S. Senate has the power to confirm the President's nominees for Justices of the Supreme Court, the EP is given no such authority for the Judges proposed by the EU member governments for the ECJ and CFI. The Senate can also approve individual members of the President's cabinet, but the EP cannot approve individual Commissioners.

The EP and the U.S. Congress are more alike in some respects than the EP and the national parliaments of the EU member states. For example, the U.S. and EU legislatures have powers to remove their executives. The U.S. House of Representatives has the power of impeachment of the President, and the U.S. Senate the power to remove the President from office through the impeachment process. Impeachment is a blunt tool and, although two U.S. Presidents have been impeached, neither was removed from office by the Senate.

In the EU, the EP cannot unseat the executive unless a motion of censure is passed. The EP's power of censure is problematic because, in theory, there would be nothing to stop the European Council from reconstituting the same Commission that was just forced to resign. In practice, the EP would not likely wish to approve a new Commission constituted solely from the old one. Still, the EP's right of or threat of censure and the House of Representatives' right of or threat of impeachment have similar effects and contribute to systems of checks and balances.

The EP's power of censure is more similar to the power of impeachment than to the process by which a national parliament withdraws its support from a government, which usually triggers the fall of the government and new elections. Therefore, the EP is somewhat more independent than national parliaments; the EU executives cannot impose their wishes on a majority in the EP as a government must do to survive in a national parliament.

Whereas in U.S. congressional elections, incumbent members' votes matter to the electorates, this is not so much the case in EP elections. Election and reelection of MEPs have less to do with EU issues and the way political groups within the EP vote than with the national political party. Since a MEP must be included on his or her national political party list to be elected to the EP (elections are based on proportional representation), a MEP will be more attentive to domestic than to European politics. However, as earlier mentioned, given the perks that come with membership in European political groups in the EP, a MEP who wishes to advance within the EP structure of power will need to be attentive to his or her own political group in the EP.

The preceding comparison of U.S. and EU governmental systems reveals some of the similarities and differences. EU governmental decisionmaking is far more labyrinthine than that of the United States, no doubt due to the complex compromises that are needed to make the EU work. The U.S. political system is the result of compromises among constituent states, not nation-states. This chapter has thus far introduced the powers and functions of the main players in EU governmental decisionmaking and has compared the EU and U.S. as polities. The closing section draws on the main conclusions of the chapter before moving on to the outputs of the black box in Chapter 6.

Review

THEORETICAL OBSERVATIONS

Institutionalist and constructivist perspectives provide helpful explanations of the growth and development of the EU as a polity. Institutionalists focus on either the path dependency of EU bodies who develop autonomously from the initial grants of delegated authority, or the rational choice of member governments who delegate authority to the common bodies to reduce their costs of doing business in the union. Constructivists remind us that the Commission and other EU bodies consist of individuals whose European preferences, values, and interests over time have been constructed in ways that influence how these individuals run the EU. This process of Europeanization is one of the most cogent explanations of how individuals work together inside the black box to make EU policy.

Member governments delegated authority to EU bodies to run the union *and* sought ways at times to calibrate that delegation. They recognized that the EU bodies they created had grown into living organisms with proclivities linked to, yet independent of, their grantors. As EU bodies expanded their scope for autonomous agency, they drove forward both their own institutional interests and the project of European integration. EU bodies, particularly the Commission, depend on national governments to transpose EU laws and regulations into national law and on national and subnational authorities to implement EU laws and regulations. Thus, the agents of the member states in fact delegate back to the member states the powers of implementation to reduce not national, but EU, transaction costs.

EU bodies are hardly impartial. They seek to maximize their agency. They have the power to decide who gains access to and thus influences them inside the black box. The procedures EU bodies adopt make operative the powers delegated to them by governments. EU bodies add, rather than shed, layers of decisionmaking procedures that matter to the formulation and execution of EU policy.[39] Insights from principal–agent analysis, with its focus on delegation and agency, best capture the interplay between the member governments and the EU institutions. The pendulum of European integration swings between member states who retain and delegate sovereignty and EU bodies who cultivate agency.

The Commission as Treaty guardian and enforcer and initiator and executor of policy has enormous scope for agency. The Commission's mandate is to do the right thing to advance the common interest. Governments themselves are first to admit that they cannot be trusted to uphold their own interstate compacts due to the temptation to advance national over collective interests, especially when economies fall into recession. The Commission has agency when implementing its delegated authority to enforce the *acquis*. However, when governments grow skeptical of or opposed to the Commission's delegated powers and its widening scope for autonomous agency, they have on occasion sought to restrict the Commission's powers.

The Council's byzantine system of committees to oversee the Commission's implementation of legislation (comitology) is a good example of how governments endeavor to constrain the Commission's autonomy. Rational choice institutionalists predict that the Council Ministers will seek to take back powers delegated to the Commission when they wish to circumvent or undermine their own agreements. However, Council Ministers grudgingly accept the Commission's autonomous scope for agency even if they sometimes chip away at the authority delegated to it.

The Council is the fulcrum of political power in the EU. Its member governments have the power to delegate tasks to other EU bodies and the power to veto many important decisions. Further, since the Council must delegate to others much of the day-to-day work of the Council and of the EU, a principal–agent dynamic gives those on whom the Council depends scope for influence. Constructivists have much to say about the socialization effects of member government ministers working together in the Council. Governmental ministers fight for the national interest in EU legislation, but once they are in Brussels, those ministers in Council engage in a process of negotiation and compromise based on habits and customs of cooperation in the context of the *acquis*. From the ministers in Council, to the Permanent Representatives and Council Secretariat staff, and down to the working groups, a process of Europeanization occurs that allows the flexibility to balance national and European interests. This process of Europeanization shapes the relationship of national and collective interests. Since it would not be possible within the EU for one government to have everything it wants all the time, there is ample give-and-take among government ministers in the Council.

The member governments have increasingly delegated decisionmaking authority to the EP in response to widespread criticisms about the EU's democratic deficit. The more authority the member governments have delegated to the EP, the more the EP has adroitly expanded its scope for autonomous agency. The EP is less a receiver of delegated authority from the member governments than a beneficiary of the pressure member governments are under from publics to make the EU more democratic and representative. This helps to explain the growth of EP powers over time. But it is not enough. A rational choice institutionalist perspective explains how the EP has leveraged its scope for agency to push for its own institutional interests vis-à-vis the other EU bodies.

EMPIRICAL OBSERVATIONS

As demonstrated in this chapter, the EU is one of the most complicated systems of government in the world because it adds a layer of government onto the member states and it has arcane and baffling decisionmaking procedures, some far removed from the scrutiny and understanding of voters. A hybrid, still young, incomplete and messy polity, the EU is an amalgam of different governmental features. The EU is a federal, supranational, interinstitutional, intergovernmental, and transnational polity. It remains a moving target for those who study and seek to explain it, those inside the union who must abide by its decisions and indecision, and those outside the union who are affected by its action or inaction but have no say in its decisionmaking.

No one individual or body has a complete panorama view of the EU. None has the capacity to relate a set of issues being dealt with in one area of the union to those dealt with in another in order to ensure that the union's parts are related to its whole. The EU is not run by the equivalent of an effective and strong central government of a nation-state, which may have the capacity to make choices among competing policy preferences and achieve an overall purpose. The Commission and Council are divided along sectoral lines, making it hard for either to craft rounded policy that takes into account priorities and resources linked across a range of issues and choices. The EU is likely to remain a more fragmented than unified polity, and its divisions magnify those found at national level because of what the EU is. However, interinstitutional accords help in the direction of a more unified approach to EU governmental decisionmaking, especially in facilitating ways in codecision to reach accord in the first reading.[40] The EP's powers in codecision, now in the ordinary legislative procedure, have made the Commission and Council more attentive to the opinions of the EP; and the Lisbon Treaty holds out the promise of a more coherent approach to governmental decisionmaking inside the EU's black box, especially with the introduction of the two-and-a-half-year Presidency of the European Council.

If political elites and citizens perceive that the EU adds value to what the member states do, then it enjoys a period of popularity and the pendulum swings to the EU agents. When the EU is not seen as an attractive means of cooperation, the pendulum swings back to the member states. The EU will continue to function within this range of uncertainty. This is why it is unwise to apply measures of evaluation for and expectations of nation-states to the EU, since the former and latter are not the same. The EU will never be a nation-state.

Key Concepts

assent
black box
blocking minority
cabinet
codecision (ordinary legislative procedure)
comitology
Conciliation Committee
consensus
consultation procedure
qualified majority
subsidiarity
unanimity

Study Questions

1. What are the Council's intergovernmental and supranational features and the EP's transnational and supranational features? Use examples to explain each feature.
2. What are the main powers/functions of the Commission? To what extent does the Commission have agency to advance its own institutional as well as European interests? Use examples in your explanation.
3. What are four strengths and four weaknesses or shortcomings of the EP? Explain the roots of each.
4. How does a principal–agent model explain the relationship between the European Parliament and the Council? Use examples.
5. What are the steps in the passage of a legislative initiative based on codecision (ordinary legislative procedure) from its origins through enactment and implementation? Include in your explanation the role of each institution and group in the legislative process.
6. How did the ECA empower the EP to put pressure on the Santer Commission to resign? What in your view do the ECA and EP activities in this instance imply for the role of the EP in EU governmental decisionmaking?
7. What federal features do the U.S. and EU systems share (list and explain three) and in which features do they differ (list and explain three)?
8. What are four similarities and four differences you encountered when comparing both the EU and U.S. executives and the EU and U.S. legislatures? Explain each.
9. What theory or concept, or combination thereof, do you think best explains the work and influence of either the Commission, Council, or EP, and why?

Selected Readings

Elizabeth Bomberg, John Peterson, and Alexander Stubb, *The European Union: How Does It Work?*, 2nd ed. (Oxford: Oxford University Press, 2008).
Codecision website, http://EC.europa.eu/codecision/index_en.htm
Richard Corbett, Francis Jacobs, and Michael Shackleton, *The European Parliament*, 7th ed. (London: John Harper, 2007).
European Central Bank, http://www.ecb.eu/
European Commission, http://ec.europa.eu/
European Council, http://consilium.europa.eu/
European Court of Auditors, http://eca.europa.eu/
European Ombudsman, http://ombudsman.europa.eu/
European Parliament, http://www.europarl.europa.eu/
Simon Hix, *The Political System of the European Union*, 2nd ed. (London: Palgrave, 2005).
Lisbon Treaty, http://europa.eu/lisbon_treaty/full-text/index_en.htm
John McCormick, *Understanding the European Union: A Concise Introduction* (London: Palgrave Macmillan, 2008).
Neill Nugent, *The Government and Politics of the European Union* (Durham, N.C.: Duke University Press, 2003).

CHAPTER 6

The Outputs of EU Governmental Decisionmaking

Preview

In Chapter 5 we delved into the EU's black box to demystify the process of converting inputs into outputs. In Chapter 6 we turn our attention to the outputs themselves. The purpose of the EU as a polity is to make policies that enhance economic and social welfare and contribute to common stability and security. For each internal policy area, we examine its origins, objectives, and development; formulation and execution; and key elements.

This chapter finds that common policies cover a wide range of functional needs of EU citizens, such as food, water, product, and maritime safety, as well as sectoral ones, such as fisheries and agriculture. EU policies are based on either the EU's own Treaty competence (commercial policy), shared competence between the EU and the member states (energy, transport, and international trade in services), or member state competence subject to EU influence (social benefits of employment policy affecting free movement of labor). EU policies are often clusters of related policies (the internal market). Policies reflect a lopsided distribution of EU public funds—agriculture consumes the lion's share of total spending. Some policies are regulatory (workplace safety), redistributive (social policy), distributive (research and development), or macroeconomic (supply of money). Policies are subject to the pressures of reform (competition policy) and to the tests of subsidiarity (education policy) and fiscal prudence (Eurozone debt ceilings). Some are clearly mandated by the Treaty but still developing (transportation), some clearly mandated by the Treaty and fully developed (antitrust), and others not clearly mandated by the Treaty but rather developed over time and later codified in the Treaty (passport-free movement of persons). Some policies have developed from intergovernmental accords outside the Treaty to areas of supranational or intergovernmental accords brought under the Treaty remit (internal security). Policies are either internal (cohesion aid), external (association accords), or internal with external impact (environmental policy). The EU has added new policies to the remit of the Treaty since the 1980s. Most recently, the Lisbon Treaty added the following new policies for which the EU now has legal competence to take action: tourism, energy security, ecological protection, humanitarian assistance, intellectual property rights, public health, space policy, and sport. EU policies are often related to one another and to the functioning of the internal market (police cooperation necessitated by the free movement of persons).

The EU, like any polity, is judged for what it does. That judgment feeds back into new sources of policy inputs. Policy outputs that result in poorly functioning policies will, through the feedback loop, be subject to change and reform if the polity is to be responsive. No polity can survive if it does not evolve to address the needs of its citizens.[1] Chapter 6 focuses primarily on the internal policies of the EU and Chapter 7 on the external ones. It is not until Chapters 8 and 9 that we evaluate the effectiveness of the EU polity. For now, we turn to a brief explanation of the different instruments or types of EU governmental decisionmaking.

Types of EU Governmental Decisionmaking Instruments

In this chapter we turn our attention to the outputs of the EU as a polity, as depicted in Figure II.1. Although these outputs take the form of a dizzying array of different instruments when carried out by individual institutions, the EU's primary decision-making instruments are regulations and directives.

The Commission initiates a legislative proposal for consideration by one or both of the EU's colegislators—the Council and the EP. For example, the Commission initiated a legislative proposal to allocate funds for Galileo—the EU's satellite navigation program. A successful legislative proposal ends up as a **Council regulation**, a piece of legislation enacted by one or both of the colegislators. A Council regulation is binding in its entirety and directly applicable in each of the member states. This means that a regulation does not normally require implementation by the member governments. Instead, the Commission implements regulations. The financing of Galileo is an example of a Council regulation, as is the implementation of the greenhouse gas emissions trading system provided for in the Kyoto Protocol.

In a **Commission regulation**, the Commission publishes binding technical adjustments to existing legislation. Commission regulations pertain to economic policies designed to enhance efficiency and minimize market failures. Such regulations include those establishing consumer protection and technical production standards, as well as health, safety and environmental standards. A **Council directive** is a binding set of principles, objectives, and requirements in specific areas to which member governments give effect by passing individual national implementation measures. A directive may be addressed to all or some of the member governments. Proposed by the Commission, directives are subject to legislative action by one or both of the EU colegislators. For example, a Commission regulation implemented a Council directive that provided monetary compensation for crime victims paid by member state authorities on whose territory the crime was perpetrated.

As this brief overview demonstrates, EU policies are implemented through a variety of decisionmaking instruments, the most important of which are directives and regulations. Other instruments include Council decisions, resolutions, negotiating directives, conclusions, joint actions, common positions and strategies, and framework decisions; EP resolutions, opinions, recommendations, and initiative reports; and Commission legislative proposals, opinions, recommendations, competition rulings, communications, action plans, studies and reports, and White and Green Papers.[2] We now turn to some of the major EU policy areas in order to examine what the EU polity produces.

Internal Market

ORIGINS, OBJECTIVES, AND TIMELINE

The EU is many things—a peace model, a social market economy, a monetary union, a magnet for neighbors, a source of foreign aid, and a provider of external security. But of all things, it is an internal market of nearly 500 million people. The internal market is why the EU exists as an economic entity. The policies that guide the internal market and aim to complete it are the EU's most important core functions. The Treaty guarantees EU citizens free movement of goods, services, capital, and labor. However, as you are about to learn, intra-EU labor mobility and trade in services still face obstacles.

In addition to trying to complete the internal market, the EU must preserve what significant market integration has already occurred. This is especially challenging during periods of economic recession and financial crisis, when member governments are more inclined to subsidize, protect, or otherwise favor domestic producers even if such aid would contravene the rules of the internal market. For example, during the 2008–2010 recession, several Eurozone member governments raised public debt as a percentage of GDP to stimulate domestic spending. Such spending exceeded the debt ceilings established by the Eurozone countries to maintain monetary stability.

Chapter 1 covered the origins of the internal market. We already know that the aim of creating one market out of many was to benefit EU citizens (whose living standards would rise), governments (whose ability to deliver public goods would increase), producers (whose competitive positions and profits would increase), and consumers (whose choice and supply of products would be enhanced). Snapshots of the development of the internal market included

- 1957—the Treaty set into action the progressive establishment of a customs union and a common market.
- 1968—the EC completed the establishment of the customs union, followed by the development of the common market in the 1970s.
- 1960s–1970s—the pace of market integration slowed, due in part to increased resort to national trade protectionism (use of NTBs), the effects of oil price hikes and recessions, and the lack of political impetus to ensure implementation of the four freedoms (free movement of goods, services, capital, and labor).
- 1979—in *Cassis de Dijon*, the ECJ affirmed the principle of mutual recognition of national market legislation: producers who conform to the standards of one member state cannot be excluded from the markets of other member states.

- 1985—the Commission published its *White Paper on Completing the Internal Market* in response to lagging industrial competitiveness and market fragmentation. The *White Paper* served as the basis for the SEA.
- 1987—the SEA aimed to improve EC competitiveness by eliminating thousands of NTBs by 1992. It defined the internal market as an area without internal frontiers within which the Treaty ensures the free movement of goods, persons, services, and capital.
- 1992—the EU harmonized many national product and regulatory standards into mutually recognized EU standards; harmonized VAT (sales tax) and excise duties; eliminated or simplified customs formalities; opened up national public procurement to cross-border competition; eliminated controls on the free movement of capital; strengthened competition rules; introduced QMV for use in most internal market areas; and empowered the EP to amend market legislation (cooperation procedure).
- 1993, 1998, and 2001—successive Treaty revisions granted the EP the power to veto internal market legislation (codecision) and extended use of QMV in the Council.
- 2000—the HOGS adopted the Lisbon Strategy with the aim of becoming the world's most "dynamic, competitive, knowledge-based economy" by 2010. The Strategy was launched in response to trenchant problems of economic competitiveness and unemployment.
- 2002—the introduction of Euro notes and coins helped facilitate the flow of capital across the internal market.

In just over fifty years, the EU has developed the internal market from a customs union and common market to a monetary union, expanding the EP's authority over internal market legislation, and addressing remaining obstacles to full free movement of economic activity. Having reviewed major internal market developments, we turn now to how decisions are made before examining key elements of the internal market policies.

FORMULATION AND EXECUTION

The HOGS establish broad policy guidelines with regard to the internal market, charge the EU bodies with taking action in support of their guidelines, and approve treaty changes. However, daily administration is left to the Commission, which proposes and executes internal market legislation. In most instances, the Council and EP legislate together. All along the way, the Commission consults with and depends on a wide variety of players organized at the European level (e.g., special interests and standards-setting agencies). The Commission and other EU bodies attract hundreds of lobbyists from producer, labor, professional, and other groups who seek to influence internal market policy.

The Commission has built on the authority that member governments have delegated to it. It has also extended its scope for agency as a regulator of and proponent for completing the internal market. The Treaty makes the Commission the EU's good cop/bad cop. For example, the Commission promotes cooperation whereby member governments agree to directives that harmonize national production and other standards into mutually acceptable EU production standards. The Commission also shames member governments slow to transpose EU directives into national law; and, failing that, is authorized to institute infringement proceedings against them at the ECJ.

ECJ rulings and opinions have, overall, enforced the Treaty rules governing the functioning of the internal market and strengthened the Commission's regulatory powers. The member governments have delegated codecision-making authority to the EP to amend or veto most pieces of internal market legislation. For its part, the Council uses QMV in nearly all internal market areas, which eases decisionmaking.

KEY ELEMENTS

Internal Market Policy rests on two broad objectives. One objective is to retain and manage the internal market *acquis*—for example, mutual recognition of production, health and safety, and other standards; market-opening regulations and directives; antitrust rules; and worker rights, including the free movement of labor. The other objective is to extend market integration to trade in financial and other services and ensure free movement of labor—two areas of the internal market where the EU still has much to do. Two important examples of internal market policies address the responsibilities of producers (competition policy) and the rights and needs of workers (social policy).

Competition Policy: The internal market cannot feature free trade if member governments or firms engage in practices that adversely affect cross-border competition. The Treaty prohibits practices that inhibit or distort competition in the internal market with the effects of reducing economic efficiency, hindering innovation, limiting consumer choice, and raising consumer prices. More specifically, the Treaty prohibits

- a firm from creating a monopoly or otherwise engaging in a restrictive practice that would allow it to establish a dominant position in the market, reducing or eliminating competition (see Microsoft case below);
- a firm from forming a cartel that would restrict or end competition (price fixing);[3]
- firms from merging with the effect of suppressing competition in the internal market[4] (see Commission ruling on the Boeing and McDonnell Douglas merger in box 6.1); and
- state aid (subsidies, grants, tax incentives) from a government to a domestic firm that gives the firm an unfair advantage in the internal market over other firms that do not receive such aid.[5]

The member governments delegated to the Commission the authority to determine if firms and governments violate competition rules. If the Commission finds that restrictive practices do occur that adversely affect the internal market, it works with the offenders to eliminate or change those practices. When that fails, the Commission initiates a case in the CFI against those charged with violating competition

Box 6.1.   The Boeing–McDonnell Douglas Merger

A controversial Commission ruling on the merger of the U.S. firms Boeing and McDonnell Douglas underscores the power of the Commission under EU competition law. The two companies announced their agreement to merge in 1996. The world's largest and third largest manufacturers of big commercial aircraft, Boeing and McDonnell Douglas were direct competitors in the sale of large commercial aircraft, and with Airbus Consortium (a European consortium of aircraft manufacturers) they constituted the three remaining large aircraft manufacturers in the world. The merger would have formed the world's largest aircraft manufacturer and second largest defense supplier.

Although the U.S. Federal Trade Commission cleared the merger of the two firms without condition in 1997, the Commission would not approve the merger in the EU without extracting concessions from Boeing to ensure increased competition. Since neither Boeing nor McDonnell Douglas had manufacturing facilities in the EU, the Commission was concerned about the impact of their combined sales in the EU and feared abuse of dominant position.

From an EU perspective, the proposed merger held out the possibility of lost sales for Airbus Consortium. The Commission was under enormous political pressure to review the merger proposal with a fine-toothed comb. However, from the American perspective, there was the appearance of a conflict of interest because the issue was less about competition between U.S. and European firms or the relative merits of the merger itself than it was about a blatantly political act of the EU to protect Airbus Consortium from being exposed to further competitive forces within the EU. The merger plan was propelled by the need for these two companies to compete on a global scale, and that meant competing with Airbus Consortium.

The Commission successfully pressed Boeing–McDonnell Douglas to, among other stipulations, (1) eliminate its exclusive supplier contracts with various American airline carriers and refrain from engaging in such exclusive supplier contracts until 2007, and (2) offer its competitors nonexclusive licenses for patents that were developed from publicly financed research and development. Boeing and McDonnell Douglas had no choice but to consent to the Commission's demands; otherwise the merger would not have been approved, thus blocking the newly constituted company from doing business in the EU.

In the end, a major trade row between the EU and the United States was averted when the Commission and McDonnell Douglas negotiated the terms of the merger, but it left a bitter aftertaste for the U.S. Government and has since led to calls for more cooperation between U.S. and EU competition authorities to minimize differences in the way the EU and the United States handle merger reviews. As a result, the EU and the United States have since expanded the terms of cooperation of their 1991 bilateral agreement on the application of competition laws.

rules. The CFI has the power to levy fines. Member state firms and governments may appeal Commission competition rulings to the ECJ.

The member governments' antitrust authorities deal with violations of competition rules within their national jurisdictions. If a domestic restrictive practice, merger, or state aid in one member state adversely affects trade and competition elsewhere in the internal market, the EU has competence to act. The EU only takes action when trade is affected between or among the member states or when foreign governments or foreign firms engage in activity that adversely affects trade among the member states. Given limits on the size of its personnel and resources, the Commission depends on member governments, firms, and individuals to bring to its attention a suspected breach of competition rules. It also depends on member governments and national courts to implement its rulings.

Competition Policy is a supranational policy. No internal market can operate in the absence of laws regulating fairness in trade and competition. Member governments not only have delegated authority to the Commission in such a politically sensitive area, they have consented to accept Commission competition rulings. Prior to the SEA, the Commission was politically timid as the policing agency for competition rules. However, as a result of the 1992 Project, Competition Policy became a primary instrument to enforce the completion of the internal market in general, and to reduce trade-distorting state subsidies in particular. Member governments knew that they could not depend on themselves to police and enforce competition rules in a free internal market. They are often under enormous pressures from some of their own domestic producers to grant subsidies and other forms of protection that could disadvantage firms from other member states. They recognized that the internal market could not function in the absence of a single body charged with ensuring that the rules of competition are fair and respected. Furthermore, the member states recognized that Competition Policy reduces their own "transaction costs" of doing business in the union. It would have been too costly for the member governments themselves to manage and enforce the common rules.

Over time, the power of the Commission in Competition Policy has grown to include invasive on-site investigations and, as mentioned, the imposition of fines on firms found guilty of violating competition rules. In 2004, the Commission found that Microsoft Corporation, leading global software publisher, used the dominant market position of its Windows product for operating systems of personal computers to restrict competition in the internal market. The Commission argued that Microsoft restricted competition in two ways. First, Microsoft refused to disclose certain technical information to competitors, so that its products communicated better with Windows than with the products of other companies. The Commission therefore required Microsoft to disclose technical information to competitors and to authorize the use of this information for the development of interoperable products. Second, Microsoft tied the sale of Windows to its Windows Media Player, thus weakening competition in the media player market where Microsoft was acquiring a leading position. As a result, the Commission required Microsoft to permit computer producers and consumers in the EU to buy Microsoft's Windows operating system without Windows Media Player.

The Commission fined Microsoft nearly €497 million for abusing its dominant position and demanded changes in its Windows operating system and other business practices. Microsoft appealed the Commission's ruling to the CFI. The case ended in 2007 when the CFI upheld the Commission's earlier decision and fine. The EU ordered Microsoft to unbundle its Windows operating system from its media player software. In 2009, a similar complaint was brought against Microsoft on the grounds that tying Internet Explorer to Windows distorted competition between web browsers. This time, Microsoft quickly agreed to eliminate the built-in browser.

In recent years, some member governments, especially France, have grown increasingly restless over the Commission's handling of competition issues, fearing that the Commission was not friendly to cross-border mergers and other practices designed to increase the global competitiveness of EU firms. Some feared that the Commission's competition powers were growing far beyond the member governments' original intention when they delegated authority to the Commission in this area. Moreover, EU and foreign firms were complaining about the economic analysis and methods used by the Commission to rule on competition cases. Pressure was on the Commission for more transparent (clear) and consistent economic analysis of the effects of restrictive practices, state aids, and mergers. As a result, the Commission proposed—and the Council approved—policy reforms in 2004. These reforms aimed to

- simplify and clarify Treaty rules to allow more certainty among firms about business practices that are inconsistent with or in breach of Competition Policy;
- apply more consistent economic criteria by the Commission in determining the economic effects of restrictive trade practices;
- increase the purview of national competition authorities in domestic market cases that do not pose a major threat to competition across the internal market; and
- enable the Commission to focus on the most egregious restrictive practices that impact cross-border trade.

The theory of historical institutionalism helps explain the exponential growth of the Commission's antitrust powers. Their scope became far greater than intended by some of the member states when they delegated authority years earlier. Principal–agent analysis, the core concept of the theory of rational choice institutionalism, focuses our attention on how member governments were tempted to take back some of the authority to govern Competition Policy delegated to the Commission in this sensitive field. In practice, however, member governments who tried to curtail the Commission's powers found that they still needed the Commission to administer the policy. Without fair and enforced competition rules, the internal market would begin to unravel. Therefore, Competition Policy had to be handled collectively and authority still needed to be delegated to the Commission.

In the end, the reforms actually strengthened the Commission's hand in enforcing the most egregious antitrust violations. Given the Commission's very limited human and financial resources to fully, consistently, and effectively conduct Competition Policy, it makes sense to encourage decisions that do not need to be made at EU level to remain with the national antitrust authorities (consistent with the principle and practice of subsidiarity).

Social Policy. The internal market is not just an area of producer interests and responsibilities. Social Policy, and its financial arm, the European Social Fund (ESF), were created by the Treaty to lend a labor or social dimension to the internal market.

The objectives are to promote social progress and employment, improve working conditions, and ensure equal pay for men and women, free movement of workers, and nondiscrimination in the workplace. The ESF was created to provide retraining and relocation for workers adversely affected by internal market developments. The member states thus delegated limited authority to the EU in labor issues, primarily on issues related to the free movement of labor. Most other areas of employment policy remained subject to the purview of the member governments.

The Commission initiates legislative proposals in the area of social policy. In doing so, it consults the EESC, the EP, and a wide variety of social partners (e.g., employer organizations and trade unions that operate at EU level). The Commission consults the EP in areas where the Council legislates on the basis of unanimity. Codecision occurs in areas where the Council legislates on the basis of QMV. The Council is assisted by COREPER and the working groups that constitute the comitology system.

The Treaty guarantee of free movement of labor meant that workers from one member state who seek work in another should not be discriminated against in terms of their employability, remuneration, and other work and employment conditions. On this basis, EU law has been extended to protect the rights of workers who cross borders to take jobs. Neofunctional theory explains the spillover from the establishment of the right of free movement of workers to the rights of workers who take jobs in member states other than their own.

In a modest move to protect workers' rights, the SEA allowed directives on occupational health and safety to be decided on the basis of QMV in the Council. This provision symbolized a shift in thinking on the place of workers both in the Treaty and in the internal market. It opened up social issues to supranational decisionmaking. However, it also undermined the principle that governments remain sovereign in areas of workers' rights. From this ceding of sovereignty on a single issue of workers' rights, the EU has incrementally extended its competence to several new areas of workers' rights.

The Commission proposed the Social Charter, a list of worker rights, adopted by the Council in 1989. It included provisions for the free movement of workers on the basis of equal treatment and opportunity, employment based on fair remuneration, improvement of working conditions, free association and collective bargaining, and protection for minors in the workplace. The right of association and the right to strike remained under the sole purview of the national governments. The Social Charter was appended to the TEU as a protocol; however, the British Conservative Government opted out of the Charter.

Three new Social Policy developments were codified in the Amsterdam Treaty. The Treaty incorporated the Social Charter into the *acquis* (the British Labour Government opted into the Charter) and provided for EU action against discrimination based on age, belief, disability, ethnicity, gender, sexual orientation, and race. The Nice Treaty authorized the Council to decide, on the basis of unanimity, when codecision can be used in such areas as protection of workers when their employment contracts are terminated and protection of the employment interests of non-EU workers.

The Treaty of Lisbon introduced new dimensions to EU Social Policy. For example, the Charter of Fundamental Rights stipulates certain workers' rights, many previously covered in the Social Charter, and the Lisbon Treaty guarantees these rights under EU law. The Lisbon Treaty also extends QMV to social services for migrant workers and empowers the European Council to decide to transfer decisionmaking from unanimity to QMV in some areas of Social Policy, such as protection of workers whose contracts are terminated.

The problem with EU Social Policy since the 1990s is that, despite the increase in new Treaty provisions to support the needs of workers, EU unemployment remains high, and workers in individual member states are still loath to move across borders to take jobs. The EU cannot legislate the removal of cultural preferences despite the right to free labor movement. Even when workers try to find work outside their home country, they face a plethora of national obstacles, as discussed in the next section.

Social Policy is an integral part of the internal market, but it would be naive to think that it has had fundamentally positive effects on employment. However, the existence of EU social legislation is still new and occurs in ways unintended by member governments who delegated the early grants of authority. We now discuss the gulf between the Treaty provisions that guarantee workers' rights and national policies governing the social terms of employment over which member governments retain legal purview. For example, member governments, not the EU, have sovereignty over workers' pay, the right of association, the right to impose lockouts, the right to strike, social security payments, and unemployment insurance.

Unemployment and Free Movement of Labor: Unemployment and economic competitiveness are among the EU's most trenchant problems. If labor can move freely in search of jobs, then in theory firms can enhance their comparative advantages by hiring workers with the skills they need. In practice, member governments and firms have manifold reasons to erect and maintain barriers to the free movement of labor. Most seek to protect domestic employment from social dumping. **Social dumping** refers to the fear in richer EU states that domestic employees will lose high-paid jobs with generous social benefits to workers from poorer EU states, who will migrate into the richer states to work for lower pay and fewer social benefits. For example, in the context of campaigning for ratification of the EU Constitutional Treaty in 2005, the icon of the "Polish plumber," as depicted in image 6.1, captured a humorous Eastern European response to fears that Eastern European workers would flood Western European labor markets.

However, unemployment, economic competitiveness, and economic growth cannot be addressed by closed labor markets. Without a free market for labor, labor costs rise, and EU products, which must reflect those costs, become priced out of European and global markets. Workers are comparable to producers. Producers sell products that consumers buy. Each producer sells and each consumer buys freely. Their commercial exchange is eased by a currency union that eliminates exchange-rate costs and risks. Workers, like producers, sell something—labor—but because there are obstacles to cross-border free movement of labor, workers in the internal market do not enjoy opportunities equivalent to those of producers and consumers.

The EU cannot ease its high rate of unemployment without ensuring free movement of labor. Yet free movement of labor cannot be achieved because there are clashes between national and EU laws and between member governments with market-oriented (neoliberal) preferences and those with social market (Keynesian) preferences. As previously discussed, the EU has sovereignty over the realm of free movement of

Image 6.1.   Polish Plumber (Polish Tourism Bureau in response to nega-tive rhetoric against cheap labor from Poland. Translation: "I'm staying in Poland; come one, come all"). Courtesy of the Polish Tourism Bureau

labor. The member states have sovereignty over the realm of social benefits associated with employment, such as welfare, health care, and housing.[6] Firms in each member state operate in a cultural-historical framework that shapes attitudes and practices with regard to such issues as commitment to lifelong employment and generous social benefits and protections for labor (as in France and Germany).

As stated above, the Treaty provides for the abolition of any discrimination against workers of the member states based on nationality with regard to employment, remu-neration, and other conditions of employment. Indeed, there have been EU regula-tions governing free movement of labor and equal treatment of nationals of one member state working in another member state since 1968. Not only does the Treaty guarantee the right of all EU citizens to work anywhere in the internal market, it also guarantees the rights of establishment—the right of individuals and firms to establish a firm in the territory of any of the other member states. EU legislation and ECJ rulings have also provided the legal bases for the mutual recognition of professional, educational, and trade qualifications. Nevertheless, it has proven much easier to facili-tate movement of persons travelling within the EU's passport-free zone (Schengen Accord) than to guarantee all EU citizens the right of establishment.

All EU member governments generally subscribe to the broad social market model of capitalism. However, they differ over the extent to which they are willing to expend public funds to retain consistently high levels of social benefits for their workers. Some neoliberal governments (e.g., in Britain and Poland) have supported rigorous market-driven economies with flexible and competitive employment practices and policies, lower taxes, and thus reduced government intervention in the economy in general. Keen to create new jobs and perform competitively on local and global scales, they still offer social protections and benefits for workers but at a level of support lower than, say, the governments of France and Germany.

France, Germany, Austria, and other member governments are concerned that the inflow of cheap labor will upset the delicate balance in their countries between employment and social benefits. These governments prefer and support social market economies with generous social protections and benefits. Now that the EU has expanded to include CEE countries, with their ample supplies of cheap labor, other member states fear social dumping. Such a fear is why some member governments and firms set up obstacles to free movement of labor in the EU.

Despite the Treaty's competence in the area of employment, the EU does not have the authority to force member governments to adopt common labor market policies. Social Policy has generally not been a major area of EU legislative action because it deals less with markets than with ideological preferences.[7] Given how structural unemployment is linked to labor market rigidities, what can the EU do, especially since it recognizes that member governments are not receptive to addressing these problems with any new legislative initiative on the scale of the 1992 Project? One response has been the Lisbon Strategy, discussed below, which was designed by the HOGS to focus on employment issues in relation to the clear need to increase European competitiveness. However, there has still been no substantial improvement in removing obstacles to the free movement of labor, although the pressure remains on governments to open up labor markets and generate new jobs.

Free Movement of Trade in Services: The Treaty guarantees free movement of trade in services. Trade in services has become the backbone of the EU's economy and the most important missing link in the completion of the internal market. Trade in services differs from trade in goods. Goods are visible. You can touch and see them—Belgian chocolates, Florentine leather, French wine, German coffeemakers, Polish crystal, and Valencia oranges. When offering a service, a vendor provides something a consumer needs that is not a good—banking, education, engineering, insurance, marketing, telecommunications, stocks and bonds, or tourism. Since trade in services refers to so many different kinds of services, it is impossible to make generalizations about whether the EU services market is open or closed.

On the one hand, national obstacles have remained fairly entrenched in some services: energy, public utilities, transportation, and retail banking and other financial services such as life insurance, savings accounts, investment, mortgage and consumer credit, and investment products. National control over financial issues and interests has meant that free trade in financial services has been slow to evolve. It is hard to integrate capital markets. On the other hand, some EU directives in banking and insurance have begun to open markets and some national markets have opened up to allow for cross-border competition in telecommunications. For example, much lower consumer telephone costs and more choices of services are now available.

There are three compelling reasons to open up trade in services. First, the service industry is the largest generator of jobs and wealth in the EU, so opening new markets generates employment. Second, the more choice businesses have in securing bank loans at competitive interest rates, the more economic growth is stimulated. Cheaper capital drives economic growth, especially for small and medium-size firms. Pooling liquidity, promoting competition and efficiency, and reducing the costs of doing business are all important for the success of the internal market. Competition in the internal market for financial services also encourages consumers to search for and obtain the best interest rates possible for their savings and other investments. Third, the internal market cannot prosper if its largest economic sector is not open to trade and competition on a European scale. The EU loses economic competitiveness, economic growth, and comparative advantage to outside countries with large integrated service sectors. For example, it costs much less to trade in stocks in the United States than it does in Europe. If the EU is to be in a position to negotiate with the United States and other major traders in services and influence global regulatory developments, it needs to have a more integrated internal market for trade in services.

The EU has responded to the fragmentation of the internal market in services with two initiatives proposed by the Commission and endorsed by the Council in 2000: the Financial Services Action Plan (FSAP) and the Lisbon Strategy. The **Financial Services Action Plan** is a cluster of forty-two legislative and other initiatives to open up the financial services market. To integrate the member states' financial services markets, FSAP aims to

- remove market and regulatory barriers that block cross-border trade in financial services (e.g., brokerage houses, banks, insurance companies);
- increase consumers' choices in procuring banking, investment, mortgage, insurance, pension, and other financial services;
- reduce the cost of capital, already too high in the EU due to a fragmented and inefficient financial market;
- help firms and governments raise capital in amounts and at rates similar to those found in the United States; and
- encourage free flow of finance into the EU in order to reduce dependence on foreign sources, particularly the United States, in raising investment capital.

Most of the FSAP directives and regulations have been enacted by the EU (e.g., passage of EU Directive on cross-border takeovers), and many experts suggest that the EU is finally moving closer to an integrated financial market. There has been an increase in the integration of corporate and government bond markets and some integration of equity markets. There is evidence of increases in cross-border flows of venture capital and private equity finances. The introduction of the euro encouraged integration of financial markets since it eliminated currency risks and conversion costs. Differences in interest rates across the internal market are now similar to differences within the member states, thus facilitating integration of money markets.[8]

However, in individual member states, obstacles remain to the free movement of services provided by the retail banking industry. Since the positive benefits of implementing the FSAP initiatives may not be experienced by the national banking industries for several years, they are reluctant to sacrifice now for benefits later. One major obstacle to free movement of retail banking services is the fact that more bank mergers occur within rather than across state borders. This may be due to national competition authorities who eschew cross-border mergers to protect national champions. Retail banks continue to operate in mostly protected home markets, charging what they wish for services in the home market, with no competition from the services of banks from other member states.

FSAP is now in the consolidation stage, but governments are slow to transpose FSAP directives and regulations into national legislation. It has proven easier to agree upon and enact new rules than it has been to implement them. Once again, the Commission as watchdog over the transposition process is critical: it tries to "name and shame" governments slow to transpose.

Recognizing the problems of unemployment and competitiveness in local and global markets and the remaining obstacles to completing the internal market, the HOGS launched the **Lisbon Strategy** in 2000 with two ambitious goals: (1) make the EU by 2010 the world's most dynamic, knowledge-based (information technology) economy; and (2) address the problem of unemployment while cultivating sustainable growth. The Lisbon Strategy lists target areas for action by member governments, but the list of things to do—for example, spend more on R&D, support investment in information technology, and reduce state aid—is no different from what the EU has been advocating since the 1980s. The Commission assesses and publishes progress reports on the individual member states' implementation of the Lisbon Strategy. It also makes recommendations, subject to approval by the Council.

Is the Lisbon Strategy too ambitious and impracticable? A midterm review of the Lisbon Strategy in 2005, led by former Dutch Prime Minister Willem Kok and his expert working group, cited the member states for failing to take sufficient action and criticized the strategy for being overloaded with targets, improperly coordinated, and thus lacking prioritization. The Kok Report was a wake-up call to member governments to redouble their efforts to achieve the Lisbon objectives.

The Lisbon Strategy is an acknowledgment that the internal market is malfunctioning in some areas, but it has not driven the kind of excitement and commitment by the EU bodies and member states to revamp the internal market as did the 1992 Project. Some are critical of the Barroso Commission for not taking the kind of initiative that Delors took in generating support for the 1992 Project and for EMU. Others lay blame on the member governments themselves, who have no appetite for any new major legislative initiative to open up trade in services.

Rather than support a major legislative initiative to address EU competitiveness and employment problems, the HOGS introduced the Open Method of Coordination (OMC) in 2000. OMC was designed to facilitate agreements on broad principles and goals related to the EU's most difficult economic problems. Governments are then expected to implement common agreements on a national basis without the need to enact and implement new EU legislation. Although the Commission is charged with overseeing the OMC process, the ECJ has no powers of judicial review. This informal decisionmaking mechanism seems to be preferred by member governments and the Commission over formal legislation, but it remains to be seen if OMC will facilitate desired outcomes.

Common Commercial Policy

ORIGINS, OBJECTIVES, AND TIMELINE

Just when the member states eliminated tariffs among themselves in 1968, they replaced their own external tariffs with the external tariffs of the EC, known as the Common External Tariff (CET). The EC thus assumed sovereignty over an area traditionally reserved to states. By extending sovereignty to the EC over the handling of external tariffs, the member states also conceded the right to negotiate and conclude trade agreements with nonmember states and international organizations. As far back as the 1960s, the EC began negotiating and concluding international trade agreements, including the Kennedy Round of GATT multilateral trade negotiations. In so doing, it took the first steps in establishing the Common Commercial Policy (CCP), a core supranational policy of the union.

The EU not only levies tariffs but is responsible for collecting the revenues earned from import levies, which in turn are used as a source of income to meet EU costs. Levying and collecting taxes as revenue is a bastion of state sovereignty. Why then have member governments surrendered sovereignty to the union to set import levies? The member states who join the union reckon that the loss of sovereignty to set tariffs and quotas is outweighed by the considerable economic gains. Member states join the union so that their firms may enjoy preferential access to a large free internal market—access not available to outsiders, who pay a tariff or meet a quota to enter. It would defeat the preferential status of member state firms if cheap imports were to enter the union from the lowest tariff point of access. Once the product of a low-cost external producer entered the union, that product would move freely within the union and possibly undercut the existing market share of a union producer. However, outside firms may enjoy the same preferential access to the internal market as insiders if they establish a manufacturing presence inside the union. Since foreign firms are treated as European ones inside the union, they pay no tariffs on intra-EU trade. Having a CET for the world's largest internal market attracts foreign firms to invest inside the EU.

FORMULATION AND EXECUTION

The European Council sets broad guidelines for the CCP and approves major international trade decisions. The Commission negotiates international trade agreements based on a Council mandate. The Council has sole power to enact international trade treaties. QMV is the standard decisionmaking mechanism in the CCP under the Treaty. However, the Council acts with unanimity in the areas of trade in services, intellectual property rights, and foreign direct investment. The Commission implements external trade agreements, such as those that arise from negotiations at the WTO, where the EU is a voting member. On WTO agreements, the EP has no veto power because codecision is not extended to the EP in this area. Instead, the EP is engaged by the Council in the consultation procedure, where it has the opportunity to influence legislation. Yet the Treaty does grant veto power to the EP on EU association and certain other trade agreements with third countries. The ECJ also rules on the CCP. Its rulings over time have generally strengthened EU competence to act in external trade on behalf of the member states. Readers will recall, however, that in Chapter 3 we learned that the Commission and the member governments share competence to negotiate WTO agreements on trade in services and on trade-related aspects of intellectual property.

KEY ELEMENTS

The CCP refers to the needs, instruments, objectives, and interests of the EU with regard to bilateral and multilateral trade negotiations, agreements, and actions. The EU is an export-driven economy. For example, it depends on export trade as a higher percentage of GDP than the United States. Thus, it needs to open up new markets around the world. Since the EU cannot expect to enhance exports without opening its own market to imports, it engages in market-opening negotiations with trade partners. The instruments of the CCP include setting tariffs and quotas with third countries or international institutions. Tariffs and quotas are designed to offer degrees of protection for and preferential treatment of EU firms in their own home market. Without the CCP/CET there would be no internal market. The member governments through the Treaty delegated power to the Commission to restrict imports if it finds that (1) foreign governments or firms are dumping goods on the EU market at below market prices (anti-dumping duty case); or (2) foreign firms' goods exported to the EU are aided by government subsidies (countervailing duty case). Import levies for agriculture are used to keep cheap imports from entering the union and undermining EU price supports for agricultural products.

The EU's competence to regulate the CET is the core instrument of the Common Commercial Policy. The CCP consists of the EU's international trade and trade-related agreements with bilateral and multilateral partners. As a contracting party at the WTO, the EU negotiates and concludes multilateral trade agreements. The EU also has bilateral trade agreements with third countries: industrial free trade agreements, association agreements, Euro–Med partnership accords, Stabilization and Association Accords (SAAs), Partnership and Cooperation Agreements (PCAs), association accords with former Soviet bloc states, economic partnership agreements, and interregional accords.

An industrial free trade agreement eliminates two-way industrial tariffs between the EU and a nonmember state. The EU has industrial free trade accords with each of the four members of EFTA (Iceland, Liechtenstein, Norway, and Switzerland) and with countries outside Europe (e.g., Chile and Mexico). The EU and the EFTA states, minus Switzerland, are members of the European Economic Area (EEA). In this area, the EFTA states agree to implement EU internal market legislation. The EU is negotiating bilateral free trade accords with India and South Korea.

An association agreement is a political and economic framework within which tariffs are reciprocally cut, the EU offers development assistance, and a political dialogue is instituted. Some association accords provide for the progressive establishment of a customs union and eventual membership. Turkey has an association accord with the EU. A Euro-Med accord establishes over time industrial free trade between the EU and nonmember Mediterranean states (e.g., Egypt and Lebanon). These accords together form what the EU refers to as the European Neighborhood Policy (ENP), designed to enhance economic development and political stability in the areas that surround the EU. The EU offers significant nonreciprocal tariff preferences (cuts) on agricultural imports. The Euro–Med accords provide for significant political dialogue between the signatories as well as for cooperation against such security threats as crime, terrorism, and proliferation of weapons of mass destruction (WMD). In 2009, the Euro-Med Partnership was relaunched as the Union for the Mediterranean, which comprises the EU and 16 non-EU states around the Mediterranean basin.

A Stabilization and Association Accord is a form of association between the EU and individual Western Balkan states. SAAs aim to bring these states closer to the EU with the possibility of future membership, while cultivating security, stability, democratic government, and economic growth in the region. The EU offers favorable terms of trade and engages these states in a diplomatic, political, and security dialogue. Cooperation with regard to anticrime and antiterrorism is emphasized. The EU has SAAs with Albania, Croatia, and Macedonia and signed but not ratified accords with Bosnia-Herzegovina (BiH), Montenegro, and Serbia. Some EU member states, the Netherlands in particular, have delayed ratification of the SAA with Serbia. Although Belgrade cooperated in the arrest of Radovan Karadzic and his extradition to The Hague to face charges of war crimes, Serbia is under pressure to arrest and extradite Ratko Mladic.

The EU has four additional types of foreign trade and political agreements under the CCP.

1. A Partnership and Cooperation Agreement promotes democratic and economic development in former Soviet-bloc countries (e.g., Russia, Kazakhstan, and Uzbekistan). However, PCAs do not provide for future EU membership.
2. In its newly developed Eastern Partnership initiative, the EU seeks to negotiate and conclude association agreements with six former Soviet republics: Armenia, Azerbaijan, Belarus, Georgia, Moldova, and Ukraine. The agreements will offer substantial financial aid and preferential terms of trade with the aim of cultivating close political and economic integration. However, as with PCAs, these new association accords will not provide for future EU membership.
3. The EU is negotiating economic and partnership accords governing trade relations and political cooperation with the African, Caribbean, and Pacific countries under the rubric of the Cotonou Agreement.
4. An interregional accord binds the EU and another regional organization into common initiatives. The EU has sought to negotiate accords with members of the Andean Community, the Association of Southeast Asian Nations (ASEAN), the Common Market of the South, and the Gulf Cooperation Council (GCC).

As much as the CCP is an instrument of EU trade policy, it is also an important instrument of the EU external relations and policies (taken up in Chapter 7) with regard to

- fostering foreign economic and social development—the EU waives import levies for the world's poorest states by offering the Generalized System of Preferences program;
- reducing or eliminating tariffs for countries in political turmoil (Afghanistan) or engaged in the fight against terrorism (Pakistan);
- supporting human rights and nonproliferation by conditioning Euro-Med and other foreign trade agreements on signatories' respect for human rights and commitment to nonproliferation (Syria);
- imposing trade sanctions, such as embargoes, or blocking preferential trade terms, with respect to countries such as China, Cuba, Myanmar, Serbia, Uzbekistan, and Zimbabwe who are determined to have breached international human rights laws and democratic norms;[9] and
- lifting trade sanctions for countries such as Libya, Serbia, and South Africa, whose governments no longer breach international legal commitments and norms.

As the world's largest importer and exporter, and the world's largest host to and provider of foreign investment, the EU is a global commercial player. As we noted above, it can offer trade benefits and impose trade sanctions that affect many of the world's countries and regions. The CET is the primary instrument of the CCP as the EU conducts international trade negotiations and relationships. A customs union requires a CET to exist, but was it an intended, unintended, or unexpected consequence of the establishment of the CET when the EU extended its tariff powers to other areas of international affairs? Institutionalists would claim that the Commission expanded its scope for agency by applying its CET to other areas of international affairs. Neofunctionalists would claim that there was a spillover from the functioning of the internal market to the outside world.

Monetary Policy

ORIGINS, OBJECTIVES, AND TIMELINE

Monetary Policy refers to the formulation and execution of decisions related to the regulation of the common currency. The European Central Bank (ECB) sets interest rates that affect the supply of money in the internal market. The Eurozone member states are obliged by common accord to practice fiscal prudence in order to keep budget deficits from burgeoning, in order to restrain inflation, and thus maintain the value and stability of the euro. The Council and Commission coordinate macroeconomic policy of the member governments and engage in surveillance of their budget deficits.

After the internal market, monetary policy is the most important supranational policy arena of the EU. The road to currency union has been long and winding. The transfer of sovereignty over Monetary Policy from member governments to the EU began with the entry into force of the TEU in 1993. The TEU provided for the progressive establishment of the economic and monetary union (EMU), culminating in 2002 when the euro replaced national currencies. Sixteen EU states have joined the

Eurozone, of which eleven were charter members. Of the older EU members, Britain, Denmark, and Sweden have opted to remain outside. Of the new members who joined the EU in 2004 and 2007, four have joined the Eurozone: Slovenia in 2007, Malta and Cyprus in 2008, and Slovakia in 2009. In 2009, the Eurozone population reached 339 million.

The establishment of the EMU was a momentous event in the history of European integration. The power to print and regulate money and set interest rates has been a bastion of state sovereignty for hundreds of years. Not only did the Eurozone member states relinquish these powers, they may no longer employ monetary policy to address periods of growth (restraining inflation by raising interest rates) and periods of recession (lowering interest rates). But in agreeing to monetary union, the member states also stood to gain economically.

EMU eliminated the costs of converting currencies in the exchange of goods and services and ended the uncertainty of fluctuating exchange rates among the member countries. For example, when the Finnish cell-phone manufacturer Nokia contracts with a Spanish importer of its product, it need not be concerned that the appreciation of the Finnish currency against the Spanish currency will erode profit margins between the time of the contract and the delivery of the goods. Additionally, the cost of converting Finnish into Spanish currency is eliminated. The spur to business—the value added to competitiveness—not only strengthens producers and benefits consumers, but helps make the EU more competitive relative to other large internal markets already equipped with their own currency unions.

Although the Treaty of Rome was silent on EMU, it did make macroeconomic policy coordination a matter of common concern. It would have made little sense to call for monetary union before the establishment of the internal market. Once the customs union was firmly established, a functional spillover from the internal market policy to monetary policy was inevitable. The idea of monetary union dates back to the 1960s and first took the form of the 1970 Werner Plan, which called for monetary union by 1980. However, the Werner Plan was derailed by the pernicious effects of the recessions of the 1970s, brought on by oil cartel price hikes and the collapse of the Bretton Woods fixed exchange system. The Bretton Woods international monetary system enabled the EC member states to enjoy the benefits of monetary stability without having to establish their own monetary union. The EC response to the collapse of Bretton Woods was to stabilize the relationships among its members' currencies by creating the snake-in-the-tunnel, an informal grid designed to keep fluctuations to a minimum. The snake remained outside the Treaty framework, and members joined and left on a voluntary basis.

The 1979 **European Monetary System** (EMS) established for the participants an institutionalized narrow grid within which currencies could fluctuate between a ceiling and a floor. At first, the margin of fluctuation in the Exchange Rate Mechanism (ERM) was just 2.25 percent (the margin was wider for Italy); in 1992–1993 the ERM was widened to 15 percent when the member states could no longer maintain such a narrow margin of fluctuation in a time of turmoil in foreign exchange markets. Indeed, in late 1992, the British pound, which had just entered the ERM earlier in the year, departed from it along with the Italian lire.

Overall, the EMS worked well to stabilize currency fluctuations from 1979 to 1992. The central banks of the EMS states intervened in currency markets. For example, if the Italian lire fell in value below the floor (which it did), reserve currencies would be purchased by the central banks to lift the value of the lire back into the grid. If the German mark rose in value above the ceiling (which it did), reserve currencies would be sold by central banks to bring the value of the mark down within the grid. However, in EMS, exchange-rate fluctuations remained (although within a narrower range), as did conversion costs.

EMS provided an element of monetary stability, although it remained completely outside the Treaty structure. In 1992–1993, during the period of turmoil in foreign exchange markets, the member states did not make a complete break with the ERM. As one of the criteria for joining the EMU, the TEU required that a candidate would have to participate successfully in the ERM for at least two years. Eight years after the creation of the EMS and ERM, the SEA stimulated new interest in monetary union, which spilled over from the momentum to engage in further economic integration during that era. With a renewed optimism about what the Europeans could do, as a result of the success of the 1992 Project, French President d'Estaing, German Chancellor Schmidt, and Commission President Delors adroitly built support for EMU beginning in the late 1980s. Their work culminated in the Delors Report on EMU in 1989. However, one huge impediment to facilitating cross-border trade flows remained: fluctuating exchange rates.

Member governments recognized that, if the monetary union were to work, it would need the Commission to play the role of watchdog—to oversee its functioning—and the ECB to regulate interest rates independently of the national central banks. Such delegation of power by national governments to EU institutions to ensure compliance and to provide for impartial monitoring is predicted by theorists of rational choice institutionalism who focus on principal–agent relations. However, there was more to the EMU's launch than reducing national transaction costs.

Political and security interests of national governments were also played out at the IGC where the member states negotiated the TEU. France not only wanted to further anchor a unified Germany in the EU at a time of epic change, but also wanted the Franco-German relationship to remain the EU's driving engine. Germany wanted its EU partners' endorsement of the unification of East Germany with West Germany and the integration of East Germany into the EU. Monetary union, therefore, was not just about institutional and individual agency and neofunctional spillover: it was also about the pursuit of national political interests in a changing world.

The TEU introduced three stages of EMU. Stage one (1990–1993) was the establishment of a free movement of capital and closer coordination among national economic policies and central banks. Stage two (1994–1998) was the creation of the European Monetary Institute, forerunner of the ECB. Stage three (1999–2002) was the establishment of the ECB and fixed exchange rates, the introduction of the euro first for cashless transactions (while national currencies remained in circulation) and then to replace national currencies. The TEU set out the criteria for the EU member states to join the Eurozone. Under the **Maastricht Convergence Criteria**, annual national budget deficits must not exceed 3 percent of GDP; total national debt must not exceed 60 percent of GDP; exchange rates must stay within the ERM range of fluctuation for at least two years before the euro's introduction; inflation must not exceed more than 1.5 percentage points over the average of the three best performing member states; and long-term interest rates must not be more than 2 percent above the average of the lowest three performing member states. The Maastricht Convergence Criteria were primarily designed to establish the conditions for each member state that wished to join the EMU.

There was concern, expressed especially by Germany in 1997, that member states who met the Maastricht Convergence Criteria and joined the EMU remain faithful to their commitments to fiscal prudence in order to strengthen the euro by keeping down government debt and inflation. Haunted by memories of hyperinflation, Germany had no intention of replacing its strong and stable Deutschmark with a weak and unstable euro. Germany wanted to compel its EMU partners not to stray from prudent fiscal spending. In response, EMU members agreed in 1997 to the **Stability and Growth Pact** (SGP). The SGP requires members to keep their budget deficits below 3 percent of GDP to (1) encourage and sustain convergence of the Eurozone member economies; (2) prevent a situation where one or more member states allows excessive deficits to undermine confidence in the stability of the Eurozone economies; and (3) discourage inflation. Errant governments who breach the 3 percent threshold are called on to provide plans for reducing excessive public spending. If that fails, the Council may impose punitive fines, which are explained in the next section.

FORMULATION AND EXECUTION

The European System of Central Banks (ESCB) is the name given formally to the EMU, but it refers technically to the ECB and national central banks of the EU. Decisionmaking in monetary policy occurs in Frankfurt and Brussels. In Frankfurt, the EU's independent Central Bank, the ECB, monitors the money supply in the Eurozone (the countries that use the euro) and sets interest rates, which affect the supply of money available in the Eurozone countries. The Lisbon Treaty officially establishes the existence of the Euro Group—the informal monthly meetings of the Economic and Finance Ministers for the Eurozone member states (currently chaired by Jean-Claude Juncker). Non-Eurozone EU members retain their own national competence in monetary policy. The ECB's enormous supranational power raises concerns among some of the member states, particularly France.

The first concern is with the legitimacy of the ECB. Few doubt that a central bank needs to be politically independent of governments in order to objectively maintain the value and stability of the euro and to cap inflation. Governments and their politicians know that they cannot trust themselves to do the hard work of monitoring and regulating the supply of money in prudent fashion. That said, the ECB has a great deal of political power for an agency independent of EU bodies and thus far removed from the EU polity. Moreover, during a period of recession, some governments would argue that it is politically imperative that the ECB lower interest rates to stimulate economic activity. Since the ECB is independent, it does not take orders from the Eurozone national capitals.

The second concern has to do with the problematic fit between ECB interest rates set uniformly for the whole of the EU and the needs of some countries (or their regions) that are in periods of recession or of growth. As discussed in Chapter 3, OCA theorists predict that a currency union cannot work or work well if members do not experience complementary business cycles. For instance, if Ireland is experiencing economic growth, it does not need to have low interest rates, but if Germany is in recession, Germany does need low interest rates. However, Germany cannot reduce interest rates because only the ECB can do that. Germany could increase governmental spending to jumpstart the recessionary economy, but that could exacerbate inflation and cause Germany to breach the SGP.

Whereas in Frankfurt money supply is regulated by the setting of interest rates completely independent of the rest of the EU polity, in Brussels, the Commission and the Council conduct surveillance of the SGP to ensure that the euro reflects sound budgetary spending policies in the member states. Ecofin is responsible for surveillance of the SGP, including monitoring members' budgetary policy and public finances and the legal and international aspects of the euro. The member states who have adopted the euro usually meet a day before Ecofin Council meetings and deal exclusively with EMU issues. When Ecofin votes on EMU-related issues, non-Eurozone member states do not take part in the vote.

In 1997, the European Council adopted Ecofin's resolution on the two regulations that together constitute the legal basis of the SGP and apply to all the member states of the EU:

- the "early warning procedure": a system of multilateral surveillance of the SGP's budget provisions and coordination of economic policies to discourage breaches of the 3 percent cap on public deficits as a percentage of GDP; a member state at risk of exceeding the deficit cap receives an early warning from the Council based on a Commission proposal (prior to the Lisbon Treaty, the Commission warning was a recommendation). For example, in 2004, the Commission recommended that the Council issue an early warning to Italy;
- the "excessive deficit procedure": when a member state's budget deficit actually exceeds 3 percent of GDP (e.g., in 2008 the Council adopted a decision on the existence of an excessive deficit in the UK and issued recommendations to remedy the situation).

The Commission as good cop/bad cop is responsible for monitoring the SGP's implementation. The Council is responsible for acting on the Commission's recommendation. It may accept or reject a Commission recommendation to activate either an early warning procedure or an excessive deficit procedure. All EU members, regardless of their membership in the Eurozone, are required by the SGP to submit annual reports to Ecofin on their budgetary objectives; these reports serve as the basis for multilateral surveillance by the Commission and Council.

If the public debt of a Eurozone member moves up toward the 3 percent ceiling, the Council may, acting on a Commission proposal, prescribe remedial action and, failing that, activate the early warning procedure. If the Council determines, based on a Commission proposal, that an excessive deficit has arisen, it issues recommendations to the concerned member state and calls on it to take action to bring down the deficit. If the member state in question does not comply with the Council recommendation, the Council may impose sanctions. Initially, the penalty takes the form of a deposit that will be converted into a fine if the excessive deficit is not reversed within two years. No fines have yet been imposed. It requires a stretch of the imagination to envision the Council imposing punitive damages on one of its own members, but the mere specter of doing so could, in time, apply sufficient pressure on an errant state to make it reduce its public debt spending.

KEY ELEMENTS

The member governments delegated authority to the Commission to conduct surveillance of the SGP's provisions and report findings to Ecofin. Theorists of rational choice institutionalism explain and predict why governments delegate elements of their sovereign authority to common bodies. In this arena, the common bodies are the Commission, which monitors, reports, and recommends, and the ECJ, which issues rulings. Eurozone member governments delegate to reduce their transaction costs of doing business in the currency union. However, powerful member governments may seek to take back the authority granted to the EU bodies when they do not like the results of that delegation.

For example, when the Commission reported to the Council in 2003 that France and Germany were in breach of the excessive deficit agreements, the Council did not act on the Commission recommendation. Instead, it decided in November 2003 to temporarily suspend the excessive deficit procedures of the SGP. The Commission took the Council to the ECJ with the complaint that the Council's nonadoption of the Commission proposals on excessive deficit procedures for France and Germany was not allowed. The Court ordered the Council to reverse the suspension of the excessive deficit procedure. The Commission then dispatched a communication to the Council in September 2004 providing "clarification" of the deficit situation in France and Germany. The Commission noted that because both countries still had an excessive budget deficit, measures to reverse the situation were imperative. The Commission also called for the reform of SGP to make it more flexible without losing its purpose of fostering fiscal prudence to support a stable euro.

The Council decided in 2005 to revise the SGP on the basis of the Commission proposal, in order to take into account special difficulties members may have in meeting their commitment to the 3 percent threshold. In other words, the member governments agreed to save the SGP by easing its requirements. It had become apparent that, according to a strict interpretation, the SGP's debt ceiling was being breached by France and Germany. The members tried to keep the SGP by making it more flexible to help governments facing low or negative economic growth or increasing short term costs arising from social security reform and high unemployment. A more flexible interpretation of the SGP debt ceiling would be acceptable so long as governments brought down deficit spending under 3 percent during better economic times. Governments agreed to the value of the surveillance system of the SGP and the usefulness of peer pressure and support in order to ensure the integrity, certainty, and effectiveness of the SGP. Flexibility is permitted in exceptional circumstances when

- there is a severe economic downturn;
- pension reform is under way;
- governments are increasing spending in areas such as R&D in ways consistent with the goals of the Lisbon Strategy;

- governments are called on to increase spending for programs abroad that deal with international security and stability and humanitarian disasters; and/or
- governments under economic duress reduce deficit spending to below 3 percent in times of economic growth.

With this new commitment to a more flexible SGP, the member governments also agreed to strengthen Commission surveillance of those members asking for special consideration when they breach the 3 percent threshold. If countries breach the cutoff, the Commission and Council assess the situation in order to recommend action for governments to bring deficits down. Levying fines is still possible in the SGP but unlikely. Is the reform a setback? Yes and no. Yes, because fiscal prudence restrains inflation and lends confidence to the value of the euro as an international reserve currency. No, because if fiscal prudence means a straitjacket in which governments cannot increase spending in the short term to address exceptional circumstances, there is no choice for them but to break with the SGP in defense of vital national economic interests.

It is still too soon to ascertain if the reform is a fundamental retreat from the members' 1997 commitment to fiscal responsibility for a strong and stable common currency. In the end, however, while member governments give and take back delegated authority, they must abide by the ECJ ruling as long as they want the euro to survive intact. They must also continue to depend on the Commission to monitor compliance.

The economic logic of monetary union is something scholars debate. Some economists maintain that member states of an internal market should not move to the next stage of economic integration—a currency union—until they constitute an optimum currency union (introduced in Chapter 3). An OCA would include countries that (1) have extensive economic integration and no longer need to rely on monetary policy—the use of interest rates—to address periods of economic downturn; and (2) have complementary business cycles. Some argue that EU members had yet to form an OCA in the 1990s and should have waited until they formed a currency union. Others argue that several EU members, especially the Rhineland countries, were advantaged by creating a currency union in the 1990s because they did constitute an OCA and thus monetary union made sense. However, economics were not the only explanation for the move from common market to monetary union.

The EU struggles to be an effective monetary union in the absence of a full economic union. The ECB sets interest rates, but when they are high, money supply is tight. A tight supply of money stifles job-creating and tax-revenue-creating investment in production of goods and services. When the EU has high interest rates, high unemployment, and low growth, the Eurozone member governments are caught between the constraints of money supply controlled by the ECB and (1) increases in government spending to address needs such as R&D; and (2) the imperative of the Lisbon Strategy to generate economic growth and competitiveness and raise employment levels. Where governments have sovereignty in fiscal policy, they cannot raise taxes too high, because that would stifle investment and dampen employment.

The recession triggered by the global banking and financial crisis beginning in 2008 put an enormous strain on the EU and its member states to stimulate economic growth by fiscal means and stabilize the banking industry without undermining the discipline of the SGP and the rules of the internal market, especially in the area of competition policy. In 2008–2010, the Commission and Council strove to find the right balance between member state deficit spending during the recession and a more flexible SGP. The ECB faced its biggest crisis since the introduction of the euro. Banks needed an injection of capital to stabilize them and allow them to do their job: finance the economy. Capital was also needed to stimulate business activity and consumer spending. In response, member governments agreed to new fiscal stimulus packages (that amounted to 1.5 percent of the EU's GDP) from the EU and national budgets. The ECB judiciously and slowly lowered interest rates while keeping a close eye on the return of inflation. The EIB substantially increased its budget for loans to distressed industries, including a loan to the car industry to manufacture "greener" cars.

Since financial regulation of the banking industry remains largely in the hands of the national authorities, the member governments were at first inclined to respond with domestic solutions. The EU is not organized to deal with banking and financial supervision. However, as the banking crisis grew, member governments began to recognize the value of using a coordinated approach to avoid upsetting the functioning and rules of the internal market and those of the SGP. It was not easy to bring together divergent national policies. Nevertheless, in 2009, the Commission adopted a report, based on the recommendation of an EU task force on EU financial supervision, that called for new EU financial regulations under the ECB's auspices to supervise banking institutions and monitor systemic risks with an early warning system.

Agriculture

ORIGINS, OBJECTIVES, AND TIMELINE

Agricultural policy, like the CCP, is a foundation block of European integration: it looms large in how the Rome Treaty came about. With memories of food shortages and starvation after the two world wars, Europeans were keen at the time of the Rome Treaty to cultivate food security. EC charter members wanted to support food production, but France in particular wanted duty-free access to the West German agricultural market. West Germany wanted duty-free access to the French industrial market. Part of the compact that resulted in the Rome Treaty, EU food policy has grown to become the most integrated—and most criticized—of the EU policies.

The Treaty established the objectives of a Common Agricultural Policy (CAP): support and increase farm income and production, retain a rural economy, and ensure food supplies at reasonable prices. Council decisions in 1962 began to establish common market organizations for individual farm products. These common market organizations have come to constitute the instruments of the CAP. Farmers were guaranteed minimum prices to ensure a return on production costs and a profit, were protected from cheap imports from outside the EC by variable import levies, and were given export subsidies to bridge the gulf between high internal price supports and the much lower world market prices.

FORMULATION AND EXECUTION

The European Council sets overall farm policy guidelines, but day-to-day functioning is handled by the Commission, which drafts and executes legislation (price supports, production quotas). Whereas the Council (of Agricultural Ministers) had decided on CAP legislative proposals on the basis of consensus in the past, the Lisbon Treaty provides for decisionmaking on the basis of QMV. The Council is assisted not by COREPER but by the Special Committee on Agriculture (SCA). Groups representing farmers, such as the Committee of Agricultural Organizations (COPA), are consulted before legislation is enacted. COPA's large and influential staff in Brussels lobbies the EU in support of the CAP. For each area of agricultural support, a regulatory or management committee works with the Commission. CAP costs are financed by the EU budget through the European Agricultural Guidance and Guarantee Fund (EAGGF).

One of the major improvements in the union's democratic governance was brought about by the Lisbon Treaty, which gave the EP co-equal decisionmaking authority with the Council in the CAP. Thus, prior to the Lisbon Treaty, the EP had no codecision powers in the CAP, which meant that this huge and costly policy area of the internal market was not subject to the EU's system of checks and balances and was a step farther removed from public accountability. A critic opined that this was an "example of what happens where there is no real link between EU institutions and EU citizens. In such a circle it is easy for governments to use the Commission as a scapegoat for decisions that they really do not want to take."[10] The issues that confront reform of the CAP are discussed below.

KEY ELEMENTS

The CAP features a common market organization for each of the farm products covered by EU farm policy (e.g., beef, cereals, cotton, dairy, fruits and vegetables, milk, potatoes, poultry, rice, sugar, and wine). A common market organization sets out common rules concerning free internal trade (elimination of intra-EU trade barriers), import levies/quotas (which give EU farmers preferential access to the EU market), competition rules, and support mechanisms (production subsidies, income support). Support of farm income has consisted of three instruments, all now subject to reform.

- *Price Supports*: Traditionally, to support farm income, the EU guarantees farmers minimum prices by buying their products when the price falls below the minimum price. The EU either stores these products until prices rise (at which time they are released into the market), exports them at subsidized prices, or donates them as food aid. Since high price supports have encouraged costly overproduction, the EU is moving away from price supports to income supports or is limiting the amount of production subject to price supports for farmers.
- *Import Levies and Quotas*: The EU imposes levies and quotas on food imports from outside the EU when world food prices fall below EU price supports. Import protection gives EU farmers preferential access to the internal market.

- *Agricultural Export Subsidies*: When EU farm prices rise above world market prices, the EU uses subsidies to pay farmers who export the difference between world and EU prices.

The CAP is controversial because (1) vital national interests are at stake in the politics of food and in the policy's redistribution of wealth; (2) consumers pay more for their food as a percentage of income than consumers in the United States; (3) CAP price supports and subsidies trigger large high-price surpluses that are costly to store or export at subsidized prices; and (4) EU export subsidies drive down world market prices or cause other farm exporting countries to subsidize their exports as well, leading to farm export subsidy wars.

The CAP is the "beauty and beast" of the EU. For some, the beauty in the CAP is that it has met its objectives through supranational integration. The CAP is an article of faith and a way of life for those who most benefit from it. For these believers and beneficiaries, the CAP has resulted in ample food supplies and sufficient income to keep enough farmers on the land to maintain a rural economy. Insofar as a rural economy and locally grown food are intrinsic to the culture of the member states, the CAP helps maintain European culture. Although the CAP is costly, its supporters point to a reduction in costs as a percentage of the total annual EU budget from a high of 70 percent in the 1980s to 45 percent in the 2000s. Supporters also point to the positive development by which farm support is changing from production to income in order to keep farmers farming and maintain rural economies without spurring unwanted overproduction.

For others, the beast in the CAP is the economic inefficiency and wastefulness of subsidized food production. This results in surpluses costly to store or export at subsi-

Image 6.2.   Dairy Farmer in Belgium. Courtesy of the Audiovisual Library of the European Commission

dized prices. In addition, environmentalists are concerned that incentives to overproduce lead farmers to overutilize land, eroding soil and depleting nutrients. EU taxpayers foot the bill and consumers pay higher prices for farm produce. Many have argued for a reform of farm policy that would replace incentives to overproduce with direct farm income payments. However, some opponents claim that direct farm income support will cost nearly as much as support for farm income linked to guaranteed prices. The beast in the CAP is that its high costs drain productive resources from areas where the EU needs to invest to be competitive, such as R&D in information technology and biotechnology (a main goal of the Lisbon Strategy). Opponents also point to the fact that large and prosperous EU farmers benefit much more from CAP price and income supports and subsidies than do smaller and poorer farmers.

It is very hard politically to reform the CAP. Although the EU's own farm population is declining, the political power of farm groups remains strong. Governments are heavily influenced by farm interests, and pro-agricultural individuals occupy the Commission and Council. Each has a stake in the status quo. Those who would like to see farm policy reform are not well organized in Europe, and thus opposition is far more diffuse than support is unified. Whether one sees the beauty, the beast, or the beauty and the beast in the CAP, it is clear that farm policy has been undergoing slow-moving reforms since the 1980s. Reform is driven by high costs associated with large surpluses, enlargement of the EU to include countries (like Poland) with large farm sectors that the old EU members do not wish to subsidize, and external pressures. External pressures to reform the CAP come from the United States, the Cairns Group (non-EU farm producing states), and the WTO. In recent years, the Council adopted Commission-proposed reforms aimed to

- progressively delink farm income from farm production subsidies by offering direct income payments to farmers (some EU production support will remain but will be progressively reduced);
- encourage farmers to plan their production to meet market needs rather than be geared toward receiving production subsidies;
- open up the EU farm sector to more rigorous market-oriented competition while maintaining farm income in order to preserve a rural economy and stable food supplies;
- link EU farm income subsidies to farmers who practice methods favorable to sustainable development, food safety, and animal welfare;
- favor smaller and poorer farmers over larger and richer ones; and
- apply cost savings from CAP reform to financing a new rural development policy.

There is cause to be a tad skeptical of CAP reform. It has been tried before, and farmer and allied interests still like to remind Europeans that the CAP is part of the mortar that holds together the EU. What has changed is enlargement, global pressure, and unsustainably high costs at a time when governments do not wish to extend the spending limits of the EU. There is thus reason to think that the EU will succeed in putting into effect some reforms and that the EU of the twenty-first century will evolve without CAP production subsidies as an article of faith.

Regional Development

ORIGINS, OBJECTIVES, AND TIMELINE

A union of states or a single state cannot hope to keep the support of its citizens if some of its regions are wealthy and others poor. From the beginning, the Treaty included regional development as a goal. Although interstate rivalries over who gets how much regional development aid are normal in the EU today, there is much to be said for a union that does not forget its most underprivileged areas. A price to pay for an internal market with a humanitarian face is regional development policy, even if governments vie with one another for a larger slice of the pie, and even if it is difficult to measure the success of the policy relative to its costs.

The Treaty calls on the EU to increase the standard of living and quality of life for all EU citizens, use its resources to reduce gaps in economic development among its members, and thus establish a more socially and economically cohesive solidarity among member states. It will never be possible for all of the regions to be equally rich, but it is possible to reduce gaps in development across regions so that the citizens of the EU will equate their prosperity with European unity. Regional aid is the second largest spending area of the EU policies after agriculture, consuming one-third of the entire budget. EU regional assistance exists concomitantly with regional assistance provided by member governments for their own citizens. Whereas regional aid distributed by national governments is designed to help depressed regions in that particular state, EU regional development aid is designed to ensure more even distribution of wealth across the union.

Although regional policy aims to distribute wealth more evenly across the union, it also promotes the preservation of regional identity. Thus, a major feature of the EU is regionalism. **Regionalism** refers to the phenomenon in which subnational entities or groups within regions of member states seek to cultivate their identity and advance their interests within, but autonomously from, the national government. EU regional development policy recognizes the importance of regionalism in a union of states, and regions recognize the importance of the EU policies to them. Nation-states are the primary actors in EU governance, but regions within each of the nation-states have their own indigenous and distinctive culture, language, and history.

Each region has its own reasons for developing a relationship directly with the EU. In Germany and Austria, regions are Länder, or states. They share power as actors in federal unions and have legislative power at national level in areas that affect the Länder. England, Scotland, Northern Ireland, and Wales in the UK—and Catalonia and the Basque region in Spain—are distinctive areas whose inhabitants have a rich subnational governmental identity within unitary systems. However, they have less autonomy than do Länder. Some regions are isolated (Finnish Lapland), some poor (Italian Mezzogiorno), and some suffering from industrial decline and capital flight (British Midlands). In contrast, some regions are quite rich, especially areas in and around London, Paris, the Low Countries, western Germany, and northern Italy. Richer regions are keen to support EU legislation that opens up internal markets where they can be competitive. Less advantaged regions or regions with a strong local identity have different reasons to be interested in the EU. They stand to

- benefit from EU development aid in addition to what they receive from their national governments: regional aid helps build needed infrastructure, stimulate investment, and generate jobs;
- develop a relationship with the EU institutions independently of their national governments, to symbolize their autonomous identity, and to cope with the impact of globalization on their identity by highlighting their distinctiveness at European level; and/or
- increase their input into EU governmental decisionmaking on regional and other policy areas through the Committee of the Regions (CoR) and other EU bodies.

Member governments have a mixed view of the activity of their regions in relationship to the EU. In a general sense, it is in the national interest of each government to see the regions of the EU improve their economic fortunes. A stronger, more prosperous internal market is good for everyone. That said, some wealthy member governments who are net contributors to EU regional funds and to the EU budget overall, such as Germany and the Netherlands, would like to see their share of those costs decline.

In actuality, the exponential growth in EU regional development spending has been broadly driven by national self-interests. Some governments leverage an increase in EU regional development aid for their constituents to garner political support at home (Spain). Member states that, like Britain, benefit less from CAP spending than do other members may seek compensation by trying to garner more EU regional development spending in their own countries. Others who seek EU regional aid do not want the Commission to completely control how aid is expended and have sought to reduce the proportion of aid controlled by the Commission. Some states with a weaker sense of national identity and unity, such as Belgium and to some extent Italy, have no problem if their regions establish direct contact with the EU. Unitary systems, such as France and Spain, are more uncomfortable because they wish to discourage national groups within their regions from declaring independence. However, it may be that the more the EU becomes a focus of interest for regions that seek more autonomy from their national governments, the less likely it will be that these regions will seek independence. For its part, the Commission is interested in a union of regions because

- the EU can help narrow the gap in income between the poorest areas of the union and the union's norm;
- regional governments or citizens who live in areas that benefit from EU aid bring the union closer to European citizens at the subnational level—half the union population has enjoyed some project financed in whole or in part by EU regional aid;
- jobs are generated and welfare enhanced by regional hubs of economic activity where producers and workers converge: for example, each workday thousands of employees from Germany, France, and Belgium commute to Luxembourg City for jobs in banking and other financial services;
- subnational governments help implement EU policies on a regional basis and thus

reduce the Commission's own transaction costs in running common programs, such as agricultural and social policies; and

- EU regional policy is an opportunity for the Commission to widen its scope for autonomous action, or agency: the Commission has wide discretionary latitude in implementing Council legislation on regional policy.

The Treaty originally planted the seeds for a future EU regional development policy, but there was little action in this arena until the 1970s. Regional development policy became the second largest area of total EU spending as the EU (1) grew in membership and attained countries with more backward regions; (2) engaged in the 1992 Project to complete the internal market, but found that regional disparities were impeding its completion; and (3) established the EMU, with its required cuts in national government spending, which affected national aid to depressed regions—the subject of which was taken up at EU level.

The European Regional Development Fund (ERDF) was established in 1975 to offer aid to depressed regions of the member states. It began with very modest funds as a percentage of total EU spending at the time. However, twelve years later, the SEA included provisions to reduce regional economic disparities between the most advanced and the most backward areas of the EU. ERDF finances for regional development projects are known as **Structural Funds**. With the passage of the TEU seven years later, and the momentous task of establishing the EMU, the member governments agreed to establish the **Cohesion Fund** to provide two kinds of assistance: aid for environmental projects and aid for transport networks. Whereas the ERDF Structural Funds are available to all member states, the Cohesion Fund is only open to the countries whose GDP falls below 90 percent of the EU average: the twelve countries that acceded to the EU in 2004 and 2007, plus Greece and Portugal.

FORMULATION AND EXECUTION

The Commission formulates and executes regional policies. It consults the CoR, the EESC, and other interested parties. The Council and EP share legislative and budgetary authority. The Council consults the various working groups and committees of the Council, and the EP engages in extensive investigation and oversight as well as in consultation with constituent interests. Although the CoR is consulted on all proposed legislation that affects regional and local authorities, its advice and recommendations may or may not be accepted by the Commission. Regional governments within the EU, such as the Basque Government, seek to influence EU governmental decisionmaking in regional policy through their own delegations in Brussels and membership in regional associations at the EU level.

KEY ELEMENTS

The ERDF provides regional assistance for depressed areas in the member states, particularly those in declining industrial areas and inner cities, in order to focus on infrastructural reform. ERDF Structural Funds support local development projects that create jobs, investments and transportation networks (highways, airports, and high-speed rail links) and that provide assistance for small and medium-size firms. The Cohesion Fund provides financing for EU policies that require environmental regulations and costs associated with transportation projects. Four other forms of assistance at regional level are aid (1) for farmers in lagging rural regions, financed by the EAGGF; (2) for those engaged in reform of the fisheries sector; (3) for workers who have lost their jobs and require retraining or relocation, financed by the European Social Fund; and (4) for countries preparing for membership in the EU (pre-accession aid for structural reform and reform of agriculture).

A union of states with an internal market can no more ignore the needs of labor and employment than it can ignore the needs of regions lagging behind others. However, EU regional policy is highly political because it entails a lot of competition between the member states and the regions who stand to benefit from the second largest area of spending in the EU budget. Still, regional policy is important because it seeks to enhance economic and social cohesion among EU citizens, regardless of where they live. To that end, regional policy serves a critical function that spills over from the existence of the internal market to a union based on social values.

Environment, Fisheries, and Food Safety

ORIGINS, OBJECTIVES, AND TIMELINE

EU environmental policy is a cluster of related policies. Each cluster stems from the functioning of the internal market and the need to take seriously the myriad threats to the natural environment locally and globally. As the EU grew over the past half-century, it became clear that internal market integration had consequences for the environment—air and water quality, climate change, biodiversity, fishing stocks, and food safety from "farm to fork."

The Rome Treaty was silent on environmental policy. The Europeans were preoccupied with establishing new EC institutions and policies related to trade in the 1950s–1960s. However, as early as 1967, the EC enacted its first environmental directive (classification, packaging, and labeling of dangerous substances). Environmental policy began to take shape in the 1970s. For examples, the EC enacted directives on measures to combat air pollution from motor vehicles and to protect birds and their habitats and introduced the first regulation in the fisheries sector. It also published its first environmental action program, which sought to limit air, water, and waste pollution. The EC extended its exclusive common fisheries zone to two hundred miles off the shores of its member states. The widened zone was open to commercial fishing from EC countries. Nonmember states had to negotiate with the EC for access to the common fisheries zone.

By the 1980s and 1990s, environmental issues became increasingly salient at the domestic and EU levels, particularly with the (1) opening up of the internal market as the result of the 1992 Project, which drew attention to the environmental impacts of increased production; (2) effects of the Chernobyl nuclear accident and its fallout of radioactive material over the European agricultural landscape in 1986; and (3) outbreaks of two infectious animal diseases, mad cow disease and foot-and-mouth, which shook consumer confidence in the safety of the EU food chain in the 1990s.

The EU established the Common Fisheries Policy (CFP), which set total allowable catches (TACs) to maintain fish stocks in the common fisheries zone; the Habitats Directive on the conservation of natural habitats and wild flora and fauna; and minimum standards for drinking water. The TEU codified the principle of sustainable development and established the legal basis for the future European Environmental Agency (established 1994). The Amsterdam Treaty introduced sustainable development as a consideration in all policy areas across the internal market and introduced codecision in most areas of the environment. In 2000 the Commission published the *White Paper on Food Safety* that served as the basis for legislation creating the European Food and Safety Agency (EFSA) and for new food safety legislation. Lastly, the EU is a signatory to over thirty international environmental conventions and agreements (e.g., the UN Conventions on Biological Diversity and Climate Change).

FORMULATION AND EXECUTION

The Commission proposes and executes environmental legislation; the Council and EP legislate using codecision; and the ECJ exercises the power of judicial review. For example, in the fisheries sector, the Council fixes the number of TACs, while the Commission, which is charged with policing the common rules, conducts inspections of fisheries. The Commission is also responsible for issuing periodic environmental action programs to the Council, the EP, the EESC, and the CoR. The first action program was adopted in 1973. *The Sixth Environment Action Program 2010: Our Future, Our Choice* was adopted by the EP and Council in 2002 and defines current priorities and objectives of EU environmental policy.

The Commission consults specialized EU agencies that deal with the environment—the European Environmental Agency (EEA) and the EFSA. Whereas the EEA, with its thirty members (EU members plus Iceland, Liechtenstein, Norway, Switzerland and Turkey), provides independent scientific information on all environmental issues, the EFSA provides advice on food safety. It also offers opinions on technical food-chain-related issues, collects and analyzes information, controls and monitors safety throughout the food chain, warns the Commission about emerging risks, advises the Commission in emergencies, and informs the public of risks. For example, within the context of the EU warning system for food and feed productions, there were 7,300 alerts and notifications in 2007.

KEY ELEMENTS

Two principles largely guide EU environmental aspirations and policies: sustainable development (an aim of the Amsterdam Treaty) and the precautionary principle (an aim of the TEU). **Sustainable development** refers to the pursuit of economic growth policies that are conducive to the protection of the land, air, and water, and of other resources and living organisms. It takes into account the cost to the environment of doing business in the union. It was on the basis of the principle of sustainable development that the EU passed dramatic climate change legislation in late 2008 (see section on climate change).

The **precautionary principle** refers to the EU policy of withholding a product from the market when the product poses a potential risk to human and animal health or to the environment, in the absence of scientific evidence to the contrary.

It was on the basis of the precautionary principle that the EU in 1999 banned release of new genetically modified seeds used in the production of crops, subjecting such seeds to strict testing before approving their release. The EU requires labeling of genetically modified organisms (GMOs) used in products if the content of GMOs exceeds 1 percent. GMOs are organisms whose genetic material or DNA has been artificially altered. The EU continues to be concerned about the long-term effects on human and animal life of GMOs. Following a complaint launched against the EU about this ban, the WTO found in 2006 that the EU law was not consistent with international trade rules. The EU was forced to reverse the legislation and allow the release of genetically modified seeds. However, individual EU member governments may take action to restrict the release or distribution of genetically modified organisms if they maintain there is a threat to human health. They may do so even if the genetically modified organism was authorized by the EFSA.

The EU's Sixth Environment Action Program (2001–2010) defines four priority areas for action on the environment: climate change, nature and biodiversity, environment and health, and management of natural resources.

Climate Change. The EU and its member states signed the Kyoto Protocol in 1998 and ratified it by 2002. The EU played an important role in building support for agreement at Kyoto and in the follow-up meetings of the contracting parties. Goals to which Kyoto signatories commit themselves include, between 2008 and 2010, reduction of greenhouse gas emissions by 8 percent, compared to 1990 levels. Through an emissions trading scheme, member states and firms that have cut emissions beyond their share may sell their surplus to others that have not made the required cuts.

To prepare for a leading EU role in the run-up to and negotiations at and after the December 2009 Copenhagen Summit on the Environment, the outcome of which is expected to succeed the Kyoto Protocol in 2012, the EU enacted major climate change legislation in late 2008. The EU legislation requires a 20 percent reduction in greenhouse gas emissions from 1990 levels by 2020; requires usage of renewable energies comprising at least 20 percent of total energy consumption by 2020; and commits the EU to improve energy efficiency by 20 percent by 2020, including a significant increase in funding to develop carbon capture and storage technology. The EU has agreed to reduce greenhouse gas emissions by 30 percent by 2020 if and when a new global climate change accord is reached.

Nature and Biodiversity. The EU and its member states have made a commitment to protect and restore ecosystems and halt the loss of biodiversity. For example, the 1992 Habitats Directive requires each member state to identify sites for habitat protection and establish management measures to protect them. The focus combines wildlife preservation with economic activity as part of an overall sustainable development strategy.

Human Health. EU food safety policy aims to introduce and enforce rules on food safety and animal feed. EU safety authorities have competence over the following areas: animal nutrition, welfare, and health; plant health; food-chain contamination; and environmental aspects of food safety, such as genetically modified agricultural products. As previously mentioned, the EFSA is the lead agency for monitoring and responding to food safety issues in the EU. When faced with a food emergency, the Commission is authorized to take direct action if there is an immediate risk in the food chain. For example, the Commission may restrict or ban the sale of food or feed products. The Commission also consults the Standing Committee on the Food Chain and Animal Health.

The EU's legal framework on food safety now consists of policies and laws that require food and feed producers to trace the sources of all ingredients in their products. The EU and its member states authorize and control the use of chemicals in food production and require labels on food that give consumers information on the composition of the product, its manufacturer, and its methods of storing and preparation. For example, labels on beef products provide information with regard to the origin and rearing of the animal and how and where it was fattened, slaughtered, and butchered. In the event of the outbreak of a disease or other food emergency, the EU can now quickly locate and quarantine the origin of the problem. The label must also indicate if GMOs have been added beyond minimal traces found in most beef and other agricultural products. The EU, citing the precautionary principle, bans the import of hormone-treated beef, which it claims is injurious to human health. This has adversely affected U.S. exports of beef to the EU. In 1997, the WTO ruled that the EU violated international trade rules by blocking the import of hormone-treated beef.

The EU has instituted restrictions on animal feed additives and has called on producers to avoid unnecessary suffering of animals in all stages of the farming process. The Food and Veterinary Office conducts spot checks on slaughterhouses and other processing facilities both within the EU and in states that export food to the EU. This organization verifies if EU rules are being enforced by conducting inspections, including unannounced inspections, at production and processing plants.

Natural Resources. The EU and the member states have expressed concern that the use of natural resources not exceed environmental carrying capacity. For example, the EU Directive on waste disposal reduction calls on member states to commit to common national measures and tools to meet these goals. The EU is committed to reducing the quantity of waste by 20 percent by 2010 and 50 percent by 2050. Such measures and tools include landfill certificates that can be traded and eco-taxes on landfilling.

The fisheries sector presents an example of an EU policy designed to protect a dwindling natural resource. Since fisheries are part of the internal market, the sector is governed by the Treaty. Originally, the CFP aimed to increase production and ensure fair remuneration to those engaged in commercial fishing and fair prices with adequate supply for consumers. However, the main problem in the industry today is the scarcity of fish, and much of the effort of the EU in recent years has been to restructure fisheries and limit catches so as to retain stocks. The policy now stresses conservation and structural management of fishery resources, organization of the market, international fisheries agreements and structural reforms (training and retraining workers, decommissioning of fishing vessels).

As mentioned, the EU established a two-hundred-mile common fisheries zone in

1983 and set quotas to avoid overfishing. Conservation and management of fisheries resources became the basis for reform of fisheries policy in a 1992 regulation. In 1993, the Financial Instrument for Fisheries Guidance (FIFG) supported the restructuring of the fleets of the member states and the training and retraining of individuals engaged in commercial fishing. The FIFG grants aid for scrapping, converting, or modernizing fishing vessels; making health and safety improvements on these vessels; training those engaged in commercial fishing in new fishing techniques; and retraining workers who had left the industry as the size of the fleet decreased. As cod and other fish stocks decreased due to overfishing, the EU enacted reforms in 2002 that aimed to reduce the size of the fishing fleet by decommissioning fishing vessels. Today, TACs are fixed to stop overfishing. The size of the fleet has been reduced, but there is more to do, especially to assist communities dependent on fishing as a way of life.

Thus far the section has focused on the cluster of policies related to the natural environment in the EU. If the EU and its member states are serious about protecting natural resources and the environment, they will have to find ways to reduce energy consumption. If the EU would reduce its energy consumption levels, it might come to depend less on foreign supplies of natural gas and oil. One of the most serious risks to EU security in the modern era is its growing dependence on imports of gas and oil, particularly from Russia. The member states are divided over how much they should depend on Russian natural gas and oil. In 2009, Russia temporarily cut supplies of natural gas and oil to the Ukraine en route to Europe over a dispute with Kiev over price and supply. The Russian action jolted some of the EU member states, who feared they would not have enough winter heating oil for consumers.

How difficult it is for the EU to maintain such high consumption of natural gas and oil is demonstrated by the serious differences among the member governments over which international pipeline projects to support. For example, whereas Germany supports the construction of the Nord Stream pipeline that would transport Russian natural gas via the Baltic Sea to Germany, Poland supports the construction of the Nabucco pipeline that would carry oil and gas from Central Asia and the Caspian Sea region through Georgia and Turkey into the EU, skirting Russian territory (in an obvious effort to reduce gas dependence on the Russians). Germany depends heavily on gas supplies from Russia, which are expected to increase significantly. Poland is upset over the Nord Stream project since the pipeline would be built completely around Poland.

The Russian invasion of Georgia in 2008 reminded the EU of the seriousness of the threat to its gas and oil supply. Georgia hosts part of the pipeline carrying Caspian region oil and gas to Europe. Differences among the member governments on the issue of the competing pipelines speak volumes to the difficulty of achieving a common EU energy policy, which also bodes ill for the goal in EU environmental policy of reducing energy consumption.

Environmental policies in the EU have grown exponentially since the 1970s. All are related either to the impact of the internal market on the environment or to the growing consciousness about the effects of human-made environmental change on human, animal, and plant life. EU environmental activism seemed more prevalent in the 1970s and 1980s. Some momentum was lost beginning in the 1990s as pressures mounted from producers to limit the costs of environmental action in conditions of cut-throat economic competition on a global scale.

Justice and Home Affairs

ORIGINS, OBJECTIVES, AND TIMELINE

Given the security threats to the EU at home and abroad, JHA and CFSP together are among the most dynamic areas of growth in European integration today. These policy areas, like those of the environment, are increasingly interrelated. Whereas JHA enhances security within the EU and along its external frontier, CFSP enhances security further afield. The more the EU engages in JHA cooperation, the more it is in a position to cooperate with other international actors, for example, the United States, in combating threats to security from transnational crime and terrorism. This section of the chapter focuses primarily on the internal aspects of JHA.

JHA was primarily housed in Pillar Three before the Lisbon Treaty entered into force. The TEU founders were unwilling to bring such core and sensitive areas of state sovereignty as national security, justice, and crime fighting into the Treaty framework. Had they done so, supranational decisionmaking procedures—QMV, codecision, and judicial review—would have applied. With the passage of time during which Europeanization gained traction with regard to JHA issues, strict distinctions among pillar structures grew increasingly porous, and some important JHA functions passed to the first pillar. However, with the end of the pillar system, all JHA issues are part of one union.

JHA refers to a broad range of EU policies designed to facilitate collaboration and cooperation among the member states in the areas of police and judicial affairs, with a focus on criminal matters. The overall objective of JHA is to establish a single area of freedom, security, and justice (AFSJ) for all EU citizens and legal non-EU residents based on common police and judicial cooperation. Such cooperation would help to combat racism, xenophobia, and cross-border crimes (terrorism, offenses against children, trafficking in persons, illicit drugs and arms, money laundering, corruption, and fraud). JHA is also an important area of growth of EU cooperation, following terrorist attacks on the United States in 2001, Madrid in 2004, and London in 2005.[11]

The Rome Treaty was silent on JHA issues, but member governments began to cooperate in the 1970s–1980s to address organized crime, terrorism, and drug trafficking. The Trevi Group operated on the basis of voluntary, informal, and intergovernmental cooperation outside the Treaty framework, in ways similar to the predecessor of CFSP—European Political Cooperation. Composed of member state security officials, Trevi initially dealt primarily with terrorism and internal security. Another forerunner of the present-day JHA policy was the 1985 **Schengen Accord**. Signatories planned to abolish their mutual internal border checks and allow the free movement of persons.[12] The charter members were the Rhineland countries—West Germany, France, and Benelux. They were eventually joined by all EU member states with the exceptions of Ireland, the UK, Bulgaria, Cyprus, and Romania, although the latter three have applied to join. Applicants must install the Schengen computer system and have their external border checks declared secure by the EU. Iceland, Norway, and Switzerland are non-voting Schengen members.[13]

Like the Rome Treaty, the SEA was silent on JHA issues. However, the SEA—and its key feature, the 1992 Project—indirectly spurred the member states to take more seriously the growing problem of cross-border crime. It was one thing in the Rome Treaty to try to advance the free movement of labor. It was another thing in the SEA to extend the free movement of labor to full free movement of EU citizens and legal residents. The former was less ambitious and constrained by the impediments of hiring labor from other EU countries, as previously discussed. The latter was more ambitious. It promised to open up national borders within the EU to large numbers of legal persons—and with them, criminals and terrorists.

Whereas Schengen developed outside the Treaty framework, the TEU brought JHA cooperation under the Treaty remit but closeted it from supranational influence by establishing intergovernmental decisionmaking rules. The TEU did not provide the ECJ with jurisdiction over the third pillar, which has prevented the Commission from using the Court to pressure member governments to implement national measures on police and judicial cooperation. However, the TEU did introduce the possibility of implementing joint JHA actions on the basis of QMV.

The TEU instituted the new JHA Council of Ministers and a Coordinating Committee of senior national officials to help prepare its work. Nine areas of common concern to member governments were targeted for joint action: asylum policy; immigration, including rules and controls with regard to the entry of persons into the EU across the EU's external borders; rights of nonmembers who reside in the EU; combating drug addiction and international fraud; judicial cooperation in civil and criminal matters; customs cooperation; and police cooperation combating terrorism, drug trafficking, and other serious crimes.

No sooner had the ink dried on the TEU than its initial provisions for enhancing internal security became far too modest to deal with the effects of the end of the Cold War and the collapse of Communism. The member states were confronted with new problems of illegal immigration, trafficking in human beings, proliferation of WMD materials, and transnational crime and terrorism. It had become clear in the 1990s that a major problem confronting national law enforcement authorities was that their efforts to address the security threat were far too fragmented. Organized crime had operated on a global scale, but crime prevention and prosecution were handled on a national and subnational basis.[14] Member states' cooperation in the fight against transnational crime was impeded by varying national criminal codes. To address impediments to police cooperation, member governments began to exchange information, cooperate in investigations, and share best practices for crime fighting. These tasks were made even more daunting with the implementation and expansion of the Schengen Accord after 1995.[15]

The member governments sought to narrow the gap between the growing internal security threats and EU capabilities to address them through the Amsterdam Treaty, which, as mentioned, brought the Schengen *acquis* inside the Treaty framework, allowed Britain and Ireland to opt-in at a later date, and moved JHA areas related to free movement of persons from the third pillar into the first pillar by 2004. These areas included asylum, visas, refugees, immigration and movement of persons across EU external borders into the union, and judicial cooperation in civil matters. The Amsterdam Treaty added the prevention and combating of racism and xenophobia to police and judicial cooperation in the third pillar. It also sought to facilitate the approximation of criminal laws among the member states (e.g., definition of crimes and lengths of sentences). Member governments were bound to "framework decisions," but each would decide how implementation were to occur domestically. In the areas that remained in the third pillar—such as combating transnational crime and terrorism and providing for police and juridical cooperation in criminal matters—the Amsterdam Treaty gave the Commission a shared right of initiative with the member governments and provided for decisionmaking based on the consultation procedure (the Council consults the EP) and unanimity in the Council. However, the Treaty allowed the Council to use QMV on implementation of policies and, after five years, to change the decisionmaking procedure in any of these areas to codecision and QMV.

By 2000, the EU articulated its goals of creating an EU area of freedom, security, and justice. In the AFSJ, the member governments agreed to (1) guarantee the fundamental rights of EU citizens and legal residents; (2) coordinate policy on asylum and immigration, issuance of visas, and policing EU external frontiers; (3) promote cooperation among national police forces, customs and immigration officers, and national courts; and (4) base the AFSJ on the principle of mutual recognition in criminal matters (e.g., criminal law and judicial judgments).

Two other JHA-related developments are worthy of attention: the introduction in 2004 of the Hague Program to address illegal immigration and combat transnational crime and terrorism in the EU; and the introduction in 2005 of an EU-wide arrest warrant (discussed below). The Hague Program, which covers the period 2005–2010, addresses all aspects of policies related to the AFSJ, including the issues of migration, border management, and civil justice. A major priority of the Program is to create a common asylum area with the goal of implementing a single asylum application procedure and uniform status for refugees throughout the EU by 2010.

FORMULATION AND EXECUTION

The Lisbon Treaty transfers the following JHA areas from the old intergovernmental method of decisionmaking to the ordinary legislative procedure (QMV and codecision): external border control, asylum, immigration, police cooperation, and judicial cooperation in criminal matters. Under the Lisbon Treaty, in the area of police cooperation and judicial cooperation in criminal matters, the Commission as well as one-quarter of the member governments may initiate legislative proposals. However, when a member government has serious reservations over a proposal in these areas, it may refer the proposal to the European Council for a decision, which is based on consensus. Should nine member governments wish to proceed with legislative action in these areas, they may do so under the conditions of enhanced cooperation. Lastly, in the area of freedom, security and justice, if one-quarter of national parliaments object to a legislative proposal, the Council must reconsider that proposal. In this way, the national parliaments seek to ensure that a proposed measure dealing with police cooperation and judicial cooperation in criminal matters complies with the principle of subsidiarity.

COREPER and the Council Secretariat assist the JHA Council, as do two coordinating committees of senior national officials, one for immigration and asylum issues and the other for police and judicial cooperation in criminal matters (Article 36 Committee). The Commission is responsible for overseeing implementation of JHA policies once legislated.

As internal security threats grew in number in the 1990s and beyond, so too did Europol's functions. Begun in 1999, Europol's original task was to coordinate national operations against illegal drug trafficking. Today, the Hague-based Europol is the law enforcement agency of the EU. It collects and handles criminal intelligence to improve cooperation among competent member state authorities. The objective is to help combat and prevent serious international organized crime and terrorism. Other areas subject to member state cooperation in Europol include efforts to combat money laundering, euro counterfeiting, illegal immigration networks, sexual exploitation of children and women, pornography, and smuggling nuclear and other dangerous materials.

Europol facilitates the exchange of information between member officers seconded to Europol by the member governments. These officers, who represent their national law enforcement agencies, provide operational analysis in support of operations. They generate strategic reports, threat assessments, and crime analyses on the basis of the intelligence supplied by the member states and third parties. They also provide expertise and technical support for investigations and operations carried out under the supervision of the member states concerned. As the EU's police coordination center for collecting, analyzing, and sharing information to assist investigations carried by the member states, Europol features a computer database of criminal suspects and stolen objects that gives law enforcement officers access to millions of shared files. Although Europol helps member governments combat transnational crimes, it has no authority to make arrests.

The newest agency in support of JHA cooperation in the fight against cross-border crime is the Hague-based Eurojust, which began operations in 2002 in response to al Qaeda's attacks on the United States. It oversees operations of a liaison network of national criminal prosecutors and judges from each of the member states; helps facilitate and coordinate criminal investigations by encouraging better contacts among investigators; helps to simplify international court-to-court requests for assistance and information; and advises Europol on its operations. Eurojust prosecutors and judges have direct access to their own national judicial authorities and share advice and information with their colleagues. The Lisbon Treaty subjects both Eurojust and Europol to the oversight of the EP and national parliaments.

Following the terrorist attack on Madrid in 2004, the EU created a new position to coordinate the union's anti/counter-terrorism efforts. The EU Counter-Terrorism Coordinator's main areas of responsibility are to prepare proposals for better coordination among the relevant EU Councils and to maintain regular contacts with member states. The Coordinator, who reports to the High Representative, maintains an overview of the instruments at the disposal of the EU and monitors implementation of the EU Action Plan on Combating Terrorism.

KEY ELEMENTS

JHA, like the internal market, is a cluster of related policies that include a wide variety of concerns, three of which are discussed below: asylum, police cooperation in anticrime and anti/counter-terrorism, and illegal movement of persons. Other important elements of JHA include judicial cooperation in civil and criminal matters and the international aspects of anticrime cooperation.

Asylum. Asylum issues increasingly preoccupy JHA principals. The EU countries are frequent destinations of individuals outside the EU who wish to be granted asylum. This has led the member states to consider developing a common asylum policy that would feature a single common asylum procedure and a uniform status for those granted asylum. The member states have agreed to rules to determine which EU country is responsible for examining an asylum application, often the country the asylum seeker entered in the first place. It is this country's responsibility to examine the application according to EU criteria and to take back any applicants who subsequently travel illegally to other countries in the EU. The EU aims to have a common asylum system set up by 2012. Europol's database Eurodac assists in the scrutiny of applications for asylum (see next section on police cooperation).

Police Cooperation. In 2003, the Council agreed to a protocol amending the Europol Convention, which authorized Europol to (1) act on the suspicion (not just evidence) of organized cross-border criminal activity; (2) extend its functions to include training, equipment, and crime prevention/investigation methods; and (3) have direct contact with subnational authorities, such as individual police forces (in addition to national units). Furthermore, the construction and use of computer databases plays a major role in EU efforts to manage its external borders and fight crime and terrorism. These include: the Europol Computer System (TECS), the Schengen Information System (SIS), and the European Dactylographic System (Eurodac) for asylum seekers. In addition, the Visa Information System (VIS) was expected to come online in the near future.

Europol's TECS entails a common pool of information given by the member states as well as analytical files created by the Europol staff. Europol collects, stores, processes, analyzes, and exchanges relevant information, including information held by law enforcement services on reports of suspicious financial transactions. SIS gives police officials and participating members access to criminal data on individuals and on stolen objects. In the future, SIS will be expanded to allow the storage of biometric data and the inclusion of future EU members in the Schengen Accord.

In operation since 2003, the Eurodac database records information on asylum applicants, including biometric data, such as fingerprints. The purpose of Eurodac is to prevent "asylum shopping"—the practice of applying for asylum in several EU member states simultaneously. The system is also designed to prevent foreign nationals previously found illegal in one member state from successfully claiming asylum in another. The new VIS will collect biometric data on visa applicants, helping to prevent individuals denied visas in one Schengen member country from making a subsequent application to another.

Following the terrorist attacks against the United States in 2001, the EU began to address the threat of transnational terrorism more seriously than it had before. For examples, the EU and its member states defined terrorism; established a list of terrorist organizations and individuals whose assets are frozen within the EU (including the political wing of Hamas); put into effect a long-delayed directive of 1999 to combat money laundering; froze assets of 279 individuals and organizations suspected of terrorism; and introduced the EU-wide arrest warrant. The EU updates its list of suspected terrorists and terrorist organizations.

The EU-wide Arrest Warrant Framework Decision requires that each member state enact legislation to implement the arrest warrant. Implementation of the arrest warrant by national governments has been slow. For those member states that have fully transposed the Framework Decision into national law, the member governments may request of one another the extradition of a suspect for whom they have issued an arrest warrant. There are thirty-two offenses for which a warrant can be issued.[16] If a suspect has not committed one of the thirty-two offenses, a warrant may still be issued if the individual is accused of an offense for which the minimum penalty is over a year in prison. In 2005, the arrest warrant framework facilitated the speedy extradition of the escaped London terror bomber from Italy to the United Kingdom.

Corruption not only undermines EU values and internal market rules, its links with national and transnational organized crime and terrorism are of serious concern to the EU. For example, in 2008, the Commission blocked €486 million in EU aid to Bulgaria for failing to address corruption. The Commission will release suspended funds if Bulgarian authorities improve their record of fighting organized crime and corruption.

Illegal Movement of Persons. The member states share with one another a common border with the outside world. With free movement of persons, all EU members, no matter what their geographic location, are concerned with illegal immigration into the union. The 2004 and 2007 enlargements of the EU and the accession of some of these states to the Schengen area increase the likelihood that criminals, terrorists, and illegal aliens will enter the union. The Schengen area now comprises 400 million people in 25 countries. The EU is seeking to further increase the surveillance of its external borders. The Common Unit for External Border Practitioners was established in 2002 to oversee a large network of national immigration officers. It directs joint operations and pilot projects, develops common training for border officers, and could serve as the precursor for the establishment of a future common border control for the EU.

The European Agency for the Management of Operational Cooperation at the External Borders (Frontex) entered into force in 2005 in order to assist the member states in this area. Frontex is a coordinated EU response to the problem of illegal immigration and the repatriation of illegal immigrants to their home countries. It has already coordinated several joint operations around the EU's external borders and at the EU's international airports. Spain has asked and received assistance from Frontex to provide sea and air patrols around the Canary Islands and to dispatch experts to the Canary Islands to assist in the repatriation of illegal migrants to their countries of origin. Since most if not all illegal migrants do not have their identity cards, it is difficult to repatriate them. Italy and Portugal have worked with Frontex in assisting Spain with sea and air patrols in the vicinity of the Canary Islands.

In sum, JHA represents a new wave of European integration. The EU will face increasing pressures from within its own ranks to develop policies to address internal security threats. It will also receive pressure from outside the union to develop policies that reflect European security interests. Government principals are likely to delegate authority to common institutions, new and old, to reduce their transaction costs in running these new policies. What is striking about JHA is that the policies that it encompasses have for hundreds of years defined core sovereign functions of the nation-state. This is why JHA policies are difficult but necessary for the member governments to reach and implement. With an internal market, there are risks to security from the movement of criminals and terrorists that cannot be combated by member states acting alone.

Review

Chapter 6 began with an introduction to the instruments of EU governmental decisionmaking and ended with a *tour de table* of many major EU policy areas that emanate from those instruments. What have we learned about policy formulation and execution in the EU polity? Do theories of integration help us explain and predict EU policy developments? As theory should never be an afterthought of history, we begin with theoretical observations and end with empirical observations.

THEORETICAL OBSERVATIONS

Principal–agent analysis, the key focus of the theory of rational choice institutionalism, conveniently frames the tension and interplay between the EU member governments and EU institutions as they formulate and execute policy. The relationship between principal/delegator and agent is essential to the functioning of any polity. Rational choice institutionalism also bridges intergovernmentalism and functionalism—theories that each emphasize different yet pertinent drivers of integration at different moments. Historical institutionalism explains how EU agencies develop scope for autonomous agency, or influence, in ways that may have been unintended by the original grantors of delegated authority. Our theory review begins with intergovernmental and functional perspectives, before turning to institutional theories.

Liberal intergovernmentalists draw our attention to the role of governments, who decide whether or not to advance the course of integration at periodic IGCs. The IGC that led to the Rome Treaty established the beginning of the common market, and the IGC that led to the TEU established the process that led to monetary union. Realist intergovernmentalists focus on the importance of national interests in decisions related to the integration process. For example, France had a national security interest in anchoring Germany into a deeper (monetary) union following German unification. Germany had a national security interest in garnering the support of its EU partners for unification and the integration of East Germany into the EC. Monetary union thus served the interests of both states at a particular moment in history.

Neofunctionalists offer different but no less useful explanations of how the EU develops from one policy realm to another, as one functional need that is addressed necessitates a new and related need. For examples, we learned that there was a spillover in function from policies related to the *economic goal* of fostering free movement of persons to policies related to the *security goal* of ensuring that criminals and terrorists do not endanger the union because of its porous internal borders. Neofunctional theory also explains the spillover from the establishment of the (1) right of free movement of workers, to the rights of workers who take jobs in member states other than their own; (2) movement of goods under conditions of fluctuating exchange rates, to monetary union; and (3) CET and Common Commercial Policy designed to protect internal producers from cheap imports, to foreign and security policies.

Conventional theories of intergovernmentalism and functionalism do not adequately explain how member governments and EU bodies, and related networks of experts and special interests, interact to formulate and execute policy inside the black box. Rational choice institutionalism emphasizes what most matters inside the EU polity: the two-way interaction between governmental principals who delegate powers and EU bodies who as agents manage, develop, and refine the union.

For example, we learned that member governments sought to reduce transaction costs of running the new monetary union by delegating authority to EU bodies to oversee, manage, and police that union. Member governments recognized that, if the monetary union were to work, it would need the Commission to be watchdog and the ECB to regulate money supply by setting interest rates. Since both had to be independent of the member governments for monetary policy to work effectively, member states had to delegate authority to EU bodies. What governments often forget is that when at a moment in time they agree to delegation of authority, they cannot know if, when, and how EU bodies will expand their scope for autonomous agency in ways not fully intended.

According to theorists of historical institutionalism, national governments may regret the initial delegation of autonomous powers to EU agents, like the ECB and the Commission, for the influence they come to wield over time. Three examples come to mind from our study of monetary and competition policies.

First, we learned that member government principals had set up rules that capped excessive deficit spending (the SGP) and delegated authority to the Commission to ensure that states would not breach the rules. When some member governments exceeded the deficit spending threshold and recoiled in the face of the Commission's scope for autonomous agency, they attempted to take back some of the Commission's authority. As it turned out, member governments could not fundamentally limit the authority of the Commission to oversee the SGP. They feared the unraveling of the monetary union, a union that still served their interests. Instead, the member governments reformed the criteria for deficit spending in order to feature more flexible criteria. In the end, Commission oversight of the SGP remained.

Second, the Sarkozy Administration has advocated making the ECB accountable to the political objectives of the member governments in the area of monetary policy. Sarkozy would prefer the Ecofin Council ministers to have a direct dialogue with the ECB in order to bring the setting of interest rates in line with political objectives of national governments. This would be particularly necessary in times of recession when some member governments may wish to lower interest rates. However, the ECB by statute is an independent EU body and its independence is strongly affirmed by countries such as Germany. An article of faith in the ECB is to cast a wary eye on interest rates so low as to stir inflation. Rational choice institutionalists explain and predict that countries like France will seek to take back authority delegated to common EU bodies, like ECB, as those bodies develop a widened scope for autonomous agency. However, in the end, Sarkozy's France is not likely to succeed in taking back the independent powers of the ECB.

Third, by studying competition policy we analyzed that as the Commission's antitrust powers grew, member governments sought to reform/curtail those powers but found the Commission's role indispensable to maintaining internal market rules. They thus did not take back authority delegated to the Commission to administer competition policy.

EMPIRICAL OBSERVATIONS

The EU exists to produce outputs or policies designed to enhance the common welfare of its citizens and address the needs of its member states. Each policy is related to the objectives of the Treaty, the creation or completion of the internal market based on the four free movements, and/or the need for a common response to an unintended consequence or spillover from an existing policy. Some policies are actually clusters of related policies. It is because all EU policies are functionally interlinked and rooted in common Treaty objectives that the most advantageous way of studying EU governmental decisionmaking is to view the EU as a single polity in the areas where it has competence. The overall state of EU policymaking reveals much about the state of the EU polity itself.

Some policies clearly originated in a Treaty provision. Other policies began as areas of intergovernmental cooperation outside the Treaty but were subsequently brought under the Treaty remit, such as passport-free movement of persons, police cooperation, and monetary coordination. None of the integration policies examined in this chapter that originated in the Treaty were subsequently moved into the intergovernmental form of cooperation outside the Treaty. Furthermore, we learned that in several instances the voting on the basis of unanimity in the Council was later changed to voting on the basis of QMV. For example, the move from unanimity to QMV in the area of regional development policy in the early 2000s heralded a more supranational and integrated approach to EU regional development policy.

The internal market is the crowning achievement of European integration, but it would be unwise to conclude that the EU has created a completed internal market. The problem is that market integration has gone as far as it can go without rubbing up against the raw skin of trenchant national economic and cultural interests and preferences that impede free movement of labor and services. This is why the EU is experimenting with more flexible means of governmental decisionmaking.

The creation of a monetary union is another major political accomplishment of the EU. However, as in the case of the internal market, there are risks associated with partial completion. If the member governments backtrack on their commitments to fiscal responsibility, and the reformed SGP does not compel the reduction of public deficit to below 3 percent of GDP, the euro risks losing value. There is good reason to think that the euro will survive in the long term because Eurozone governments cannot afford to allow it to fail. Should the euro be allowed to weaken or collapse, the effect on the entire integration project would be deleterious. This ending is always possible, but not probable.

JHA is a promising area of growth of regional integration. It is interesting to note that there is more forward activity in JHA, an area far removed from the original compact that created the EU over fifty years ago, than there is in the internal market, where stubborn obstacles remain to finishing Europe. Once again, the external threat to Europe (this time transnational crime and terrorism) is catalyzing growth in JHA. As member governments engage in this old reflex to cooperate in facing down an external threat, they will continue to struggle to reach and implement common agreements in response. Judging by our review of EU policy outputs, we reconfirm that the EU is a messy polity with many unfinished and overlapping policies.

Key Concepts

Cohesion Fund
Commission regulation
Council directive
Council regulation
European Monetary System
Financial Services Action Plan
Lisbon Strategy
Maastricht Convergence Criteria
precautionary principle
regionalism
Schengen Accord
social dumping
Stability and Growth Pact
Structural Funds
sustainable development

Study Questions

1. Why is the internal market a work in progress rather than a terminus?
2. Why is regional development policy important to the EU?
3. Can the EU in its agricultural policy reconcile the need for reform with the deep roots in European culture for agricultural support?
4. How is the CCP an instrument of EU foreign policy? Give three examples.
5. What are two overarching principles of EU environmental policy? Provide an example of how each principle is manifested.
6. To what extent is neofunctional spillover present in EU monetary, regional, and JHA policies and why?
7. How does principal–agent analysis help explain EU Competition Policy?
8. What is the difference between the Lisbon Strategy and the Lisbon Treaty?

Selected Readings

Kenneth Dyson, *The Euro at 10* (Oxford: Oxford University Press, 2009).
Sophie Meunier and Kathleen McNamara, eds., *Making History: European Integration and Institutional Change* (Oxford: Oxford University Press, 2007).

John Occhipinti, "Policing across the Atlantic: EU–U.S. Relations and International Crime Fighting," *Bologna Center of International Affairs* 8 (Spring 2005): 1–12.

Ingeborg Tommel and Amy Verdun, eds., *Innovative Governance in the European Union: The Politics of Multilevel Policymaking* (Boulder, Colo.: Lynne Rienner, 2008).

CHAPTER 7

European Union Foreign Policy

Preview

The establishment of the internal market constituted the first generation of European integration. Foreign policy is the next. There are three principal reasons to make such a bold statement: (1) support for common responses to global problems is strong among member state publics (see Chapter 9); (2) threats to member states' economic, political, and security interests within, on, and outside the borders of the EU are growing; and (3) external pressures on the EU to act as an effective player in global security affairs continue to mount. It is no longer accurate for the EU to be viewed as an economic superpower and a "political dwarf"—a payer but not a player in the affairs of the world.

Certainly common accord on foreign policy issues can never be assured among twenty-seven sets of national interests. There are times when member states' national interests and preferences are so far apart that a common policy cannot be achieved. For examples, the members were terribly divided over how to respond to the genocide of the Tutsis by the Hutus in Rwanda (1994), the collapse of civil order in Albania (1998), the U.S.-led invasion of Iraq (2003), and the reform of UN institutions (2005). When there is division, there is no common position, and the economic superpower appears weak and ineffectual to the outside world. However, as this chapter demonstrates, member states often agree on collective action, and, when they do, the EU matters. When this happens, the EU raises its level of confidence as a global player, more new sources of foreign policy action are generated, and the world raises its expectations of what the EU can and should do. Chapter 7 posits four empirical and theoretical observations:

- EU foreign policy mirrors national and European identities and values (social constructivism) and draws legitimacy from national publics who overwhelmingly support the role of the EU in world affairs.
- EU foreign policy is influenced by the changing distribution of power in the world that restricts or enhances the EU's global influence (neorealism). The end of the Cold War catapulted the EU into a position of leadership in Europe before the EU itself was ready. The end of a bipolar international system dominated by the United

States and the Soviet Union unleashed new opportunities for the Europeans to exercise collective political influence abroad. External demands on the EU to act in international politics have always outpaced the EU's ability to process and respond to them. In response to external stimuli, member governments may decide at periodic IGCs and at European Council Summits to change/expand the Treaty to give more powers to the union (liberal intergovernmentalism). They do so because it is in their national interests.

- Over time, member governments delegate administration of common foreign policy actions to EU institutions to reduce transaction costs and ensure adherence to common accords (rational choice institutionalism). Member states recognize that it can be more effective/less costly to respond together to influence international issues too large for any one of them to handle well alone (**politics of scale**).[1] As member states delegate foreign policy powers to EU institutions, the scope for autonomous agencies of those institutions increases in ways not always intended or expected by the original grantors (historical institutionalism).

- The EU will further establish, consolidate, and expand its foreign policies as it engages in the processes of Europeanization and international learning (historical institutionalism and social constructivism). **Europeanization** here is the process by which institutionalized habits of foreign policy cooperation form. **International learning** here refers to the extent to which the EU builds on the experience of past foreign policy action/inaction in order to avoid mistakes, initiate new actions informed by improved knowledge, and thus maximize effects. Figure II.1 depicts the feedback loop that juxtaposes policy outputs to new sources of inputs.

Why has foreign policy become such an active area of EU governmental decision-making? Internal, border, and external security have all received more attention since the terrorist attacks on New York, Washington, Madrid, and London between 2001 and 2005 and in response to such security threats as proliferation of WMDs, transnational crime, and illegal immigration. Moreover, efforts to enhance the effectiveness of EU foreign policy have responded to the inability of the EU, despite its best efforts, to end the wars of national dissolution in former Yugoslavia.

There is a cognitive lag between the growth of EU foreign policy actions and the recognition of that growth by many leading realist and other theorists of international politics, such as Robert Kagan, John Meirsheimer, and Robert Keohane. Indeed, it is easy not to recognize the EU as an international actor. After all, its place in international affairs is new, unorthodox, sui generis, and counterintuitive to those who only see a world of Westphalian states. A hallmark of state sovereignty is control over foreign policy. Unlike states, the EU is not responsible to a single electorate for the defense of the union. Thus, many scholars assume a group of states cannot have common foreign policies. It is time for students of international politics to take a closer look at what the EU is doing abroad. They will be surprised.

While the EU has common foreign policies, it does not have a single foreign policy like that of a state. Nevertheless, the EU is a large, active, and influential player in world affairs. For examples, the EU sends and receives diplomatic representatives from over 130 governments and international institutions. It has the power to grant or withhold diplomatic recognition of state and non-state actors. It has close cooperative relations with the world's major international institutions and is a magnet for NGOs represented in Brussels. It decides on the fates of nations when they apply for membership: the EU may accept, reject, or postpone a bid to join or it may instead offer association but not full membership. The EU negotiates and concludes international treaties covering trade, human rights, criminal justice, the natural environment, and nonproliferation, among others. The union is a leader in international efforts to mitigate climate change, ban capital punishment, and stem the proliferation of WMDs. The EU influences the national economic security interests of many states who depend on access to the world's largest market for goods and services.

The EU and its member states provide 60 percent of the world's official development assistance (ODA) and humanitarian aid to 160 countries. It contributes approximately €1 billion annually to UN agencies and programs, up from €150 million a decade ago. It leads international efforts to raise funds from donor states to war-torn countries across the world. The EU holds regular summits with privileged partners on every continent of the world. It actively supports other regional integration movements as a reflection of its own experience in overcoming interstate conflict and enhancing human welfare and security.

The EU supports countries engaged in establishing the rule of law, democratic institutions and elections, and market economies. It conditions the granting of development aid and tariff cuts to countries with close historical and geographical ties on their commitments to human rights, the rule of law and nonproliferation. The EU often imposes sanctions on foreign governments who violate international norms governing basic human rights, the rule of law, and democratic practices. However, it also lifts punitive measures when those violations end. EU foreign policies aim to prevent wars before they start, stop wars once they have begun, and create postwar conditions of stability and security once wars end. The EU has taken twenty-two actions under the rubric of the CSDP since 2003.

Having attempted to characterize the union as an international actor, we need to understand the basic vocabulary of EU foreign policy. The repository of all common foreign policy practices and actions and international legal commitments is referred to as the *acquis politique*. In this chapter, EU foreign policy is referred to by its acronym, EUFP, to denote all EU foreign and security policies. Taken together, such policies do not form a single foreign policy associated with that of a nation-state. Instead, **EU foreign policy (EUFP)** is broadly defined as the range of values, interests, policies, actions, and instruments of the EU and the member states when they act collectively abroad.[2] EUFP covers trade and economics (participation in G-8 Summits); development and postwar reconstruction (leader of world donor efforts to rebuild Afghanistan, Kosovo, and Lebanon); politics (opposition to detention of prisoners at Guantanamo Bay); security (dispatch of combat or police forces for peacemaking, postwar stabilization, conflict prevention and/or peacekeeping); disarmament (operations to disarm belligerents, active support of bilateral and multilateral nonproliferation efforts); humanitarian aid (dispatch of food convoys and rescue tasks); law (support for the International Criminal Court); and functional cooperation (leader in climate change treaties and in efforts to stop trade in conflict diamonds).

Unlike NATO and its member states, the EU is primarily a **civilian power**. A civilian power is an economic-diplomatic player in world politics who has recourse to military means to defend its values and principles in conducting its foreign policies and supporting humanitarian, peacekeeping, and other defensive security operations.

However, a civilian power has recourse to military means only as a last resort. Chapter 7 introduces readers to the origins, institutions, and decisionmaking procedures of EUFP before describing individual multilateral and bilateral relationships and policies. By examining EUFP, we round out and complete our study of Part II of the book—the EU in practice, before turning to Part III, which focuses on the effects of EU policies. A key question we want to ask and answer is difficult but necessary: does the EU learn from its foreign policy actions as it creates new ones? A union of states is pointless if it does not enhance its members' interests at home and abroad.

Origins, Objectives, and Timeline

The Rome Treaty set up what became the EC internal market, but the Treaty had as much to do with international politics as it did with economics. The Treaty institutionalized the Franco-German relationship into an institutional structure of peace that was extended to other European states over time. The EC as a system of interstate relations is by extension a foreign policy instrument of its member states. As discussed in Chapter 6, the Treaty provided for the foreign commercial and political interests of its member states, who granted EC preferential trade and aid benefits to former colonies and overseas possessions. It also provided for future membership in or association with the EC for neighboring countries. However, the origins of a more explicit EUFP date back only to the 1990s, when suddenly the EC was catapulted into a European Union after the fall of communist rule and the vacuum of power left behind by the Soviet Union. The EU by default was the primary international leader of the democratic transitions and market economic reforms of the former Soviet bloc states. After unsuccessful diplomatic efforts to mediate and end the wars of national dissolution in former Yugoslavia in the 1990s, the EU organized new institutions of foreign and security policy cooperation and implemented common policies on a more global scale. EUFP has evolved over four general phases following the collapse of the European Defense Community in 1954.

PHASE ONE, 1958–1970: EMBRYONIC FOREIGN POLICY

The EC began to develop its foreign policy through Treaty-based economic instruments, such as the CET, to conclude highly political association agreements with Greece and Turkey. It introduced its Mediterranean Policy to engage nonmember Mediterranean states in closer trade and political ties with the EC through bilateral accords. These accords served to enhance EC security interests in a region vital to its foreign trade and energy supply. The EC concluded a pact with former colonies (Yaounde and Lome Conventions) to offer significant trade concessions and political dialogue, and it concluded multilateral trade liberalization agreements at the GATT.

The EC imposed economic or diplomatic sanctions against Rhodesia (human rights violations) and Greece (military junta) and instituted improved relations with Central and Eastern Europe (CEE) by granting unprecedented trading benefits. It established diplomatic relations with many of the world's countries and obtained observer status at various international organizations. As the EC grew in importance in the IPE, more nonmembers sought membership in, association with, or other trade and diplomatic benefits from the EC. As time passed, the member states felt unable to respond to external demands on the EC without a foreign policy consultative mechanism. However, they were not ready to revise the Treaty to include foreign policy instruments, which the French, in particular, were loath to share on a supranational basis. The compromise between addressing the need to respond to a demanding and changing world and addressing the need to protect such a critical area of state sovereignty came in 1970. It was then that the member governments established European Political Cooperation (EPC), which ushered in the next phase of EUFP development.

PHASE TWO, 1971–1990: FORMATIVE YEARS

During this time, the international system began to shift from Soviet-American bipolarity to a more multipolar configuration of players, including the EC, China, India, Japan, and the nonaligned movement of states. In a bipolar world dominated by the superpowers, the scope for influence of the EC as an international actor was constrained. The multipolar world, with its diffusion of economic and political power and players, opened up new possibilities for a union of states to influence international politics. The establishment of EPC, outside the Treaty rubric, enabled the member governments to begin to make common foreign policy declarations and coordinate actions in response to a demanding world. However, EPC had no international legal standing. Most EPC actions had to be put into effect by the EC with its budget resources, Commission delegations, and competences to act in international law.

Following the accession of the UK, with its global interests and presence, the EU morphed into a far more important global foreign policy player. Nonetheless, when faced with a threat to its vital economic and political interests by the oil cartel price hikes and embargo of 1973–1974, the member states failed to respond collectively, despite the Commission's best efforts to forge a common foreign energy policy. However, out of that debacle, international learning within the EC took place. The member states began to address collective security interests and threats more carefully. The EC and EPC addressed regional and global economic, political, and security issues in ways not previously entertained by the EC. For examples, in the 1970s, the EC established the Euro–Arab Dialogue; revitalized its Mediterranean Policy; participated as a bloc and initiated actions at the Conference on Security and Cooperation in Europe; and expanded its policy of *ostpolitik* (improving relations with the East) by offering special trade benefits to Soviet-bloc states, including the Soviet Union itself. After the fall of the Berlin Wall in November 1989 and the end of the Cold War soon thereafter, the EC was forced to assume the central leadership role in the democratic and market reforms of post-communist Europe.

In the world outside Europe, the EC participated in the Tokyo Round of GATT multilateral trade negotiations; imposed or lifted sanctions on Turkey, Afghanistan, and Vietnam; endorsed the participation of its member states in the Sinai Disengagement Force; established high-level consultative relationships with each of the developed countries; entered into a wide variety of international commodity, functional, and environmental agreements and treaties; granted aid to Palestinian refugees; and called for a Palestinian homeland and Palestinian participation in peace talks.

After enactment of the SEA, which brought EPC closer to the Treaty framework and explicitly extended EPC to include international security issues, the EC expanded its foreign policy activities. It imposed sanctions against Argentina, Grenada, Israel, Libya, Poland, South Africa, Syria, and the Turkish state on Cyprus; concluded trade pacts with other regional actors, such as the Andean Pact; offered new trade concessions to Gaza and the West Bank; and provided diplomatic and other assistance to Iraqi-occupied Kuwait.

PHASE THREE, 1991–1999: END OF INNOCENCE

With no recourse to military capabilities, the EC was marginalized by the U.S.-led coalition forces that liberated Kuwait from Iraq in 1991. That sense of powerlessness encouraged the EC to take the lead international role to mediate the Yugoslav conflict starting in 1991–1992. This period of development began with the Yugoslav wars and the introduction of the CFSP, which succeeded the old EPC in 1993, and ended with the introduction of ESDP in 1999. It was to be a decade of international learning for the EU member states and institutions.

As the EU was just establishing the new CFSP institutions and procedures following enactment of the TEU, it grappled with the effects of the end of the Cold War, the need to lead the international response to the democratic transitions in CEE, the pressing need to end the horror of ethnic cleansing and war in former Yugoslavia, and major transitions in the transatlantic relationship. To prepare post-communist states who wished to join or associate with the EU, the EU enunciated the **Copenhagen Criteria**. Successful applicants must function as constitutionally representative European democracies and market economies. The EU went on to negotiate and conclude association accords with most of the CEE states eligible to join the EU.

Exercising leadership in CEE proved far easier than dealing with the breakup of Yugoslavia. The EC was keen to take the lead international role as mediator when Yugoslavia disintegrated into war. No other major international player, including the U.S., the UN, and NATO, stepped in quickly to mediate. As earlier mentioned, a European Community Monitoring Mission helicopter was shot down by the Serb-dominated Yugoslav air force, killing all five EC officials on board. The author has referred to this experience as a baptism by fire[3] as the Europeans came to realize that without recourse to the full range of foreign policy instruments—particularly the military means to back up diplomacy—EC personnel would be vulnerable to attack abroad. Moreover, the EC would not be taken seriously as a world player. Serbia, for example, never took any of the EC-brokered ceasefires seriously and consequently broke most of them.

After both the EU and later the EU and UN working together were unable to secure permanent ceasefires—and after the atrocities of ethnic cleansing continued unabated—a sustained air bombardment of Serbian forces by the United States and NATO eventually brought the war to an end. American diplomatic leadership ensured conclusion of the peace plan among the belligerents at Dayton in 1995. The Europeans were again sidelined despite their huge four-year investment of diplomatic capital.

Yet their earlier diplomatic efforts served as a basis for eventual NATO action and their humanitarian assistance helped rescue and feed hundreds of thousands of refugees.

International learning by the EU was an important factor in inducing change in the way the EU as an institution conducted foreign policy. It was in the Amsterdam Treaty in 1998 that the EU responded to its deficiencies by establishing the position of the CFSP High Representative, incorporating the old Western European Union into the EU, establishing a foreign policy planning unit, and codifying the so-called **Petersberg Tasks**. These tasks refer to peacekeeping, humanitarian and search-and-rescue tasks, and tasks of combat forces in crisis management, including peace enforcement.

In retrospect, the deaths of 200,000 civilians in BiH and elsewhere in former Yugoslavia and the shortcomings of good diplomatic intentions marked the end of innocence and naiveté in the external dimension of European integration. Dayton did not end the fighting in all of former Yugoslavia. The conflict between the Albanian majority and the Serb minority in Kosovo—an autonomous region of Serbia—worsened toward the end of the decade. Despite EU diplomatic efforts to end the violence, particularly Serbian ethnic cleansing of Kosovar Albanians in 1999, military force was needed to end the atrocities. The United States and its NATO allies bombed Serbian targets, which finally brought the humanitarian crisis to an end in June 1999. Again, the EU was sidelined in its own backyard by the leadership of a non-European power. Moreover, and quite troubling for the transatlantic alliance, the military campaign revealed enormous technological weaknesses of the air forces of EU member states participating in the NATO strikes. Never before had the gap between European and American military capabilities been so exposed.

Although the EU could not stop ethnic cleansing in Kosovo, it played a key role in the way the war in Kosovo ended. Diplomatic coordination among the EU, Russia, and the United States resulted in a trilateral agreement on the terms of settlement. These terms were presented to the Serbian President, Slobodan Milosevic, in Belgrade by EU Balkan envoy Martti Ahtisaari, accompanied by Russian Balkan envoy Victor Chernomyrdin. Milosevic finally agreed to end hostilities and withdraw from Kosovo. EU diplomacy, Russian support for ending the war, and the threat of continued NATO action together worked in favor of bringing the conflict to a close. Kosovo remained a UN protectorate until it declared independence in 2008. Today, security in the country is provided by a "cascade of responsibility." Kosovo security forces are first-responders to an outbreak of violence, EU police forces are second-responders should Kosovo authorities require assistance, and NATO troops are only called in as a last resort. The EU leads economic reconstruction efforts and the restoration of civil society in Kosovo.

The EU went through an historic metamorphosis as a foreign policy player during the different phases of the Yugoslav wars. An outcome of its perceived shortcomings came in December 1998 when Britain and France agreed at St. Malo to develop a European security and defense policy. Such a policy would equip the EU to deploy troops in support of its peace and diplomatic operations without duplicating NATO. For the first time since the collapse of the EDC in 1954, the EU members were taking seriously the need to cooperate on security issues. St. Malo led to a series of agreements among the EU countries to create and operationalize the ESDP.

ESDP was an historic breakthrough for EUFP. Previously, Britain had eschewed any concept of EU security that threatened the primacy of NATO. However, the British recognized that the EU could not defend its values without recourse to military action and that the ESDP could be made to complement both NATO and EU security. France was keen to build up a European security identity autonomous of NATO. St. Malo papered over these different emphases. Despite the EU's preoccupation with the Balkans during the third phase of EUFP development, the EU actively led international negotiations that resulted in establishing the International Criminal Court (ICC) and in the signings in 1998 of the Rome Statute and the Kyoto Protocol on climate change. As the 1990s gave way to the start of a new millennium, EUFP entered a new phase of development, during which time it began to apply the lessons of engaging in international politics and security from the past decade.

PHASE FOUR, 2000–PRESENT: INTERNATIONAL LEARNING

What the EU's experience in the Western Balkans demonstrated was that the "S" in the CFSP was missing—security. The EU was unable to act as a civilian power with recourse to military capability, if only for defensive and humanitarian purposes. As a consequence, the European Council introduced the goal of ESDP in 1999 as the appropriate framework to operationalize the Petersberg Tasks. The EU member states agreed that the union must have the capacity for autonomous action based on credible military forces, the means to decide to use them, and the readiness to do so in order to respond to international crises where NATO does not wish to be involved. Between 2000 and 2002, the EU established ESDP institutions, and the EU and NATO established procedures for EU use of NATO assets when NATO did not wish to be involved in a security operation. Just as the EU was developing the new ESDP institutions, its response to the U.S.-led invasion of Iraq in 2003 was very divided. Some members supported the invasion; others did not. EUFP was again weakened by the EU's own divisions.

Back in the troubled Western Balkans region, the EU and NATO worked in coordinated fashion to achieve a peace agreement between the government and rebel forces in Macedonia, thus helping to avoid a new war. The EU deployed a military force and police mission to help stabilize Macedonia. In BiH, the EU took over security operations from NATO and negotiated association accords with the region's states as a first step toward preparing them for membership in the EU.

Searching for direction and priorities to guide EU foreign policy, CFSP High Representative Javier Solana released in late 2003 the EU's first *European Security Strategy Paper*. This paper articulated strategic objectives in response to threats to European security.[4] The Strategy Paper, which was updated in 2008,

- listed terrorism, WMD proliferation, regional conflict, state failure, and organized crime as the main threats to EU security;
- emphasized that these security threats must be confronted at home and abroad;
- emphasized that the security of the EU must first be enhanced by stabilizing the Western Balkans and resolving the Israeli-Palestinian conflict; and
- articulated the principle of **effective multilateralism** as the cornerstone of EUFP:

the EU would lend its support to uphold and develop international law and strengthen the UN Charter.

Since 2003, the EU has deployed 22 ESDP actions in Europe, the Middle East, Africa, and Asia. ESDP missions have dealt with peace enforcement, police and police training, post-war peace monitoring, rule of law, and security sector reform. We examine these ESDP operations for their intended purposes later in this chapter and again in Chapter 9 for their effects. Having briefly scanned over fifty years of EUFP development, we now turn to how the EU initiates and executes its foreign affairs decisions.

Formulation and Execution

Although the bases for EUFP decisionmaking and action were divided among its three pillars, the outside world viewed the EU as an international actor regardless of where the competence to act originated. The Lisbon Treaty ends the EU pillar structure; however, differences will remain between the two cultures of EU governmental decisionmaking: the supranational features associated with foreign economic and diplomatic policy (QMV voting, codecision); and the intergovernmental features with regard to decisions on the deployment of force (consensus or unanimity). Regardless of the legal or political basis for foreign policy action, members are bound to accept the *acquis communautaire* and the *acquis politique*.

INSTITUTIONS AND DECISIONMAKING

The Commission initiates and executes EUFP actions where the Treaty gives it competence and the Council decides, in most instances, by QMV or consensus. The EP and Council have budgetary powers, and the EP has powers of oversight and assent (questioning the Commission and Council, voting on enlargement and most international accords). The EP makes recommendations and passes resolutions related to EUFP. The Council is obliged by Treaty law to keep the EP informed of CFSP/CSDP developments. The ECJ has purview over aspects of EUFP which are related to EU competences under the Treaty.

The Commission oversees the daily functioning of external commercial, development/humanitarian aid, and other areas related to its Treaty competences, including all matters pertaining to nonmember states seeking membership in the union. The major players in the Commission are the Commission President (responsible for representing the Commission in foreign affairs); the Commission Vice President (who as the High Representative of the Union for Foreign and Security Policy bridges the Commission and the Council in the area of foreign affairs); and the Directorate-General for External Relations (responsible for the day-to-day handling of the international work of the Commission). Other DGs have significant international responsibilities, namely the DGs for Agriculture and Rural Development, Development, Ecofin, Enlargement, Environment, Fisheries and Maritime Affairs, Humanitarian Affairs, and Justice, Freedom, and Security.

Prior to the Lisbon Treaty, the Commission's external relations service staffed and ran over 130 missions to individual countries and international organizations. The Council had a limited number of its own delegations. The European External Action Service (EEAS), established by the Lisbon Treaty, will eventually succeed all existing EU delegations abroad. The EEAS will come under the authority of the new High Representative of the Union for Foreign and Security Policy (High Representative). In November 2009, the European Council named Baroness Catherine Ashton as the new High Representative. As the new EU diplomatic service, the EEAS will consist of Commission and Council staff and diplomats seconded from the member states. The High Representative participates with the Presidents of the European Commission (José Manuel Barroso) and the European Council President (Herman Van Rompuy) in annual bilateral summits with third countries. Although the High Representative is responsible for the day-to-day functioning of the CFSP/CSDP, the President of the European Council is responsible for formally representing the EU abroad.

The HOGs set overall foreign policy objectives, and the Foreign Affairs Council (FAC) is the lead agency for the formulation and execution of CFSP and ESDP actions (ESDP hereafter is referred to as the Common Security and Defense Policy or CSDP following the change in name brought about by the Lisbon Treaty). Baroness Ashton chairs the FAC and preparations for FAC ministerial meetings are handled by expert working groups, the Political and Security Committee (see below), and COREPER. Although the Council is the lead agenda-setter in CFSP/CSDP, the Commission shares the right of initiative with the member governments, although not in the area of defense, and plays an active role in civilian aspects of CFSP and CSDP. The Commission is also involved in executing CFSP/CSDP decisions when its instruments and resources are needed. Unanimity or consensus in the FAC is the decisionmaking method used on all issues related to the deployment of forces abroad. In most other areas of EUFP, QMV is used. The Lisbon Treaty provides for a new form of decisionmaking for CSDP: permanent structured cooperation. This new form of cooperation is designed for member governments whose military capabilities are at a sufficiently high level to allow them to commit to demanding CSDP actions.

EU Foreign Ministers meet from time to time in an informal retreat setting called "Gymnich meetings" to discuss specific and pressing foreign policy issues facing the EU. Defense Ministers of the EU have also begun to meet informally. A "Jumbo Council" of EU Foreign Affairs, Development, and Defense Ministers is also convened periodically.

The High Representative is assisted by Directorate-General E (Political and Military Affairs) of the Council Secretariat (providing military and political analysis in support of CFSP/CSDP) and the CFSP/CSDP units described below. Eleven EU Special Representatives (EUSRs), appointed by the Council, are posted to trouble spots around the world to help foster effective implementation and coordination of EUFP actions and programs. EU Special Representatives (EUSRs), who report to the High Representative, are posted to the Western Balkans, southern Caucasuses, Central Africa, the African Great Lakes region, Afghanistan, and other troubled regions of the world.[5]

Four principal CSDP institutions are located in the Council. The Political and Security Committee (PSC)—member state Ambassadors and the Commission—monitors the international situation, makes policy recommendations to the Council,

Image 7.1.   CFSP High Representative Javier Solana in Chad (2008). Courtesy of the Council of the European Union

and exercises strategic direction for and political control of CSDP operations. The PSC receives information and draft recommendations on the civilian aspects of crisis management from the Committee for Civilian Aspects of Crisis Management (CIV-COM). The EU Military Committee (EUMC), the highest military institution in the Council, consists of Chiefs of Defense of the member states or their military representatives in Brussels. The EUMC provides advice and makes recommendations on military matters to the PSC. The EU Military Staff (EUMS), which consists of military and civilian experts seconded by the member states to the Council, provides expertise and advice to the EUMC and PSC on defense issues. It is responsible for early warning, situation assessment, strategic planning, and implementation of policies determined by the EUMC. It is the only permanent integrated military structure of the EU.

The Civilian Planning and Conduct Capability (CPCC) unit plans and conducts civilian CSDP operations under the control of the PSC. The unit provides assistance and advice to the High Representative, the Presidency, and other Council bodies, and it cooperates with the European Commission. The CPCC director is the EU Civilian Operations Commander, who exercises command and control at strategic level for the planning and implementation of all civilian crisis management operations.

Closely related to these CSDP bodies are the European Defense Agency (EDA), the EU Satellite Center, the EU Institute for Security Studies (EUISS), and the European Gendarmerie Force (EGF). The EDA is designed to support efforts of the member states to develop EU defense capabilities in crisis management, cooperate in procurement of armaments and defense equipment, and improve and develop the technological and industrial bases of European defense. For example, the EDA is launching programs to develop a European transport helicopter based on a Franco-German initiative. Directed by the High Representative, EDA is answerable to the Council. Although charged with a broad remit, it has no independent power other than to cajole member governments to do what they said they would do.

The EU Satellite Center provides analytical reports based on satellite imagery in support of CSDP operations (e.g., the naval operation off the Somali coast, the military operation in Eastern Chad, and the monitoring mission in Georgia). The EUISS conducts and publishes research on security issues, including analyses of CSDP operations. The Vicenza-based EGF, launched by the EU Defense Ministers, consists of members of the police forces (with military training) from six of the member states with a tradition of gendarmerie forces: France, Italy, the Netherlands, Portugal, Romania, and Spain. The EGF aims to deploy within short notice a rapid intervention force in support of CSDP operations.

INSTRUMENTS AND MILITARY CAPABILITIES

Instruments. The EU had four decisionmaking instruments for CFSP: common positions, joint actions, common strategies, and declarations/conclusions. EUFP actions will continue to reflect these kinds of instruments. In a common position, the member states are obliged to comply with an EU position in the implementation of their national foreign policies. Examples include levying sanctions on countries such as Belarus, Ivory Coast, Liberia, Myanmar, and Zimbabwe. The EU has a 2008 common position on defining the rules on the control of exports of military technology and equipment. A joint action puts into operation a common position. Examples include the deployments of an EU police mission to the Democratic Republic of the Congo (DRC) and a peace monitoring mission to Georgia.

A common strategy establishes overall policy guidelines for relations with individual states and regions where member states have common interests. Common strategies guide EU relations with Russia, Ukraine, and the countries of Central Asia (Kazakhstan, Kyrgyzstan, Tajikistan, Turkmenistan, and Uzbekistan). A 2003 common strategy dealt with proliferation of WMDs. The EU makes declarations or reaches conclusions on a wide variety of international issues. For examples, in 2002 it announced its opposition to the U.S. position on the creation of the ICC, and in 2008 it presented a communication to the Council proposing trilateral (EU–China–Africa) cooperation to promote political, food, and energy security in Africa.

Military Capabilities. It has been far easier for the EU to announce its intentions to implement the Petersberg Tasks than to deliver on the promise. The member states together field approximately 1.6 million men and women in national uniforms, but those troops have been trained for territorial defense in response to a potential ground war (e.g., with the Soviet Union during the Cold War). Members struggle to train and deploy troops for EU civilian and military operations abroad. The gap between the equipment and personnel the EU member states need to deploy and what they currently have is referred to as **capabilities shortfalls.** Examples of shortfalls include air and sea lift, air-to-air refueling, attack helicopter and reconnaissance and liaison helicopter battalions, combat search and rescue, communications equipment, early warning and distant detection intelligence-gathering satellites, cruise missiles and precision-guided munitions, force headquarters, imagery and signal intelligence collection, interoperability of armed forces, rapid deployment, precision-guided weapons, strategic airlift, tactical ballistic missile defense suppression of enemy air defense, and transport docks.

The EU aims to be able by 2010 to deploy 60,000 troops in sixty days for civilian and military operations. However, the 2010 goal follows earlier deadlines that the member states failed to meet. The primary means to deploy force will take the form of a battle group.

A battle group is a form of rapid response—a combined-arms, battalion-sized, high-readiness force of 1,500 troops from participating EU member states reinforced with combat support elements. These elements include relevant air and naval capabilities, which can be launched on the ground within ten days after the EU decides to act. Each battle group has a Force Headquarters and pre-identified transport and logistics elements. Deployment of a battle group is designed to support and reinforce the peace operations of the UN, NATO, and regional security organizations, such as the AU. The EU currently has two battle groups ready for deployment. Neither has yet been deployed.

To illustrate the gap between rhetoric and capability, one need only refer to the repeated delays in the member states' ambition to rapidly transport forces far from European shores. Several member states placed orders for 170 A400M Airbus strategic air-lift carriers for rapid deployment. However, delivery is delayed as costs soar and governments grow reticent about the implications for their national budget deficits. Indeed, EU member governments' costs associated with filling the major capabilities gaps are estimated to exceed €50 billion.

Having briefly outlined some of the main elements of EUFP institutions, instruments, and capabilities, we now turn to outputs of EUFP—policies on multilateral functional and security issues and on bilateral relationships.

Key Elements—Multilateral Functional Issues

This section focuses first on multilateral functional issues because this is where the EU takes experience from home abroad. It does this by promoting human welfare and security sector-by-sector across national frontiers. As the EU itself is an intense experiment in regional multilateralism, it comes as no surprise that the *European Security Strategy Paper* stresses the importance of "effective multilateralism" as the cornerstone of EUFP. There are few international functional areas where the EU does not have an interest, position, or policy. This section briefly surveys policy where the EU is no stranger: trade, foreign development and humanitarian aid, human rights, democratic governance, climate change, and criminal justice. The next section focuses on international security issues where the EU is a newcomer.

MULTILATERAL TRADE, FOREIGN DEVELOPMENT, AND HUMANITARIAN AID

Since the EU accounts for about a fifth of total world trade, it runs an active foreign trade policy. As a contracting party to the WTO, it plays a critical role in trade liberalization negotiations. Its position is instrumental to the conclusion of the long-stalled Doha Round of WTO negotiations. The EU is active in WTO dispute settlement procedures both as a complainant (it initiates cases) and defendant (it is the target of cases). For example, in 2008, it was involved in thirty-three WTO trade disputes, fifteen as complainant and eighteen as defendant. Since it has to certify that applicants for WTO membership are market economies, the EU has influence over which countries join. Having supported the recent accession of China and Ukraine, the EU has indicated its support for the accessions of Russia, Vietnam, and Algeria.

The EU is active in highly political international trade issues. For example, it has been a leading member of the Kimberly Process—an international regime whose members agree to monitor an agreement to end purchases of diamonds from conflict areas. Moreover, the EU lowers tariffs to developing countries who respect the labor conditions established by the International Labor Organization. The EU offers subsidized loans from the European Regional Development Fund with special focus on aid to prevent and treat HIV-AIDS and other infectious diseases and on cooperation to combat illicit production of and trade in drugs, among other priorities.

Offering aid and cutting tariffs are the two primary means of EU support for countries in need of assistance. The EU and its member states are the developing countries' largest importer of goods and largest donor of aid for economic development and humanitarian assistance, providing 60 percent of total world ODA. The EU's goal is to increase ODA to 0.7 percent of the members' gross national product by 2015. The bulk of the EU's €940 million in annual humanitarian relief aid offered by the EC Humanitarian Office (ECHO) is contracted to UN and nongovernmental organizations. Humanitarian aid includes food aid and support for refugees, displaced persons and victims of drought and war. Fifty-five percent of EU humanitarian aid goes to NGOs and the remainder to UN and other intergovernmental organizations. The African, Caribbean, and Pacific (ACP) states, all former European colonies, and the nonmember Mediterranean states receive over €700 million of all EU humanitarian aid.

Principal beneficiaries of economic assistance include Croatia as it prepares to join the EU, Kosovo as it rebuilds its economy and establishes new national institutions, and Afghanistan as it fights the Taliban and other insurgencies. The EIB, one of the principal EU bodies dedicated to providing economic development assistance, provided nearly €5 billion in support for the ACP states in 2008.

As discussed in Chapter 6, the EU reduces or eliminates tariffs for most of the world's poorest states through its Generalized System of Preferences program. In another program, "Everything but Arms," the EU grants duty-free access for all products other than weapons to about fifty developing countries. The idea behind cutting or eliminating import levies is to help poor countries produce for foreign markets so that they can earn profits, provide jobs, and collect much-needed foreign exchange to purchase technologies and commodities necessary for internal development.

HUMAN RIGHTS AND DEMOCRATIZATION EFFORTS, CLIMATE CHANGE, AND CRIMINAL JUSTICE

The EU supports multilateral efforts to enhance human security to advance both its own security interests in an unstable world and its own values of human rights, the rule of law, civil society, market economics, and representative democracy. It also recognizes that development assistance is good not only for countries trying to increase the standards of living of their peoples, but also to keep individuals seeking a better economic way of life from migrating, legally or illegally, into the EU. The EU seeks to avoid an exodus of economic migrants into Europe, swamping member-state capabilities to manage their numbers and provide jobs and social services for them.

The EU is a major player in the international human rights arena when the member states stick to a common position. For example, the members have been unanimous in their strident opposition to capital punishment, viewing it as a violation of basic human rights. The EU not only seeks to isolate the United States on this issue, but outlaws the practice among its own members and requires applicant states to outlaw it as well if they want to join the union. The principal means by which the EU exercises human rights policy are through its participation in international institutions, issuance of demarches (protests), addition of human rights clauses in some of its international agreements, and use of sanctions.

At times, the EU acts in unison at the UN Human Rights Council in Geneva. However, this is not always the case. For example, at the 2009 UN Conference on Racism (Durban II) in Geneva, the union was terribly divided. Some member governments boycotted the conference for its bias against Israel (Greece, Italy, Poland, and the Netherlands). Other member governments and the Czech EU Presidency attended the conference, but left in protest after the Iranian President called Israel a racist state. Clearly the EU member states could not agree on a common position before the start of the meetings.

The EU issues demarches to foreign governments on human rights violations. For example, the EU in 2008 issued demarches on human rights abuses to Bolivia, China, Sri Lanka, and Sudan, among other countries. The EU requires the inclusion of human rights clauses in its association accords with nonmember states. The EU imposed sanctions on the military government of Myanmar for the house arrest of the Nobel peace prize recipient Aung San Suu Kyi and for the suppression of democracy in the former Burma; and an arms embargo on Uzbekistan for its human rights violations, including the incarceration of political prisoners.

Assisting countries in the process of a democratic transition or consolidation is a functional and not just a purely political issue. The EU actively promotes respect for the rule of law and free and democratic elections. It is an important contributor to election monitoring in democratizing countries worldwide. It carried out over seventy electoral observation and related missions from 2000 to 2008. For example, in 2008 it sent observers to the parliamentary elections in Bangladesh, Cambodia, and Pakistan. The EU is also a powerful voice within the Organization for Security and Cooperation in Europe (OSCE), and the two organizations work closely in monitoring elections and building conditions for democracy and civil society in war-torn areas of the Western Balkans.

Farther afield, the EU has taken an interest in the absence of democracy in Cuba. It has blocked Cuba from the benefit of EU tariff cuts afforded to other developing states that are former colonies of EU members (Cotonou Agreement) until Havana improves its human rights record and respect for democracy. The EU supported a resolution against Cuba by the UN Human Rights Council in April 2000. It has imposed sanctions on Nigeria, Zimbabwe, and other signatories of the Cotonou Agreement when violations of human rights and democratic principles have occurred.

However, the EU also lifts sanctions when previously targeted states have shifted policy. For examples, the EU lifted sanctions against Libya in 2004 after Tripoli (1) made restitutions to the families of victims of the terrorist bombing of Pan Am Flight 103 over Lockerbie, Scotland in 1992; and (2) took measures to assuage EU concerns over Libyan policies in support of WMDs and terrorism. In 2008, the EU lifted a visa ban on Uzbekistani government officials over the jailing of political prisoners and other human rights issues; and lifted sanctions on Cuba over its human rights abuses (even though the EU continued to call on Havana to release all political prisoners).

Lastly, the EU is most active in promoting human and minority rights in its own neighborhood and in its relations with states with whom the EU has association agreements. States who wish to join the EU must end discrimination against minority groups. For examples, the CEE states had to address discrimination against the Roma people before they joined the EU and Turkey was pressed by the EU to change its constitution to provide for the linguistic and other rights of its Kurdish minority. As previously mentioned, the EU makes human rights clauses a condition of all association agreements with countries in the Mediterranean and Africa. The pursuit of EU human rights with individual countries is taken up in the section on Bilateral Relations in this chapter.

The EU lobbied hard to help win the signing and passage of the 1997 Kyoto Protocol on Global Warming and the 1998 Rome Statute establishing the ICC, despite enormous opposition from the United States. As the Kyoto Protocol expires in 2012, the EU is actively supporting negotiations for the next climate change treaty. Its leadership of these talks is strengthened by the passage in December 2008 of legislation accelerating EU cuts in emissions of greenhouse gases. With similar alacrity, the EU was a major force behind the creation of and support for the ICC, lobbying foreign governments to commit to voting in the affirmative for the Rome Statute.

Key Elements—Multilateral Security Issues

In multilateral cooperation, the EU operates in the world as it does at home, seeking compromises among sovereign states to enhance human welfare and national interests when functional needs arise that cannot be satisfactorily addressed on a single-state basis. In the area of multilateral functional cooperation, the EU has long-standing experience. It is often, but not always, prepared to act with common positions. Conversely, in international security, the EU is a relatively new actor on the world stage. As described in the previous section and elsewhere in the book, Treaty-based foreign policy activities of the EU over the past half-century have had security and political implications. What has changed since the late 1990s is the willingness of the member states to act on their collective diplomacy by backing positions, interests, and values with security operations in the context of CSDP and in addressing the threats to their own and international security.

This section begins with an overview of the EU-NATO relationship given the large overlap of EU and NATO members, continues with a brief introduction to the twenty-two CSDP operations since 2003, and ends with discussions of EU positions on international security issues, including nonproliferation and anticrime/antiterrorism.

RELATIONSHIP WITH NATO

The EU and NATO Secretaries-General demonstrated the value of a coordinated EU-NATO approach to security when the EU's Solana and NATO's Robertson worked closely together to help bring about and secure the ceasefire between the Albanian minority in Macedonia and the Macedonian Government in 2001 (Ohrid Framework Agreement). The road to EU-NATO cooperation has been long, winding, and difficult given how different the two organizations' missions are, despite the fact that their memberships substantially overlap. Twenty-one EU members are NATO members (Austria, Cyprus, Finland, Ireland, Malta, and Sweden are not in NATO). The EU and NATO hold meetings together; the EU has a small planning cell in NATO—Supreme Headquarters Allied Powers Europe (SHAPE)—while NATO has a liaison office at the EU Military Staff.

In 2003, the two organizations negotiated the so-called **"Berlin Plus" arrangement**, which allows EU access to NATO assets/capabilities in security operations when NATO does not wish to act. With some notable exceptions (e.g., the CSDP operations in BiH and Kosovo), the Europeans have demonstrated their preference for taking CSDP actions without recourse to NATO assets.

From the present vantage point, the Berlin Plus arrangement is becoming outdated for two principal reasons. First, the EU has demonstrated its wish to deploy force autonomously from NATO. Second, Turkey has blocked or could block Berlin Plus and other EU-NATO formal arrangements, given its opposition to EU policy on Cyprus and the blocking by Nicosia of further progress in the EU-Turkish accession negotiations. The sooner the EU and Turkey can work out a compromise over the division of Cyprus, the better relations will be between the EU and NATO in the conduct of international security operations that interest and involve both organizations. If that scenario is not likely, either the EU and U.S. could collaborate on international security operations (which would leave out non-EU NATO countries, especially Canada and Norway) and/or the EU and NATO may continue to work quietly together in areas where the two organizations are present on the ground in common areas of operation. They already do so without Turkish opposition in BiH and Kosovo and on the east coast of Africa and are expected to coordinate further in Afghanistan.

The EU and NATO do not yet have the same kind of structured institutional relations of summits and working procedures as do the EU and the U.S. The two Secretaries-General meet, as do the North Atlantic Council and the EU's PSC. However, not much happens at these meetings, given the still-apparent differences in NATO and EU cultures and over the Cypriot problem.

EU SECURITY OPERATIONS

Table 7.1 lists and map 7.1 depicts the location of all CSDP operations. Given the very early stage in the development of CSDP, these operations are test-cases of the

Table 7.1: CSDP Operations by Country, Date, and Type of Decisionmaking, 2003–Present

Operation	Country	Date	Type/Description
Operation Concordia	Macedonia	2003	a military force deployed to oversee EU–NATO sponsored ceasefire between government and rebel forces and to replace the outgoing NATO force.
Operation Artemis	Democratic Republic of the Congo	2003	a military force of 1,800 deployed to the Ituri region, requested/ mandated by the UN and placed under French command, to provide security and humanitarian support as UN peacekeepers were rotated in and out of Bunia.
Police Mission	Bosnia and Herzegovina	2003–	a police force deployed to assist in the establishment of a multiethnic police force to enhance local stability and fight organized crime. The force of 440 police officers and 60 civilian experts replaced the outgoing UN police force.
Operation Proxima	Macedonia	2003–2005	a police force of 200 officers deployed to assist with border management, anti-crime efforts, and reform of the interior ministry.
Operation Althea	Bosnia and Herzegovina	2004–	a military force of 2,000 deployed to BiH, based on the Berlin Plus arrangement, to replace NATO forces and provide security and stability. The EU has executive authority, meaning it takes constitutional, governmental, and judicial action in the context of its operations.
EUJUST Themis	Georgia	2004–2005	a rule of law mission dispatched to assist in the reform of the criminal justice system.
Monitoring Mission	Indonesia	2005–2006	an EU-ASEAN mission of over 200 monitors in Banda Aceh to oversee the implementation of the ceasefire agreement between forces and the Indonesian Government, including the laying down of arms by rebel forces.
Police Mission	Macedonia	2005–2006	a mission to support police reform and cooperation between the police and the judiciary
EUPOL Kinshasa	Democratic Republic of the Congo	2005–2007	a police mission deployed to assist the government in the establishment of effective police programs. A successor mission, EUPOL Congo, was established in 2007.
Security Sector Reform	Democratic Republic of the Congo	2005–2009	a mission to offer assistance for security sector reform to help create an integrated army and coordinate international efforts to support army reform.
Civilian-Military Support Action	Sudan	2005–	a program of assistance to support African Union peacekeeping, civilian policing, and humanitarian efforts in Darfur, Sudan.
Integrated Rule of Law Mission	Iraq	2005–	a mission to train and/or mentor senior police officers, judges, prosecutors, and prison officials.

Table 7.1: CSDP Operations by Country, Date, and Type of Decisiommaking, 2003-Present (continued)

Operation	Country	Date	Type
Border Assistance Mission	Moldova, Ukraine	2005–	a training and monitoring mission to provide assistance for police and customs officials on the Moldova–Ukraine border to help prevent smuggling, trafficking, and customs fraud.
Border Assistance Mission	Gaza/Egypt border	2005–	a mission to monitor the Rafah border crossing between Gaza and Egypt (operation suspended in 2007, but EU is prepared to redeploy).
Support for UN Mission	Democratic Republic of the Congo	2006	a deployment of rapid reaction and standby troops to provide support for the UN forces and security before/during presidential and legislative elections.
Police and Rule of Law Mission	Palestinian Territories	2006–	a mission to train police and support the rule of law
Police and Rule of Law Mission	Afghanistan	2007–	a civilian mission of over 300 personnel to assist with training of law enforcement and justice officials, police reform, anti-corruption, and related rule of law issues.
Monitoring Mission	Georgia	2008–	a deployment of 370 peace monitors on the administrative boundary lines between Georgia and the Russian-occupied breakaway regions of Abkhazia and South Ossetia
Security Sector Reform	Guinea-Bissau	2008–	a mission to provide assistance and advice to officials of the military, police, and judiciary engaged in reforms in and restructuring of the security sector.
Naval Protection Force	Somalia	2008–	a deployment of 13 warships and three maritime patrol air surveillance aircraft off the Somali coast to escort shipments of the World Food Program and to deter and interdict pirates seeking to commandeer ships of EU member states and other countries.
EUFOR	Chad, the Central African Republic	2008–2009	a deployment of 3,100 EU military personnel to assist humanitarian workers and protect civilians, especially refugees and displaced persons, as a result of the worsening crisis in Darfur, and protect UN staff.
Rule of Law Mission	Kosovo	2009–	a deployment of 1700 personnel (with executive authority) to Kosovo to monitor, mentor, and advise judicial, law enforcement, and other national authorities in establishing the rule of law. US judges and police officers participate.

Map 7.1. CSDP Operations by Geographic Region: Overview of the missions and operations of the European Union. Data courtesy of the Council of the European Union.

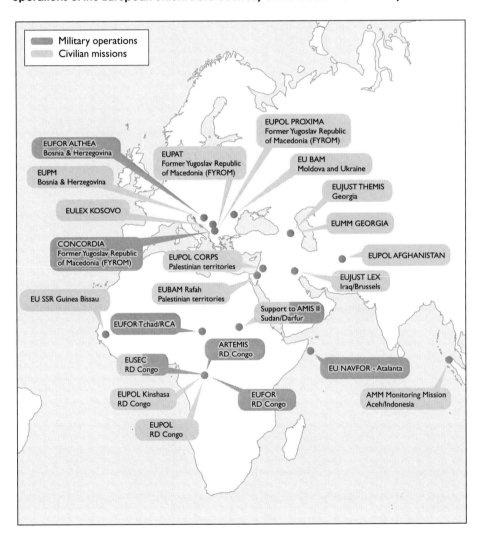

EU's new-found role in global security issues. Suffice it to say that by virtue of the demand for EU operations—and their range, type, and geographical reach—the EU is gaining experience in international security. This should not mask the limited resources and military and civilian capabilities of the EU. Moreover, CSDP operations have thus far been deployed to relatively permissive environments, which means the EU has not yet been tested in a dangerous theatre of operation such as Afghanistan.

Yet CSDP is still new, international learning is occurring, and the EU has recourse to the full range of foreign and security policy instruments for the first time. Demand for CSDP operations emanates from the Europeans themselves, who want to give back security to the world, and from the outside world, which looks to the EU as a security provider. Only time will tell what the future holds for CSDP, but there is good reason to think the Europeans are, at last, putting the "S" into the CFSP. We will return to the study of EU security operations when we examine their effects in Chapter 9. Beyond the new CSDP actions, the EU is otherwise engaged in the gamut of international security issues: nonproliferation, disarmament, arms control, and combating transnational crime and terrorism. It is to these areas we now turn.

NONPROLIFERATION, DISARMAMENT, AND ARMS CONTROL

The EU views WMD proliferation as a threat to its security. It has a policy of support for multilateral and bilateral cooperation in nonproliferation and has demonstrated that it can (1) overcome policy differences among the member states on nonproliferation issues; and (2) proffer proposals on nonproliferation at multilateral conferences and seek support for them. The EU was active and constructive in the negotiations for the indefinite extension of the Nuclear Nonproliferation Treaty (NNPT) in 1995, for which it lobbied hard, and during the Review Conference (2000). Although the 2005 NNPT Review Conference ended in failure, the EU arrived at the conference armed with a common position that reflected compromises among nuclear and non-nuclear EU members. The EU also had an impact on the Conference's final recommendations. However, some analysts suggest that the EU could have played a more effective role had it released and lobbied for its ideas months before the conference convened, not days, as was the case.

EU disarmament policy regarding nuclear weapons is another matter. As nuclear weapons states, France and Britain have interests that align with other nuclear weapons states. This makes it very unlikely that the EU will develop a nuclear disarmament policy. However, the EU actively pursues policies regarding nonproliferation of nuclear and other weapons of mass destruction. For example, it is standard in EU association accords with third countries to include a clause committing the signatories to nonproliferation and to signing/ratifying the Nuclear Nonproliferation Treaty, the Chemical Weapons Convention, and the Biological and Toxin Weapons Convention, among others. The EU could impose sanctions if the signatory does not fulfill its international obligations.

The EU offered developing country signatories to the Chemical Weapons Convention financial assistance in order to meet their international obligations with respect to the destruction of stocks of chemical weapons and production facilities. The EU has also actively sought international support for the ban on the production of and trade in antipersonnel landmines. As a signatory to the Antipersonnel Landmine Treaty banning landmines, the EU is a major financial contributor to efforts to clear antipersonnel landmines. To help stem nuclear proliferation in East Asia, particularly in North Korea in the 1990s, the EU joined and helped finance the Korean Energy Development Organization (KEDO). KEDO, unfortunately, did not succeed in stopping North Korea's pursuit of a nuclear weapons program.

The EU has grown increasingly concerned over Iran's pursuit of a nuclear energy program that is expected to result in the production of nuclear weapons. Since 2005, the EU and United States have begun to work closely together to coordinate pressure on Iran to bring its nuclear program in compliance with UN International Atomic Energy Agency (IAEA) regulations. This coordination signified a major shift from years of EU-U.S. disagreement on how to address Iran's nuclear program. The IAEA has called on Iran to suspend uranium enrichment while the country continues to develop centrifuges to enrich what could be weapons-grade uranium as well as medium-range or long-range ballistic missiles that could carry nuclear warheads reaching Israel and the EU's eastern fringe. EU sanctions on Iran include the freezing of assets in the EU of persons and entities indirectly or directly associated with Iran's nuclear program activity (e.g., Bank Melli). The EU also withholds the granting of export credits and guarantees. Since the U.S. and Iran do not have diplomatic relations, the EU plays a critically important role as the West's interlocutor with Tehran.

COMBATING CRIME AND TERRORISM

The fight against transnational crime and terrorism is a growth area of European integration in both its internal and external dimensions. Many EU foreign policy actions addressing the world's international issues, states, and regions are infused with JHA objectives. The EU reacted with uncharacteristic speed to the terrorist attacks on the United States in 2001. It proposed and is seeking to implement an EU-wide arrest warrant to simplify and expedite extradition among the member states. It put into effect a long-delayed directive of 1999 to combat money laundering, and it froze assets of twenty-seven groups and individuals thought to be linked to the terror attacks on the United States, including the political wing of Hamas. Following the terrorist attack in Madrid in 2004, the EU created a new position, a Counter-terrorism Coordinator, to enhance the counter-terrorism work of the Council in this field.

Pursuant to the continuing terrorist threat, the EU receives and analyzes information from the member states' security and intelligence services and when appropriate from Europol. The EU maintains a list of individuals and groups determined to be involved in terrorist acts whose assets must be frozen, and the EU Money Laundering Directive is being extended to cover terrorist financing. The EU engages in counter-terrorism cooperation in all its foreign relationships at bilateral, regional, and multilateral levels and provides assistance to third countries who aim to enhance their efforts in this area.

Last but not least, antipiracy is now a concern of the EU. Its naval operation off the coast of Somalia (see Chapter 9), coupled with continuing and expanding support for the besieged government in Mogadishu, suggests a new commitment to combating one of the world's oldest forms of crime and terror. The EU is paying closer attention as well to the relation of organized crime and terrorism with drug trafficking between West Africa and Latin America.

Key Elements—Bilateral Relations

After having scanned the major elements of the EU's multilateral policies across civilian and military spheres, we now turn to the rich array of relations between the EU and the world's states and regions. Our *tour de monde* begins with Europe and the Mediterranean Basin and moves south to Africa and east to the Levant and Asia, before ending further east with the Americas.

WESTERN EUROPE AND THE WESTERN BALKANS

The last four states of Western Europe not in the EU are members of the European Free Trade Association (EFTA)—Iceland, Liechtenstein, Norway, and Switzerland. Although Norwegians twice rejected EU membership in referenda, a future Norwegian membership perspective is in the realm of possibilities. Iceland applied for EU membership in 2009. The EU has been a powerful magnet, attracting EFTA members to join it since the 1970s.

The EU and EFTA share an industrial free trade area. EFTA states (except Switzerland) and the EU created the so-called European Economic Area in 2004. This allows the EFTA states to participate in the internal market (e.g., be consulted by the Commission on legislative proposals and accept the internal market legislation as national legislation), while not assuming the full responsibilities of EU membership. EFTA states (except Liechtenstein) also enjoy membership in the Schengen Accord. The EFTA states often endorse EUFP positions and have participated in CSDP operations; for example, Norway and Switzerland participated in the 2005 CSDP peace monitoring mission in Banda Aceh, Indonesia; and Norway participates in the EU antipiracy mission off the Somali coast.

The EU is also a magnet for the Western Balkan states (Albania, BiH, Croatia, Kosovo, Macedonia, Montenegro, and Serbia). Even if peoples and governments in this region are ambivalent about joining the EU, the costs of staying outside—while important decisions concerning them are made inside without them—are too great to ignore. For states with small populations, free access to a market of nearly 500 million consumers and billions of euros in pre-accession development aid are powerful inducements to joining the union.

With Romanian and Bulgarian accession to the EU in 2007, the nonmember states in the Western Balkans have become an enclave surrounded by the EU. It is because this enclave is so important to the security of the EU that the region is such a high foreign policy priority. If the EU can help these states overcome armed conflict and reconcile their differences, it can avoid the resumption of war, and it can help states develop unified national institutions with democratic features and market economies. Of equal concern to the EU is to help these states bolster their defenses against transnational terrorism and crime, particularly drug and human trafficking, money laundering, illegal immigration, and proliferation of WMDs. All these maladies adversely affect EU security.

The Western Balkans have historically been a transit or source for criminal activity between east and west. Thus, as the EU and the area's countries begin to reduce and possibly eliminate barriers to the movement of goods and persons across their borders, the EU risks importing illegal persons. The more the EU can strengthen the Western Balkan states' external borders, internal police, and judicial and overall rule of law capabilities to fight crime, the better. This is why the EU has made a commitment to these states to bring each of them closer to the integration process with the eventual objective of accession.

The decision to enlarge (or not to enlarge) the union to new members is the most important instrument in the EUFP toolkit. This is because when a foreign government wants to join the EU, it must adapt national law to meet the Copenhagen Criteria and to conform to the *acquis communautaire*. For example, there was sufficient EU leverage on Turkey to provide new constitutional protections for the rights of the Kurdish minority and to ban capital punishment. However, the more the EU expands to include European states, the less relevant enlargement becomes as a foreign policy instrument. EU publics are increasingly wary of or opposed to further enlargement. Thus there is no incentive for Belarus or Moldova to bend to EU rules and demands if EU membership is either not possible in the foreseeable future or too distant a possibility to fathom.

Among the Western Balkans, Slovenia led the way when it joined the EU in 2004, and Croatia and Macedonia have received candidate status in 2004 and 2005, respectively. Montenegro applied for membership in 2008. The path to joining the EU is through the medium of Stabilization and Association Accords (SAAs), which the EU has with Albania, Croatia, and Macedonia. It also has signed, but not yet ratified, accords with BiH, Montenegro, and Serbia. Each SAA provides the basis for the establishment of free trade with the EU, substantial EU assistance for democratization and market economic reforms, and high-level political dialogue on all major functional and security issues. The EU aims not only to bind these states closer to itself, but to encourage freer trade, reconciliation, and political cooperation among them. The feather in the cap of each SAA is the EU's commitment of future membership for the signatory if the criteria for joining are met.

Croatia. The EU-Croatia SAA was not concluded until Zagreb responded to pressure to cooperate fully with the International Criminal Tribunal for Former Yugoslavia (ICTY) by extraditing to The Hague Croatian citizens charged with war crimes or crimes against humanity committed during the Yugoslav wars of the 1990s. Croatia is a major beneficiary of EU pre-accession aid to assist with needed reforms to prepare for membership, Croatia and the EU have opened negotiations for twenty-two of the thirty-five chapters of the future accession treaty and have closed seven.

Serbia. Although the EU and Serbia concluded negotiations for an SAA in 2008, the accord has not yet been ratified by the EU. The Netherlands and Belgium are waiting for full Serbian compliance with the ICTY. Belgrade arrested Radovan Karadzic and extradited him to The Hague in 2009 to face charges of war crimes, crimes against humanity, and genocide. However, the EU is still pressing Serbia to arrest other war crimes suspects—including Ratko Mladic and Goran Hadzic. Montenegro, which declared its independence from Serbia in 2008, is negotiating an SAA with the EU.

Bosnia-Herzegovina. The EU signed an SAA with BiH in 2008, in an important complement to the EU's efforts to help stabilize the multiethnic country. Besides its deployment of military and police forces to help ensure stability and implementation of the Dayton Peace Accords, the EU is leading and financing the country's dramatic postwar economic reconstruction efforts.

Macedonia. In 2004, Macedonia applied for membership in the EU and in 2005, the EU and Macedonia entered into an SAA. In that same year, the Commission delivered a favorable opinion on Macedonia's application to join the EU, and the European Council granted candidate country status. Despite these positive indicators, accession negotiations have not yet begun. However, in late 2009 the Commission announced that since Macedonia had met the Copenhagen Criteria, it recommended to the Council that accession negotiations be opened with Skopje.

The bilateral relationship got off to a rocky start when Greece vetoed EU diplomatic recognition of the newly independent Macedonian state in 1991. Since Greece has its own region called Macedonia and felt threatened by a new state that in theory could lay claim to Greek Macedonia, the Greeks forced the EU and Macedonia to agree to refer to the republic not as Macedonia but as the Former Yugoslav Republic of Macedonia (FYROM). Once this accord was reached, the EU and Macedonia established diplomatic relations. The EU played a key role with NATO in 2001 in helping to secure a ceasefire between the Government and rebel Albanian forces. In 2003, the EU deployed Operation Concordia, a military force in conjunction with NATO that succeeded the NATO force there. The EU also deployed Operation Proxima, the EU police mission, from 2003 to 2005. As the European Council decision to open accession negotiations with Skopje requires unanimity, Greece and Macedonia will need to come to an understanding over the issue of Macedonia's name.

Kosovo. After Kosovo declared independence from Serbia in 2008, the EU was divided. Five of the twenty-seven members decided not to recognize Pristina but were willing to support the deployment of the EU rule of law mission in 2009. Previously, Kosovo, which had been a province of Serbia, had been under the administration of the UN Mission in Kosovo (UNMIK), supported by NATO-led peacekeeping forces (Kosovo Force or KFOR). The EU is in charge of economic reconstruction and cooperates closely with NATO on the ground, especially in areas where there is a Serbian community (e.g., in Mitrovica, northern Kosovo).

EASTERN EUROPE, THE CAUCASUSES, AND RUSSIA

How far can the EU expand to include all of Europe while deepening the union and maintaining the *acquis communautaire*? Concerns abound in countries like Austria, France, and Germany over reaching or exceeding the EU's "absorption capacity"—its ability to grow further and maintain cohesion as a union. One approach to its relations with the non-member states in Eastern Europe and the Caucasuses for whom membership is not likely is to offer these states close association with the EU. Such association would feature access to and acceptance of the rules of the internal market, substantial development assistance, and high-level political dialogue at head of government and ministerial levels. The EU is particularly interested in cooperating with these states, which are either sources of or transit for natural and gas supplies, especially after the Russian invasion of Georgia in 2008 and the Russian cut-off of natural gas supplies in price and supply disputes with Ukraine in 2009.

The EUFP framework for enhancing relations with Armenia, Azerbaijan, Belarus, Georgia, and Ukraine is the newly established Eastern Partnership designed to more closely associate these former Soviet republics with the EU. The Eastern Partnership has bilateral and multilateral tracks: association accords between the EU and its eastern partners, which feature free trade provisions, and regional cooperation among all to promote political stability, democratic governance, economic integration, convergence with EU internal market policies, and energy security. The newly negotiated association accords will replace the existing PCAs.

Belarus. Relations with Belarus are difficult, given EU concerns over human rights violations, flawed elections, and the imprisonment of political opponents in 2008. The EU imposed travel bans on Belarusian officials, including the President, but lifted them in 2009. Still, rule of law and human rights issues remain of concern.

Georgia. The Russian invasion of Georgia in August 2008 helped refocus EUFP attention on the southern Caucasuses. After all, the Russians had invaded a democratic country whose pipelines carry natural gas to Europe. The French EU Presidency negotiated a ceasefire in August and an agreement with the Russians and Georgians in September to deploy a monitoring mission on the administrative borders between South Ossetia and Georgia and between Abkhazia and Georgia. The EU deployment was based on Russia's agreement to withdraw all troops from the security zones on the Georgian border adjacent to the two breakaway regions and to allow EU access to all Georgian territory. Neither has happened. The Russian-backed South Ossetian army still occupies Akhalgori, a Georgian village near but outside the administrative border between South Ossetia and Georgia. No EU monitors have been allowed to enter the breakaway republics. This has led some to suggest that the EU presence implicitly recognizes new international frontiers, even though the EU is unambiguously supportive of Georgian sovereignty over its entire territory and condemned the Russians for recognizing the independence of these regions.

The European Union Monitoring Mission was rapidly dispatched to the administrative boundary regions and fully deployed by the end of 2008. The mission consists of 340 observers, costing the EU about €500 million annually. The OSCE and UN monitoring missions in Georgia were not renewed in 2009, thus leaving the EU behind as the only international monitoring presence in the country.

Ukraine. Ukraine expressed its interest in joining the EU before the Orange Revolution of 2004. However, it was far from meeting the Copenhagen Criteria, and was therefore disappointed by the EU decision not to open accession negotiations. It appeared initially that the Orange Revolution had changed the dynamic between the EU and Ukraine. First, the EU in general and some of its members (Poland, Germany, and Lithuania in particular) were important players in pressing Ukraine to hold democratic presidential elections. Second, the Government of Ukraine preferred accession to the EU over a mere PCA. The EU was under enormous pressure from Kiev to hold out the promise of future EU membership. Ukraine has aligned some of its foreign and security policies with those of the EU and participates in CSDP operations. In response to a request from the Ukraine and Moldova, the EU launched a border assistance mission in 2005 to assist officials of both countries to address the problems of weapons trafficking, drug smuggling, and organized crime.

As the glow of the Orange Revolution ebbed, and Ukrainian politics grew more divided, the EU backed off from making any promises of membership. Indeed, today Ukraine is split over its long-term relationship with the EU. Many in the western part of the country wish to join the EU, but many in the east prefer closer relations with Russia. By placing Ukraine in the context of the Eastern Partnership, the EU is sending a signal: no membership for now. This does not mean membership is precluded in the longer-term. At the same time, the EU itself is becoming increasingly divided over the scope of its absorption capacity—and one wonders when and how it will be able to meet the promise of membership for the SAA states. Short of full membership, the EU and Ukraine can work together to achieve common goals. The forum for relations will be the new EU-Ukraine association accord, which is under negotiation. The future accord is expected to feature free trade provisions and high-level EU-Ukrainian cooperation on foreign and security policy issues, including further participation by Kiev in CSDP operations.

The EU has actively mediated the dispute between the Ukraine and Russia over the price and supply of natural gas that transits the country from Russia to Europe. As mentioned, Russia had cut off the supply in its dispute with Ukraine. The EU is concerned about a potential repeat of such a cutoff, which would threaten winter fuel deliveries to millions of EU citizens.

Russia. EU-Russian relations are strained and troubled. EU member states are at times divided over how best to respond to such Russian actions as shutting off gas supplies to Europe through Ukraine and invading Georgia, or to the suspicious murders of Russian journalists who are out of favor with the government. The former Soviet republics and Eastern bloc states in the EU are far more skeptical of Russia than are, say, the French, Germans, and Italians. Primary among all of these EU concerns is the reliability of Russia as a major supplier of natural gas and oil to many EU member states. The EU needs to engage Russia not only to procure energy supplies but to cooperate in the fight against transnational terrorism and crime and proliferation of WMD and to address issues of nuclear safety. Is Russia interested?

Since the EU lacks a coherent foreign energy policy and is divided over how best to deal with Russia, it is disadvantaged in its relations with Moscow. Conversely, the Russians are keener to deal bilaterally with the member states most dependent on their supplies of natural gas and oil and tend to dismiss or ridicule the EU as a paper tiger. Still, what the EU does has implications for Russian interests, so it may be fallacious to assume Russia does not take the EU seriously. For example, the EU has failed to assuage Russian concerns over the Eastern Partnership initiative for its goal of bringing the six former Soviet republics closer to the EU without including Russia.

Kaliningrad provides another example of how an EU policy adversely affected Russian interests. The EU-Russian dispute over Kaliningrad—a Russian enclave surrounded by the EU after Polish and Lithuanian accession—began in 2004. After tense negotiations, an accord between the EU and Russia over Kaliningrad was reached. Under the agreement, the Russians were obliged to concede to EU demands that when Lithuania joined the EU, the people of the Kaliningrad region, who previously enjoyed free movement between the enclave and Russia, would have to be issued visas by Lithuania, effective January 1, 2005. It was a bitter pill for the Putin Government to swallow, and it posed serious constraints and costs on both the Kaliningraders and the Lithuanians. For the EU, which is bound by the Schengen Accord to enforce tight controls along all EU frontiers, the issue was one of security. Kaliningrad has high rates of drug abuse, drug trafficking, prostitution, money laundering, and other organized criminal activity, as well as the highest rate of HIV infection in Europe. It is a major source of pollution in the Baltic.

The EU-Russian PCA of 1997, which expired in 2007, featured four priority areas of cooperation: economic and energy issues, foreign and security policy, domestic security and judicial cooperation, and education and culture. The EU and Russia began negotiations for a new agreement in July 2008. However, the EU suspended those talks in August after the Russian invasion of Georgia. It resumed them in November 2008 after Russian troops withdrew from the adjacent zones between each of the two breakaway regions and the Republic of Georgia.

At the 2009 EU-Russia Summit, the two sides failed to bridge their differences over bilateral trade and energy issues. The strained energy relationship is illustrated by competing planned natural gas pipeline projects, which divide not only the EU member states themselves but EU-Russian relations. One project, Nord Stream, would carry Russian natural gas to Germany via the North Sea, thus angering the Baltic Republics and Poland. A competitor, Nabucco, would carry Caspian Sea natural gas to Europe, skirting the Russian Republic. Nabucco's future is uncertain, given questions about the willingness of Iran, the Kurdish region of Iraq, and other suppliers to participate. Recently, the Russians broached with Austria, Croatia, and other states the possibility of another pipeline, South Stream, to transport natural gas to Central and Southern Europe, bypassing Ukraine.

In sum, it is important to note that the EU imports nearly 30 percent of its oil and 40 percent of its natural gas from Russia. This heavy dependence on energy imports is not reflected in common EU policies regarding foreign energy policy and Russian relations. A divided EU ought to heed the lessons of 1973. Despite the Commission's best attempts to forge a common policy on relations with the oil producing states, which had tripled prices and cut supplies, the then European Community failed to act together.

MEDITERRANEAN BASIN AND TURKEY

The EU has had a coherent policy toward the nonmember Mediterranean states since the 1970s—and for good reason. The bulk of EU imports and exports travel through the region, including imports of energy sources from North Africa and the Middle East. Moreover, the region is a source of illegal movement of persons into the EU. The more the EU can help stimulate economic development in the Mediterranean region, the more likely workers in neighboring states will remain employed at home, rather than seek illegal entry into the EU. Moreover, the more the EU can help these states stop illegal movement of persons into their own territories, the less likely illegal migrants, criminals, and terrorists will enter the EU.

The Mediterranean Basin. In its Mediterranean Policy of the 1970s, the EU offered tariff preferences and substantial development aid to countries in the region. However, by the 1990s, it became clear that the region's economies were not much better off as a result of EU trade concessions and aid. As a result, the EU initiated a new process to enliven and strengthen its policy in the region in a summit with the Mediterranean states in 1995. In the so-called Barcelona Process, Mediterranean states and the EU agreed to engage in regular dialogues in order to increase cooperation in trade, development, cultural understanding, and security. The summits and other meetings of the Barcelona Process offered rare venues where Israeli and Arab representatives gathered in the same room and had opportunities for exchange not normally afforded elsewhere.

By 2004, the Barcelona Process morphed into the European Neighborhood Policy (ENP). Nonmember Mediterranean states are invited to negotiate action plans and association accords. Such accords feature free trade and visa liberalization measures and provisions for political dialogue on human rights, energy, democratization, market economic reforms, nonproliferation, anticrime and antiterrorism. The ENP also aims to create a free trade area among the states of the region. However, this is more an aspiration than a likely scenario since what the nonmember states want most is not free trade among themselves, but free access to the EU market. Nonetheless, the EU is in the process of negotiating and ratifying individual association accords with each of its Mediterranean partners, as it has already done with Egypt and Israel. It is making slow progress in fostering south–south trade. However, Egypt, Jordan, Morocco, and Turkey have been engaged in an initiative to increase trade among themselves. Given the normalization of EU-Libya relations, the two sides are weighing the possibility of commencing negotiations for a new bilateral trade accord.

In 2008, the EU French Presidency hosted a summit of forty-two EU members and nonmember Mediterranean states to launch the Union for the Mediterranean, which aims to raise the political importance of EU-Mediterranean relations by holding biennial summits that cover issues of concern to the countries of the region. Three obstacles to the success of the new initiative are the divisions among the Mediterranean states themselves, which are many; the lack of political-economic complementarity among them; and the difficulty of forging cooperation given the seemingly elusive nature of peace between Israel and Palestine.

Turkey. Turkey is the Mediterranean state most critical to EU security, yet it is often neither understood nor appreciated for the stability and security it lends to the EU. The EU needs to develop an effective foreign policy toward Ankara worthy of such an important neighbor. This is because of Turkey's democratic and secular state and market economy, its strategic Asia Minor location, the size and power of its armed forces, its ability to communicate with Israel and the Arab states, its role as a market for European goods and services, and its cultural and historical ties with Europe. Turkey's future as a Western secular state is of vital interest to the EU, which is reflected in the growth and institutionalization of EU-Turkish relations over the past five decades.

The EU-Turkish association agreement dates back to 1963; its main feature is the EU-Turkish customs union established in 1995. Turkey applied to the EU in 1987 and the EU granted it candidate status in 1999. The EU and Turkey began accessions talks in 2005. However, only minor chapters of the accession treaty have been completed. The EU-Turkish dialogue on membership has yielded mixed results, which students of EUFP need to understand.

On the one hand, the EU has adroitly used the Copenhagen Criteria to leverage changes in Turkey, for example, changes now made to the Turkish constitution to outlaw capital punishment and to guarantee the language and other rights of minorities such as the Kurdish population. Turkey has made significant progress in meeting EU expectations for political and economic reforms. On the other hand, the EU and Turkey face at least three serious roadblocks to achieving Turkish membership. First, public support for Turkish accession is weakening in the EU. French President Nicolas Sarkozy and German Chancellor Angela Merkel support close Turkish association with, but not membership in, the EU—even though the EU and its member states have declared Turkey a candidate country. However, the Ankara Government has expressed interest only in full membership. Second, public support for Turkish accession is also weakening in Turkey. The country is increasingly divided between secular and religious trends. A more fundamentalist brand of Islam is gaining currency in Turkey, a development that opens up questions about the future of a secular Turkey and its goal of joining the EU.

Third, the EU and Turkey are badly divided over the issue of Cypriot unification. The impasse over its resolution is having adverse effects on EU-Turkish relations. Turkish troops have occupied northern Cyprus, where the Turkish Cypriots live, since their invasion in 1974 to stop the union of Cyprus with Greece. Turkey recognizes the Northern Cypriot Turkish state as a sovereign republic, but no other state extends such recognition. Cyprus joined the EU in 2004 before the Greek and Turkish Cypriot communities were able to reach a settlement and unify the island. A 2004 vote on the UN plan for reunification was accepted by a majority of the Turkish Cypriots, but not of the Greek Cypriots. In retrospect, it was a huge mistake for the EU to extend membership to Cyprus before unification because, as an EU member, Cyprus can veto EU agreements with Turkey and the Cypriot conflict is now an EU one.

The core problem for Turkish accession to the EU is that Ankara neither recognizes the Nicosia government nor permits Greek Cypriot ships to enter and use Turkish ports and Greek Cypriot airlines to land in Turkey. If Turkey and the EU are still committed to membership, Turkey will need to recognize Cyprus and end all impediments to the movement of goods and persons from Cyprus. An additional complication due to the Cypriot impasse is that Cyprus blocks Turkey's full participation in the EDA and CSDP, and Turkey blocks formal EU-NATO security cooperation and retains a veto over the EU's use of the Berlin Plus arrangement. In sum, it is clear that the EU-Turkish relationship hinges on many uncertainties, yet the interdependence between the two partners is complex and in most ways mutually beneficial. Should accession negotiations eventually lead to a successful conclusion, there is a great risk that one or more of the member states will not ratify the accession treaty or will subject the treaty to a referendum that results in a no vote. Should this happen, one can imagine that the Turkish relationship with the EU would sharply deteriorate.

SUB-SAHARAN AFRICA

The EU has long-term historical, commercial, political, and strategic interests in Sub-Saharan Africa. Its policy in recent years is guided by the EU Strategy for Africa adopted in 2005. The EU's Strategy seeks to strengthen African, AU, and UN capabilities to predict, prevent, and mediate conflicts on the continent. The EU holds regular summits with the African Union and individual African states, for example, South Africa. The EU employs all instruments of EUFP in the region—economic, trade, development assistance, diplomatic, and security.

Cotonou Agreement. The main element of EU Africa policy is the Cotonou Agreement, signed by the EU and seventy-eight ACP states in 2000. Although the accord is between the EU and ACP states, most of the signatories are African states. The Cotonou Agreement features tariff reductions, economic aid, and political dialogue on human rights, democratization, energy, anticrime/antiterrorism, nonproliferation, and other major security issues. The EU negotiates individual accords with the African states and participates in EU-African summits of heads of government and state. With China's growing influence in the region and the investment and aid China offers without conditions, the EU faces more limits to its diplomacy in the region than, say, in the Western Balkans, where membership in the union is a significant inducement to change.

African Great Lakes Region. Since the genocide of the Rwandan Tutsis by the Hutus in 1994, and the humanitarian disaster brought about this and other manmade and natural disasters, EUFP is increasingly focused on the African Great Lakes region (DRC, Rwanda, Uganda, and Burundi). The EUSR in the African Great Lakes region oversees peace agreements and CSDP operations, fosters reconciliation, promotes respect for human rights and the rule of law, coordinates EU humanitarian and famine relief, and supports international efforts to stabilize the region and to bring to trial those who have been charged with crimes committed during the Rwandan genocide.

The EU has demonstrated support for security and stability in the DRC through four CSDP operations, all listed in table 7.1. First, in Operation Artemis (2003), within two weeks after a request by the UN Security Council, the EU deployed a French-led military force over a three-month period. The EU force stabilized the town of Bunia and reinforced an existing UN force. Second, in 2005, the EU, in close coordination with the UN, launched a police mission to Kinshasa, in response to an invitation from the DRC Government. It was the first civilian mission for crisis management in Africa within the framework of the CSDP. Third, an EU advisory and assistance mission, established in 2005 at the request of the DRC Government, provides advice and assistance to the Congolese officials in charge of security, while ensuring the promotion of policies compatible with human rights and international law. Fourth, in 2006 the EU deployed troops to the DRC (and standby troops in neighboring Gabon) in response to a request by the UN to assist UN personnel with regard to the holding of presidential and legislative elections in the DRC.

Somalia. The EU deployed its first maritime CSDP action in 2008 to assist World Food Program (WFP) shipments to Somalia and to deter, interdict, and arrest pirates off the Somali coast (EU NAVFOR Atalanta). The maritime mission features thirteen warships and three marine surveillance aircraft of six EU member states: France, Germany, Greece, Sweden, Italy, and Spain. The Netherlands and Belgium are expected to join the mission. France has proposed a CSDP action that builds on a program it wishes to introduce to train Somali governmental security forces to complement the union's antipiracy mission.

Sudan. The EU and its member states chose not to intervene directly in the humanitarian crisis in Darfur in 2004, despite the massive killings of civilian populations, victims of rebel aggression or of rebel aggression backed by Sudanese Government troops. However, in 2004 and 2005 the EU began providing a wide range of financial, technical, and logistical support, personnel, and equipment for the peace-keeping troops of the AU, which are in the region to oversee a ceasefire between government and rebel forces and to stop what the U.S. Government has called a genocide. The EU is training African troops, supporting the police component of the AU effort, assisting in transporting AU battalions, providing aerial observation, providing logistical support and training, supporting salaries, and funding insurance for AU troops. EU military personnel are participating in the AU ceasefire commission. The EU aids AU peacekeeping operations in Darfur and elsewhere on the continent. In 2005, the EU Council adopted a joint action appointing a EUSR to Sudan to coordinate EU aid in support of AU peace efforts. In 2008–2009, the EU deployed 3,100 EU military personnel to Chad and the Central African Republic to assist humanitarian workers and protect civilians, especially refugees and displaced persons, as a result of the worsening crisis in Darfur, and to protect UN staff.

THE MIDDLE EAST

In February 2006 the EU and its member states woke up to just how volatile relations were between the Islamic and European worlds. The publication in Denmark and elsewhere in Europe of cartoons depicting the prophet Muhammad, considered a sacrilege for Muslims, was met with massive protests, attacks on the EU mission in Gaza and the Embassy of Denmark in Damascus, and boycotts of Danish and EU goods in countries such as Iran. As demonstrated by these protests, the Middle East is a source of risk, as well as opportunity, for the EU. The EU depends on exports to and imports from the region, particularly oil imports. It also depends on political stability in the region, without which trade would be disrupted, and on social, political, and economic development in the region to dissuade large numbers of migrant workers from illegally seeking entry into the EU. This section begins with a brief overview of EU relations with the core protagonists of the Mid-East conflict, Palestine and Israel, before providing a thumbnail sketch of EUFP with regard to the rest of the Arab world and Iran.

Palestine. The EU supports an independent and democratic Palestine at peace with Israel. Its aid takes three forms: economic, political, and security. The EU is the world's largest donor of aid to the Palestinian Authority and to Palestinian refugees through the UN Relief Works Agency (UNRWA). It not only underwrites the P.A. institutions, but contributes to the operating budget of the P.A. The EU has an association accord with the P.A. that provides substantial economic assistance, tariff cuts, and ongoing political dialogue.

The EU funds a wide variety of projects and programs in the P.A., from election preparations and monitoring to training the Palestinian customs service, and from funding electric supply, water treatment, and waste disposal operations to assisting in border control and management. Election preparation and monitoring assistance in support of democratization are other essential ingredients in working toward a final settlement. Without institutions of civil society taking root in the P.A.—independent police and judiciary, functioning hospitals and universities, and government bodies

Image 7.2.   Palestinians Burn Danish Flag to Protest Publication of Cartoons of Muhammad, 2006. Courtesy of Reuters

able to perform their work in the absence of corruption—the Palestinians will not be in a position to negotiate with Israel for a final settlement.

Along with economic and political assistance, the third dimension of EU aid to the P.A. is to help the Palestinian Territories become more secure and safe. The EU dispatched a police mission for the Palestinian Territories in 2006. The purpose of that mission continues to be to help the P.A. establish an effective, modern, civilian police force through advising, mentoring, and training police and judicial officials. The EU border-crossing mission to support the opening of the Gaza-Egypt border at Rafah in 2005 was emblematic of EU support both for the P.A. and for Israeli security needs until the crossing was closed in 2007. After Hamas won the Palestinian elections in 2006, the EU and the United States froze millions of euros and dollars in aid to the Government of the P.A. and instead sought to funnel assistance to the Palestinian people through NGOs and other means. The EU and the United States, among other international donors, did not want to directly assist the Hamas Government, which

Image 7.3. Rafah Border Assistance Mission (2006). Courtesy of the Council of the European Union

has accepted neither Israel's right to exist nor previous Palestinian agreements with Israel. Hope that the Rafah crossing could soon be reopened anytime was dashed after the massive Israeli bombardment of Gaza in 2009 in response to rockets that Hamas had fired from Gaza against Israel.

Israel. The EU-Israel association accord provides Israel with substantial tariff cuts on agricultural exports to the EU and creates an industrial free trade area between the two partners. The EU also extends to Israel privileged access to science research and development projects. The accord features an action plan that reconfirms and deepens political bilateral cooperation in a wide variety of issues pertaining to Israel and its regional relationships, anticrime and antiterrorism efforts, science and technology, and justice and home affairs. What continues to block trust between the EU and Israel is Israel's deep-seated distrust of the EU for what it considers a pro-Arab Mideast policy. The EU is highly critical of the building of Israel's security wall and the construction of Israeli settlements in the occupied territories. The EU does not recognize Israeli sovereignty over East Jerusalem. Yet Israel is highly dependent on access to the EU market and on the beneficial effects of EU aid to stabilize, develop, and support civil society and democratization in the P.A.

Syria. The EU conditions association accords with the Mediterranean states on two clauses: (1) all signatories must commit to honoring human rights; and (2) all signatories must abide by international agreements on nonproliferation. These conditions were especially important when the EU and Syria negotiated but did not conclude and ratify an association agreement in 2004. Some EU member states, particularly France and the UK, opposed the agreement because of Syria's interference in Lebanon and open hostility to Israel. The EU, pressured by the United States, is also interested in ending Syrian support for international terrorism. However, the two parties have recently resumed negotiations.

Gulf Cooperation Council (GCC). A cornerstone of EUFP is to support other regional integration efforts around the world while at the same time pursuing EU economic, political, and security interests. The EU and the GCC (Bahrain, Kuwait, Oman, Qatar, Saudi Arabia, and the United Arab Emirates) have a cooperation agreement designed to increase two-way trade and to provide the basis for a future FTA. The cooperation agreement features a political dialogue, annual summits and ministerial meetings, and other forms of cooperation, in such areas as security, energy, agriculture, health, education, and culture. The GCC is a major energy supplier to the EU and is the EU's sixth largest export market. The EU is the GCC's largest export market. The EU's interest in the region is also fueled by the important strategic location of these countries on or near the Persian Gulf and the importance of supporting the regimes that resist Islamic fundamentalist extremism.

Afghanistan. The EU has provided significant financial and political support for the post-Taliban Afghan Government and the country's postwar reconstruction. Twenty-three EU member states account for approximately 25,000 troops as part of the UN-mandated deployment of the International Stabilization Force in Afghanistan (ISAF). The EU and its member states are the world's largest donors to Afghan reconstruction. To bolster the Afghan Government and coordinate EU aid, the EU in 2002 opened a Commission Delegation and an ECHO Office in Kabul, and in 2004 sent an EUSR. The EU has demonstrated its support for democratization in Afghanistan by providing significant financial aid to support presidential elections.

One particular object of aid important to the EU is support for counter-narcotics operations. Ninety-nine percent of heroin sold in the EU is thought to originate in Afghanistan. Given the relationship of illicit trade in opium to organized crime, counter-narcotics is important to the reconstruction and stability of Afghanistan. The EU police and rule of law mission dispatched in 2007 trains Afghan police and judges. However important the EU efforts are in Afghanistan, they are largely confined to civilian arenas, while certain EU and NATO member states are engaged in operations to combat Taliban and insurgent forces.

Iran. EU-Iran relations are troubled primarily over concerns related to Iran's pursuit of a nuclear energy policy expected to contribute to the development of a nuclear weapons capability; Iran's hostile and provocative position toward Israel; and Iran's financial and political support of terrorist organizations, such as Hezbollah. As previously mentioned, the EU has imposed sanctions against Iran, including financial sanctions against Iranian banks for their role in the financial aspects of Iran's nuclear program.

For over twenty years, the EU and Iran have engaged in a dialogue on bilateral issues—trade, human rights, democratization, proliferation of WMDs, and terrorism. The EU prefers a diplomatic negotiation approach in order to achieve the goal of compelling Iran to suspend its nuclear program for non-civilian purposes and to comply with its commitment to the IAEA inspectors.

Given its oil resources and strategic location, Iran is a major focus of EUFP. As Iran and the U.S. have not had diplomatic relations since 1979, the EU is the most important representative of the West in Iran. France, Britain, and Germany on behalf of the EU have engaged with Iran on the issue of the consistency of Iran's nuclear energy program with Iran's commitments to the NNPT. The EU, like the United States, is concerned over Iran's nuclear ambitions, efforts by Iran to hide a uranium enrichment program and to carry out undeclared plutonium experiments, and Iran's failure to report the use of imported uranium for testing centrifuges at undisclosed sites. The EU has stuck overall to a common diplomatic approach to Iran.

Iraq. Although the EU failed to speak and act with one voice over the U.S.-led invasion of Iraq in 2003, individual member states are participating in the multinational force in Iraq, and the EU is increasingly active in helping to rebuild the country. The EU is one of the leading donors of reconstruction and humanitarian aid, much channeled through the UN and the World Bank. The EU is supporting Iraq's membership in the WTO and the two parties are negotiating a Partnership and Cooperation Agreement.

Two important developments in EU-Iraq relations occurred in 2005 and 2006. In 2005, the EU initiated an integrated rule of law mission for Iraq. The mission has trained 2,500 Iraqi judges, senior police, and prison officers in managing the criminal justice system. Although the training has occurred outside of Iraq, the EU is planning to conduct training in Iraq itself in the near future. In 2006, the Delegation of the European Commission opened in Baghdad. What continues to hamper the delivery of EU and other international aid in Iraq is the persistent violence perpetrated by those opposed to the democratic government of Iraq, especially suicide bombings of civilian targets.

ASIA

Until recently, Asia did not figure prominently in EUFP. For most of the EU's history, Asia was viewed primarily in commercial terms. However, in recent years the EU has grown more active in the political-security situation in the various regions that make up Asia. For examples, it grants North Korea food aid and has sought to condition that aid on agricultural reform; it deployed a peace monitoring mission to Banda Aceh, Indonesia; it imposed sanctions on China after the student massacre at Tiananmen Square; and it has supported regional integration in ASEAN. The EU holds annual summits with Australia, China, Japan, New Zealand, and South Korea, and the EU and Asian countries hold annual meetings on international economic and financial issues.

Central and South Asia. The EU has been slow to develop its relations with the countries of Central and South Asia. However, since 2006, the EU has posted a EUSR to the region and has introduced a Common Strategy for a New Partnership with Central Asia. Although the EU holds regular summits with Pakistan and with India, its relations with these Asian powers are slowly developing. The underdeveloped relationship between the EU and Pakistan is anachronistic, given the importance of Pakistan to EU and global security concerns. To encourage Pakistan's continued support in the war against al Qaeda and the Taliban, the EU has offered more generous trade terms to Pakistan through the EU-Pakistan Cooperation Agreement. The EU has recently extended the remit of its EUSR in Afghanistan to include Pakistan. However, the EU seems ill-equipped and certainly not ready to confront the serious challenges to its own regional and global security should extremist Islamic fundamentalist forces topple Pakistan's secular government and take control of the country's nuclear weapons. Moreover, EUFP extends in a serious manner neither to the Indo-Pakistan conflict over the disputed region of Kashmir nor to the terrorist attacks on India from bases in Pakistan. Although the EU and India are negotiating a free trade accord, the bilateral relationship remains underdeveloped relative to the complementary values of two of the world's largest democracies.

Southeast Asia. In 2005, the EU, in coordination with ASEAN, supported a ceasefire in Banda Aceh, Indonesia, following the tsunami devastation there. The mission monitored the implementation of the peace agreement signed between the Indonesian Government and the Free Aceh Movement in 2005. The 219 unarmed monitors—from the EU, Switzerland, and Norway and from five ASEAN countries (Thailand, Malaysia, Brunei, Philippines, and Singapore)—were responsible for patrolling/inspecting the demobilization of the Free Aceh Movement, including the destruction of its weapons. The mission served as a liaison between the parties of the peace agreement and handled complaints of violations of the agreement. Elsewhere in the region, the EU imposed sanctions on Myanmar (Burma) for not honoring the results of democratic presidential elections and for the house arrest of Aung Sang Suu Kyi. The EU and ASEAN, who hold regular meetings, are negotiating a free trade accord. The EU is seeking new partnership and cooperation agreements with Brunei, Indonesia, Malaysia Singapore, and Thailand.

Northeast Asia. The EU and South Korea have completed negotiations for a free trade agreement; talks had languished for years over trade in automobiles. When the EU extended diplomatic recognition to North Korea in 2001, it used the occasion to engage the North Koreans in the advancement of human rights and market economics in that country. With North Korea, the EU has been active in two ways. It has been a provider of food aid to North Korea and has attempted to condition that aid on reform of the farm sector. It also, in the 1990s, joined the Korean Development Organization (KEDO), a group that includes the United States, South Korea, and Japan. KEDO was committed to assisting North Korea to secure energy supplies in exchange for agreement not to pursue a nuclear energy program.

China. In 2007, the EU and China agreed to negotiate a new PCA to replace their 1985 bilateral trade and cooperation agreement. The EU and China hold annual summits. However, in 2008 China cancelled the EU-China Summit because of the visit of the Dalai Lama to France. Like the United States, the EU is concerned about its increasingly large trade deficit with China. Today, China is the largest importer of EU goods in the world. The EU supported China's accession to the WTO in 2001.

In 1989, following the Chinese Government's crackdown on pro-democracy student demonstrators at Tiananmen Square, the EU imposed a military trade embargo on China that China is lobbying hard to remove. Some EU members such as France and Germany have expressed interest in ending the embargo, given the importance of trade with China. However, the EU has held back due to pressure from the United States not to take action that could destabilize the balance of security situation, for example, between China and Taiwan. The EU is also under pressure from international human rights NGOs to maintain the arms embargo, given China's continuing poor human rights record.

WESTERN HEMISPHERE AND THE UNITED STATES

The EU's interest in Latin America and the Caribbean is largely stimulated by trade, investment, and human rights issues, since there are few security risks in the hemisphere. The EU and Latin American and Caribbean states hold annual summits. The EU has free trade accords with both Mexico and Chile. In the negotiations for the EU-Mexico free trade accord, Mexico opposed but, in the end, was forced to accept the accord's stipulations on human rights. The EU and the Andean Pact (Bolivia, Columbia, Ecuador, and Peru) and the EU and the Common Market of the South (Argentina, Brazil, Paraguay, and Uruguay) hold regular summits, engage in political dialogue, and are negotiating new trade agreements. The EU-Caribbean trade agreement seeks to stimulate trade, investment, and sustainable development, conduct political dialogue, and build on trade among the Caribbean states themselves.

In 2003, the EU suspended official contacts with the Government of Cuba over the imprisonment of political opponents and other human rights abuses. It also blocked Cuban participation in the EU-ACP agreements. Although the EU continues to be concerned over the human rights situation on Cuba, it lifted restrictive measures in 2005 when Havana suspended laws that provided for the imprisonment of dissidents.

The EU and Canada, who have a close bilateral economic and political relationship, meet in an annual summit and work together on many global issues. For example, Canada contributes to CSDP operations in BiH, DRC, the Darfur region of Sudan in cooperation with the AU, and elsewhere. The EU and Canada are negotiating a new trade and cooperation accord that would broadly embrace liberalization of trade in goods and services.

The United States is the largest and most important interlocutor of the EU in the international system. The complex interdependent relationship is built on two foundations: economic relations and cooperation in political and security issues. Although there is neither an EU-U.S. association accord nor a PCA, relations have been structured since 1995 by the so-called "New Transatlantic Agenda and Joint Action Plan," which provides for meetings and venues to cooperate on foreign policy issues. The annual EU–U.S. Presidential Summit, the multiple ministerial meetings each year between government officials, and the working group meetings and day-to-day interactions provide a framework, if messy, that allows the two sides to cooperate and coordinate when they can agree and minimize differences when they cannot agree.

The EU-U.S. commercial relationship (two-way trade and investment) is the world's largest.[6] The two are each other's largest export markets. The U.S. imports more from the EU than from any other partner and the U.S. is the EU's largest importer of goods after China. Few trade disputes threaten to disrupt the flow of commerce. However, disputes over GMOs, farm subsidies, and aircraft subsidies do risk unleashing retaliatory measures if bilateral or WTO trade dispute settlement procedures do not result in resolution. Disputes are usually settled bilaterally or at the WTO. The WTO is in many ways the institutional framework for EU-U.S. trade relations, and the G-8 and other multilateral fora serve as venues for cooperation in global financial, development, and other related issues. Various transatlantic councils (e.g., the Transatlantic Business and Consumer Dialogues and the Transatlantic Eco-

Image 7.4.   EU–U.S. Summit, November 2009, Washington, D.C. Courtesy of the Swedish Presidency of the EU

nomic Council) help bring together public and private sector players in transatlantic relations. The two sides are bound by bilateral agreements, such as the air transport and civil aviation safety agreements. The two also cooperate in such areas as competition policy, regulatory policy, and intellectual property rights.

The political-security relationship between the U.S. and EU is new and growing in importance. For all the ways the EU and U.S. are different, they share many complementary values in international affairs (support for democratization, market economics, human rights, and the rule of law) and interests in international affairs (antiterrorism, nonproliferation, and conflict prevention and resolution). It may be inevitable that two such large foreign policy players—each with a global perspective and reach—are bound to cooperate when values and interests converge. This is especially true since the two together dominate world development assistance. The more the EU develops CFSP/CSDP, the more EUFP gains traction, the more the EU-U.S. relationship is likely to be taken up by international security issues.

Twenty-one EU members are U.S. allies in NATO, which means that NATO remains the most important institutional bridge between North America and Europe. Although there is some NATO-EU interinstitutional rivalry and competition (e.g., over respective missions in Africa), and the frozen conflict in Cyprus continues to block any new formal or high profile EU-NATO cooperation, the two security organizations work well together on the ground. EU and NATO commanders in BiH and Kosovo have good working relationships and agreements. It was only a few years ago that the EU and NATO—neighbors in Brussels for decades—almost never talked to each other.

The EU and United States need each other to address global problems too big for either one to handle effectively alone. As there are very few areas where the EU and U.S. have direct foreign policy differences, they tend to be drawn into cooperation in areas of the world where their interests and values converge. In some areas, the U.S.

takes the lead—in Afghanistan, Pakistan, the Middle East Peace Process (MEPP), and the North Korea nuclear program. In others, the EU takes the lead—providing security in BiH, helping end the Russia-Georgia war and monitoring the ceasefire agreement, and garnering worldwide support for the creation of the ICC and the ratification of the Kyoto Protocol. In some areas, the U.S. and EU work together—stabilizing the security situation in Macedonia and Kosovo, coordinating support for the AU in Darfur, participating in the Mid-East Quartet (the U.S., the UN, Russia, and the EU), coordinating policy in response to Iran's uranium enrichment program, and supporting human rights in Myanmar. Each brings a different set of instruments and experiences that the other needs. The EU and U.S. have increased bilateral cooperation in such international security areas as nonproliferation, disarmament, and anti-terrorism.

There are instances where the Europeans are keen to distinguish their common foreign policies from those of the United States—when values or interests do not converge and there are substantial policy differences—in order to develop an identity and autonomy for EUFP. The EU often underscores its support for and U.S. opposition to the Kyoto Protocol and the Rome Statute for the ICC. It actively opposes as violations of basic human rights the practice of capital punishment in the United States and the use of the U.S. naval base at Guantanamo Bay to hold enemy combatants. Still, as demonstrated in this section, there is far more to unite the EU and U.S. on most international issues than there is to divide them. Moreover, a major irritant in bilateral relations began to heal in 2009 when the Obama Administration announced that it would close the U.S. detention camp for terror suspects in Guantanamo Bay. The Europeans are now under pressure from Washington to accept some of the detainees who cannot be safely returned to their home countries for fear of persecution or death.

This section explores EU-U.S. relations with regard to countries, regions, and key international issues. Chapter 9 provides an analysis of the effects of EUFP actions on the interests of the United States.

The EU and United States with Regard to Countries and Regions. The EU and United States share common objectives in the Western Balkans and have worked closely together and with NATO in Macedonia, BiH and Kosovo. A significant development in EU-U.S. security relations occurred in 2008 with the deployment of ninety U.S. police officers, judges, and prosecutors to Kosovo under the command of the EU rule of law mission there. This is an important, symbolic, and historically unprecedented U.S. validation of CFSP/CSDP.

The EU and U.S. share concerns about the backwards movement of democracy in Russia, the Russian shut-off of natural gas to Europe through Ukraine, the need to integrate Russia into the global political economy, and the Russian invasion of Georgia. As a result, EU, NATO, and U.S. relations with Ukraine and Georgia are being strengthened.

The EU and the United States share a common commitment to a democratic and secular Turkey and to the reunification of Cyprus. Given the limits to EU mediation of the Turkish-Cypriot dispute since Cyprus became an EU member, the U.S. may be the best and only diplomatic bridge between the EU and Turkey regarding resolution of this frozen conflict.

In Africa, the EU and U.S. are heavily involved to combat HIV/AIDS; address the humanitarian disasters in Sudan, the DRC, and elsewhere on the continent; support AU peacekeeping efforts; combat piracy off the Somali coast and help stabilize the internal situation in Somalia; and promote democratization and market reforms throughout the continent. However, the duplication of NATO and EU efforts to train the AU in Sudan points to the need for more common cause. In addition, it is not clear how much coordination occurs between the NATO and EU antipiracy maritime missions off the coast of Somalia.

Throughout the Middle East, the EU and United States share a common cause in supporting secular states to further democratize while strengthening their economic, social, and political systems to resist the spread of extremist ideology. The EU and United States ultimately share the same goals in the Holy Land: a sovereign Palestinian state, stable, secure, and democratic, living in peace alongside Israel. There was a time in the 1980s when the EC began recognizing Palestinian interests in a future peace process with Israel, a commitment the U.S. was not prepared to make publicly. However, by the 1990s the U.S. and EU joined together in pursuing a two-state solution. They cooperate extensively in the Mid-East Quartet to press the core protagonists to return to the road map to peace. Both sides have relayed financial and economic aid to the besieged Gazans through NGOs so that such aid could not be used by the Hamas Government (which recognizes neither the State of Israel nor Palestinian-Israeli peace agreements). The considerable financial and political capital of both the EU and United States will be needed to ensure that if and when a final settlement occurs, significant political and economic resources will be available for its implementation. The EU-Palestinian and U.S.-Israeli relationships keep lines of communication open and offer critical support if the MEPP can be brought back on track.

In Afghanistan, U.S. and U.S.-led NATO forces are struggling to contain the return and spread of the Taliban. The EU deployed a police and rule of law mission to assist the Afghan authorities and is the lead organization contributing to and organizing international donor support for reconstruction. However, the imbalance between U.S.-led NATO and EU efforts in the country is stunning, and the U.S. presses its NATO allies in the EU to commit more troops to assist the Kabul government to fight the Taliban. The increasing threat of insurgency in neighboring Pakistan also threatens to marginalize EUFP, which is why the EU should develop a common strategy for such an important country on such a critical international fault-line.

The EU policy of diplomatic engagement of Iran to address such issues as Iran's support for international terrorism, hostile opposition to the existence of the State of Israel, efforts to enrich uranium, and suppression of basic human and minority rights at home has borne little if any fruit over the past thirty years. The U.S. approach has been the converse of that of the EU. The U.S. policy had been to isolate and punish Iran for its support of Hezbollah, violations of the NNPT, to which Iran is a signatory, and human rights violations. However, in recent years, both Republican and Democratic administrations in the United States have supported EU efforts to seek a diplomatic solution with Iran over its suspected nuclear weapons program. As Iran continued its uranium enrichment program, especially since 2005, the EU and United States engaged in serious cooperative efforts to press Iran to cease its activity.

The EU had no unified policy on the U.S.-led invasion of Iraq in 2003, but differences among the EU members and between the EU and U.S. over the reasons for starting the war are now history. The Europeans and Americans are likely to increase cooperation for postwar reconstruction and democratization. The EU's rule of law mission to help train Iraqi magistrates and police is a first step, along with EU reconstruction aid, to address the needs of the Iraqi people and Government. However, as in Afghanistan, the U.S. perception is that the EU and some of its member states are not doing enough to help Iraq confront al Qaeda and the insurgent forces, given the scale of European resources and the impact of the security situation on European interests if Iraq does not finally stabilize.

Asia is a region where the EU and United States have yet to cooperate seriously in many areas of mutual interest, such as integrating China into a position of leadership and responsibility in the IPE (and in the management of the IPE's rules and institutions), reducing EU and U.S. trade deficits with China, and dealing with nuclear proliferation issues on the Korean peninsula. The EU has only recently begun to engage in the affairs of the Asian regions in areas outside purely commercial pursuits. EU involvement in North Korea—its decision to extend diplomatic recognition, its food aid, and its participation in KEDO—enhances important U.S. security interests in the region. The EU arms embargo on China is important to the United States, given the need for a coordinated international response to China's human rights record, as well as in the context of U.S. relations with Taiwan. The EU and United States continue to coordinate policy regarding Myanmar and to impose economic and diplomatic sanctions in response to Myanmar's continued disregard of democratic elections and the house arrest of Aung Sang Suu Kyi. Conversely, EUFP appears underdeveloped in South Asia, where Pakistan is struggling to maintain government control of large swaths of its territory now controlled by insurgent forces and where Indo-Pakistan relations remain volatile. The more the EU can inject needed diplomacy and resources to help lend stability in the region, and the more the EU and U.S. can cooperate to achieve these ends, the better for EU-U.S. political relations.

The EU and United States with Regard to International Security Issues. The fastest areas of growth in EU-U.S. foreign policy cooperation have been in anticrime/antiterrorism efforts and in international security where the EU is inserting itself as a new contributor. For example, the EU and U.S. have accelerated their joint cooperation in all areas of nonproliferation, especially during the Obama Administration. EU-U.S. anticrime and antiterrorism cooperation is growing more important year after year since the 2001 al-Qaeda attack on the United States. The two partners exchange information on terrorist and criminal activity for purposes of interdiction and criminal prosecution. Europol and the U.S. Department of Homeland Security place officials in each other's headquarters to enhance cooperation. The U.S. Attorney General, Secretary of Homeland Security, and Secretary of State meet with their EU counterparts yearly, if not more frequently, and senior-level working groups of EU and U.S. officials meet twice yearly to exchange information. The EU and United States have established a high-level dialogue on transportation and border security issues to discuss common interests in such areas as visa policy, biometrics, data sharing, sky marshals, and cargo security. Lastly, U.S. anticrime and antiterrorism efforts are enhanced by the adoption of the EU-wide arrest warrant and the EU policy to freeze terrorist assets. EU-U.S. negotiations for mutual legal assistance on extradition of criminal and terrorist suspects have made progress, as have negotiations for information exchange between police and intelligence authorities. In 2003 the EU and the United States agreed to an extradition agreement, with the proviso that the United States not apply capital punishment to any person extradited from the EU to the United States who is found guilty in a court of law in the United States.

Moving from the struggle against transnational crime and terrorism to interstate and intrastate conflicts, the EU and U.S. are stepping up their cooperation. This is largely because the EU is playing a role as a provider of security. Although the twenty-two CSDP operations taken thus far were in relatively permissive environments, the step-by-step experience the EU is gaining in the work of international security builds confidence, even if some suggest the EU should be doing more work in less permissive environments. The time will come, soon, when the EU's mettle will be tested. The more the EU takes over from NATO troops in the Balkans, as it has in BiH and is likely to do so in Kosovo in the near future, the more those NATO troops are available for more dangerous duty elsewhere.

For fifty years, the Americans pressed the Europeans to do more to contribute to international security. Now that they are, the Americans are beginning to take note, especially at the end of the second Bush Administration and the early years of the Obama Administration. No longer is CSDP seen by the U.S. and NATO as a threat to the transatlantic alliance. It is in the EU and U.S. interests for the EU and NATO to work out new cooperative accords to replace what now appears to be the dated Berlin Plus arrangement. But, as we learned in this chapter, that will have to await a settlement on Cyprus. Until then, the EU and NATO will work on the ground to sort out the mechanisms of cooperation, and the EU-U.S. relationship will develop an explicit security cooperation dimension. In that regard, it will help to replace the New Transatlantic Agenda and Joint Action Plan of 1995 with an updated framework for relations to meet the challenges of a world far different from that of 1995.

Review

This chapter has surveyed the broad outlines of EUFP with regard to multilateral issues, countries, and regions. In concluding the chapter, how do we best explain the growth of EUFP since the 1990s, and what can we deduce from the survey? We started and now end with the thesis that EUFP is the next generation of European integration. The impetus behind the growth of EUFP is three-fold. First, the more the EU grows in membership and expands its territory, the more it faces security risks within, on the borders of, and from outside the union territory: security at home and security abroad are increasingly linked. As a result, the EU is becoming an important player in combating crime, and it is beefing up external borders and helping neighbors to do likewise. Second, external pressures are mounting on the member states to act effectively in global security affairs. As a result, the number of CSDP operations continues to increase. A third impetus explains the importance of European identities and values and the strong public support behind EUFP. The role of public opinion is one of the measures of EUFP effects covered in Chapter 9.

THEORETICAL OBSERVATIONS

This chapter identified four bodies of theoretical thought that broadly explain why EUFP exists: social constructivism and historical institutionalism; realism—particularly the variants of liberal intergovernmentalism and neorealism; and rational choice institutionalism. Social constructivists recognize that EUFP mirrors national and European identities and values, and historical institutionalists recognize that, for the EU to play an effective role in world affairs, national governments need to delegate authority to the union. They often cannot accomplish alone what they can together. Over time, the Europeans learn to make foreign policy more effectively through two processes: international learning, whereby mistakes of the past are avoided and lessons learned; and Europeanization, whereby the process of developing new habits of cooperation among old nation-states gains traction. Even when member governments may seek to curtail the functions of the EU in handling world affairs, they will be constrained because the costs of separate national action can be higher than sticking together.

The process of learning by doing is captured in figure II.1, which depicts the feedback loop that situates policy outputs to new sources of inputs. Even when the EU should or could have acted in world affairs, or could have acted more effectively, its foreign policy presence is based on solid foundations, the *acquis communautaire* and *acquis politique*, which provide elements of continuity, certainty, and reliability in EU foreign relations. There is an enduring logic to regional economic integration with regard to foreign and security policy.

Neorealism focuses our attention, rightly, on how EUFP is influenced by a changing distribution of power in the world that restricts or enhances its global influence. The outside world has no patience to wait until the EU sorts out if and how it is going to make decisions and finance its foreign policy actions. Russia, China, and even the United States tend not to take the EU seriously if the union does not act as an effective player on issues of concern to them. Even if the EU wanted to hide from international politics, it would not be able to do so. External demands on the EU to act in international politics have always outpaced the EU's ability to process and respond to them. Put differently, external demands draw the EU ever more deeply into the currents of international politics even though it is still learning to swim in deep water.

In response, according to liberal intergovernmentalists, member governments may decide at periodic IGCs to change/expand the Treaty to give more powers to the union. The EU acts in international politics because it is in the self-interests of member states to cooperate with one another and common institutions to pursue collective interests and objectives. Clearly, national interests drive the development of CFSP/ CSDP. Member governments exercise the most influence over the direction of EUFP either at periodic IGCs where Treaty reform and change are negotiated or at European Council Summits.

Rational choice institutional theory helps us to understand that, over time, member governments delegate administration of common foreign and security policy actions to EU institutions to reduce transaction costs and ensure adherence to common accords. Member states recognize that they can be more effective at less cost if they respond together to influence international issues too large for any one of them to handle well alone (concept of politics of scale). Rational choice institutionalism also helps us to put into perspective the constraints on national power and interests within a regional grouping of states. The EUFP of the future will continue to be cast as a dynamic between principals and agents and between national and European interests. The balance between individual and collective preferences is played out continuously inside the EU black box.

EMPIRICAL OBSERVATIONS

The chapter has demonstrated the growth and development of EUFP from its early modest reach in foreign economic diplomacy to today's foreign and security policy actions that stretch across the world's major issues, regions, and countries. The EU is in the process of becoming a global player. When it fails to act as a collective, it is weak, divided, ineffective, and marginalized. The fear of failing helps drive EUFP.

The EU has strained relations with Russia and Iran. Its failure to develop a common energy policy alongside a common Russia policy exposes weaknesses and divisions that will disadvantage the EU and weaken EUFP. With Iran, the EU has a common policy, but, as in the case of the U.S., its policy has not deterred Tehran from enriching uranium. EU relations with China, Japan, and India are underdeveloped but have potential to mature and become mutually beneficial. The EU has been slow to recognize the importance of Pakistan and the countries of Central Asia to European security and energy interests. The destabilizing situation in Pakistan also exposes limits to the EU's reach in this part of the world. As Central Asia is a region of risk and opportunity for the EU, EUFP is likely to expand its reach to developing relations with the governments of the region to pursue policies that enhance stability and provide a stable supply of natural gas and oil to Europe.

The EU is critical in helping the Palestinians and Israelis overcome their conflict if and when the belligerents finally agree to a structure of peace. However, the EU appears weak and divided over how best to assist the Government of Afghanistan. Although many of its member states contribute to the UN-sanctioned NATO force in Afghanistan, especially France, Germany and the UK, the EU itself is more a payer than a player. Its mission to mentor the police and judges is laudable but pales in comparison to what its own member governments, NATO, and the U.S. are doing militarily to keep the country free of Taliban control. Closer to home, the EU actively pursues issues of stability and security in the Mediterranean and surrounding areas. It is a critical partner of the UN and AU in dealing with Africa's many man-made and natural humanitarian disasters.

For all of the EU's foreign policy aspirations, CFSP/CSDP resources are small and EU capabilities still lag behind what is needed. A staff of about two hundred personnel with a budget of just €100 million in 2008 illustrates the gap between rhetoric and action. This chapter ends where it began. The EU is in the process of becoming an influential foreign policy player far different from its modest roots as an economic integration experiment to put an end to war. EUFP remains unprecedented in the history of the Westphalian nation-state system, but the EU needs to sustain the political will and garner the resources to finance needed capabilities to deploy and use force rapidly and effectively. It cannot afford to fail.

We have now completed Part II of the volume, with its focus on the EU in practice. We have studied the existence of common policies at home and abroad that result from decisions made in the EU polity. How effective the EU is in the execution of its common policies is the subject to which we now turn in Part III. If the EU cannot produce policies that effectively address the needs of citizens and governments, it is not likely to flourish and could decline. This is why it is important to conclude the book with an evaluation of what the EU means to Europeans and to the world.

Key Concepts

acquis politique
Berlin Plus arrangement
capabilities shortfalls
civilian power
Copenhagen Criteria
effective multilateralism
EU foreign policy
Europeanization
European Security Strategy Paper
executive authority
international learning
Petersberg Tasks
politics of scale

Study Questions

1. What did the author mean when he wrote, "The establishment of the internal market constituted the first generation of European integration. Foreign Policy is the next"?
2. What four major observations do you make and why of the evolution of EUFP across its four phases of development?
3. What are five examples of major EUFP actions that reflected unity among the member states and five examples when unity eluded them and the union failed to respond to a significant international issue or event? What are the consequences of such failure to act?
4. In your view, what theory or concept, or hybrid thereof, best explains the reach of, and limits to, EUFP action?

Selected Readings

Council of the European Union, "1999–2009: Ten Years of CSDP" in *CSDP Newsletter* (Brussels; Council of the European Union, Autumn 2010).

Council of the European Union, *President's Report on CSDP* (Brussels: Council of the European Union, 2009).

Alvaro de Vasconcelos, ed., *What Ambitions for European Defence in 2020?* (Paris: EU Institute for Security Studies, 2009).

Roy H. Ginsberg, *Ten Years of European Foreign Policy* (Berlin: Heinrich Boll Foundation, 2002).

———, *The European Union in International Politics: Baptism by Fire* (Lanham, Md.: Rowman & Littlefield, 2001).

Javier Solana, *A Secure Europe in a Better World: European Security Strategy* (Brussels: Council of the European Union, 2003).

Part III

EVALUATING EUROPEAN INTEGRATION

In Part II we deconstructed the European Union as a polity into its component parts, but we did not yet close the circle of EU governmental decisionmaking. In Part III we reconstruct the pieces of European integration to form a more rounded understanding of what the EU means and how it works. A final question remains that Part III asks and tries to answer: what effect does the EU have? After all, the EU exists in order to enhance the welfare of its member citizens and states. Does the EU have influence or agency to affect its member citizens and governments in terms that meet their needs and expectations? How is effect measured? For social scientists, measuring effect is hard and yet imperative. If we are ever to know whether the EU matters to its member citizens and governments—and if the EU is to evolve, retreat, or even wither away—we must seek to understand its effect.

Effect is both cognitive (what people think the effect of the EU has been on them) and empirical (what has actually happened because of an action or inaction of the EU). Defined as impact or influence, effect can be positive or negative, or neither. Figure II.1 depicts the critical link in the feedback loop from outputs of the EU polity to new sources of inputs, vital to any political system's effect and longevity. Feedback measures include public opinion of EU citizens and international learning by national governments and EU bodies.

Public opinion—a critically important element in the democratic politics of the EU and its member states—captures effect. The means to capture what people think about how the EU affects them are imperfect and inexact, but to avoid analysis of popular opinion would leave our study of European integration incomplete. If EU citizens equate EU policy outputs that have positive effects on them with EU institutions, the consequences could strengthen the role of those institutions as they engage in new decisionmaking initiatives.

International learning refers to the lessons EU member governments and common bodies draw from past mistakes as reflected in the actions the EU takes. Indeed, the EU's founding was a product of international learning. Without international learning, the future of the EU is at best uncertain and at most bleak because past mistakes will be repeated. Decisionmaking outputs are generic—for example, directives and regulations. Outputs provide the basis for EU policies. When outputs have effect, they become outcomes. Feedback provides the nutrients needed for the polity, like any organism, to function healthily.

The feedback loop in figure II.1 also depicts the notions of path dependency and unintended consequences, which are central to the effective functioning of the polity. Institutionalist theory of integration focuses on the relationship between principals (governments) and agents (central institutions) in EU governmental decisionmaking. When principals delegate authority at a single juncture in time to EU agencies to run the union and reduce transaction costs, they cannot know the long-term consequences of that initial grant of delegation. Delegation often, but not always, occurs as a result of a Treaty change. An unintended consequence of a delegation of authority from principal to agent may be the growth and development of an EU institution that exhibits wide scope for agency independent of the controls of national governments. When this happens, some member governments may seek to curtail autonomous agency as central institutions begin to cut too deeply into national prerogatives and sovereignty. The EU depends on a balance between the legitimacy offered by the participation of its member governments and the utility of common bodies to uphold the rules and act in the common interests. As demonstrated in Part II, member governments, in the end, are forced to accept some scope for autonomous agency of central institutions. Without these autonomous institutions, the union would grow lawless and fall apart. Therefore, not only is public opinion critical in the feedback chain linking outputs to outcomes and new sources of inputs, but so too are EU institutions and their relationship to the member governments.

Chapter 8 explores the effect of internal EU policies and institutions on member citizens and governments. Chapter 9 explores the effect of EUFP on the outside world and on the union itself. The more the EU enhances the welfare of its citizens through effective institutions and policies, the more the EU as a polity is likely to survive and grow. The more the EU has influence beyond the confines of Europe, the more the model of regional integration and peace it represents is of moment to the world outside.

CHAPTER 8

The Internal Dimension of European Integration

Preview

Chapter 8 explores the effective functioning of the internal dimension of European integration—EU institutions and policies—by focusing primarily on public opinion data. The chapter begins with a brief overview of other **measures of effect** such as demographic (growth of membership), economic (increase in intra-EU trade), monetary (growth in the euro as a world reserve currency), and parliamentary (results of EP elections and outcomes of votes on ratification of EU treaties by national parliaments). There are many additional measures of effect, far too numerous to list and evaluate here, but the author encourages readers to think creatively about how to determine what the EU means by exploring and testing some of these and other measures. Measuring European integration will be a process as much subject to refinement as is the process of European integration itself.

GROWTH OF MEMBERSHIP

A key measure of effect is the decision taken by nation-states to apply for membership and to remain in the EU after accession. The EU is a **pole of attraction** for its neighbors and for those with close historical and commercial ties who seek either membership (Britain in 1973), association (Turkey in 1962), or partnership (Russia in 2001) with the union. As the EU grew more attractive relative to the other trade bloc in Europe—EFTA—most of the EFTA states over time joined the EU. If membership entailed more costs than gains, the EU would not have grown in membership from six to twenty-seven over the past half-century and be considering further expansion. In 2005, the EU agreed to begin accession negotiations with Croatia, Macedonia, and Turkey. In 2008, Montenegro applied for membership, followed by Iceland in 2009.

No member state has seceded from the EU.[1] Thus the EU continues to retain its members, who would be disadvantaged if they left the EU or the EU fell apart.

Members join for various reasons, such as national commercial and political advantage (Britain in 1973) or to avoid the disadvantage of being left outside of EU governmental decisionmaking (Sweden in 1995). Europeans tend not to want their country to leave the EU, and they would not want the EU to fall apart.

The EU has grown to embrace nearly all of Western and Central Europe, and it has made a long-term commitment to membership for the Western Balkans under the right conditions. Moreover, the EU is a locus of economic and political power in the wider area. The EFTA states, especially Norway, closely follow EU foreign policy positions and participate in CSDP and CFSP actions. EFTA, candidate countries, and other closely associated neighbors peg their currencies to the euro, engage in euro-denominated trade, and/or hold euros in official reserves.

The TEU limits the expansion of the EU to countries in Europe who meet the Copenhagen Criteria. Years ago, the EU turned down overtures from Morocco and Israel to join. There are alternatives to full membership in the EU, and over time the number of states with formal association and partnership agreements with the EU has grown. Since not all countries in and adjacent to Europe can join the EU, the EU has established a range of associative relationships and partnership agreements binding the entire area closer to but not inside the EU. Therefore, as depicted in figure 8.1, a view of Europe described by former Commission President Delors as a set of **concentric circles**, with the union at its nucleus, is a useful way to map the evolution of the European geography in the early twenty-first century.

INTRA-EU TRADE AND THE EURO AS A WORLD RESERVE CURRENCY

Growth of intra-EU trade (trade among the members) relative to extra-EU trade (trade between the members and nonmembers) is another indicator of effect. Customs union theory, discussed in Chapter 3, predicts that once an internal market like the EU is established, trade among members will grow relative to trade between members and the outside world. The removal of tariffs and NTBs on internal trade, while maintaining the CET, has resulted in increased intra-EU trade. In historical terms, intra-EU trade between 1960 and 2000 grew by approximately 1200 percent in real terms, while extra-EU trade grew at 730 percent.[2]

In more recent years, according to Eurostat, the data collection agency of the EU, intra-EU trade (imports and exports) between 1992 and 2006 increased from €1.6 trillion to €4.9 trillion, an increase of about 205 percent. According to Eurostat data, intra-EU imports as a percentage of total EU imports remained steady at roughly 65 percent between 1992 and 2006. Similarly, intra-EU exports as a percentage of total EU exports remained steady at roughly 68 percent from 1992 to 2006.[3]

These data indicate that intra-EU trade has increased significantly over time. However, this increase has not occurred at the expense of EU trade with the outside world, which has increased slightly more than intra-EU trade. EU citizens have the best of two worlds: the benefits of intensified trade among themselves, which generates wealth that stays in Europe, and the benefits of imports to and exports from the outside world, which historically have always constituted a large portion of European wealth. Despite fears in the 1980s that the EU would become a "Fortress Europe" in

Figure 8.1. Europe of Concentric Circles

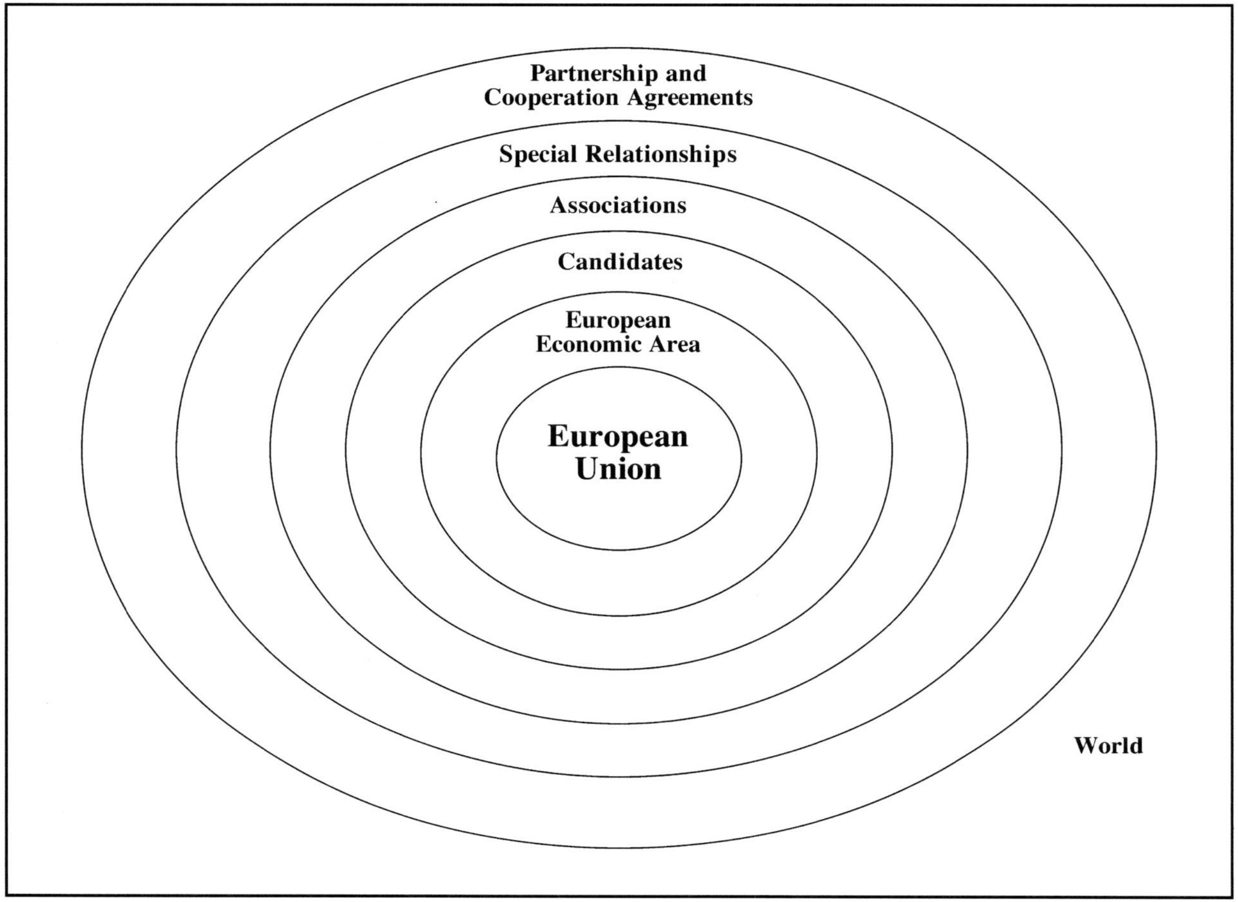

World

Partnership and
Cooperation Agreements

Special Relationships

Associations

Candidates

European
Economic Area

**European
Union**

trade terms, the EU has increased internal and external trade in ways beneficial both to Europe and to the world.

Another economic measure of EU effect is the growth in Eurozone membership and in the use of the euro as a foreign exchange holding of nonmember states. The Eurozone membership increased from eleven charter members in 1998, to sixteen members when Slovakia joined in 2009. In 2006, the total value of euro notes in circulation overtook that of dollar bills; 27 percent of the world's official currency reserves were held in euros in 2008, up from 18 percent ten years earlier. Conversely, the dollar's share fell from 71 percent to 63 percent over the past ten years.[4] According to Professors Menzie Chinn and Jeffrey Frankel, the euro could overtake the dollar as the preeminent world reserve currency by 2024 if Britain, Sweden, Denmark, and the twelve new members who joined the EU in 2004 and 2007 were to adopt the euro.[5]

EP ELECTIONS AND RATIFICATION PROCEDURES FOR EU TREATIES

Another measure of EU effect is voter turnout for EP elections. In terms of this measure of effect, the EU fares very poorly just when it needs public support for its only democratically elected, and thus most legitimate, body. In the seven EP elections from 1979 to 2009, average voter turnout in the EU declined from 62 to 43 percent. Voter turnout among the six original EU members, historically among the most committed to European integration, declined: for example, in Italy from 86 to 65 percent; in France, from 61 to 41 percent; in Germany, from 66 to 43 percent; and in the Netherlands, from 58 to 37 percent.

Voter turnout among other members is also in decline. For example, in Austria, turnout declined from 68 percent in 1996 to 46 percent in 2009, and in Portugal, from 72 percent in 1987 to 37 percent in 2009.[6] Voter turnout in the 2009 EP election was exceedingly low for the newest members, particularly Slovakia (20 percent), Lithuania (21 percent), Poland (25 percent), and Romania and Slovenia (28 percent). Surely a lack of awareness and understanding of the importance of the EP explains in large part why these voters failed to show up in larger numbers at the polls.

The EU is not seen as having a positive effect on its own electorate. Low voter turnout does little to help the EU gain and keep legitimacy in the eyes of its own citizens. While voter turnout rates in some national and local elections may also be declining, voter turnout is even more important for EP elections than it is for national and subnational elections. Since the EU as a polity is an experiment in the history of interstate cooperation, it feeds on the legitimacy given to it by publics. The nation-states of Europe can survive without the EU, but the EU cannot survive without the support of its member states and citizens. The EU has to rise to a higher level of democratic legitimacy than that of the constituent member states. Low voter turnout weakens the EU as a polity because it deprives it of democratic legitimacy. These data point to the need for the EU to demonstrate its effect on voters in the EU's newest and some of the older members in order to avoid a repeat of these bleak turnout numbers in the next EP elections in 2014.

National parliamentary votes and popular referenda on EU Treaty changes provide another measure of EU effect. The gulf between the two can be staggering. When the member governments complete negotiations for, and sign, a new EU treaty, it must be ratified by each of the national parliaments and receive the EP's assent. In some countries, there is a constitutional requirement to hold a popular referendum, while in others the government may itself decide to hold a popular referendum.

Danish voters in 1992 and Irish voters in 2001 were the first and second electorates in EU history to rock the foundations of European integration by voting no in referenda on new EU Treaties. Although the Danish parliament voted by a margin of 130 to 25 in favor of the TEU in May 1992, the Danish electorate rejected the Treaty in a June 1992 referendum by a razor-thin majority of 50.7 percent (49 percent for), based on a voter turnout of 83 percent. After Copenhagen renegotiated certain Treaty terms with its EU partners to assuage the concerns of Danish voters, a second referendum was held in May 1993: 57 percent voted for and 43 against, based on a voter turnout of 86 percent.

Although the Irish parliament voted by a margin of 98 to 13 in favor of the Nice Treaty in October 2002, the Irish electorate rejected the Treaty in a June 2001 referendum by a margin of 46 percent for and 53 percent against, with a voter turnout of 35 percent. After Dublin renegotiated certain terms with its EU partners to assuage the concerns of Irish voters, a second referendum was held in October 2002: 62 percent voted for and 37 percent voted against the Treaty, based on a voter turnout of 49 percent.

Up until the time of the Irish and Danish no votes, there was always an assumption that publics and their elected representatives would vote for whatever EU Treaties their governments negotiated and signed. These referenda indicated that the positions of governments and parliaments were not consonant with the thinking of the publics whom they represented. What Irish and Danish voters did was to strengthen the EU by rooting it not in the constituent governments and their parliaments, but in the constituent citizens. No parliament has rejected ratification of a new Treaty. Public opinion is more unpredictable. The trick for the student of European integration, when examining why electorates vote down Treaty changes, is to differentiate between those who vote no for reasons having nothing to do with the Treaty itself (e.g., to protest against a national government or recoil against globalization) and those who vote no for reasons directly related to the EU. In the former, there is little if anything the EU and its member states can do, but in the latter the member governments and EU bodies can adjust the Treaty to address concerns and try to make the EU more acceptable overall to citizens who doubt its value or oppose its existence.

Ratification of the doomed Constitutional Treaty began with each of the Heads of Government and State signing the Constitutional Treaty. Fifteen parliaments of the member states that held ratification votes voted overwhelmingly to ratify the Constitutional Treaty. These data point to very strong support among members of national parliaments for the Constitutional Treaty that their governments negotiated and signed.[7]

In popular referenda in France and the Netherlands in May and June 2005, respectively, voters rejected the Constitutional Treaty. In France, 45 percent voted yes and 54 voted no, based on a turnout of 69 percent. In the Netherlands, 38 percent voted yes and 62 percent no, based on a 63 percent turnout. These votes contrasted with public opinion polls taken in 2005 (before the referenda) of 1,000 French and 1,000 Dutch citizens over the age of sixteen, randomly chosen. When asked if they were for or against the Constitutional Treaty, 60 percent of French respondents indicated that they were for the Treaty and 28 percent were against, while 53 percent of Dutch respondents were for the Treaty and 38 percent were against.[8] Public opinion reflected in polls was clearly different from the voting in referenda during the same period of time. As a result of the French and Dutch no votes, the EU was forced to postpone the ratification process for the Constitutional Treaty until after a period of reflection.

Although the no vote constituted a small majority in France, most analysts recognized that a significant portion of that negative vote was related to opposition to the French government in the context of the coming of the 2007 presidential election. Surely many French voters who indicated they did not support the Treaty also reflected a fear in France of the loss of French identity in a changing Europe and world. Far more damaging to the EU construction was the large Dutch no vote. This is because many Dutch who voted against the Constitutional Treaty were not voting against the EU or any one aspect of the EU, but rather against the decreasing influence of the Netherlands in a larger and more diffuse Europe.

The irony of the ratification process for the Constitutional Treaty was that despite the defeats in some referenda, (1) the fifteen national parliaments voted to ratify with huge majorities; and (2) public opinion polls on the Constitutional Treaty indicated substantial majorities of support for the Treaty in each of the member states. For its first half-century, the EU was elite-driven. In its second half-century, if the EU is to endure, citizens must be more aware and engaged.

In 2007, the Constitutional Treaty was replaced with a less contentious "reform treaty," the Lisbon Treaty. In Ireland, a nationwide referendum on the Lisbon Treaty was held in June 2008. In echoes of the 2001 Irish referendum on the Nice Treaty, 53 percent voted against and 47 percent voted in favor of the Lisbon Treaty. Voter turnout was 53 percent. Many voted no in the referendum because they felt they lacked sufficient knowledge and information about the Treaty to lodge an affirmative vote. Subsequently, Ireland and the EU agreed that Ireland would hold another referendum (in October 2009), after the EU addressed various concerns raised by voters (as discussed in Chapter 2). In the second referendum, 67 percent voted for and 33 percent voted against the Lisbon Treaty. Voter turnout was 59 percent.

Opposition in democratic systems of government like the EU and its member states is a good thing. That said, however well referenda reflect the will of the people, they do capture public feelings and fears that may be tangential to or unrelated to the matter put to a vote in a referendum. When a referendum focuses on a single issue, such as a tax or a government reform, there is less scope for voters to consider other related and unrelated issues or to be confused. In the case of EU Treaties, where issues are complex and intertwined with national and global issues, referenda may be inexact measures of public opinion. In the end, it matters little if the Dutch, French and Irish no votes were due primarily to domestic or to European politics. What matters now is that the EU has to consider the effect it is having on Europeans. In the end, this is a good thing for Europe, because a union that does not engage its citizens is a weak union with an uncertain future.

PUBLIC OPINION

This chapter draws on public opinion data from **Eurobarometer**, the name of a series of surveys measuring historical and current public opinion on EU issues. Eurobarometer is funded and administered by the Commission's Directorate-General for Press and Communication. The Commission subcontracts national pollsters to conduct the interviews that are designed to gauge the level of EU citizens' support for European integration and to measure their reactions to questions about individual EU policies, institutions, and democracy. The first survey was released in 1974, a year after the first expansion of the EC. The main type of Eurobarometer report, released twice yearly, is the Standard Eurobarometer. In most of the surveys, 1,000 face-to-face interviews of EU citizens (over the age of fifteen) in each of the member states are conducted in their own homes and languages. However, 2,000 citizens are interviewed in Germany, 1,300 in the United Kingdom, and 600 in Luxembourg. Pollsters take into account gender, age, region, and size of locality in their random sampling.[9]

Complexities and risks are necessarily associated with data gathered across twenty-seven countries using different languages and amalgamated into EU averages. This is why it is important to take into account a standard deviation of plus or minus 3 percent for Eurobarometer public opinion polls. This helps to limit errors in measurement. This said, Eurobarometer is the only poll that asks the same questions over time and place, thus helping to capture overall trends in citizens' perceptions of the EU.[10] When Eurobarometer public opinion data are juxtaposed with other measures of EU effect, we have the opportunity to observe the gulf between what people say in polls, how they vote in referenda, and how their representatives vote in their legislatures.

Historical Data and Overall Perceptions

This section of the chapter identifies and analyzes public opinion data on the importance of the EU to its citizens, support for European unification, the benefits of being a member of the union, trust in the EU institutions, the image of the EU, and the position of the member governments in the EU. In each area, historical data are presented first, followed by more recent data in order to identify trends over time.

IMPORTANCE OF THE EUROPEAN UNION AND SUPPORT FOR POLITICAL UNIFICATION

When asked in Eurobarometer surveys from 1975 to 1992 if respondents felt that the EC was important to them, between 67 and 85 percent of the respondents said that it was important. Roughly 12 percent indicated that EC matters were not important to them.[11] The data suggest that between British accession, the oil cartel crisis, and direct EP elections in the 1970s, and the enactment of the SEA and conclusions of the TEU negotiations in the late 1980s and early 1990s, a large majority of EC citizens polled felt that the EC was important.

When asked from 1982 to 1996 if they supported European political unification, roughly 70 percent of respondents said yes. Between 10 and 20 percent, rising to 24 percent in 1996, responded in the negative. Over 80 percent of respondents in Italy, Luxembourg, and Ireland indicated the strongest support for unification. Support in Greece, the Netherlands, Portugal, Spain, and France ranged between 70 and 80 percent. Support for European unification dropped to 60 percent or below for the United Kingdom, Austria, Finland, and Sweden.[12] Overall levels of support for unification were strong during the time in review. However, evidence indicates that such support was lower for many of the countries who joined the EU years after the charter members. Subsequent data support the observation that publics in the Nordics, particularly Sweden, and in the United Kingdom were not comfortable with the idea of political unification. Over time, support for unification would decline, as demonstrated by the data below.

When asked again in 2006 if they supported European political unification, 54 percent of respondents said yes (down from about 70 percent in the 1982–1996 period) and 30 percent said no. Between 65 and 77 percent of respondents said they supported unification in Slovenia, Slovakia, Greece, the Czech Republic, Cyprus, Lithuania, and Spain; between 13 and 23 percent said they did not. Support was weakest in the United Kingdom (31 percent in support; 54 percent against). Just 36 percent of Finns supported unification (50 percent against), 40 percent of Austrians (43 percent against), 42 percent of Swedes (47 percent against), and 42 percent of Danes (44 percent against).[13] Enlargement has widened the EU, but it has diluted support for political unification.

A word of caution about the question of support for political unification. The choice of words means different things in different member states. For some, unification is a process that binds the member states closer to a union but not to a United States of Europe. For others, unification is a euphemism for a federal Europe, which is anathema to respondents in such countries as Britain, Sweden, and Denmark. Therefore, because the term *unification* is so value-laden, it may not be a wise choice for future Eurobarometer questions. It is a question that was more pertinent to the union of six than to that of twenty-seven. The future of the EU is more likely to be characterized by the concomitant existence of the state and the union rather than by the supremacy of one or the other.

BENEFITS OF MEMBERSHIP

The question of membership benefits cuts more directly to the specific interests of EU citizens than does their support for political unification. When asked from 1983 to 1995 if they had on the whole benefited from membership in the EU, between 45 and 60 percent of respondents said that they had benefited. However, the Eurobarometer reported that only 23 percent felt that they had not benefited in 1983. According to figure 8.2, covering the years 1996–2009, those who said they had benefited from membership dropped to a low of 41 percent in 1997, before rising to a high of 59 percent in 2007. Those who reported that they did not feel they benefited fluctuated between a high of 36 percent and a low of 26 percent between 1996 and 2002. In recent years, approximately one-third of respondents continue to feel their country has not benefited from membership in the EU. What is most important about the data is that those who responded that they did not know if their countries had benefited substantially decreased from a high of over 20 percent in 1999 to a low of 13 percent in 2009.[14] The data thus suggest that respondents over time have more information about the EU in order to know whether or not their country has benefited from membership. In order to gauge changes in how Europeans have responded to the

Figure 8.2. **Benefits from EU Membership, 1996–2009.** *Source: Standard Eurobarometer 71, Fieldwork: June–July 2009*

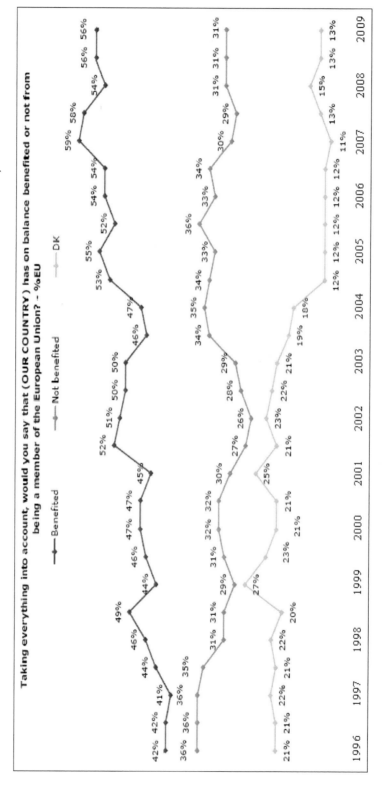

question of benefits from membership, it is illustrative to compare and contrast the data of 1996 and 2009.

When Eurobarometer asked in 1996 if respondents felt they benefited from EU membership, 42 percent responded in the affirmative. Of those respondents who felt they most benefited from membership, the Irish were first (86 percent), followed by the Dutch (70 percent), and the Portuguese (68 percent). In contrast, 36 percent of EU respondents felt they did not benefit from membership. For example, just 17 percent of Swedes and approximately one-third of Austrians, Finns, Britons, Danes, and Belgians felt that they benefited from membership. Fifty-six percent of Swedes felt they did not benefit from membership, followed by the Finns (49 percent), Austrians (46 percent), Britons (43 percent), and Danes (40 percent).[15]

In 2009, 56 percent of EU respondents felt that they benefited from membership. Those countries whose respondents felt they most benefited from membership included Slovakia (80 percent), Ireland (79 percent), Estonia (78 percent), Denmark (77 percent), Poland and the Netherlands (74 percent), Luxembourg (72 percent), Lithuania (71 percent), Spain (70 percent), and Belgium (68 percent). Just under one-half of respondents from Sweden and Austria indicated that they benefited from membership. In contrast, 31 percent of EU respondents felt they did not benefit from membership. Just 34 percent of Britons felt they benefited from membership, 36 percent of Hungarians, and 38 percent of Latvians.[16] These data indicate that in 2009 substantially more Danes, Swedes, Belgians and Austrians felt they benefitted from membership than those polled in 1996. Support for membership remained high among Irish respondents.

When respondents were asked what they thought of their membership in the EU between 1981 and 1994, those who responded by saying that the EU was a "good thing" ranged between roughly 50 and 70 percent. At the time of the SEA in 1987, those who felt the EC was a good thing increased to 63 percent, and the number peaked at 70 percent at the time of the TEU negotiations in 1991. Only roughly 10 percent of respondents claimed that the EU was a "bad thing." Those who responded by saying the EU was neither a good thing nor a bad thing ranged between 20 and 28 percent. Figure 8.3 depicts what respondents across the EU thought of their membership between 1995 and 2009. Just over one-half of respondents said that the EU was a "good thing," and roughly 15 percent said that it was a "bad thing." Just over a quarter of respondents felt the EU was neither good nor bad.[17]

In 2009, 53 percent of total EU respondents felt that their country's membership was a good thing. Luxembourg, Dutch and Spanish respondents were most affirmative (79, 72 and 71 percent, respectively), followed by Ireland, Romania, Slovakia, Belgium, Denmark, Germany, Poland, Estonia, Lithuania and Malta (between 57 and 69 percent). Roughly one-half of respondents thought their membership was a good thing in France and Portugal. Latvian, British and Hungarian respondents were least affirmative (25, 28, and 32 percent, respectively).[18] What is significant and alarming about these data is that in 2009 respondents from only sixteen EU member states felt that their country's membership in the EU was a good thing.

Between 1971 and 2003, Eurobarometer asked respondents if they would be "sorry," "indifferent," or "relieved" if the EU were to be "scrapped" (there are no new data since Eurobarometer no longer asks this question). About 40 to 50 percent of respondents claimed that they would be sorry (with the exception of 2001, when

Figure 8.3. Support for EU Membership, 1996–2009. *Source: Standard Eurobarometer 71. Fieldwork: June–July 2009.*

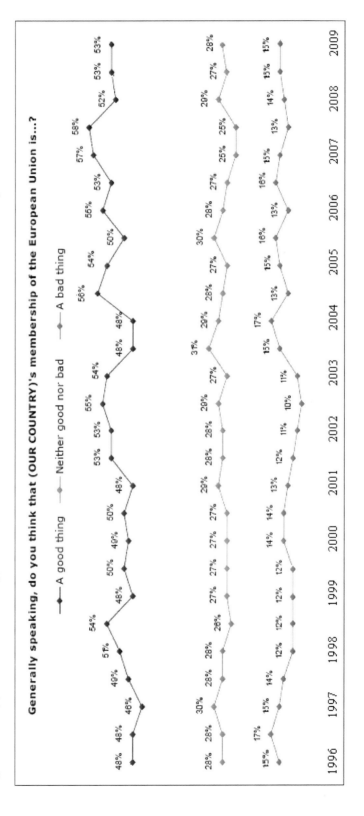

Generally speaking, do you think that (OUR COUNTRY)'s membership of the European Union is...?

—◆— A good thing   —◆— Neither good nor bad   —◆— A bad thing

that percentage dropped to 30 percent); fewer than 40 percent said that they would be indifferent (with the exception of 2001, when the response rose to 45 percent); 10 percent claimed that they would be relieved or did not know.[19] These data did not offer the EU a wide margin of support. That about half or nearly half of respondents would be sorry if the EU were to be scrapped is consistent with other data collected over time. However, the EU was clearly not having an effect on the 40 percent of respondents who indicated that they were indifferent about the possibility of scrapping the EU. Indifference, while not opposition, still weakens the EU and could further weaken it if the EU cannot demonstrate its positive effect on this large segment of European public opinion.

In 1996 Eurobarometer asked (but has not asked since), "If a referendum on continued membership in the EU were held tomorrow in your country, how would you vote?" Sixty-five percent of respondents said they would vote to retain membership, 11 percent said they would vote to leave, and 9 percent did not know. Support for continued membership was strongest in Ireland (84 percent), Netherlands (82 percent), Italy (81 percent), and Greece (76 percent), and weakest in Finland (57 percent), the United Kingdom (52 percent), Austria (45 percent), and Sweden (38 percent).[20] Although over a decade old, these data suggested that in all EU members, with the exception of Austria and Sweden, a majority of respondents preferred to remain in the EU. However, the data also indicated that segments of the EU public are ambivalent about the benefits of membership or hold, as discussed below, a negative image of the EU.

IMAGE OF AND NATIONAL POWER IN THE EUROPEAN UNION

Figure 8.4 depicts the responses to a Eurobarometer question asked between 2001 and 2009 about the image of the EU. Respondents who have a positive image ranged between 42 and 52 percent. In contrast, approximately 17 percent of respondents have a negative view of the EU. Between 31 and 36 percent of respondents had a neutral image of the EU.

In 2009, forty-five percent of EU respondents had a positive image, 16 percent a negative image, and 36 percent were neutral. Although the majority view is still positive, there are now fewer Europeans who have a positive image of the EU. Respondents from countries with the most positive image (those who responded with 52 percent and over) came from Romania, Bulgaria, Ireland, Italy, Luxembourg, Slovakia, Cyprus, Spain, and Poland. Respondents from countries with the least positive image (those who responded with fewer than 40 percent) came from the United Kingdom, Latvia, Hungary, Finland, Austria, and the Czech Republic. These data suggest not only that most of the EU's newest members (those that joined in 2004 and 2007) view it in positive terms, but that in all charter members the percentages of positive responses are above or close to the EU average.[21]

In 2004 and 2007, Eurobarometer asked respondents if they felt their country's voice, as well as their own voice, counted in the EU. In 2007, 61 percent of respondents felt their country's voice counted in the EU, down from 68 percent in 2004. In

Figure 8.4. Image of the European Union, 2001–2009. *Source: Standard Eurobarometer 71, Fieldwork: June–July 2009*

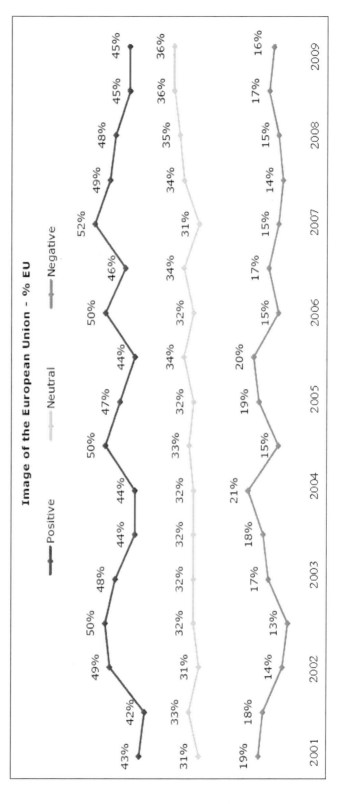

Image of the European Union - % EU

2007, respondents who felt their country's voice counted in the EU included a high of 86 percent in France, 80 percent in Denmark and between 72 and 79 percent in Luxembourg, Germany, Sweden, Malta, Belgium and the Netherlands. Between 35 and 48 percent of respondents felt their country's voice counted in Bulgaria, Cyprus, Czech Republic, Romania, Latvia, Italy, Portugal, Greece, Austria, Slovakia, United Kingdom and Lithuania. [22]

In sharp contrast, only 30 percent of individuals felt their voice counted in 2007, down from 39 percent in 2004. There were only four member states where respondents who felt their voice counted in the EU exceeded 49 percent: Denmark (58 percent), and France, Luxembourg and the Netherlands (50 percent). Just 14 percent of Czechs, 16 percent of Bulgarians, 17 percent of Italians and Britons, and 20 percent of Portuguese, Romanians, and Slovaks felt their voice counted in the EU.[23] These data measuring respondents' perceptions of whether their voice matters are highly problematic for the EU and point to the need to reduce the democratic deficit (discussed further below).

Institutions and Democracy

This section examines data on trust in and knowledge of the EU and ends with data on support for the Constitutional/Reform Treaty. With regard to overall trust in the EU in 2009, 47 percent of respondents claimed that they trusted the EU, while 41 percent claimed that they did not. The Estonians, Romanians, Slovaks, Bulgarians, Maltese, Belgians, Cypriots and Lithuanians most trusted the EU (62 to 68 percent). The Britons, French, Latvians and Austrians least trusted the EU (45 percent and below).[24]

These data concerning trust in the EU contrast with responses to another question comparing trust in EU institutions with trust in other institutions at national and international levels. Eurobarometer asked in 2007 how EU citizens tended to trust the following six institutions: UN, national legal system, EU, national parliaments, national governments, and political parties. Fifty-three percent of respondents ranked the UN first, followed by the EU (48 percent), the national legal system (47 percent), the national parliaments (35 percent), the national governments (34 percent), and national political parties (18 percent).[25] These data indicate that there is widespread mistrust of democratic institutions within the member states and that the EU garners higher levels of trust than those of national political institutions.

When Eurobarometer asked between 2000 and 2005 how much respondents felt they knew about the EU and its institutions and policies, 2 percent said that they knew a great deal, between 23 and 27 percent knew quite a lot, and between 50 and 55 percent said that they knew a little. Between 17 and 22 percent knew almost nothing.[26] These data reflect the need for the EU and its member governments to expand education among EU citizens about the integration process.

When respondents were asked in 2005 if they were in favor of or against the EU Constitutional Treaty, 48 percent responded in the affirmative and 18 percent in the negative, while 18 percent did not know. Belgians were most in favor (71 percent), followed by Germans (59 percent), Slovaks (57 percent), Poles (54 percent), and Luxembourgers (50 percent). Those least in favor were the Hungarians (26 percent),

Britons (31 percent), Czechs (35 percent), and Irish (37 percent).[27] These data were and remain worrisome. Although Europeans claimed they wanted a more effective and efficient union, especially in EUFP and JHA, fewer than half of those polled supported the Constitutional Treaty, which was designed to address those concerns. Furthermore, the gap between governmental and public support for the Constitutional Treaty was startling. Not only did member governments negotiate, conclude, sign, and thus support the new Treaty, but fifteen of their national parliaments ratified it by large majorities, and the EP voted in favor of the Treaty as well.

SUPRANATIONAL INSTITUTIONS

As the two most supranational institutions of the EU with the most scope for autonomous agency, the ECJ and Commission are recognized and trusted by significant numbers of Europeans. For example, in 2007, 64 percent of respondents said they were aware of the ECJ and 50 percent said they trusted it. Seventy-nine percent of respondents in 2007 indicated that they were aware of the Commission, and 50 percent trusted it. The 2007 data on trust followed a low of 40 percent in 1999 and a high of 52 percent in 2004.[28] In 2009, trust in the Commission declined to 44 percent. Trust in the Commission was highest (56 to 62 percent) among Belgians, Slovaks, Estonians, Dutch, Maltese, Danes, Portuguese, and Finns; trust was lowest (22 to 43 percent) among Britons, Latvians, French, Germans, and Austrians.[29]

In 2007, Eurobarometer asked respondents if they were aware of and had trust in the EP. Eighty-eight percent indicated that they were aware of the EP and 55 percent trusted it. Respondents who indicated that they trusted the EP did so in the range of 50 to 59 percent between 1999 and 2007.[30] In 2009, trust in the EP declined to 48 percent. The EU countries whose populations most trusted the EP were Slovakia, Belgium, Malta, Denmark, Estonia, and Romania (62 to 67 percent); those who least trusted the EP were the United Kingdom (22 percent) and Latvia (40 percent).[31]

INTERGOVERNMENTAL INSTITUTIONS

Respondents' awareness of and trust in the Council have been lower than for the EP, Commission, and ECJ. In 2007, 62 percent of respondents indicated that they were aware of the Council, and 44 percent trusted or tended to trust the Council. Awareness of respondents whose countries hold the European Council Presidency has generally been low; large numbers of respondents have not been aware that their country was holding the Presidency. In 2007, only 57 percent of Portuguese respondents were aware that their country was holding the Presidency. Nevertheless, when asked if they thought the Presidency was important, large majorities (77 percent) responded in the affirmative.[32] The following paragraphs provide data between 1986 and 2007 on the levels of awareness by respondents of their countries' EU Council Presidencies.

Only 22 percent of British respondents were aware of their Presidency in 1986, although 59 percent reported that they thought it was important. During their 1998 Presidency, 36 percent were aware and 63 percent thought it was important.[33] In the spring 2005 run-up to the British Presidency, which began in June, respondents were asked, "Have you recently read, heard or seen anything about the UK's Presidency?" Thirty-eight percent responded in the affirmative and 57 percent in the negative, while 5 percent did not know. When asked if the British Presidency was important regardless of whether or not they were aware of it, 71 percent said it was important, 21 percent said it was not, and 9 percent did not know.[34]

In the 1989 and 1995 French European Council Presidencies, approximately 42 percent of French respondents were aware of the Presidency and 64 percent thought it was important. In 1994, 41 percent of Germans were aware of their Presidency and 45 percent thought it was important. At the other end of the spectrum of opinion, 92 percent of Danish respondents were aware of their Presidency in 2002 and 77 percent thought it was important; for Sweden's 2001 Presidency, 92 percent were aware and 72 percent thought it was important; for Finland's 1999 Presidency, 87 percent were aware and 72 percent thought it was important; and for Greece's 2003 Presidency, 84 percent were aware and 82 percent thought it was important.[35] Two observations are worthy of our attention: (1) respondents from smaller member states were more aware when their countries held the European Council Presidency than respondents from larger member states; and (2) respondents who were less aware when their country held the Presidency tended to emphasize the importance of their Presidency more than well-informed respondents from other countries.

DEMOCRACY IN THE EUROPEAN UNION

Scholars have referred to a **democratic deficit** in the EU—a gulf between the powerful decisionmaking authority of government at national and EU levels and the perception among citizens that decisionmaking is cloaked in secrecy and made in the absence of sufficient checks and balances, far from home and public scrutiny. When respondents were asked in 2007 if they were satisfied with the way democracy worked in the EU, 52 percent stated that they were satisfied, 32 percent dissatisfied, and 16 percent did not know. The satisfaction with the functioning of democracy in the EU steadily increased from a low of 35 percent in 1996. The countries most satisfied with how democracy worked in the EU were Poland, Belgium, Spain, Denmark, and Slovenia (60 percent or more). Respondents in the United Kingdom, Finland, Bulgaria, Netherlands, Sweden and Portugal were less satisfied with how democracy worked in the EU (46 percent or less).[36] These data will remind the EU and its member governments to make the EU more democratic, representative, and transparent.

When asked in 2007 if respondents were satisfied with the way democracy worked in their individual countries, 58 percent were satisfied and 39 percent were not. Between 1995 and 2007 these data remained steady.[37] Therefore, levels of satisfaction and dissatisfaction with the way democracy works are similar for the member governments and the EU, and fears of a democratic deficit are warranted at both levels of government. When asked in 2005 if they thought that the EU would be more democratic if the Constitutional Treaty were ratified, 64 percent of respondents agreed, 20 percent disagreed, and 16 percent did not know. When asked if the EU would be more efficient, 63 percent agreed, 20 percent disagreed, and 16 percent did not know.[38] The irony is that voters in France and the Netherlands rejected the Constitutional Treaty that was supposed to make the EU more democratic and efficient. With the passage of the Lisbon Treaty, however, there is hope that the democratic deficit will be reduced.

Policies of the European Union

The EU polity exists to advance the interests, values, and welfare of its member citizens and governments. Eurobarometer offers a rich range of public opinion data on the internal market, the euro, environmental policy, and JHA issues. However, Eurobarometer is far more reticent in asking EU citizens tough and critical questions about the CAP and its high costs relative to other EU budgetary priorities. As a result, the availability of public opinion data on EU policies depends on which questions Eurobarometer chooses to ask and when.

INTERNAL MARKET POLICY AND ECONOMIC ISSUES

Chapter 6 examined the EU's most trenchant economic problem—unemployment exacerbated by lagging economic competitiveness. It should come as no surprise that EU citizens cite unemployment as their chief economic concern. When asked in 1996, 2004, and 2008 what were the most important issues in need of priority action facing the EU, employment was chosen by 85 percent of respondents in 1996, 44 percent in 2004, and 26 percent in 2008.[39] When asked in 2009 what were the most important issues facing the upcoming EP election campaign, the top concern was again unemployment, voiced by 57 percent of respondents from the twenty-seven member states.[40]

When asked in 2005 which level of government was most suited to solve the problem of unemployment, 60 percent said the EU, 24 percent said national government, and 12 percent said regional government.[41] However, when respondents were asked in 2007 about their view of the role played by the EU in fighting unemployment, only 25 percent had a positive view, 24 percent negative, and 40 percent neither positive nor negative.[42] As unemployment is a function of economic growth, Eurobarometer asked respondents in 2007 which level of government is most suited to solve the problem of economic growth. Fifty-seven percent said decisions should be made by the national government, and 40 percent said that such decisions should be made jointly with the EU.[43]

Eurobarometer turned its attention in 2005 to issues of European competitiveness in information technology and R&D. As discussed in Chapter 6, the Lisbon Strategy was adopted in 2000 to set the goal of creating the world's most competitive information economy by 2010. Investment in R&D is a priority of the Lisbon Strategy. When asked in 2005 which level of government was most suited to address the issue of R&D, 47 percent said the EU, 42 percent national government, and 6 percent regional government. When asked which level of government was suited to address the issue of access to new information and communications technology, 42 percent said national government, 41 percent EU, and 11 percent regional government.[44] In 2007, 23 percent of respondents said R&D decisions should be made at the national government level, while 72 percent considered decisions should be made jointly with the EU.[45]

Free trade in services is a goal long desired by the EU. When asked in 2005 if the increase of competition in the internal market in such service sectors as transport, telecommunications, banking, and insurance was having positive or negative effects, 22 percent of the respondents said negative and 60 percent said positive.[46] The Lisbon Strategy's goal that the EU should become a top economic power in the world was reflected in a question Eurobarometer asked in 2005. When asked if the EU could become a top economic power in the next five years, 38 percent said either yes or probably yes, 54 percent said either no or probably not, and 9 percent did not know.[47] The large no vote reflects the reality on the ground of very slow progress across the EU in meeting the goals of economic competitiveness established by the Lisbon Strategy.

MONETARY POLICY

Eurobarometer has been interested in measuring public support for the euro before, during, and after its introduction. Europeans have generally supported the idea and reality of the euro. For example, when asked in 1996 about levels of support for the introduction of the euro, 47 percent expressed support while 33 percent were against. Support was strongest in Greece, Ireland, the Netherlands, and Italy (64 to 78 percent) and weakest in Sweden, Austria, the United Kingdom, Finland, Denmark, and Germany (27 to 40 percent). From 1997 to 2002, Eurobarometer asked respondents to what extent they thought the success of the euro was a priority: between 55 and 62 percent said it was a priority, 25 percent not a priority, and 10 percent did not know.[48]

Figure 8.5 depicts support for and opposition to the single currency among EU members (regardless of their participation in the Eurozone) from 1999 to 2009. Overall, EU support has ranged between 55 and 67 percent. Opposition to the single currency has remained relatively steady, between 25 and 35 percent since the late 1990s.[49] In 2009, 61 percent of respondents indicated support for the euro, while 33 percent were opposed. Support for the euro was stronger (69 percent) among respondents from the Eurozone countries; favorable opinions ranged from 89 percent in Slovakia to 41 percent in Greece. Support for the euro was strongest in Slovakia, Slovenia, Ireland, Luxembourg, Belgium, Finland, and the Netherlands (81 to 89 percent). British, Czech, Danish, Swedish, Latvian and Polish respondents registered the most opposition (41 to 66 percent against).[50] Overall, the data from the Eurobarometer surveys suggest that the EU is having a positive effect on citizens' perception of the euro. Europeans are aware of the ECB. For example, in 2009, 75 percent said that they were aware of the ECB, and 44 percent said they trusted the ECB.[51]

AGRICULTURAL AND ENVIRONMENTAL POLICIES

Eurobarometer surveys have not asked relevant questions about the high costs of farm support in the EU. Thus Eurobarometer offers no public opinion data on the CAP. Yet the CAP consumes 47 percent of the total EU budget and competes with other priority spending areas with regard to the Lisbon Strategy. Despite the importance of

Figure 8.5. Support for the Single Currency, 1999–2009. *Source:* Eurobarometer 68, Fieldwork: October–November 2007 and Eurobarometer 71, Fieldwork: June–July 2009

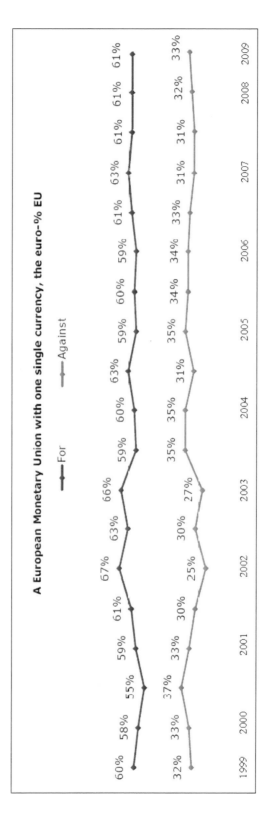

A European Monetary Union with one single currency, the euro-% EU

the CAP in EU decisionmaking, Eurobarometer has focused only on citizens' concerns about agriculture in general. For example, in 1996 when Eurobarometer asked respondents what their biggest fears were, loss of small farms was listed by 62 percent.[52] When asked in the same year what the top priorities of the EU were, 69 percent said agricultural and fisheries problems.[53] When asked in 2009 what were among the most important issues ahead of the next EP election, only 17 percent replied agriculture.[54] Agriculture is on the minds of Europeans, but less so now than in years past. The environment is also on the minds of Europeans, for which there is far more Eurobarometer public opinion data than for agriculture.

Europeans think the EU ought to and will play an increasingly important role in addressing the environment. For example, when asked in 1996 what the top priority of the EU was, 83 percent of respondents said joint efforts to protect the environment.[55] When asked by Eurobarometer between 1997 and 2002 if the EU would play a more or less important role with regard to the environment, 80 percent responded that the EU would play a more important role and only 10 percent said it would play a less important role.[56] When asked in 2009 what were the most important issues for the next EP election, 29 percent said the fight against climate change.[57] When asked in 2007 at which level environmental protection decisions should be taken, 73 percent of respondents said the EU, and only 24 percent said the national government.[58]

When Eurobarometer asked in 2007 about respondents' perception of the EU's role regarding environmental protection in their country, 52 percent of respondents had a positive view, 14 percent had a negative view, and 24 percent had neither a positive nor negative view.[59] When asked in 2005 what level of government was most suited to provide solutions for environmental protection, 45 percent said the EU, 37 percent national government, and 15 percent regional government.[60] In 2005, 63 percent of respondents said protecting the environment was a priority over economic competitiveness and 24 percent said it was not a priority over economic competitiveness.[61] Asked that same year about the role played by the EU in protecting the environment at the national level, 52 percent responded positively, 16 percent negatively, and 23 percent were neither positive nor negative. When asked what top three actions the EU should follow in order of priority, 19 percent said that environmental protection should be one of the top three priorities.[62] There is thus a wide scope of popular support for EU environmental policy action, which demonstrates the real and putative effects of the EU in this area of public concern.

JUSTICE AND HOME AFFAIRS

Chapter 6 argued that JHA was a growth area of integration. Public opinion in the EU appears to be driving support for immigration and anticrime policies at EU level. Asked in the 1990s about the fight against drugs, between 55 and 68 percent of respondents said that policy ought to be decided jointly by the EU and national governments, and between 20 and 25 percent said that policy ought to be handled by national governments alone.[63] When asked in 1996 what respondents most feared, 69 percent said the increase in drugs and organized crime.[64]

When asked in 1996 what they thought were the top priorities for the EU in this area, 97 percent of respondents said the fight against organized crime, 86 percent fighting drug trafficking, and 76 percent immigration.[65] Between 1997 and 2002, 85 percent of respondents perceived positively the EU response in the fight against crime and drug trafficking, only 7 percent perceived the EU response negatively, and 5 percent did not know.[66]

After the terrorist attacks on Washington and New York in 2001 and on Madrid in 2004, Europeans added terrorism to their list of concerns at EU level. When in 2004 respondents were asked what were the most important issues facing the EU, between 15 and 26 percent responded crime. Forty-seven percent of respondents in the Netherlands listed crime, followed by 39 percent in Ireland, 37 percent in the United Kingdom, and 31 percent in Denmark.[67] When asked to identify the most important issue facing their country in 2008, 17 percent of the respondents said crime, 9 percent said immigration, and 5 percent said terrorism.[68] When asked in 2009 what the most important issues were for the next EP election, 33 percent said crime, 29 percent said immigration and 28 percent said terrorism.[69] In 2004, Eurobarometer polled EU citizens to learn their perceptions of the role of the EU in dealing with terrorism, crime, and immigration. Fifty-three percent of respondents had a positive perception of the role of the EU in fighting terrorism, 17 percent a negative perception, and 20 percent had neither a positive nor negative perception. On fighting crime, 39 percent had a positive perception, 18 percent had a negative perception, and 35 percent had neither a positive nor negative perception. On immigration, 24 percent had a positive perception, 40 percent a negative perception, and 26 percent neither a positive nor negative perception.[70] The data suggest that EU citizens are more comfortable with a strong EU role in fighting terrorism and transnational crime than in dealing with the sensitive issue of immigration.

In 2005, citizens in the EU were asked about the role played by the union in national issues. In the area of fighting terrorism, 55 percent had a positive perception of the EU role, 15 percent a negative perception, and 22 percent had neither a positive nor negative perception. In the area of fighting crime, 42 percent had a positive perception of the EU role, 15 percent had a negative perception, and 36 percent neither a positive nor negative perception. On the issue of immigration, 28 percent had a positive perception of the EU role, 38 percent had a negative perception, and 20 percent had neither a positive nor negative perception.[71] When asked in 2008 what respondents thought were the most important areas the EU should address, 36 percent said fighting crime, and 33 percent said fighting illegal immigration.[72] It is no surprise that in the growth area of JHA cooperation, publics support collective action.

Review

The effect of the EU is felt by its member governments and citizens, but even though the former represent the latter, the two do not always share the same views toward the EU. The question of how representative democratic governments are of their electorates has long interested scholars of comparative government and democratic theory. EU member governments and their parliaments decide to join and remain in the EU. Governments negotiate and sign new EU Treaties, and national parliaments ratify them. The EU exists because it enhances the interests of member governments. Some would go so far as to say that the EU has rescued the European nation-state by making the state more important at the collective level. It is interesting to note that the views of national representative bodies and the views of national publics measured by Eurobarometer polls are difficult to reconcile, because the former, overall, support European integration and the latter are divided.

In some of the member states, both over time and more recently, significant segments of the public have expressed the opinion that the EU is not such a "good thing" and that the EU as a polity is too far removed to allow them to feel that their voices matter. Yet the EU exists to take action to enhance the welfare of its citizens. However, publics appear more inclined to support and welcome individual elements of regional integration than they are to embrace the EU overall. Our analysis of EU public opinion data suggests a union that is not capturing, retaining, or increasing public support. Publics are not well informed about EU issues, policies, and institutions and feel they are unable to influence them. In particular, significant segments of public opinion in the Nordic countries, Britain, and Austria are ambivalent about their membership in the EU.

Europeans support EU action in areas of concern to them—immigration, crime, agriculture, and the environment, to name a few—and they support the euro. Support and trust exist for individual EU institutions, especially the Commission, ECJ, and ECB. Surprisingly, the EP has the most legitimacy of the EU bodies but commands the least trust among respondents. Since Europeans want a more democratic and efficient union in which they feel their voice counts, significant numbers of them support treaty reform. Although many Europeans are more inclined to be skeptical or ambivalent about their membership in the EU, a majority of them wishes to remain in the union and would not want the EU to fall apart. In other words, Europeans find fault in the way the EU works but not enough fault to want to leave.

Particularly alarming is the EU's failure to capture the support of the 40 percent of respondents who indicated they were indifferent over the possibility of the EU being scrapped. Indifference, but not opposition, is weakening the EU and could further weaken it if the EU cannot demonstrate its positive effect on this large segment of European public opinion. An equally alarming development is that only 53 percent of respondents felt that the EU is a good thing. British, Nordic, and Austrian respondents were among those polled who did not think the EU is a good thing and have not for some time.

The data suggest that the farther removed the EU is from its citizens, the more the EU needs to be brought closer to them after a half-century of an integration process that was driven by elites. Large numbers of EU citizens fail to vote in EP elections, and the turnout rate is declining. The EU needs its citizens to vote in EP elections to enhance the democratic legitimacy of the union and its only elected body. As important as voter turnout is for national and subnational elections, it is more important for EP elections. This is because the nation-states of Europe can survive without the EU, but the EU cannot survive without the support of its member states and citizens. The EU has to rise to a higher level of democratic legitimacy than that of the constituent member states because it is still new, young, and untried.

If the EU is to matter to its citizens and to justify the resources of time and capital to support an institutionalized structure or polity that produces welfare-enhancing policies, it needs to work at national and subnational levels to enhance education about and awareness of the EU. Most Europeans polled think more education about the EU would be better. Europeans want a union that addresses their core problems and needs. They want a union in which their voices count. These are the same things publics want of their national governments. The crisis of the EU is also a crisis of the EU member governments.

Public opinion is the main source of feedback in the EU polity as in other pluralistic governmental polities. Whereas unemployment driven by lagging economic competitiveness is the EU's most trenchant economic problem, lackluster and ambivalent support for the EU as a decisionmaking polity is its most trenchant political problem. EU and national leaders need to pay attention to the problems their constituents have with how the EU and national governments work. If they can address that feedback, the EU polity ought to garner more support and trust in the future. What the EU and its member governments first need to do is to reverse the decline in public perceptions of the EU through education, effective governance, and helpful policymaking, and then, in the longer term, work to increase public acceptance of and support for it. The EU was built by elites for elites during its first half-century. The public opinion data generated in this chapter remind EU and national political elites that a union that is not rooted in the imagination and support of its people is a union whose future cannot be assured. If European integration can now focus on engaging Europeans to embrace their union, the EU as a polity will have a far more secure future than a union that remains aloof from those whom it serves.

Key Concepts

concentric circles
democratic deficit
Eurobarometer
measures of effect
pole of attraction

Study Questions

1. What is meant by "effect" in the context of the European Union, and why is it important to measure and evaluate at the EU level?
2. What are three measures of EU effect that were not covered in this chapter? How would you test these measures?
3. What in your view can the EU and its member governments do to garner additional support for the EU, so that more citizens feel they have a voice in the EU polity and benefit from it? Be specific.

CHAPTER 9

The External Dimension of European Integration

Preview

Chapter 7 introduced readers to the evolution and types of EUFP actions but did not focus on their effects. Measuring effects is difficult but necessary if we are to learn anything about the EU role in the world. Chapter 8 focused on the internal effects of European integration on EU citizens. Now, in Chapter 9, we turn to the effects of EUFP actions in international affairs as well as on the Europeans themselves. The data and analysis in this chapter demonstrate the following.

- There is no ambivalence about the importance of and need for EUFP among EU publics. No other policy arena of the EU has as much public support.
- There is no major issue of international functional or security affairs for which the EU and its member states do not have interests at stake and often common policies in support of those interests.
- The outside world is affected by what the EU does (and does not do). Countries look to the EU for commercial, diplomatic, political, security, and other forms of engagement, aid, assistance, and recognition. Some look to the EU as an alternative to U.S. leadership in certain areas of international affairs. These areas include climate change, criminal law, development assistance, and deployment of civilian missions to help prevent and end wars and establish the rule of law in violence-prone countries.
- The more the EU acts with effect in international politics and security, the more the EU directly affects U.S. foreign policy interests. Many solutions to world problems require responses from the world's two largest and richest democratic centers of power (the EU and the U.S.) with the resources to make a difference on a global scale. The more EU and U.S. foreign policy values and interests converge, the more the two together can address solutions to global problems too big for either of them, or any other global player, to address effectively alone.

Member Governments as a Measure of EU Foreign Policy Effect

When the EU acts in international affairs, it often has an effect. This effect may be positive or negative, marginal or considerable; or the EU's effect may be nil. The EU had a positive and considerable effect on establishing the conditions for security in Macedonia in 2003 when, with NATO, it pressed rebel forces and the Government in Skopje to agree to a lasting ceasefire. Conversely, the EU had a considerably negative effect when in 1991 it prematurely extended diplomatic recognition to Croatia, unintentionally helping to fan the flames of war in neighboring BiH. Emboldened by the EU's recognition of Croatia, Sarajevo declared independence and sought international recognition before the multiethnic country was ready.

In other instances, the EU may act, but the effect is marginal or negligible. Imposition of EU sanctions on China after the 1999 Tiananmen Square student revolt did not alter China's human rights posture (although its impact on China has been to press the EU to end those sanctions). In other instances, the EU may choose not to act when it could or should have. For examples, there was no common EU position on the anti-racism Durban Review Conference in 2009, which reflected poorly on the EU itself as a champion of human rights on a global scale. There was also no common EU position on reform of the UN in 2005, which reflected poorly on the EU given that "effective multilateralism" is a cornerstone of EUFP.

Finally, there are times when the EU decides not to take international action because the member states lack a consensus over its utility. For example, to avert a humanitarian disaster in eastern DRC, UN Secretary-General Ban Ki-Moon asked the EU in late 2008 to intervene by deploying military forces to protect and bring aid to 250,000 refugees. The UN wanted humanitarian supplies to reach those fleeing the fighting between government and rebel forces in North Kivu province and asked the EU to fill the gap until UN peacekeepers were reinforced in the region in four months' time. Some members wanted to intervene (Finland, Ireland, and Netherlands) while others did not (UK and Germany). The EU members who opposed intervention did so in part because they felt the UN mandate and objective were not clear, and the entrance and exit strategy for the deployment of an operation involving EU troops too vague. In the end, the EU chose not to comply with the UN's request.

For most of its members, the EU has become the most important forum of foreign policymaking, especially in conjunction with the UN and, for twenty-two of its twenty-seven members, with NATO. France has always viewed the EU as the means to develop common foreign policies, especially those that are autonomous of the United States and NATO. However, France and Britain, both nuclear powers, are permanent members of the UN Security Council, which affords them a global forum for diplomacy beyond Europe. Conversely, Germany has a long tradition of support for European integration in general and for EUFP: both are important to German national interests. The framework of EUFP is flexible enough to accommodate neutral countries in the union (Austria, Finland, Ireland, and Sweden) who may not wish to associate themselves with certain EUFP actions, but do not block the adoption of these actions. The EUFP framework also accommodates Denmark, a NATO member and thus not neutral, who negotiated opt-outs with regard to participation in CSDP.

EU members who wish not to be involved in an EUFP action may engage in what is known as "constructive abstention." States who do not wish to take a common action do not block others from doing so. For example, Cyprus did not veto the deployment of the EU's rule of law mission to Kosovo in 2008, but did not wish to be involved in it. By using the constructive abstention mechanism, Nicosia could make the political point that it did not support the mission without vetoing it.

This chapter begins with an analysis of public opinion data and member government support as key measures of EUFP effect. It then defines and applies the concept of "external political impact" to EUFP with regard to global and other security issues and players.

Public Opinion as a Measure of EU Foreign Policy Effect

EU publics demonstrate overwhelming support not only for EUFP but for military means to back that policy. Figure 9.1 depicts the level of support for EUFP from 1996 to 2007.[1] Eurobarometer surveys during this period show a consistent pattern of support, ranging from 63 to 72 percent. In 2007, 70 percent of respondents said they supported EUFP. However, about one-fifth of respondents throughout this period said they were against EUFP. Fifty-eight percent or fewer of Portuguese, Maltese, Swedish, and British respondents supported EUFP, while levels of support exceeded 75 percent for respondents from a number of other member states, for examples, Greece (88 percent), Germany (85 percent), Cyprus, Slovakia, and Slovenia (81 percent), Hungary and Poland (79 percent), and Belgium (78 percent).[2]

EU citizens have long supported CSDP in large numbers. Figure 9.2 depicts support for a common security policy from 1996 to 2007. In 2007, 76 percent of respondents said they supported CSDP, confirming no change in this high level of support through the period covered in figure 9.2. Opposition remained unchanged at roughly 14 percent throughout the period.[3] Over 50 percent of respondents in each of the member states replied that they supported EU security policy. Support was strongest in Cyprus (90 percent), followed by Greece and Slovakia (89 percent), Belgium and Germany (88 percent), Luxembourg and Slovenia (86 percent), and the Czech Republic and Estonia (85 percent). Opposition was strongest in the United Kingdom (53 percent) and Sweden (54 percent).

Large segments of EU publics polled perceived that the EU role in the world is becoming more important, that the EU will become stronger in the world once the Treaty is reformed, and that defense policy decisions ought to be made at the EU level. When EU citizens were asked in 2005 how they saw the role of the EU in the world compared to five years earlier, 62 percent said the EU role had become more important, 24 percent that it had not changed, 6 percent that it was less important, and 7 percent did not know.[4] More than 50 percent of respondents in each of the member states, except Britain and Austria, thought the EU role had become more important. When respondents were asked in 2005 if the adoption of the Constitutional Treaty (now the Lisbon Treaty) would make the EU stronger in the world, 71 percent agreed, 15 percent disagreed, and 15 percent did not know.[5] Even in

Figure 9.1. Support for EU Foreign Policy, 1996–2007. *Source:* Eurobarometer 68, Fieldwork September–November 2007

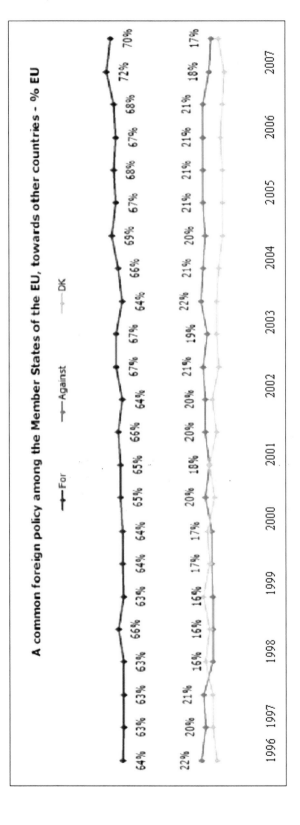

A common foreign policy among the Member States of the EU, towards other countries - % EU

Figure 9.2. Support for EU Security Policy, 1996–2007. *Source:* Eurobarometer 68, Fieldwork September–November 2007

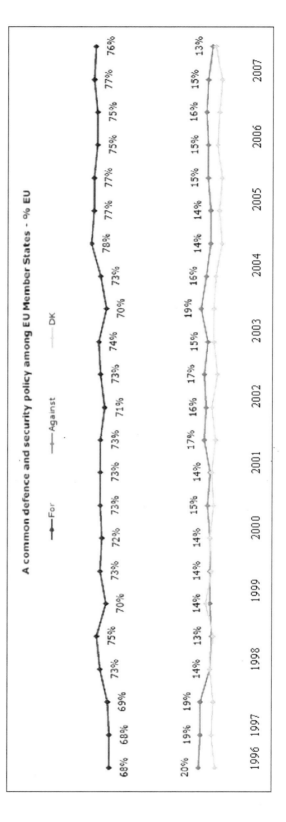

Euroskeptical EU members, there was overwhelming agreement that the treaty reform would make the EU stronger in the world. In Sweden, 75 percent concurred, in Britain, 61 percent, and in France, 70 percent.

European security policy decisionmaking occurs in three major realms: the national governments, NATO, and the EU. When asked in 2006 where defense policy decisionmaking should occur, 49 percent of respondents said the EU, 21 percent national governments, and 17 percent NATO. The EU was the first choice for respondents in all the EU member states except for Denmark and Ireland.[6] When Eurobarometer asked respondents in 2007 if they supported EUFP independent of United States foreign policy, 78 percent responded in the affirmative. In all member states, more than half of the respondents supported this view. The most enthusiastic supporters of this idea were the Greeks (94 percent), Germans (91 percent) and Cypriots (89 percent). The weakest support was in Romania (64 percent), Portugal (66 percent) and Italy (67 percent).[7]

Europeans overwhelmingly support the growth and development of CSDP. The problem for CSDP is not whether publics support it, because they do (70 percent of respondents in 2004 indicated support for the deployment of a rapid reaction force to handle international crises).[8] However, Eurobarometer does not couple its questions about CFSP and CSDP with questions concerning the costs of developing and deploying military capabilities. Given widespread fears of losing social benefits to new areas of spending, such as defense, it is likely that a good number of respondents in favor of CSDP would not want to pay for needed capabilities. Declining defense budgets as a percentage of GDP in several EU member states, such as Spain, confirm the observation that some in the EU do not want to put the full range of Petersberg Tasks into operation.

Having briefly surveyed Eurobarometer public opinion data on EUFP, we now turn to one of the most important and difficult questions of the book and one of the most important questions about the EU: does the EU matter in the world? The point of having EUFP is to shape a world that reflects the values and interests of the EU members collectively. Without political impact on international politics, the EU loses external influence and legitimacy as well as internal and external confidence. When an individual EUFP action has a political impact on a nonmember's foreign policy or on an issue area in international politics, the outcome closes the circle of EUFP decisionmaking depicted in figure II.1. Without outcomes, there are no links back to the sources that initiate action, there is no expectation of effective action, institutional memory breaks down, the efficiency and legitimacy of the EU to act internationally suffer, and the Europeans continue to react to world political events shaped by others.

External Political Impact as a Measure of EU Foreign Policy Effect [9]

External political impact refers to the effects of EUFP on nonmembers such that (1) nonmembers modify or change the direction or substance of a domestic or foreign policy in ways that would not likely have occurred in the absence of the EU stimulus (or EU stimulus accompanied by influence from other international actors); (2) nonmembers' interests are beneficially or adversely affected by EUFP action; or (3) non-members' interests are beneficially or adversely affected by EUFP inaction. External political impact also refers to the effects of EUFP activity on international political and functional issues such that the processes or outcomes of negotiations are modified or changed in ways that would not likely have occurred in the absence of EU stimulus or EU stimulus accompanied by stimuli from other international actors. When an EU member state or group of EU member states takes a foreign policy action outside of the EU context, such action is not considered an EU foreign policy action.

How do we know when the EU has political impact? Conventional wisdom based on *realpolitik* and balance of power politics suggests that foreign policies belong only to states. Thus many do not think to look to the EU as a *source* of foreign policy actions or to the international actors and issues that are *objects* of EU foreign policy actions. The more external political impact the EU has, the more the EU will develop a viable foreign policy decisionmaking system. Without outputs with impact—or outcomes—the EU will never develop the inward and outward capacity and confidence to act more effectively in international politics.

As observed in Chapter 8, measuring effect is hard but not impossible, and such measurement is necessary.

The EU has external political impact for *what it is*—the power of its ideas and the scale of its resources. The EU is a regional community of values and interests whose policies abroad reflect what the EU has achieved at home—peace and stability, interstate reconciliation, and enhanced human welfare and security. Even if the EU chooses not to act in a particular international issue, it has impact for what it is—a large internal market and monetary union with enormous influence in both diplomacy and the international political economy.

The EU has external political impact for *what it does* (empirical power). For examples, it underwrites the Palestinian Authority to create institutions of civil society needed to secure statehood and peace with Israel pending a final settlement; actively supports passage of new international treaties in criminal justice and global warming; provides military and civilian forces to stabilize regions at risk of war or in the process of postwar reconstruction; and leverages states wishing to join or associate with the EU to commit to guaranteeing human rights and nonproliferation.

The EU has external political impact for *what it is becoming* (putative power). By developing JHA and CFSP/CSDP actions, the EU gains traction as an important player as it combats transnational crime and terrorism and assists countries and regions in the areas of conflict prevention, crisis management, and postwar reconstruction. The EU is just at the cusp of contributing to international security as it draws on all instruments of foreign policy for the first time in its history and gains experience and traction by deploying military and civilian personnel to troubled lands around the world.

Inaction as a Measure of EU Foreign Policy Effect

In evaluating EUFP outcomes, a dose of sobriety is needed because the EU remains a thoroughly unorthodox and often uneven international player. It is not a state with a clearly recognizable foreign policy; it has neither historical nor contemporary precedents. The methodology of testing the political impact of any one actor or phenomenon on another requires care and rigor. At the same time that EUFP activity has spread across continents and issues, there are many instances when the EU could or should have acted in international affairs but did not because it neglected a responsibility, failed to patch together a common approach, or felt it could not act because it was not ready. When the EU fails to act in defense of its interests and values, its inaction may have adverse effects on its own or outside interests. The most egregious failure of the EC to stick to a common foreign policy position came in 1973–1974 when the member states did not adhere to a common approach to the oil cartel actions of OAPEC that singled out the Netherlands in an act of economic warfare (the Dutch suffered an embargo of oil supplies). The EU has failed to forge a common approach or take direct action in the following instances, among others:

- When the United Kingdom was at war with Argentina in 1982, Italy and Ireland backed away from EC economic sanctions against Argentina.
- The EC responded so belatedly as to have no political impact during the 1986 crisis between Libya and the United States that ended in U.S. air raids on Libyan targets.
- Due to a Greek veto, the EU was unable to extend diplomatic recognition to the new state of Macedonia from 1992 to 1995, depriving Macedonia of urgently needed diplomatic and other support. In this instance, a single member blocked what would have been unanimity on an important foreign policy decision.
- Before and during the outbreak of genocide in Rwanda in 1994, the EU did not have a common policy to help stop the carnage.
- The Greek-Turkish dispute over the sovereignty of Imia, an uninhabited Aegean islet, had to be mediated by the United States in 1997.
- An EU initiative condemning China's human rights policy at the 1997 UN Commission on Human Rights was blocked by France, contravening a prior accord reached within CFSP.
- When the Albanian government nearly collapsed in 1997, Italy was forced to organize a non-EU international humanitarian and military response. This was a lost first opportunity to put CFSP into action and may have given a boost to Kosovar Albanians in their quest for independence from Belgrade.
- Before and during what the United States called a genocide in Darfur, Sudan, in 2004 and 2005, the EU did not have a common policy.
- In the aftermath of Russia's shut-off of natural gas supplies to Europe through Ukraine in winter 2009, the EU has not developed a common policy on how best to limit dependence on supplies of Russian natural gas and oil to the EU.

The above examples list instances when the EU failed to act as a foreign policy collective. However, for each inaction, there are many more examples of EUFP action. Since it is important to establish and measure the scope of action, this chapter focuses on when the EU did act in international politics and with what effect. The following sections offer some observations of EUFP effects with regard to multilateral functional and security issues and organizations.

Effects on Global Issues and Players

The EU is the world's premier example of multilateral cooperation among sovereign states on a regional basis and the world's most important supporter of multilateralism on a global basis. The EU does abroad what it does well at home. Multilateralism refers to the practice by which several states and groups of states cooperate institutionally to advance common functional or security needs. Support for multilateralism abroad has always been a cornerstone of EUFP, but it figured prominently as the centerpiece of the 2003 *European Security Strategy Paper*. The EU's greatest effect on world affairs is its contribution to multilateralism.

The EU, as one of the most influential members of the WTO, has the power to support or block completion of the Doha Round of multilateral trade negotiations. It also has enormous influence over the admission of new members into the WTO, such as China (which has joined), and Russia and Ukraine (which wish to join). A stronger, more global WTO as a democratizing and liberalizing force in the world is good for EU and U.S. interests. Failure of the EU, the U.S., and the other WTO contracting parties to overcome final differences to reach a conclusion of the Doha Round threatens to adversely affect these interests.

The EU and its member states together are the world's largest providers of ODA. ODA is channeled through intergovernmental organizations, such as the UN Relief Works Agency (UNRWA) in the West Bank and peacekeeping operations of the African Union (AU) in countries like the Sudan and DRC. ODA is also channeled through nongovernmental organizations, especially those working in Africa and the Palestinian Territories. It is difficult to know the effects of EU foreign aid, but EU projects help establish or reestablish institutions of civil societies in war-torn regions from Afghanistan to Lebanon and Palestine and in areas where there are natural disasters, such as famine in North Korea and Sudan. EU members give more generously to ODA as a percentage of GDP than does, say, the United States. The United States, unlike the EU, is more inclined to provide aid bilaterally than through multilateral aid agencies.

Human rights and now criminal justice on a global scale are main concerns of EUFP. Besides conditioning its vast network of bilateral trade agreements with third countries on respect for human rights, the EU has gone on a worldwide campaign to ban capital punishment, which it considers a human rights violation. Indeed, the EU members will not agree to extradite any criminal or terrorist suspect wanted in the United States without having a guarantee that the individual will not be subjected to capital punishment if she or he is found guilty in a U.S. court of law.

The EU actively lobbied governments around the world to sign and ratify the Rome Statute establishing the ICC. The ICC entered into force in 2003, and all EU member states ratified it. The EU resisted efforts by the United States to pressure its members and applicant states to sign bilateral accords with the United States exempting American citizens from ICC jurisdiction in their countries. By so actively supporting the ICC and challenging U.S. interpretations of it, the EU has added to the isolation of the United States on matters related to the emergent international criminal justice system. However, the EU could be a more effective player in the area, particularly at the UN Human Rights Council in Geneva, where its members have voted differently on individual cases of human rights violations.

International security is a new area of EUFP. The EU endeavors to act in international security across the range of the Petersberg Tasks. CSDP operations are designed to provide security in states that request EU support or in states where such a request is made by an international security organization. Such operations also aid the EU itself as it addresses transnational crime and terrorism and illegal immigration, so that illicit activity is confronted on the doorsteps of Europe and beyond, rather than inside the EU. As described in Chapter 7, the EU has deployed twenty-two CSDP actions—military actions, police actions, and rule of law, border, peace monitoring, naval patrol, and other missions. This section introduces readers to an examination of some of the impacts of CSDP actions on states that request and benefit from CSDP actions (e.g., Georgia), on other international security providers (NATO) and on the EU itself (member states, EU bodies, and the interplay between the EU's civilian and military instruments).[10]

The more the EU builds confidence in itself as a provider of international security, the more the international community perceives that the EU can be relied on to organize, provide, and lead security actions effectively. The non-EU member states that serve under EU command of CSDP operations gain experience working with the EU, and use the opportunity to draw closer to and support EU foreign policies—for examples, Norway in the EU naval mission off the Somali coast; Russia in the EU military operation in Chad and the CAR; Ukraine in the EU police missions in Macedonia and BiH; and now the U.S. in the EU rule of law and police mission in Kosovo. The more the EU attracts nonmember state participation in its CSDP operations, the more the EU becomes a magnet for other security players who want to contribute to international peace and security but would prefer for whatever reason not to join a NATO or UN operation.

Croatia and Turkey contribute to CSDP operations while seeking closer ties with, or aiming to join, the EU. The participation of Ukraine and Russia in CSDP operations reminds us of the importance of EU relations with these states, especially given the recent strains in EU-Russian relations over natural gas supplies and the invasion of Georgia. Active Canadian participation is another reminder of the close EU-Canadian partnership in international affairs.

Finally, it is worth noting that non-EU member states bring to CSDP operations their own assets (Ukraine, Russia, Turkey), resources (Switzerland, Norway), and experience (Canada).

CSDP operations have impact on international organizations. Increasingly the UN calls on the EU to deploy military and civilian missions. The more the EU can help the UN Secretary-General, General Assembly, and Security Council enhance international peace and security, the better it will be for the UN peacekeeping forces, already strapped for personnel and funds, who are needed in other conflict areas. The EU provides support for the International Criminal Tribunal for Former Yugoslavia (ICTY) by detaining indicted individuals in BiH. The EU-AU relationship is quickly developing as the EU increasingly lends it financial, diplomatic, humanitarian, and military support for AU efforts to help the dire situation in Darfur. CSDP also affects NATO. The more the EU can do to relieve NATO of troop deployments in the Western Balkans, the more NATO troops can deploy to Afghanistan, where Taliban and other insurgents control large swaths of territory and threaten the Government's survival. The more the EU builds its capacity to deploy force rapidly and effectively abroad, the more NATO benefits, given the huge overlap in membership between NATO and the EU and the convergence of many NATO and EU interests. A weak CSDP is of no consequence to NATO.

The growing number of requests for EU security operations by countries and international organizations is an indicator of the EU's empirical and putative impact on international security issues. The EU is filling a niche as a unique provider of security, unique in the sense that its forces, always invited by the host government or mandated by the UN, are viewed as providers of humanitarian aid and support for civil society rather than as invaders. CSDP operations are not those of a single state or a single great power with a national or hegemonic agenda.

DEPLOYMENT OF COMBAT FORCES

Table 7.1 lists the twenty-two CSDP operations undertaken since 2003. Of those, five were combat operations: Macedonia and the DRC, both in 2003; BiH (2004–present); the DRC (2006); and Chad and the CAR (2008–2009).

Macedonia. In its first troop deployment, the EU's Operation Concordia consisted of 350 lightly armed personnel from twenty-six countries. The EU, which replaced an outgoing NATO force, patrolled ethnic Albanian regions on Macedonia's frontiers and engaged in surveillance, reconnaissance, and other security tasks. Macedonia requested the EU deployment to help oversee implementation of the ceasefire accord in 2001 between the government and rebel forces, an accord cosponsored by the NATO and EU Secretaries-General. The EU force replaced the outgoing NATO force. The EU military deployment, which was succeeded by an EU police mission deployment (Operation Proxima; see next section), helped solidify EU-NATO gains in securing a peace agreement. Overall, Macedonia today is more stable and secure than it was at the time of the EU deployment; however, the country continues to struggle to combat crime and corruption, which impede the start of accession talks with the EU.

Since the EU received UN authorization to act and took responsibility for security from NATO, it had a positive impact on the UN and NATO, allowing these security organizations to deploy their resources and personnel to other far less stable and thus needful areas of the world. Concordia was also a measure of how the EU–NATO relationship would work using the Berlin Plus arrangement. There were tensions between the EU command of the Operation and NATO over use of assets; however, overall Concordia went smoothly, and, encouraged by this success, the EU launched its police mission to Macedonia once it was clear that the overall security situation had improved.

Democratic Republic of Congo. The EU's second deployment was in Africa, a projection of force far from Europe and essential to the global reach of CSDP. Operation Artemis, a military force of 2,000 troops, was dispatched to the unstable eastern region of the DRC (Ituri province) at the request of the UN Secretary-General and mandated by the Security Council. The UN asked the EU to deploy in 2003 to relieve 750 UN peacekeepers in the region until a larger UN force could be deployed. The mission objective was to provide security and improve the humanitarian situation in Bunia. EU troops helped internally displaced persons (IDPs) return to their homes, helped reopen markets, protected refugee camps, secured the airport, and ensured the safety of civilians and UN and humanitarian aid workers. Since the EU lent stability to the region while the UN prepared for redeployment, it aided both the humanitarian and security effort in Bunia at a time when the potential for more violence against civilians was very high.

The EU deployment gave the UN the breathing space it needed to restructure its mission in the DRC. For countries whose contingents joined the EU mission (Brazil, South Africa, and Canada), the EU mission provide an opportunity to work with and expand cooperation with the EU as a new international security provider. The EU had an impact on NATO and the United States by demonstrating a willingness to take an action without recourse to the Berlin Plus arrangement. At first, the U.S. and some in NATO were alarmed that the EU would take an autonomous military action. The United States wanted NATO (and by extension the United States) to vet all CSDP military operations, even those that did not require access to NATO assets. The United States wanted to make certain that the two organizations did not work at cross-purposes, that they avoided duplicating assets, and that the EU did not engage in military action outside the NATO context that could later draw in NATO forces should the EU require assistance in a nonpermissive (dangerous) security environment.

However, as it has turned out, the U.S. and NATO generally no longer have serious reservations about autonomous CSDP operations. The more the EU acts with confidence and capability in international security, the better for NATO. NATO forces are suited for different kinds of operations. Their biggest and most dangerous deployment in Afghanistan is such an overriding priority that NATO needs to count on the EU to do what it can to enhance security in the Western Balkans and Africa.

In Operation Artemis, the EU gained experience in its first military deployment outside Europe. It began drawing on the full range of foreign policy instruments in a country where it, and especially some of its member states, such as France, had had long-standing diplomatic, humanitarian, and economic relations and interests. The EU applied the lessons learned to future military operations. The French led the operation and provided the majority of troops deployed. The more individual EU member states take leadership of EU troop deployments, the more CSDP itself develops in the context of EUFP.

Bosnia-Herzegovina. The EU's third military deployment—Operation Althea—occurred in BiH in 2004 with a force of 7,000 troops from twenty-two EU and non-EU member states. The UN-authorized force succeeded the NATO force that had been there. Althea's primary purposes are to ensure compliance with the Dayton Peace Accords; maintain a secure and safe environment; support local authorities in combating organized crime; provide support for the ICTY, including detention of indicted individuals; and contribute to defense reform. The EU is particularly eager to work with BiH authorities to strengthen border controls, given concerns over the movement of terrorists and criminals into EU territory through BiH—a traditional conduit for illicit east-west activity, including drug and human trafficking.

When evaluating the effectiveness of Operation Althea, it is important to note that in recent years the EU police mission in BiH (see below) has taken over the lead function of enhancing security. An indicator of how far the security situation has improved in BiH was the EU's decision in 2007 to reduce the number of troops to 2,200 with plans afloat to further draw down troop levels. Still, the country's three main ethnic communities are not integrating into a single national political culture as hoped years ago at Dayton: Bosnian Croatians look to Zagreb and Bosnian Serbs to Belgrade for leadership. Bosnian Muslims feel increasingly uneasy over their potential isolation from the rest of Europe. However, a cold peace is better than no peace, and with EU security assistance BiH enjoys more security and safety now than at any time since the 1991–1995 war.

Operation Althea is the result of a UN Security Council mandate, so the UN system has much at stake in how well the EU conducts a military operation on its behalf. UN peacekeeping forces had struggled to maintain stability and security in the war-torn country since the 1990s. To underscore the quality of EU-UN cooperation, it is useful to note that the EUSR in BiH double-hats as the UN Special Representative. The more the EU succeeds there, the more the UN can focus efforts elsewhere where the need for assistance is greater—in the DRC and Sudan. As Althea is a critical test of EU–NATO cooperation under the Berlin Plus arrangement, it is worth noting that both sides state that operational cooperation on the ground in BiH is very good. The EU's presence in BiH allows NATO forces to redeploy in Afghanistan. Just as the EU mission helps free up UN and NATO personnel to deploy elsewhere, the operation attracts contingents from other states. Nine non-EU member states lend troops to the operation: Albania, Argentina, Canada, Chile, Morocco, New Zealand, Norway, Switzerland and Turkey.

The mission is important for the EU because, as with operations in Macedonia, it allows the union to draw on and bring together the full range of foreign policy instruments—civilian and military. The EU is still learning how to (1) better co-manage military and police operations (see below); (2) couple military and civilian operations with the work of the Council, the Commission, and other EU bodies present in the country to help it rebuild and prepare for possible future EU membership through its SAA; and (3) work with other security providers under its own command.

Democratic Republic of Congo. The fourth military operation (EUFOR DRC), requested by the UN Department of Peacekeeping Operations, came and went in 2006. The EU deployed 1,100 rapid reaction forces to Kinshasa, DRC, and 1,100 stand-by troops to Gabon to provide both support for the UN police mission in the DRC (MONUC) and general security before and during the presidential and legislative elections. EU troops worked well with MONUC and the DRC government in deterring violence, containing the spread of violence in general, and responding to the attack on the residence of the Congolese Vice President. MONUC requested EU assistance when needed during the operation, for example, when disturbances occurred at the Congolese Supreme Court. EU forces remained neutral even as they responded to violence. By helping to limit violent disruptions to the election process, the EU with MONUC played a critical role in helping the democratic transition gain traction in the war-torn country.

The mission was an important learning experience for CSDP. Twenty-one member states and Turkey participated. Germany hosted strategic operations headquarters in Potsdam, and France took command of the operational headquarters in Kinshasa.

The larger and more powerful EU member states worked with one another—and the smaller member states offered their troops to serve alongside those of the larger states. A process of Europeanization helps CSDP gain traction.

Chad and the Central African Republic. The fifth EU military operation occurred in 2008–2009. The EU deployed 3,700 troops from twenty-six member and nonmember states in eastern Chad and northern CAR (EUFOR Chad/CAR). Refugees and IDPs were being driven from their homes into refugee camps in Bunia, DRC as a result of the fighting in Darfur. They were also being attacked by Chadian rebel forces and bandits and by Sudanese-sponsored militias in the DRC.

The UN requested the EU to provide assistance and security for its own personnel, other humanitarian workers, and civilians; and to prepare for the deployment of UN peacekeeping troops in the region in one year's time. As with the other EU military deployments, the mission had impact on the ground, on other international security providers, and on the EU itself.[11]

The EU's job was to get humanitarian aid to the refugees and IDPs in camps in the region. Its core mission was to protect international personnel and civilians while remaining neutral in the battles between government and rebel forces. Although its troops came under fire, it steered clear of engaging in combat. The EU helped thousands of refugees and IDPs return to their villages, provided medical care, and deactivated unexploded bombs. It helped deter attacks despite the many threats in the region: the anarchic conditions in Chad, the war in Darfur, bandit attacks on refugees, and efforts to recruit child soldiers.

The UN Security Council authorization for the EU deployment signaled a growing dependence of the UN on the EU to provide multilateral security assistance and the increasing importance of EU-UN cooperation and coordination. The EU was quick to respond to the UN Security Council request for deployment. EU forces assisted the UN by escorting UN food aid convoys and conducting operations to secure the areas around the UN's future areas of deployment. Many troops from EU member states who served in the EU operation were re-hatted as UN peacekeepers once the EU mission ended. The EU succeeded in buying a year's time for the UN to deploy its own peacekeepers in the region in 2009. However, it is important to note that huge differences in institutional cultures and decisionmaking practices, including budgetary/funding procedures, presented serious obstacles to interinstitutional cooperation in the implementation stages of the mission.

The mission was important to the AU and NATO. For the AU, the EU mission helped alleviate some of the adverse effects on civilians as a result of the spillover of the conflict from Sudan, where the AU and UN were present, to the neighboring areas. Indeed, the EU viewed the mission not only in terms of the dire humanitarian crisis in CAR and Chad but in relation to the continuing crisis in Darfur and its support for the AU-UN mission in Sudan. The EU mission also affected NATO. The EU demonstrated its ability to deploy troops far from Europe without recourse to NATO assets. Some in NATO lamented the lack of EU-NATO coordination and usage of the Berlin Plus arrangement, while others have begun to accept the value of autonomous EU military deployment. The more the Europeans gain experience and confidence in African security operations, the more this bolsters CSDP, and by extension NATO, since many of the same troops service both EU and NATO operations. The EU and NATO share complementary interests in enhancing African security.

The more the EU can contribute to African security, the more NATO is able to focus on Afghanistan.

The mission had impact on governmental and nongovernmental organizations alike. The mission affected three non-member states who sent contingents (Albania, Croatia, and Russia). Russian helicopters were procured for the mission beginning in December 2008. The EU has reported that these helicopters helped increase the mobility of EU forces as they conducted over five hundred air missions. Apparently the EU asked the United States for lift support in Chad and turned to the Russians when the U.S. declined the EU request. The Americans feared a growing CSDP dependence on the use of American assets and an unwillingness on the part of the Europeans to pay for their own needed capabilities.[12] The participation of the Western Balkan states in CSDP operations allows these states to demonstrate their value to the EU as they aim for closer association with and membership in the EU. The EU also affected NGOs by helping them bring aid to refugees and IDPs. Having done so under rebel attack, the EU helped mitigate some of the worst and most excessive violence that now normally exists in the country.

It is difficult to measure the impact of any international security contributor to Chad. For the EU, the "endgame" was to do what it was asked to do and depart, so at least what it accomplished in a finite period of time can be evaluated. Sadly for Chad, there is no endame in sight: some consider the country to be broken, others a failed state. Chad will require the support of the international community for a long time. However, the mission had important effects on the EU itself.

The operation was important to build internal EU experience and confidence in a large deployment far from Europe to a region roughly half the size of France. The EU was able to draw on all its foreign policy instruments in the country: security, diplomatic, financial, and humanitarian. For example, ECHO, the EDF, and the Commission provided loans, grants, and diplomatic assistance to complement the work of the military mission. The EU fulfilled the missions of protecting international personnel and civilians, security refugees and IDP camps, facilitating and providing humanitarian relief, and bridging a dangerous security and dire humanitarian situation with the deployment in March 2009 of UN forces. EU forces secured the area of operation by conducting over 2,400 patrols, deactivated hundreds of unexploded ordinances, and provided medical aid to the local population. Health care, water purification, emergency shelters, and food aid were provided for hundreds of thousands of refugees and IDPs in the DRC and Chad. Moreover, the EU was able to deploy forces quickly across inhospitable terrain with severe water shortages and other logistical challenges related to fielding an operation in such a remote location. Indeed, the mission's startup was delayed over rebel attempts to overthrow the Chadian government.

The EU has been criticized for fielding a mission that was dominated by French troops (French forces comprised about half the EU deployment). Critics have also charged that the mission was too modest relative to the scale of the crisis and that the EU left the country to further rebel violence and banditry once the year-long mission ended and there was a transfer of authority to the UN. That said, it would have been unwise for the EU to get drawn into the violence between rebel and government forces, as the mission was defined to provide humanitarian support while the UN prepared to deploy. Thus, the EU took care to remain strictly neutral and steer clear of the extant French force already operating in Chad and of France's support of Chad's President Deby. While it is true that France wanted to lend stability to a regime it already supported and to use the UN request as an opportunity to build experience for the CSDP, the operation was still an important learning experience for CSDP. Indeed, EU forces came under attack by rebel forces, yet managed to steer clear of civil conflict, and dealt surprisingly well with highly difficult circumstances on the ground. Moreover, the EU stresses that the EUSR and the European Commission remain in the region and continue to offer and coordinate humanitarian aid, that many member states have joined the UN forces, and that the problem in the region and neighboring Darfur is far larger than the mission the EU was asked to do by the UN.

In that vein, and as an early military deployment mission, it had more impact on the EU itself in terms of learning than on the long-term security and stability of Chad. The Chad mission afforded the EU a new opportunity to work creatively and coherently in a country far from Europe and within which the union was represented by different and often competing bodies (e.g., the Commission and Council). The mission also provided an invaluable experience for smaller EU member states to send contingents to serve alongside the French and other larger member states, allowing them to gain experience in a theatre that would not otherwise have opened up for them and to demonstrate their commitment and mettle in a hostile terrain under difficult circumstances.[13] EUFOR Chad/CAR was not just about bridging EU and UN missions; it was about building EU internal confidence in an early major CSDP military operation.

DEPLOYMENT OF POLICE AND RULE OF LAW MISSIONS

If the EU were to register a trademark for the CSDP, it would be its civilian missions, namely police and rule of law missions. These missions draw on a strong gendarmerie and constabulary tradition in the southern EU member states, on long traditions of legal justice in the northern member states and throughout the EU, and on EU preferences for enhancing security through civilian means in areas of the world where it has interests. In terms of the global security architecture, the EU is providing much-needed expertise with these and other civilian operations, while NATO, UN, and AU troops remain more focused on military operations. In-as-much as military operations are targeted in task and time and have a clear exit strategy, they are easier to evaluate or "benchmark." This is not the case with civilian missions, which are far more complicated and prolonged in duration.

Table 7.1 lists seven police or police/rule of law missions since 2003. Short of the deployment of troops, the EU assists countries in transition struggling to establish the rule of law and the establishment of independent judicial systems by offering to (1) deploy police forces to provide security in divided countries while enhancing local security and fighting organized crime (BiH, Kosovo); (2) train police forces and customs officials to perform needed functions such as border management and anticrime support (Macedonia); and/or (3) improve the functioning of the criminal justice system (Macedonia, DRC, the Palestinian Territories, Georgia, Iraq, Afghanistan, and Kosovo). Improvement of the criminal justice system focuses on the reform of the police and the judiciary (so that once the police arrest a suspect there will be a court that will know how to prosecute) and on the protection of the rights of the accused and the imprisoned. In other words, a rule of law mission aims to assist foreign governments with the creation of conditions necessary for the establishment of an effective police force working cooperatively with an independent judiciary. Such missions train and/or mentor senior police officers, judges, prosecutors and prison officials.

As this section demonstrates, the more the EU reaches out to border areas and beyond to help empower police, justice, and governmental officials in troubled lands to enhance security, bolster customs, and fight crime, the more the EU enhances its own security by limiting the flow of criminals and illegal aliens into EU territory. The more the EU does civilian operations well, the more it increases internal confidence and international learning as well as external confidence.

An indicator of EU external impact is the growing demand for EU police operations. Police actions outside Europe demonstrate a global commitment to helping countries establish the rule of law. The EU has much work ahead of it in terms of applying a single standard of policing to vastly different countries and in delivering the capabilities needed. There is also a need for EU police missions to address not only what most interests the EU—anticrime cooperation and border control—but also what most interests average citizens of the recipient states—street crime. That said, the EU has an important niche to fill in international security in ways complementary to the UN, NATO, AU, and the United States, among other international security providers.

Macedonia. In 2003, the EU deployed its first police mission of two hundred officers and personnel, Operation Proxima, to Macedonia at the request of the Macedonian Government as a follow-up to Concordia, the EU's completed military mission. Operation Proxima sought to monitor, mentor, advise, and reform the police, help fight organized crime, promote sound policing standards, promote border management and the creation of a border police, and support a political environment conducive to facilitating the Ohrid Framework Agreement. Twenty-four EU member states and Turkey, Norway, Switzerland, and Ukraine participated in the mission.

The mission was important to Macedonia as a measure of continued support for the country's peaceful transition and closer relationship with the EU. However, the country continues to suffer from human rights problems, corruption and crime, and proliferation issues. The mission served UN and NATO interests in a country where both had stakes in stemming the tide of war between Albanian rebel forces and the Skopje Government and building the basis for a new and stable state in the heart of the volatile Balkans. Like other police and military missions, Proxima was important to the EU: it helped strengthen the external borders of the EU against the inward movement of criminals and terrorists while assisting Macedonia as it prepared to meet the requirements for an SAA and, of course, to eventually meet the Copenhagen Criteria for EU membership. Since 2003, the EU had recourse to all instruments of foreign policy in Macedonia, which could increase the union's effectiveness and coherence as it helps Macedonia develop conditions for stability, security, prosperity and democracy.

Bosnia-Herzegovina. The EU Police Mission (EUMP), deployed to BiH in 2003, replaced the existing UN police mission in the country. The purpose of the mission is to assist BiH in establishing a professional multiethnic police service in close coordination with the EUSR. The EUPM focuses on fighting organized crime, inspecting and monitoring police operations and investigations, and offering assistance to enhance the operational capacity of the BiH police system. The mission helped establish and works with new state agencies, such as the Ministry of Security and the State Border Service. It also helped transform the BiH Police Academy into one with enhanced powers to fight organized and other major crime.

The mission has helped provide security in a country whose constituent elements have still not been stitched together into a unified polity and national political culture. Thus the EU's police mission continues to be needed in BiH to help enhance security in a country that has yet to fully develop national institutions, especially as Operation Althea continues to reduce the size of its force presence. The primary threat to security in the country now originates less from a resumption of military hostilities, which Althea was created to address, and more from crime and violence that requires civilian police action and rule of law support. One indicator of impact is how EUPM has begun to eclipse the importance of Althea. Another indicator of the EU's impact on the country is captured by the dilemma both BiH and the EU would face should the EU decide to withdraw the mission. Most think an EU departure would raise criminal activity in BiH.

The mission has major effects on UN and NATO interests and on other security providers in the region. Since the EU mission succeeded the UN International Police Task Force, it allowed the UN to deploy elsewhere. Moreover, as the mission takes over more security responsibilities, it frees up NATO resources for redeployment to Afghanistan. NATO has an interest in this mission because it is governed by the Berlin Plus arrangement. Eighty officers and other personnel from non-EU member states—Canada, Iceland, Norway, Switzerland, Turkey, Ukraine, and Russia—participate in this multinational mission.

Early shortcomings of EUPM in BiH were attributable to the insufficient and ineffective coordination between the military mission, Operation Althea, and the police mission; difficulty in recruiting officers, training, and assignment of personnel; uncertainty about identifying and implementing "best" police methods (no one size fits all); and a relatively modest budget for an operation that at its height comprised five hundred police officers and thirty civilian employees. The mission has shifted from its early focus on developing police capabilities to focus on a more coordinated approach to organized crime and police restructuring.

As it dispenses diplomatic and economic assistance and prepares the country to take advantage of the SAA, the EU is finally able to deploy the full range of foreign policy and security instruments: the work of the military mission, the police mission, and the Commission. Only time will tell us about the EU's measure of success, but at least the union can operate with a full foreign policy toolkit in a region where limited civilian-only diplomacy failed to meet the test of effectiveness in the 1990s. The challenge of EUFP is no longer not having access to the full range of foreign policy instruments, but using those instruments with coherence and positive effect.

Kosovo. In 2008, the EU deployed a police/rule of law mission of 1,700 police officials and judges with executive authority to Kosovo (EULEX KOSOVO). Ninety U.S. police and judges participate in the mission. The Americans are joined by personnel from Norway, Switzerland, Croatia, and Turkey. These states lend their imprimatur to the EU's mission, which increases confidence both in the EU and on the ground. The mission, which took over from the UN mission (UNMIK), assists the new national government to establish the rule of law, patrol national frontiers to deter criminal movements and other illegal activities, and deter clashes between the Serbian minority in northern Kosovo (Mitrovica) and elsewhere and the Albanian majority. While deterring a resumption of military conflict is handled by NATO's military force of 16,000 troops (KFOR), the EU mission is responsible for deterring civil unrest and combating crime and corruption by supporting the police and judiciary together.

It is highly difficult to evaluate the effects of the mission to date, not only because it is new but because Kosovo is a very complex and politically charged environment in which to operate. Nonetheless, the mission is as important to the country's stability as it is to EUFP. If the EU cannot help establish the rule of law in Kosovo, where can it do so successfully? We begin with some of the challenges the EU faces in having impact on the ground.

Although five EU member states do not recognize Kosovo's independence, they did not block the decision to deploy EULEX. As a result, the EU is helping Kosovo establish the rule of law and training the police in a country to which it does not grant de jure diplomatic recognition. EULEX Kosovo is a status neutral mission. Adding grist to the mill, the Kosovo government does not exercise full control over the north of the country around the Mitrovica region, where there is a predominantly Serbian community on the Kosovo frontier with Serbia. In order to enhance EU access to the north and to help provide security there, the EU works with Serbia—a country that is a critical link in securing peace in the region, given its influence over the Serbs in northern Kosovo. This disturbs Kosovo, which claims sovereignty over the region but does not exercise control there. It is also difficult for the EU to speak with one voice in the country. The EUSR double hats as the UN High Representative, which means that out of one office the EU must try to help Kosovo while representing the entire membership of the UN, including Serbia. In addition to the EUSR, the EU is represented by the commander of EULEX and the head of mission of the European Commission office. Other players are the commander of NATO's KFOR and the multitude of foreign embassies, international organizations (UN, OSCE, Council of Europe), and NGOs. The EU has to distinguish the value of its own presence from that of the UN and, with the other security players, help Kosovo solve its security problems.

However, since the territory is small, there are many opportunities, formal and informal, for the members of the international community to work together and cooperate. The head of mission of EULEX and the EUSR/UN High Representative meet regularly. They are well advised to do so and also to meet with the KFOR commander, as the problem for Kosovo and for the entire international community in Kosovo is the sad reality that the territory remains one of Europe's largest conduits for human trafficking and other illegal activities.

Despite the challenges on the ground, EULEX and KFOR are working well together after a rough start. For example, after a dangerous situation occurred in December 2008 in the Mitrovica area, EULEX police, still quite risk-averse, called in KFOR for assistance prematurely. Since then, however, the two commanders agreed to parallel agreements with Kosovo to handle the threat or outbreak of violence in what is known as the **cascade of responsibility**. If a situation of potential violence occurs, the first responder is the Kosovo police. If the Kosovo authorities require EULEX to intervene, the EU is the second responder, and if the EU needs assistance, KFOR is prepared to intervene. Although it is a fact that the EU needs to be able to handle risky security situations, it is also a fact that EULEX, given its inexperience and limited capabilities, coupled with a culture of risk aversion, cannot manage two crises simultaneously. Nevertheless, in spring 2009, the EU did not need to call in KFOR reinforcements when it used tear gas bullets to contain the outbreak of violence in Mitrovica as Serbs protested the return of Kosovar Albanians to reconstruct their homes. So long as NATO and the EU commanders commit to working together informally, Turkey will not exercise a veto, but if the agreement on the cascade of responsibility were to be codified in Brussels, Ankara would veto it.

The EU patrols the north and maintains an office there, but does not patrol overnight. EU judges have begun to hold trials in the north during the day. Since the EU has executive mandate in Kosovo, its judges are holding trials and trying to chip away at the huge backlog of cases. EU judges have begun to hold trials to unstop the long backlog of cases but are stymied by the lack of prison space for those found guilty of crimes and given jail sentences. The shortage of prison cells means the convicted have to wait to serve a sentence. Another challenge of adjudicating in a region such as Mitrovica and elsewhere is the fact that in a small country the accused, the accusers, the judges, the prosecutors, the police, and the prison authorities all know one another. In the absence of impartiality, it is difficult to ensure and dispense justice. The EU mission is also working with Kosovo and the Mitrovica and Serb authorities to begin collecting customs duties on trade between Serbia and Kosovo.

By all accounts, the EU and international community have to make a long-term commitment to helping Kosovo change a long-standing culture. Police and justice reform will take years. However, the EU recognizes that Kosovo is a space for EUFP action, given the country's proximity and the reality that KFOR will continue to decrease the size of its presence. Overall, on the ground there is a broad stability within which economic reconstruction is taking off with the benefit of foreign aid. Two persistent problems require agility and creativity on the part of the EU. It needs to establish an effective presence in the north with more effective outreach, and it needs to support the police to fight crime; the judiciary so that there is a viable and efficient court system once criminal suspects are arrested; and the prison system to implement sentences once there are convictions.

Africa and the Middle East. In 2005, the EU began to dispatch police missions outside of Europe, first in the DRC, then in the Palestinian Territories, and now in Afghanistan. In the DRC, the EU assisted the transitional government with new police programs in close cooperation with the UN missions in the country. It also established the Coordination Office for Palestinian Police Support in the Palestinian Territories to advise, mentor, and train police and judicial officials. The mission's reach is limited since the Palestinian Authority is divided between the Fatah-based government in the West Bank and the Hamas-based government in the Gaza Strip. Fifty EU personnel help advise justice and prison officials.

Approximately two hundred to three hundred civilian personnel from seventeen states participate in the EU police and rule of law mission in Afghanistan launched in 2007. The mission, which builds on an earlier police mission in Kabul, is designed to strengthen the capacity of Afghan police officers to enforce the rule of law. However, it struggles to acquire traction, have effect, and gain visibility. The EU deployed slowly and had trouble recruiting police officers to serve in Afghanistan. It is difficult to assess the effect of the mission on the ground. However, officials of the EU mission are now placed in the Afghan Ministry of the Interior, where they are advising and mentoring senior police officers. The EU has agreed to increase the size of the force to four hundred, although the problems of police training and reform in the country are so vast that they will dwarf what the EU proposes to do. The reach of the EU mission is limited by Turkey's opposition to an agreement between the EU and ISAF to provide security for EU staff. This limits EU staff to Kabul or regions of the country where Provincial Reconstruction Teams, run by countries such as Germany, agree to provide security.

The EU struggles to shine light on its policies and programs in Afghanistan for a number of reasons. First, the EU is represented by the EUSR and the Commission Delegation, plus EU member states with major aid programs and with troops in ISAF. Second, the EU either competes with or gets overshadowed by the work of other security providers, principally NATO's ISAF, U.S. Forces, Germany's Provincial Reconstruction Team, which has a long history of support for Afghan police training efforts, the UN agencies, and the work of NGOs in the country. There are too many international security and humanitarian players without a collective international leadership in the country, trying to help civil society. The EU is not able to provide that leadership. ISAF has limitations in bringing security to the streets for average Afghans, as the U.S. is coming to recognize.

The EU began training Iraqi officials in 2005, and in 2009 it began conducting training programs inside Iraq. The EU has also offered training and mentoring programs in the EU states for 2,700 Iraqi judges, prosecutors, senior police officers, and prison officials. Officials are trained to improve skills and procedures in criminal investigation. The problem of the EU in Iraq is one of visibility and perceived relative weakness. On the one hand, EU aid to the country comprises one-third of the world total, which should give the union influence. On the other hand, the EU appears weak in Iraq relative to the heavy lifting and fighting some of its member states are engaged in as part of the international force attempting to provide security and stability for the Iraqi Government.

DEPLOYMENT OF OTHER CSDP MISSIONS

Other CSDP missions, covered in this section, include border patrol, peace monitoring, and naval patrol and interdiction. The EU also supports the reform of the armed forces, principally in the DRC and Guinea-Bissau, and is offering financial, military, diplomatic, and humanitarian assistance to AU forces in Sudan.[14]

Border Patrol. A border patrol or border assistance mission helps countries with issues of customs and the movement of persons across troubled international frontiers. The EU assists customs and police officials on the Moldova-Ukraine frontier to help prevent smuggling, trafficking, and customs fraud. Not only does EU assistance help enhance security on this international border, it reduces the movement of criminals, terrorists, and illegal aliens into the territory of the EU. However, border problems persist, and the EU will have a long-term interest in cooperating with Moldova and Ukraine customs and police.

The now suspended EU mission in Rafah is another example of a border assistance action. In 2005, in response to an invitation from Israel and the P.A., the EU dispatched a monitoring mission to provide a third-party presence at the Rafah border crossing. The purposes of the mission were to monitor the P.A. performance; to support the Palestinian capacity to monitor border control and customs; and to contribute to the liaison between P.A., Israeli, and Egyptian authorities. Palestinians were charged with staffing and management of the border crossing. EU monitors supervised the crossing, and Israel monitored the crossing by camera. The EU monitoring mission had the authority to order the reexamination of any passenger, vehicle, or luggage. The EU monitored, verified, and evaluated the P.A. performance at the crossing with regard to the provisions of the agreement governing the border opening—provisions for which it retained authority to ensure compliance. Seventy staff members of the mission were mostly seconded from the EU member states. The value of having the EU mission on the border-crossing was that it (1) eased the flow of legal traffic between Gaza and the outside world through Egypt; (2) monitored the movement of criminals and terrorists across this border; and thus (3) assuaged Israel's legitimate security concerns about the openness of the Gaza–Egypt border-crossing.

The opening of the Rafah border crossing was an important step toward Palestinian statehood and to the Middle East Peace Process (MEPP). However, as earlier mentioned, the mission was suspended in 2007 when Hamas gained control of the Gaza Strip. Reopening was pushed further into the future after the 2009 Israeli bombardment of Gaza in response to the rockets Hamas fired from Gaza into Israel. The EU keeps the operation on call should conditions improve and the mission could assume its duties. Unfortunately, that is not likely any time soon since it would require the accord of Hamas, Egypt, and Israel.

Peace Monitoring. The EU conducted a ceasefire agreement in Indonesia (2005–2006) and is monitoring a peace agreement in Georgia (2008–present). In the Aceh Monitoring Mission, 80 monitors from the EU, Norway, and Switzerland were joined by ASEAN monitors for deployment to Banda Aceh to oversee the ceasefire between the Free Aceh Movement and the Indonesian Government, following their peace agreement in 2005. That agreement was facilitated by the UN and its crisis management initiative, which received financial support from the EU. Rapidly deployed, the EU's six-month mission to Aceh, the first CSDP operation in Asia, was designed to monitor the two parties' compliance with the terms of the peace accord. The mission was innovative for helping Indonesia settle a crisis situation. The EU ensured that the parties met their targets for decommissioning and destroying weapons belonging to the Aceh rebels, demobilization and integration of Aceh rebel members, and withdrawal of Indonesian troops and police units from the Aceh region. The mission also observed the human rights situation in Banda Aceh. For the EU, the mission was important as a confidence-building exercise in an area of the world where traditionally the EU's interest had been more commercial than political. The EU helped the country end decades of armed conflict that had resulted in thousands killed and many more displaced. The EU contributed to the long-term development of Indonesia as it helped solidify the peace process in Aceh. By working with ASEAN members, the EU began to deepen political and military cooperation with East Asian states. It was the first, and surely not the last, CDSP mission in Asia. Having worked with ASEAN, the

EU created a model for what regional institutions may accomplish together around the world.

Over two hundred EU unarmed monitors were dispatched to Georgia in 2008 to patrol the administrative borders between Georgia and each of the two breakaway republics, Abkhazia and South Ossetia. As discussed in Chapter 7, the two republics declared their independence in August 2008 after a brief war between Georgia and Russia. Russia and Venezuela recognized the sovereignty of both republics in Fall 2008.

The monitors were deployed rapidly after the EU concluded the terms for deployment with Georgian and Russian officials in September 2008, and Russian troops withdrew from their Georgian positions outside Abkhazia and South Ossetia. Monitors patrol the regions adjacent to the breakaway republics and report on cease-fire violations. The mission contributes to stability and security and to confidence-building as the EU lends its support to a lasting solution. As the OSCE and UN missions were ended in 2009, the EU remains the only international organizational presence in Georgia. However, incidents of violence continue to threaten the safety of EU personnel, who are distributed in field offices across Georgia.

The EU mission in Georgia is important to the international community, given that EU monitors offer a stable presence that is in the interests of all sides to the conflict on one of the world's dangerous political fault-lines. The mission has an impact on Georgia, which counts on an international presence to deter a Russian invasion. The Georgians are particularly keen to have the EU stay now that the OSCE and UN have gone. However, they are very uncomfortable with the EU's deployment on only the Georgian side of the administrative borders, in contravention to the terms of the EU deployment. The EU monitors are blocked from patrolling inside the two breakaway republics; thus, they cannot observe conditions in those regions and where the Russian are present. The inability to patrol all of Georgia adversely affects Georgia's sovereignty, for it gives an impression that the EU presence affirms new international frontiers, which of course is not the EU's intention. However, the EU presence does calm Georgian nerves and also decreases the likelihood that Tbilisi will take any action that would precipitate a Russian invasion. For all these reasons, the mission is also consistent with core Russian interests. That is, EU monitors likely reduce the possibility of a resumption of hostilities from the Georgia side, are not allowed in the areas the Russians control, and unintentionally complement Russian interests in seeking de facto international recognition of new borders.

The EU's mission in Georgia also furthers the interests of EU members, the UN, the U.S. and NATO. The mission is important for some EU member states because they have a genuine interest in supporting an independent and democratic Georgia, and for others because Georgia is important strategically given that its pipelines carry oil to them from the Caspian and Black Sea regions. The mission aids the UN because it is not present. It has a favorable impact on the U.S., which applauded the EU's quick diplomatic response to the outbreak of the war, the ceasefire it negotiated, and the monitors it dispatched. The U.S. would not otherwise have been able to deploy monitors, given the proximity to the Russian border. The more the EU can help stabilize Georgia's border areas, the better for the U.S. No one outside Georgia wants a U.S.-Russian military confrontation over Georgia. NATO too is affected by the EU presence in Georgia, given the close NATO-Georgian relationship as represented by the Partnership for Peace and the possibility of future Georgian membership in NATO.

The EU may have to remain in Georgia for a long time, now that no other international security organization is deployed in the country. A sudden withdrawal could leave behind a dangerous security vacuum. Although EU monitors continue to ask for entry at the borders with the two breakaway republics, they are denied access; thus it is impossible for the EU to monitor conditions and to develop relations with the authorities and peoples of these regions and to offer development aid. The mission is the first of its kind for the Europeans. They deployed quickly and are doing effective work in the country. The EU continues to work on a coherent and coordinated approach to Georgia, not easy with the presence of the EUSR for Georgia, the EUSR for the south Caucasuses, the head of the Commission delegation, the EU member states present, and all the other governmental and nongovernmental representatives. The EU continues to struggle to find the right balance among recognizing the territorial integrity and sovereignty of Georgia, maintaining relations with Russia in order to deal with natural gas supplies and other critical issues, making contacts with the breakaway republics, and deterring a resumption of hostilities. This mission has been a learning exercise for the EU, but there is reason to be concerned that the EU may be stuck in another frozen conflict.

Naval Operation. A naval protection force is a deployment of EU naval forces to protect international shipping of humanitarian and other supplies and/or to combat piracy. In 2008 the EU deployed Operation Atalanta off the Somali coast to deter, repel, repress, and interdict piracy that menaces and threatens the flow of much of European and world trade. Nine EU member states and Norway provided thirteen frigates and three maritime patrol air surveillance aircraft, with 1,200 personnel involved, to escort shipments of food from the World Food Program (WFP) and patrol waters in the Gulf of Aden, the southern Red Sea, and parts of the Indian Ocean (roughly the size of the Mediterranean Sea).

However, most agree that what the EU needs to do now is to support stability and security on land in Somalia—much more difficult than by sea. Gravely weakened by the departure of Ethiopian forces from Somalia in 2009, the transitional federal government continues to face Islamist rebel forces fighting it and each other. As the security situation deteriorates following the departure of Ethiopian troops who helped provide security, the EU has been able to help by escorting WFP vessels to deliver food aid safely to 1.5 million persons. The EU recommends that shipowners register with the website of the Maritime Security Center for the Horn of Africa and advises ships to remain six hundred miles off the Somali coast when possible. The EU and Kenya negotiated an agreement in 2009 whereby, in exchange for EU financial support for the Kenyan judicial and prison systems, pirate suspects interdicted and arrested by EU forces are handed over to Kenyan authorities for incarceration and trial. The EU is seeking similar agreements with the Seychelles and Tanzania. However, although Kenya receives EU aid for trial and imprisonment of pirates, one wonders about this burden on a poor country and its legal system when the EU member states could, but do not want to, bring to trial and imprison pirates in European countries.

The mission affects the security interests of Somalia's neighbors and the trading nations of the world, including the U.S., Japan, Russia, China, and India, whose navies are present off the Somalia coast, and NATO. The EU and NATO cooperate with each other and with the world's navies to deter and interdict piracy. Atalanta cooperates with ships from Russia, China, Brazil, and Ukraine. However, although the EU and NATO cooperate in antipiracy patrols, they also compete: neither organization wants to cede leadership to the other. The benefit of a NATO-led mission is that it would include the U.S., Canada, and Norway. The benefit of an EU-led mission is that the EU has an accord with Kenya to house and try the pirate suspects, while the U.S. and NATO maritime group (CTF151) does not. The EU, therefore, has more flexibility and effectiveness in deterring piracy than NATO.

The mission's impact on the EU is of interest. By leading the operational headquarters in the UK, Britain is able to invest politically in CSDP, from which it is often absent given its large troop deployments in Iraq and Afghanistan (Britain did not participate in CSDP operations in Chad and DRC). In terms of EU experience, the deployment was rapid. The member states generally claim that the mission has gone surprisingly well for the EU's first and that a sea mission helps support CSDP overall. EU naval forces have deterred or thwarted pirates from taking control of merchant vessels and have captured pirates and their equipment. Moreover, EU naval forces have successfully escorted merchant vessels across the length of the Somali coast to get WFP and other food delivered safely to port cities.

The mission has more to do with EU strategic interests than with solving Somalia's manifold problems on land. However, the EU is supporting the transitional government in Somalia and UN efforts in the country. The EU is considering a French proposal that the EU train and pay the salaries of Somali soldiers and police loyal to the transitional government in a first concrete step to help the country establish the rule of law and conditions for its return to civil society.

Review

The chapter began and ends with two probing questions: does the EU matter in the world and, if so, how do we know it? Yes, the EU matters; and we know it because the indicators described in this chapter point to external political impact—for what the EU is, what it does, and what it is becoming.

Publics in the member states support EUFP. Member governments are vested in the success of EUFP. The union is one of the world's centers of economic and democratic power. It is a magnet for those who want to join, associate, or partner with it. Measures of EUFP impact include the extent of EU influence over the functioning of the international political economy and over the world of diplomacy, law, and human rights and the development of many major international issues. We learned that the EU is entering a new world in which it can give back security and stability to regions at risk of war, at war, ending war, and rebuilding after wars. The EU has had impact on the ground where its deployments have operated and on other providers of international security, who now recognize that the EU matters. More importantly, EUFP is having an impact on the EU itself because it is learning how to dispense international security.

We have seen a strong demand for EU security contributions from the world's leading international security organizations and countries in dire need of the EU's conflict prevention and resolution skills. We have seen the EU implement a variety of security actions across time, place, and function. The EU has relieved UN and NATO civilian and military forces for deployment elsewhere. Only recently is the EU finally able to operate in various troubled lands with recourse to the full range of foreign policy instruments—civilian and military. The cliché of the EU as an economic superpower and a political dwarf is outdated. The more the EU can draw on the nexus of civilian and military instruments, the more it can implement rounded and effective foreign and security policies.

However, the day will come when the EU will have to perform in a nonpermissive security environment, deploy its battle groups, possess the lift power to transport its troops, and demonstrate that it is not always risk-averse. Just as it has found its voice in international affairs, so too will it have to demonstrate that behind that voice is a set of capabilities ready for deployment. The longer the gap persists between the rhetoric and promise of EUFP and the capabilities needed for operationalization, the more the EU risks losing its international political luster and credibility. It can no more risk failure than if it were to allow the euro to collapse or the internal market to fail or the *acquis communautaire* to unravel.

We have discussed the impact of the EU for what it is and what it does. But what is more important to the future of the EU as an international actor is where EUFP is going. Will the EU act on the world stage only in bit parts or will it be able to perform the large roles? All signals indicate the EU will become more important in the decades ahead in the fight against transnational crime and terrorism, in coping as a region with the risks and opportunities of economic and other forms of globalization, and in enhancing human and international security through civilian and military deployments. The world needs the security, stability, and example the EU offers from its own experience of overcoming interstate conflict and enhancing human welfare and security. EUFP is the external dimension of European integration. If European integration is to endure at home, the union will have to act in defense of European interests and values abroad.

Key Concepts

cascade of responsibility
external political impact

Study Questions

1. Why do EU publics support CFSP and CSDP?
2. What are three examples of the EU's external political impact, and when and where did they occur?
3. What are three examples of the inability or unwillingness of the EU to take joint foreign policy action?

4. What is the difference between the EU's putative and empirical foreign policy power, and why is this difference significant?

Selected Reading

Roy H. Ginsberg and Susan E. Penksa, *The European Union in Global Security: The Politics of Impact* (London: Palgrave Macmillan, 2011).

CHAPTER 10

Conclusions

The logic of regional integration endures. Europeans still draw on an old reflex to cooperate in facing new and common security threats and other problems too large for any single state to address effectively alone. States join and remain in the European Union because the benefits of being inside the union outnumber the costs of being outside. We have studied theories that help us to explain why states join, remain in, and benefit from an economic and monetary union with a common foreign and security policy. It remains worthwhile to be a member of the EU even if it is imperfect and incomplete. Many states who remain outside seek to associate or partner with the EU to limit the costs of being outside and to seek cooperation with the world's largest, richest, and most influential regional union of states.

The union began as a pact of peace in the aftermath of war through limited and sectoral integration. In time it grew functionally to cover many other areas of public and international policy designed to enhance the welfare of citizens and the interests of governments. Europeans benefit materially by exploiting economies and politics of scale within the union, but they also gain from a process of Europeanization based on common habits of cooperation and similar values and interests. They do all of this while retaining their own separate and unique statehood and political culture. The EU and its member states exist concomitantly. The EU as an experiment in regional interstate cooperation endures because it is based on a foundation of common denominators—a shared geography, history, religion, economy, and civilization among likeminded states. These common denominators, essential ingredients in regional integration, have fostered peace, security, stability, and prosperity.

In the mid-twentieth century, the imperative of postwar reconstruction and the response to the external threat of totalitarianism helped catalyze regional integration and cooperation. In the early twenty-first century, the imperative to respond to the risks and opportunities of economic globalization and to transnational threats to human and state security are new catalysts for regional integration and cooperation.

The European Union's First Half-Century

The recent fiftieth anniversary of the entry into force of the Treaty of Rome is a good place to evaluate the course of integration from a continent at war with itself to one at peace—and to consider the EU's future course. One cannot understand the EU from the perspective of any single snapshot in its history. A half-century retrospective reveals the union's peaks and troughs and provides a more panoramic, thus more accurate, view of overall trends and patterns. In only fifty years, these nation-states have overcome centuries of internecine warfare to create a structure of democratic peace and reconciliation that seems likely to endure despite its fits and starts. The EU represents nothing less than a transformation in the behavior of Westphalian nation-states.

The EU remains a work in progress. This book has demonstrated that most of the EU policy areas are incomplete and overlapping. There is insufficient effort to relate the policy elements of the union into a more unified whole in which EU and national leaders make more informed choices about how to prioritize public expenditures. At the same time, the EU struggles to bring itself closer to its citizens and to narrow the democratic deficit. The Lisbon Treaty was designed to improve the functioning of the EU at home and abroad after several recent rounds of enlargement and to enhance the union's democratic representative features. The EU cannot expect to function well and address the needs of its citizens if it continues to widen but not deepen.

In its next fifty years, the EU is likely to address many of these unfinished areas, rather than take on new and difficult areas of cooperation in the absence of tectonic changes in European and world affairs that would jolt the membership into a new epoch of economic integration. The two exceptions are JHA and CFSP, given the new security threats facing the old states of Europe in the twenty-first century. While the EU addresses new security threats and plays a more active world role, the EU and its member states will need to make the union more relevant to their citizens. EU citizens want to learn more about their union. At the same time, the EU and its member states need to accelerate efforts to integrate new immigrant communities into the European political, economic, and social mainstream as the union grows more multicultural. It would be ironic for a union based on interstate reconciliation in the twentieth century to fail to engage in the economic, cultural, and social integration of its own peoples in the twenty-first century.

As the EU and its member governments and citizens face the challenges of the future, the *acquis communautaire* is likely to remain the union's bedrock. This is because the body of law that governs how the union works meets the interests of the member states. The path of cooperation will always be rocky. The member states' responses to the effects of the recent global financial and banking crisis tested the logic of a collective response while threatening to unravel some of the EU's important rules governing the functioning of the internal market. In the end, the member states agreed to common approaches, and the *acquis communautaire* continued to serve as a brake against the temptation to breach the union's long-standing common rules and agreements for short-term gain.

The European Union at the Intersection of Theory and Practice

The EU is a living laboratory of regional interstate cooperation. It is not enough to study the practice of the EU without explaining it. Explanations are found in theories.

The most effective method of explaining European integration is therefore to test theoretical concepts against the real-world practice of the EU. Each of the theories of integration examined offered important insights, and each helped to sift through what is most important about how the EU works.

A major theoretical conclusion of our study of the EU polity is the importance of the dynamic between principals and agents inside EU governmental decisionmaking—the tension between governments as principals and the agents that they establish to run the business of the union. The book has demonstrated that EU institutions and leaders can and do develop their own influence over EU integration. Without EU institutional agency, European integration would long ago have evolved more like EFTA and NAFTA than the EU. Member governments decide at episodic conferences if new powers are to be given to the EU institutions. Even though governments may try to take back agency from EU institutions long after they have delegated power to those institutions, those same governments know that the EU cannot run effectively without the institutions they have created to enforce the rules and act in the common interest.

Also important is the logic of functional spillover which helps us to explain how cooperation in one area to raise human welfare may stimulate cooperation in another, related area that also raises human welfare. The process of expanding EU cooperation from one to another policy area was never linear but does help us to understand how a small coal and steel community can evolve over time into a large economic and monetary union.

Demystifying the European Union

By demystifying the EU, this book has sought to challenge assumptions about war and peace and what sovereign states can do together. The EU still remains a mystery to its own citizens. Many sense that it is important, but they neither understand how it works (for its infinite complexity) nor feel as though their voice in it matters (for its distance and lack of transparency). The EU is now far removed in time from the ravages of the twentieth century's world wars and the role European integration played in putting those terrors to rest. On the one hand, the EU has moved beyond its roots in the Franco–German reconciliation to a much broader enterprise, which testifies to the success and strength of the union. On the other hand, if Europeans grow complacent about the origins of their union, the communitarian logic could again be tested by the ghosts of wars past.

The EU has been a transformative experience for the European nation-state. It needs to have a transformative effect on the European citizen. Europeans are still baffled by the EU polity, for its arcane and complicated—nay, byzantine—nature. This is not sustainable. For the EU to grow and develop in its second half-century, Europeans need to know and have a say in how it works. For the union to endure beyond an economic or political logic, and to have legitimacy, it will have to capture the support and imagination of Europeans. Students are well advised to apply to European integration the insights and lessons of a social constructivist perspective, which stresses the importance of identity and values.

This book has taken interdisciplinary and comparative approaches to help readers understand what the EU is. The EU is far too multifaceted and complex to be captured by any single disciplinary perspective. None has a monopoly on knowledge of integration, and yet together, history, law, economics, and politics provide a rich, rounded, and more complete understanding. The most effective way to understand how the EU as a polity works is to compare and contrast its essential features to those of other polities. We have compared the European Union to another union of states across the Atlantic, the United States, in order to highlight and explain the EU's own federal features. The logic of comparative government can just as easily extend to the study of other federal or federal-type political systems (e.g., the EU and Brazil, the EU and Canada, or the EU and Switzerland).

Constructing and Deconstructing the European Union

This book has sought to demystify the EU by (1) constructing it as a fact of history and a product of law and political and economic theory; (2) deconstructing it in order to examine its key elements in relation to the whole; and (3) reconstructing it as a polity with effect on its citizens and the world outside. We have constructed the EU as a phenomenon rooted in history, informed by the economic and functional logic of a customs union to enhance human welfare, and practiced in law. We have deconstructed the EU to examine the whole range of institutional and decisionmaking actors and processes, with a focus on the two-way relationship between nation-state principals and EU agents and their scope for agency. The EU depends on a balance between the legitimacy offered by the participation of its member governments and the utility of common bodies to uphold the rules and act in the common interests. As earlier concluded, Europe of the twenty-first century will be inhabited by the nation-state and the European Union, concomitantly.

When reconstructing the EU, we focus on identifying and evaluating effects. For social scientists, measuring effect is hard, not impossible, and imperative. Without effect, there is no point to having a union of states. We have reconstructed the EU to focus on the effects of its internal and external policies on those for whom they are intended, and on the effectiveness, even existence, of the EU polity itself. The EU is judged for what it does, which feeds back into new sources of policy inputs. Policy outputs that result in poorly functioning policies will, through the feedback loop, be subject to change and reform if the polity is to be responsive. No polity can survive if it does not evolve to address the needs of its citizens. The book focused on various measures of evaluating the EU, the most important of which is public opinion. Thus it pays to reemphasize that the EU exists to enhance the welfare of its citizens; therefore, what those citizens think of the union and their level of awareness and trust in the union matter.

In this book, in sum, to build our knowledge of the EU we have rooted its construction in history and law and in economic theory and institutional practice. We have examined its key elements before putting the pieces back together to form a more coherent and unified whole. By constructing our knowledge of the EU piece by piece, we have come to learn how important the EU is to Europeans and to the rest of the world.

The Importance of the European Union

The EU is important to Europeans because it has so drastically influenced the international relations of the continent, as well as the domestic politics and economics of the member states, that the resurgence of war among them is unimaginable. At the same time that the Europeans have developed a union of values and institutions to structure peace and stability over the past half-century, they have also managed to preserve the diversity of their separate states and peoples within the unity of collective and complementary interests.

The EU matters in international affairs. It has a power of attraction for what it is, what it believes, what it does, and what it is becoming. It is because of its power to attract and influence that the EU has political impact on the world outside Europe. The European Union is without precedent in international affairs, and at the same time it is establishing a precedent for overcoming interstate hatreds and war. It is because it is sui generis as an international phenomenon that studying, traveling, living, or working in the European Union is worthwhile and different. It remains a great experiment in international cooperation in a region that was home to the First and Second World Wars. If the lessons of Europe's past are to matter over time—to have universal appeal—they must apply outside Europe. The European Union is important to the world as an experiment in regional peace and prosperity and as a provider of stability and security. The EU becomes relevant beyond its narrow confines when it serves as a model of regional cooperation elsewhere.

Glossary of Major EU Institutions and Policies

Key concepts, institutions, and policies related to European integration are bolded and defined in each chapter and listed at the end of each chapter.

Committee of Permanent Representatives: COREPER, which comprises the permanent representatives or ambassadors of the member governments, assists the Council by seeking accord on legislative proposals before they are sent to the Council for legislative action. COREPER lays down guidelines for, and supervises the work of, expert advisory committees. COREPER I consists of the Deputy Permanent Representatives; COREPER II consists of the Permanent Representatives.

Committee of the Regions: The CoR is an advisory body of local and regional authorities in the member states, whose views with regard to local and regional interests (e.g., education, environment, transport, vocational training) are considered by the Commission, Council, and EP in the context of preparing new legislative initiatives. The CoR issues its own opinions as well.

Common Agricultural Policy: A premier and costly sector of integration, the CAP is designed to support farm income through production, income, and export subsidies. For each of the farm products covered by the CAP, common market organizations provide the rules governing competition, production, trade, and financial supports. The CAP also emphasizes food safety, environmental objectives, and rural development.

Common Commercial Policy: The policy springs from the establishment of the customs union and the Common External Tariff. It provides the legal basis for the EU to conduct and conclude trade negotiations with nonmember states and international organizations and to either lower tariffs to help developing countries increase their exports to the EU or raise tariffs when the EU wishes to impose economic sanctions on foreign governments violating international norms.

Common Foreign and Security Policy: The CFSP consists of joint actions, common positions, and common strategies that direct or frame EU foreign policy action with regard to individual nonmember states, regions, and institutions and non-state actors, as well as international political and security issues and problems.

Common Security and Defense Policy: CSDP is the framework within which the member states seek to develop civilian and military capacities for the Petersberg Tasks of crisis management, conflict prevention, humanitarian search and rescue, peacemaking, and other tasks at international level. CSDP is the military arm of the Common Foreign and Security Policy.

Competition Policy: The Treaty prohibits single firms from establishing a dominant position in the internal market as a result of mergers, cartel actions, or state aids. The Commission monitors and prohibits such anticompetitive activity that could distort competition in the internal market.

Conciliation Committee: This committee of representatives of the Council and EP, which is convened under the codecision procedure (now known as the ordinary legislative procedure), aims to reach accord between the two institutions when there are differences over a legislative proposal. The Commission, which assists the Conciliation Committee, encourages the Council and EP to reach a joint text.

Council of the European Union: The Council, previously known as the Council of Ministers, consists of the ministers of the member governments who enact legislation. In most areas of the internal market and monetary union, the Council shares legislative decisionmaking with the EP. The composition of the ministers depends on the subject to be discussed.

Court of First Instance: This Court, renamed the General Court by the Lisbon Treaty, has the jurisdiction to hear certain cases not handled by the ECJ, namely certain preliminary references, most direct actions brought by individuals against EC bodies, most administrative and staff disputes, and certain appeals from Commission competition rulings.

Economic and Social Cohesion Policy: The purpose of this policy is to reduce disparities in wealth among the EU's regions through Structural and Cohesion Funds. The four Structural Funds are the European Regional Development Fund (to support infrastructure and investment designed to create jobs); European Social Fund (to support worker retraining); European Agricultural Guidance and Guarantee Fund (to support farm income and rural development); and Financial Instrument for Fisheries Guidance (to support reform of the fisheries sector). The Cohesion Fund grants financing for environment and transport infrastructure projects for the neediest member states.

Environmental Policy: EU environment policy seeks to preserve, protect, and improve the quality of the environment and promote measures at international level to deal with worldwide environmental problems. The policy features two guiding principles: sustainable development, to take into account the natural environment in economic decisions, and the precautionary principle, to ban production or the release of a technology that could harm human health. Areas subject to the common policy include food safety, fisheries, water, land use, and emissions of greenhouse gases.

European Central Bank: The ECB is responsible for maintaining price stability in the Eurozone by controlling money supply through setting interest rates and by monitoring price trends related to price stability. The ECB manages the euro, conducts foreign exchange operations, ensures smooth operations of payments systems, and formulates and executes EC economic and monetary policy.

European Commission: The Commission, the coexecutive and bureaucratic arm of the EU, promotes, defends, and safeguards the broad interests of the EU. It initiates and executes legislation and enforces EU law as the "guardian" of the Treaty. The Commission is responsible for planning and implementing common policies, drafting and executing the budget, and managing EU programs. It manages the day-to-day functioning of the EU.

European Council: The European Council, which refers to the summit gatherings of the EU Heads of Government and State, sets the broad political directions and priorities of the union. The President of the European Commission and the High Representative attend and participate. The President of the European Council chairs meetings, sets agenda, seeks consensus, and represents the European Council to other EU bodies and to the outside world.

European Court of Auditors: The ECA audits the implementation of the EU budget and the revenues and expenditures of the EU bodies to ensure the union's sound and legal financial management.

European Court of Justice: Renamed the Court of Justice of the European Union by the Lisbon Treaty, the ECJ enforces Treaty law, ensures that EU law is uniformly interpreted by the member states, and rules on the interpretation of Treaty law at the request of national courts. The ECJ most often deals with annulment, infringement, and responses to preliminary rulings.

European Economic and Social Committee: The EESC, which consists of representatives of employers and workers, is consulted by the Council, Commission, and EP in the context of new legislative initiatives.

European Investment Bank: The EIB finances investment projects that promote European integration and economic development in countries closely associated with the EU as well as those who are candidate countries.

European Parliament: The EP is the assembly of the directly elected representatives of the citizens of the EU member states. Members of the EP sit in the assembly on the basis of transnational European political groups rather than as representatives of the member states. The EP has the power to legislate with the Council in areas subject to the ordinary legislative procedure, enact the annual EU budget, and engage in oversight of the other EU institutions. The EP's assent is needed for the EU to enter into association accords with third countries and to enlarge the EU to include new members. The EP confirms the Commission—and has the power to censure it.

European Police Office: Europol provides a structure for police cooperation among the member states in order to prevent and combat transnational organized crime, such as drug trafficking, trafficking in human beings, child pornography, money laundering, and terrorism.

Justice and Home Affairs: JHA focuses on the goal of creating an area of freedom, security, and justice among the member states to prevent and combat racism, xenophobia, and transnational crime. Cooperation extends to combating such crimes as trafficking in human beings, drug trafficking, fraud, and corruption. JHA policy also extends to asylum, immigration, and free movement of persons; justice cooperation in civil and criminal matters; and customs and police cooperation.

Political and Security Committee: The PSC follows international developments for the CFSP and CSDP, and it helps to define and monitor common policies. Under the authority of the Council, it is responsible for the political control and strategic guidance of crisis management operations. Composed mainly of national representatives, the PSC is at the heart of crisis management activities.

Social Policy: Through the Social Fund and other mechanisms, the EU promotes social progress, employment, improved working conditions, equal pay for men and women, free movement of workers, and nondiscrimination in the workplace.

Notes

Introduction

1. For pathbreaking scholarly work on the concept and case studies of interstate reconciliation, particularly with regard to Germany's postwar relationships with its neighbors, see Lily Gardner Feldman, "The Principles and Practices of Reconciliation in German Foreign Policy: Relations with France, Israel, Poland, and the Czech Republic," *International Affairs* 75, no. 2 (1999): 333–396; and Lily Gardner Feldman, *From Enmity to Amity: Germany's Reconciliation with Her Neighbors* (Lanham, Md.: Rowman & Littlefield, forthcoming).

2. Although there are other examples of regional integration, no other regional integration movement in the world has achieved the unity of the European Union. The Nordic Council and the Gulf Cooperation Council (GCC) deepen an already peaceful relationship among the member states. The Association of Southeast Asian Nations (ASEAN), like the European Union, fosters reconciliation among formerly hostile states (Vietnam joined ASEAN, formerly an anti-Vietnam/anticommunist bloc, in 1995) as well as economic integration.

Chapter 1: Unity and Disunity

1. Unlike the Roman Empire, ancient Greece did not impose unity on Europe, but it did cultivate the idea of a common civilization, forerunner of European civilization, and it bequeathed to the future European civilization philosophy, science, and new forms of social and governmental organization.

2. For further insights into the period, see Charles W. Kegley Jr. and Gregory A. Raymond, *Exorcising the Ghost of Westphalia: Building World Order in the New Millennium* (Upper Saddle River, N.J.: Prentice Hall, 2002).

3. Quincy Wright, *A Study of War* (Chicago: University of Chicago Press, 1965), 244.

4. Henry Kissinger, *Diplomacy* (New York: Simon and Schuster, 1994).

5. Britain supported independence of the Latin American republics and also supported the Greek and Belgian revolutionary aspirants.

6. For a thorough historical account of the Zollverein, see Ronald H. Price, *The Evolution of the Zollverein* (Ann Arbor: University of Michigan Press, 1949).

7. Kissinger, *Diplomacy*.

8. For further analysis of the League of Nations as heir to nineteenth-century international cooperation and with reference to modern European integration, see Inis Claude Jr., *Swords into Plowshares: The Problems and Progress of International Organization* (New York: Random House, 1956).

9. Claude, *Swords into Plowshares*, 47.

10. Winston Churchill, "A Speech at Zurich University," in *The Sinews of Peace*, ed. Randolph S. Churchill (Boston: Houghton Mifflin, 1949), 197.

11. Seymour E. Harris, *The European Recovery Program* (Cambridge, Mass.: Harvard University Press, 1948), 76. Early American postwar reconstruction efforts in Europe were focused on individual national economies. However, the Americans determined by 1947 that a piecemeal approach to reviving the European continent was not yielding expected results and that the Europeans needed to work jointly on a European scale to increase economic efficiency and reduce barriers to the flow of trade and capital. Although agricultural and industrial production and consumption were still low, European economies were beginning to revive, but not soon enough for the Americans. The White House and the State Department—and a large majority in Congress—were concerned about the need to integrate the western occupation zones of Germany into the wider European economy and to build up Western Europe as a hedge against the communist subversion and Soviet expansionism.

12. "For European Recovery, the Fiftieth Anniversary of the Marshall Plan," Library of Congress, www.loc.gov/exhibits/marshall.

13. Jean Monnet, *Memoirs* (Garden City, N.Y.: Doubleday, 1978), 292.

14. Monnet, *Memoirs*, 295.

15. Schuman Declaration, "Declaration of 9 May 1950," European Commission, http://europa.eu.int.

16. Treaty of Paris, "Selected Instruments from Treaties," European Commission, http://europa.eu.int.

17. John Gillingham, *Coal, Steel, and the Rebirth of Europe, 1945–1955: The Germans and French from Ruhr Conflict to Economic Community* (Cambridge: Cambridge University Press, 1991), 372.

18. For an analysis of the ECSC's accomplishments, see Stephen Frank Overturf, *The Economic Principles of European Integration* (New York: Praeger, 1986). For a critique of the ECSC, see Gillingham, *Coal, Steel, and the Rebirth of Europe, 1945–1955*.

19. Monnet, *Memoirs*, 397.

20. Monnet, *Memoirs*, 394.

21. Gillingham, *Coal, Steel, and the Rebirth of Europe, 1945–1955*, 361.

22. For a transcript of the Messina Declaration, see Leiden University, http://www.eu-history.leidenuniv.nl/index.php3?c-52.

23. EC competition policy was based on antitrust regulations in the United States, extended to firms that are government owned or subsidized. Indeed, competition lawyers from the United States assisted in drafting the articles in the Rome (EEC) Treaty that dealt with EC competition policy. For more focus on competition policy, see chapter 6 of this book, and Simon Hix, *The Political System of the European Union*, 2nd ed. (London: Palgrave, 2005), 242–245.

24. Egyptian President Gamal Abdel Nasser nationalized the Suez Canal, energy lifeline to Europe, in 1956. In response, France and Britain, together with Israel, invaded Egypt, but American pressure to end their invasion exposed the reality of a weakened Europe when faced with the enormous relative power of the United States. This added grist to the mill of those, particularly in Paris, who argued for more European integration as a means to regain influence lost to the United States. The fracture in U.S. and European relations was an important determinant of Britain's reassessment of its decision to remain outside the EEC in 1957.

25. Rome Treaty, "Selected Instruments from Treaties," European Commission, http://europa.eu.int.

26. The author thanks the students in his Spring 2005 class, Political Economy of European Integration, for suggesting that we not conclude that the EU has exorcised the ghosts of Europe's past because we cannot be sure what the future holds.

Chapter 2: Theory and Practice of Modern European Integration

1. This section draws from the work of Sandi E. Cooper, ed., *Five Views on European Peace* (New York: Garland, 1972); Hendrik Brugmans, ed., *Europe: Dream, Adventure, Reality* (New York: Greenwood, 1987); and Walter Lipgens, *A History of European Integration* (Oxford: Clarendon, 1982).

2. Inis Claude Jr., *Swords into Plowshares: The Problems and Progress of International Organization* (New York: Random House, 1956), 25.

3. Hendrik Brugmans, ed., *Europe: Dream, Adventure, Reality* (New York: Greenwood, 1987), 59.

4. Brugmans, *Europe*, 59.

5. Chris Brown, Terry Nardin, and Nicholas Renger, eds., *International Relations in Political Thought: Texts from the Ancient Greeks to the First World War* (Cambridge: Cambridge University Press, 2002), 394–398.

6. Immanuel Kant, *Perpetual Peace* (New York: Columbia University Press, 1939).

7. Brugmans, *Europe*, 69.

8. Brugmans, *Europe*, 15.

9. Brugmans, *Europe*, 19–20.

10. Randolph S. Churchill, ed., *The Sinews of Peace: Postwar Speeches by Winston S. Churchill* (Boston: Houghton Mifflin, 1949), 199–201.

11. Churchill, *The Sinews of Peace*, 100–102. A close associate of Churchill, Robert Boothby, Conservative member of the House of Commons, echoed Churchill's ideas on Europe. On February 20, 1946, Boothby stated that, given the arrival of a postwar international order based on the overwhelming power of the United States and the Soviet Union, "the smaller nations of Western Europe, of whom we are one, cannot hope to survive, politically or economically, in isolation. Unless we get together in pursuit of a common political and economic policy, we shall inevitably, sooner or later, be absorbed into one or other of these two great economic and political blocs which surround us, one in the East and the other in the West." Lipgens, *A History of European Integration*, v.

12. Lipgens, *A History of European Integration*, 17.

13. Monnet drew on his experiences in international trade in cognac and as a Deputy Secretary-General of the League of Nations and his work as a coordinator of Anglo–French arms during World Wars I and II. Just ahead of the fall of France in 1940, he called for Anglo–French union with a single parliament, army, customs union, and currency. Monnet recognized before most that the European powers after World War II had grown smaller in a world of superpowers and new centers of powers released from the constraints of colonization. The Europeans could not achieve separately the means to survive. Monnet believed that institutions can create opportunities for new habits of thought and action. After both World Wars I and II he was interested in winning the peace. After World War I, he was inspired by Wilson's Fourteen Points, a general association of nations to afford mutual guarantees of political independence and territorial integrity to great and small states alike, but grew disillusioned with the return to national politics as usual and the limitations of the League. He lamented the lack of enforcement powers of the League, which is why he fought hard to empower the ECSC to have some sovereignty. For more information, see Jean Monnet, *Memoirs* (Garden City, N.Y.: Doubleday, 1978).

14. David Mitrany, *A Working Peace System* (1943), as quoted in Brent F. Nelsen and Alexander Stubb, eds., *The European Union: Readings on the Theory and Practice of European Integration*, 3rd ed. (Boulder, Colo.: Lynne Rienner, 2003), 118.

15. Ernst Haas, *The Uniting of Europe: Political, Social, and Economic Forces, 1950–1957* (Stanford, Calif.: Stanford University Press, 1958).

16. Leon Lindberg, *The Political Dynamics of European Economic Integration* (Stanford, Calif.: Stanford University Press, 1963).

17. Leon Lindberg and Stuart Scheingold, *Europe's Would-Be Polity* (Englewood Cliffs, N.J.: Prentice-Hall, 1970); Philippe Schmitter, "Three Neofunctional Hypotheses about International Integration," *International Organization* (Winter 1969): 161–166; and Philippe Schmitter, "A Revised Theory of Regional Integration," *International Organization* (Autumn 1970): 836–868.

18. Stanley Hoffmann, "Tradition and Change," *Daedalus* 95, no. 2 (Summer 1966), as quoted in Nelsen and Stubb, 163–177.

19. Robert Keohane and Joseph Nye Jr., *Power and Interdependence* (Boston: Little Brown, 1977, revised 1987).

20. Andrew Moravcsik, *The Choice for Europe: Social Purpose and State Power from Messina to Maastricht* (Ithaca, N.Y.: Cornell University Press, 1998).

21. Moravcsik, *The Choice for Europe*, 472.

22. This survey is largely limited to the internal development of the EC over the past fifty years. For a survey of the EC's external relations, see Chapter 7.

23. In 1962 the Council of Ministers adopted a financial regulation on how the Common Agricultural Policy (CAP) would be financed through July 1965. In December 1964, the Council asked the Commission to present, by April 1, 1965, a proposal for financing the CAP for the period between July 30, 1965, and January 1, 1970. In March 1965 the Commission presented its proposal, which surprised member governments, especially France, for its boldness in advancing the influence of EC institutions. The Commission proposed that (1) revenues from EC farm import levies/duties would accrue to the EC, thus giving the EC financial independence from the member states, and (2) in enacting the Commission's annual budget proposal, the EP would have more influence over the amendment process and the Council would vote on the proposed budget on the basis of a majority. Commission President Walter Hallstein presented the proposal to the EP rather than the Council, as convention dictated, thus raising the ire of some member governments and giving the Gaullist Government in Paris an opportunity not only to oppose the Commission proposal but to seek a wholesale restriction of the political influence of the Commission relative to that of the Council in EC governmental decisionmaking. The Commission's strong-arm tactic had backfired.

The Commission proposal to endow the EC with its own resources, which would have shifted the balance of power from the Council to the Commission and thus strengthened the supranational tendency of the EC, came at a bad time. The Rome Treaty stipulated that by 1967 important political decisions in the Council previously made on the basis of unanimity could be made on the basis of a majority vote. President de Gaulle and his government were keen to forestall the coming of majority voting, so France's opposition to the Commission proposal on CAP financing was the green light it needed to press the issue of French concern about the future supranational direction of the EC. The Gaullist Government preferred an intergovernmental union where the member governments in the Council drove the integration process and made important decisions on the basis of unanimity, with the Commission playing the role of mediator. France was not alone among the member governments with these concerns.

For these reasons, France rejected the Commission proposal on CAP financing, preferring instead to commit for another five years to the same way the EC had handled CAP financing in the previous five years. Paris could merely have opposed the Commission proposal but instead took more draconian measures. On June 15, 1965, France, holding the EC Council Presidency, recalled its permanent representative to the EC and began a boycott of the ministerial meetings of the Council. However, lower-level French officials represented the government's interests in some areas of EC activity. On June 29–30, 1965, the Council met and decided against transferring farm import levies and customs duties to the EC, but that did not bring France back into the fold. In July the Commission proposed transitional financial arrangements for the CAP for the 1965–1970 period but stated the EC should have its own resources from farm import levies and duties beginning in 1970. The modification of the Commission's proposal did not satisfy the French, who continued their boycott. France was insistent on carrying out the boycott even though its European partners and the Commission were prepared to work on a resolution satisfactory to all.

24. In 2014 a QMV will be calculated on the basis of a double majority of member states and their populations—a double majority will be a decision taken by 55 percent of the member states comprising 65 percent of the EU population. For the full text of the Lisbon Treaty see http://europa.eu/lisbon_treaty/full_text/index_en.htm.

25. Monnet, *Memoirs*, 318.

26. Monnet, *Memoirs*, 85.

27. For a succinct introduction to these three revisionist perspectives, see Mark A. Pollack, "Theorizing EU Policy-Making," in *Policy-Making in the European Union*, ed. Helen Wallace, William Wallace, and Mark A. Pollack (Oxford: Oxford University Press, 2005); and Antje Wiener and Thomas Diez, *European Integration Theory*, 2nd ed. (Oxford: Oxford University Press, 2009).

28. See Mark A. Pollack, *The Engines of European Integration: Delegation, Agency, and Agenda Setting in the EU* (Oxford: Oxford University Press, 2003).

29. For introductions to the logic of constructivism, see Thomas Christiansen et al., *The Social Construction of Europe* (London: Sage, 2001); Jeffrey T. Checkel, "Social Construction and European Integration," in *The Social Construction of Europe*, ed. Thomas Christiansen et al.; and Thomas Risse, "Social Constructivism and European Integration," in Antje Wiener and Thomas Diez, *European Integration Theory* (Oxford: Oxford University Press, 2009)

Chapter 3: The Economic and Legal Foundations of the European Community

1. The author wishes to express his gratitude to Professors Mehmet Odekon and Joerg Bibow, Department of Economics, Skidmore College, for their invaluable comments on this chapter. These sections also draw on Willem Molle, *The Economics of European Integration: Theory, Practice, Policy* (Aldershot: Ashgate, 2001), 13–28; Stephen Overturf, *The Economic Principles of European Integration* (New York: Praeger, 1986), 26–53; R. G. Lipsey, "The Theory of Customs Union: A General Survey," in *Readings in International Economics*, ed. Richard E. Caves and Harry G. Johnson (Homewood, Ill.: American Economics Association, 1968), 261–280; Jacob Viner, *The Customs Union Issue* (New York: Carnegie Endowment for International Peace, 1950); and Bela Belassa, ed., *European Economic Integration* (Amsterdam: North-Holland, 1975).

2. See Viner, *The Customs Union Issue*.

3. The author thanks Professor Odekon for his explanations of trade diversion.

4. Overturf, *The Economic Principles of European Integration*, 27.

5. Belassa concludes that trade creation exceeded trade diversion several times, that the elimination of tariffs and quantitative restrictions among the member states resulted in a sixfold increase in intra-EC trade over the 1958–1970 period, and that imports from nonmembers increased, but by only three times. See Belassa, *European Economic Integration*, 116–117. Molle argues that internal trade increased among clusters of members, rather than among all members simultaneously. See Molle, *The Economics of European Integration*, 116.

6. Overturf, *The Economic Principles of European Integration*, 47.

7. Molle, *The Economics of European Integration*, 31. See also Robert Mundell, "A Theory of Optimum Currency Areas," *American Economic Review* 51 (1961): 657–665. It is hard to know what the optimal size of the EMU ought to be for the European Union. The EU is not

certain how far it wishes to expand to countries such as Ukraine and Turkey. Where does Europe end and where does Asia begin? One possibility is to have the EMU open to those members of the EU who wish to join. This is what the EU has done. Britain, Sweden, and Denmark have stayed out of the EMU, and the new members who joined the EU in 2004 are not yet eligible to join the EMU.

8. Molle, *The Economics of European Integration*, 32.

9. Overturf, *The Economic Principles of European Integration*, 51.

10. Simon Hix, *The Political System of the European Union*, 2nd ed. (London: Palgrave, 2005), 322.

11. The notion of the EC's "imperfect constitution" is discussed by Renaud Dehouse, *The European Court of Justice* (New York: St. Martin's, 1994). The author wishes to acknowledge his appreciation for the lucid studies of EC law done by Dehouse and the following scholars whose work has influenced the writing of this chapter: Anthony Arnull, *The European Union and Its Court of Justice* (Oxford: Oxford University Press, 1999); and Grainne de Burca and J. H. H. Weiler, eds., *The European Court of Justice* (Oxford: Oxford University Press, 2001). The author also wishes to express his appreciation to two individuals who were immensely helpful in the legal section of this chapter. Professor Beau Breslin, Department of Government, Skidmore College, provided invaluable comments on the comparisons of the powers, institutions, jurisdictions, and influences of the U.S. Supreme Court and ECJ. Kenneth Olmstead, one of the author's research assistants, not only researched the cases for this chapter but worked closely with the author to explain the essential elements of EC law for students at an introductory level.

12. This analysis of the classification of the ECJ draws on de Burca and Weiler, *The European Court of Justice*, 6; and Dehouse, *The European Court of Justice*, 34.

13. Since 1989, most administrative disputes, such as staff disputes, have been heard by the Court of First Instance (CFI), for which the ECJ has appellate jurisdiction.

14. Upon holding oral hearings on questions of fact, law, applicable texts, and precedents, the Advocates General provide opinions to the ECJ to help the Judges arrive at their decision. An Advocate General is assigned to each case and gives an opinion before the Judges deliberate. This opinion sets out the relevant facts and legislation, analyzes the issues raised and the relevant case law, and concludes with a recommendation. The Treaty of Nice empowered the ECJ to rule without first hearing the opinion of the Advocates General. ECJ Judges and Advocates General are appointed by common accord of the member governments on staggered terms; one-third are up for appointment every three years. Acting unanimously, the Council may increase the number of Advocates General. The Lisbon Treaty provides for future increase in the number of Advocates General from eight to eleven and establishes a seven-person panel to offer an opinion on the suitability of candidates for ECJ judges and Advocates General.

15. Although member governments through the Treaty delegated power to the ECJ Judges to uphold and interpret the law of the EC, they were not completely comfortable with offering life terms. There are pros and cons associated with short renewable terms. On the one hand, the member governments' power to appoint gives them enormous influence over the Judges at the time of reappointment that could allow for a degree of politicization in the recruitment of Judges, casting a shadow over the independence of the ECJ. A Judge's record in the ECJ will be assessed by the national government in power back home. On the other hand, since the ECJ's deliberations are secret and the Court takes decisions by consensus (or by simple majority if necessary), it is difficult to attribute opinions to individual Judges. Once the appointment process is over, the Judge enjoys full independence during his or her term. See Dehouse, *The European Court of Justice*, 7, 12. Another benefit of not having life terms is that ECJ Judges and Advocates General return to their national judiciaries where, as influential players, they are equipped with EC experience and are generally pro-integration. They help to bring EC law home. For further comparison of ECJ and U.S. Supreme Court terms, see Leslie Friedman Goldstein, *Constituting Federal Sovereignty: The European Union in Comparative Context* (Baltimore: Johns Hopkins University Press, 2001). Thus, although the member governments have

through the Treaty delegated powers to the ECJ, they have sought to limit the scope for autonomous agency (see Chapter 5) of the ECJ by limiting rather than having life terms.

16. The ECJ sits in grand chamber when an EC body or member state is party to the proceedings and makes such a request, when cases are brought before it with regard to certain Treaty articles, and when, after hearing from the Advocates General, the Court considers a case brought before it to be of exceptional importance. A chamber of three or five Judges hears other cases. The President of a five-Judge chamber is elected for three years and the President of a three-Judge chamber for one year.

17. The CFI Judges elect their President for a renewable term of three years. The CFI Judges deliver a single collective judgment; no dissent is offered. The scope for appeal of a CFI judgment to the ECJ has expanded over time to include all direct actions brought by individuals, member states, or EC bodies. The CFI, like the ECJ, makes a collective judgment with no dissent. The CFI appoints its own rapporteur. Unlike the ECJ, the CFI is not assisted by Advocates General.

18. Three ECJ legal secretaries assist Judges and Advocates General with research and assist in drafting judgments and opinions (similar to the role played by law clerks assigned to each of the U.S. Supreme Court Justices). See Dehouse, *The European Court of Justice*, 4. A Court Registrar, appointed by the Court for a renewable six-year term, directs ECJ records and cases and handles administrative and financial issues. The ECJ President appoints a Judge to serve as a rapporteur responsible for producing the final report and a summary of arguments for each case, which gives this individual significant influence over the final deliberations.

19. Arnull, *The European Union and Its Court of Justice*, 35. The Treaty in its original form did not subject the EP to the annulment legislation because the Treaty did not empower it to adopt measures designed to have legal effect on third parties. However, when the EP later adopted measures that did have legal effects on third parties, the ECJ ruled that the EP was subject to annulment procedures.

20. Arnull, *The European Union and Its Court of Justice*, 38. The *Chernobyl* decision was reconfirmed in *European Parliament v Council* (1990). The ECJ again ruled that proceedings for annulment brought by the EP against an act of the Commission and Council are permissible if the action by the EP seeks to safeguard its prerogatives and is founded on submissions alleging their infringement.

21. Arnull, *The European Union and Its Court of Justice*, 26–27. For further analysis of the rights and duties of the Commission with regard to enforcement actions against member states, see Arnull, 23–29; de Burca and Weiler, *The European Court of Justice*, 14; and Dehouse, *The European Court of Justice*, 18–19.

22. Arnull, *The European Union and Its Court of Justice*, 50.

23. Weiler stresses a major difference between the U.S. Supreme Court and the ECJ. The latter's relationship with and dependence on the national courts is "far more delicate and sensitive." See de Burca and Weiler, *The European Court of Justice*, 221. The system of EC law depends on the quality of the dialogue between the ECJ and national judges. A separation of judicial functions exists by which the ECJ interprets EC law and national courts apply the interpretation to the dispute issues. Dehouse, in *The European Court of Justice*, 51–53, warns that this division of labor may prove one day to be a source of friction if tensions between EC and national courts develop.

24. Arnull, *The European Union and Its Court of Justice*, 51.

25. See Dehouse, *The European Court of Justice*, chap. 2, for a more comprehensive analysis of direct effect.

26. On a formal level, the Dutch administrative tribunal in *Van Gend en Loos* was asking the ECJ to interpret what the Treaty meant, yet the ECJ was also being asked to rule whether the Dutch decision to change the tariff classification conformed with EC law. Dehouse, *The European Court of Justice*, 49.

27. Dehouse, *The European Court of Justice*, 38.

28. Dehouse, *The European Court of Justice*, 49–51.

29. Dehouse, *The European Court of Justice*, 125.

30. Dehouse, *The European Court of Justice*, 39–51.

31. See de Burca and Weiler, *The European Court of Justice*, 28.

32. See de Burca and Weiler, *The European Court of Justice*, 28.

33. Dehouse, *The European Court of Justice*, 42–43, 50.

34. Dehouse, *The European Court of Justice*, 41.

35. Dehouse, *The European Court of Justice*, 42.

36. Arnull, *The European Union and Its Court of Justice*, 99; and Dehouse, *The European Court of Justice*, 42–45. National measures that encroach on the field within which the EC exercises its legislative power or that are otherwise incompatible with EC law could not be allowed any legal effect.

37. Dehouse, *The European Court of Justice*, 43.

38. Arnull, *The European Union and Its Court of Justice*, 29.

39. Arnull, *The European Union and Its Court of Justice*, 29. Despite the robust ECJ interpretation of EC supremacy and EC enforcement proceedings in *Francovich*, the Court in subsequent rulings tempered its approach. In *Procureur de la Republique v Waterkeyn* (1982), the ECJ determined that its judgments do not in themselves confer rights on individuals but rather establish whether a member-state action conforms with Treaty law. When the ECJ determines that a member state breaches a provision of Treaty law that produces direct effect, "the national courts must draw the appropriate consequences and protect rights claimed by individuals under that provision." Arnull, *The European Union and Its Court of Justice*, 30. In *Greenpeace* (1998), the CFI ruled that it would not hear individual cases, such as *Frankovich*, if the point of contention only concerned an individual "in a general and abstract matter." In *Greenpeace*, three associations and a number of individuals concerned about environmental protection sought annulment of a Commission decision providing financial aid to Spain's construction of electric power stations in the Canary Islands. These associations claimed the right under EC law to challenge the Commission's action on the grounds that it breached EC rules protecting the environment. The CFI did not accept the argument that the individual and association applicants were individually concerned, as others who lived and worked in the Canary Islands were equally affected. For further analysis, see Arnull, *The European Union and Its Court of Justice*, 45–46; and de Burca and Weiler, *The European Court of Justice*, 22.

40. Dehouse, *The European Court of Justice*, 54.

41. For further analysis of this case, see Alaine van Hamme, "The ECJ: Recent Developments," in *The State of the European Community*, vol. 1, ed. Leon Hurwitz and Christian Lequesne (Boulder, Colo.: Lynne Rienner, 1991).

42. Arnull, *The European Union and Its Court of Justice*, 95. See also Klaus-Dieter Borchardt, *The ABC of Community Law* (Brussels: European Commission, 2000), 105, for a list of cases related to the primacy of EC law. Another source is the ECJ website: http://europa.eu.int. Click on the "institutions" tab and then on the link labeled, "Court of Justice of the European Communities." In the ECJ website you can find detailed explanations of the functions of the different bodies of the Court. There is also an extensive body of ECJ and CFI case law. The legal summary of the cases is in English, but other records of the cases are in French. The case summaries are in legal terminology not easily accessible to the lay reader but are very useful for any student wishing to know more details about a case.

43. For a frontal assault on an intergovernmental approach to the study of EC law and a cogent defense of neofunctionalism, see Alec Stone Sweet, "European Integration and the Legal System," in *The State of the European Union: Law, Politics, and Society*, ed. Tanja Borzel and Rachel A. Cichowski (Oxford: Oxford University Press, 2003), 37. Stone Sweet argues the *Cassis* ruling suggests that the Treaty implied, or even required, mutual recognition of national product standards. After *Cassis*, no national product standard or regulation would be exempt from the rulings of the EC Courts.

44. Dehouse, *The European Court of Justice*, 46. The Treaty of Amsterdam, which reinforced the protection of fundamental rights in the EU, stipulated that the EU is "founded on princi-

ples of liberty, democracy, respect for human rights and fundamental freedoms, and the rule of law—principles common to the member states."

45. William R. Slomanson, *Fundamental Perspectives on International Law* (Belmont, Calif.: Thomson Wadsworth, 2007).

46. Dehouse, *The European Court of Justice*, 57.

47. Dehouse, *The European Court of Justice*, 151.

48. *General Report on the Activities of the European Union 2002* (Luxembourg: European Commission, 2003), 432. The Treaty guarantees the right of individuals and firms to establish a firm in the territory of any member state.

49. *General Report on the Activities of the European Union 2002*, 433.

50. Goldstein, *Constituting Federal Sovereignty*, 15.

51. See Arnull, *The European Union and Its Court of Justice*, chap. 5; and Dehouse, *The European Court of Justice*, 4, 115, 143, 153.

52. Goldstein, *Constituting Federal Sovereignty*, 176.

53. See de Burca and Weiler, *The European Court of Justice*, 216.

54. The Treaty of Nice (2001) permits the Statute of the EC Courts to be amended by the Council (acting unanimously) at the request of the ECJ or Commission. Changes in ECJ and CFI rules may be decided in Council on the basis of qualified majority voting. The Lisbon Treaty does little to change the ECJ and CFI. As mentioned, it does change the name of the ECJ to the Court of Justice of the European Union. The CFI will be renamed the General Court. The new Treaty establishes a seven-member panel to give an opinion on candidates' suitability to be a Judge or Advocate General before decisions on their appointment are made by the member-state governments. Panelists are to be selected from among former ECJ and General Court members as well as recognized jurists and members of national supreme courts. The ECJ will be granted jurisdiction in some areas of the JHA and jurisdiction to interpret implementation of the Charter of Fundamental Rights. However, the ECJ will not have jurisdiction in such areas as police operations and national measures to maintain law and order and safeguard internal security. Poland, the UK, and the Czech Republic have opted out of the Charter of Fundamental Rights. For more information, see *Treaty of Lisbon*, 156-157 in http://europa.eu/lisbon_treaty/full_text/index_en.htm.

55. See de Burca and Weiler, *The European Court of Justice*, 216–217. See pages 219–226 for Weiler's prescriptions for a more robust reform of the EC judicial system. In particular he calls on the ECJ to introduce separate and dissenting opinions (along the lines of the U.S. Supreme Court) and for the establishment of one nonrenewable term for ECJ Judges to remove even the hint of dependence on a member government.

56. *Bulletin Quotidien*, no. 9848, February 25, 2009, 16 and *Annual Report of the EC Court of Justice* (2008) in http://curia.europa.eu/. In 2008, the CFI settled 605 cases, a 52 percent increase over 2007. The number of hearings doubled in 2008 to 341 over 172 in 2007.

57. For example, in the 1990s, national constitutional courts began to defy the supremacy of the ECJ. The German Constitutional Court ruled in 1994 that national authorities may disregard EC legal measures if they fall outside the competences of the EC as understood by German governmental bodies.

Part II: The European Union in Practice

1. See David Easton, *A Framework for Political Analysis* (Englewood Cliffs, N.J.: Prentice-Hall, 1965). Figure II.1 draws on a model of EU foreign policy decisionmaking that first appeared in Ginsberg, "Narrowing the Theoretical Capabilities-Expectations Gap."

2. For a lucid study of principal–agent relations in the EU, see Mark A. Pollack, *The Engines of European Integration: Delegation, Agency, and Agenda Setting in the EU* (Oxford: Oxford University Press, 2003). See also Alexander Wendt, "The Agent-Structure Problem in International Relations Theory," *International Organization* 41 (Fall 1987): 417–446.

3. Pollack, *The Engines of European Integration*, 3–17.

4. Pollack, *The Engines of European Integration*, 382–383.

5. John Peterson and Elizabeth Bomberg, *Decisionmaking in the European Union* (New York: St. Martin's, 1999), 23.

Chapter 4: The Contexts and Actors of EU Governmental Decisionmaking

1. Roy H. Ginsberg, *Foreign Policy Actions of the European Community: The Politics of Scale* (Boulder, Colo.: Lynne Rienner, 1989); and Roy H. Ginsberg, *The European Union in International Politics: Baptism by Fire* (Lanham, Md.: Rowman and Littlefield, 2001).

2. See Thomas Frellesen and Roy H. Ginsberg, *European Union–United States Foreign Policy Cooperation in the 1990s: The Elements of Cooperation* (Brussels: Center for European Policy Studies, 1994); Kevin Featherstone and Roy H. Ginsberg, *The European Union and the United States in the 1990s: Partners in Transition* (New York: St. Martin's, 1996); Roy H. Ginsberg, *Ten Years of European Foreign Policy: Baptism, Confirmation, Validation* (Berlin: Heinrich Böll Foundation, 2003).

3. Karin M. Fierke and Knud Erik Jorgensen, eds., *Constructing International Relations: The Next Generation* (Armonk, N.Y.: M. E. Sharpe, 2001).

4. For example, the CoR adopted an opinion in June 2004 in favor of the development of low-cost airlines that provide air services between regional airports, which it viewed as favorable to regional economic development in the EU.

CoR members must have an electoral mandate from the authorities they represent or be politically accountable to them. The bureau of the CoR consists of a President, Vice President, and Chairpersons of the major political groups. Bureau members are elected for two-year terms. Five Commissions handle the work of the CoR: Economic and Social Policy; Cohesion Policy; Constitutional Affairs and Governance; External Relations; and Sustainable Development. The CoR has a staff of about 230. The influence on EU governmental decisionmaking of the CoR is limited, as is the case with the EESC. The Council or Commission may set a deadline too short for the CoR to deliver an opinion. Subnational authorities have access to the Commission, Council, and EP, which diminishes the uniqueness and influence of the CoR.

5. EESC members, appointed by member governments but independent once appointed, serve renewable four-year terms. EESC members elect a President, two Vice Presidents, and a bureau. The EESC Presidency rotates among the three constituent groups—employers, labor, and other interests. The Vice Presidencies are filled by the two groups not holding the Presidency. The EESC has a staff of about 500.

In actuality, the EESC has limited influence because there are other avenues for access by interest groups (e.g., Commission working groups, EP political committees); and the Commission or Council can give the EESC a short deadline to submit an advisory opinion, so short that if the EESC misses it, the views of its members are not taken into account. EESC views are solicited so late in the legislative process that final decisions already have been made. Furthermore, the Commission and Council are not bound by the Treaty to incorporate EESC opinions into proposed legislation; and the EESC does not have the resources to examine legislative proposals as closely as other EU bodies do, especially given the fact that its members serve the organization on a part-time basis. For more information about the EESC, consult www.esc.eu.int.

6. MEPs are particularly prone to influence by lobby groups, since the EP does not have the same rules as, say, the Commission and the three branches of the U.S. Government, which restrict outside income and provide for disclosure of investment income. The *Wall Street Journal* reported that MEPs with ties to the banking industry have sought to water down the EU's Third Money Laundering Directive designed to tighten financial crime laws, which is germane to the fight against international terrorism. See Glenn R Simpson, "Lobby in Europe Helps Sway Law on Terror Funding," *Wall Street Journal*, May 24, 2005, A3. For further evaluation

of lobbying in Brussels and Strasbourg, see Rory Watson and Michael Shackleton, "Organized Interests and Lobbying," in *The European Union: How Does It Work?* ed. Elizabeth Bomberg, John Peterson, and Alexander Stubb (Oxford: Oxford University Press, 2008).

7. Hazel Smith, *European Union Foreign Policy and Central America* (New York: St. Martin's, 1995).

8. Richard N. Haass, *Economic Sanctions and American Diplomacy* (New York: Council on Foreign Relations, 1998), 96.

9. Timothy J. Conlan and Michelle A. Sager, "The Growing International Activity of the American States," in *Policy Studies Review* 18, no. 3 (2001): 13–16.

10. Ginsberg, *Foreign Policy Actions of the European Community.*

11. *Bulletin Quotidien*, February 8, 2006, 4.

12. *Bulletin Quotidien*, February 1, 2006, 4.

Chapter 5: Inside EU Governmental Decisionmaking

1. John Peterson and Elizabeth Bomberg, *Decisionmaking in the European Union* (New York: St. Martin's, 1999), 16.

2. Peterson and Bomberg, *Decisionmaking in the European Union*, 9.

3. In January 1999 the EP investigated allegations of financial mismanagement, fraud, and nepotism in the Santer Commission. The EP passed a motion that put the Commission on probation until a committee of independent experts established by the EP reported on the allegations. The College of Commissioners resigned a day before the vote on a motion of censure was scheduled to be held in the EP. The censure motion was defeated by a 293–232 vote. For more information, see Committee of Independent Experts, *First Report on Allegations Regarding Fraud, Mismanagement, and Nepotism in the European Commission* (Brussels: European Parliament, 1999). The Prodi Commission endeavored to improve its mechanisms for monitoring and controlling national and subnational agencies who in turn administer 80 percent of the EU budget—namely agriculture and structural spending. See Committee of Independent Experts, *Second Report on Reform of the Commission: Analysis of Current Practice and Proposals for Tackling Mismanagement, Irregularities, and Fraud* (Brussels: European Commission, 1999).

4. Professor Neill Nugent argues that the insistence (in the Treaty) that Commissioners remain completely independent of their national politics ought to be interpreted flexibly; that is, it is useful for the Commissioners to maintain links back home in order to explain to the College what is likely to be acceptable back home. A Commission that is naive about politics and national interests in the member states is not likely to be effective in producing proposed legislation that will make it through to fruition. See Neill Nugent, *The Government and Politics of the European Union* (Durham, N.C.: Duke University Press, 2003), 115.

5. Commission President Prodi introduced a new policy for the cabinets in order to make them more multinational in composition, and thus less focused on the nationality of the Commissioner. Each cabinet is expected to comprise aides from three different member states. The *chef* or deputy *chef de cabinet* ought to come from a member state other than his or her Commissioner. The weekly meetings of the chefs de cabinet are chaired by the Secretary-General in advance of Commission meetings. Commissioners consult and interact among themselves when necessary between meetings. *Chefs de cabinet* seek accord on as many items on the agendas of their Commissioners as possible in order to leave to the Commission those politically sensitive issues that were not solved at lower levels.

6. The DGs and other services of the Commission are: Agriculture, Budget, Competition, Development, Common Service for External Relations, Economic and Financial Affairs, Education and Culture, Employment and Social Affairs, Energy and Transport, Enlargement, En-

terprise, Environment, European Anti-Fraud Office, External Relations, Financial Control, Fisheries, Group of Policy Advisors, Health and Consumer Protection, Humanitarian Aid Office, Information Society, Internal Audit Service, Internal Market, Joint Interpreting and Conference Service, Joint Research Center, Justice and Home Affairs, Legal Service, Personnel and Administration, Press and Communication, Publications Office, Regional Policy, Research, Taxation and Customs Union Secretariat-General, Statistical Office, Trade, and Translation Services.

7. To work as a civil servant in the Commission is to have the likelihood of a long, well-paid career, but one in Brussels, Luxembourg, or foreign posts far from one's home country. The *concours*, the entrance exam, must be passed. Fluency in two of the EU's official languages and a university degree are required. For those candidates who wish to work in the policymaking or policy management areas of the Commission, a quota system based on nationality exists to ensure that no one country or group of countries has disproportionate influence.

8. The Commission issues a formal warning notice to a member government that has not complied with EC legislation, and the Commission expects a reply. If compliance is still not forthcoming, the Commission issues what is called a "reasoned opinion" in which it explains why it thinks the member government is not in compliance. Usually the Commission and the member government in question work out an understanding to the satisfaction of each; however, in a small percentage of cases, continued noncompliance forces the Commission to take the errant government to the ECJ. The ECJ not only makes a determination but may also levy a fine, which the Commission collects.

9. European Commission, *General Report of the Activities of the European Union, 2002* (Luxembourg: Office for Official Publications of the European Communities, 2003), 95.

10. In the spirit of the principle of subsidiarity, the Amsterdam Treaty established the Conference of Community and European Affairs Committees of Parliaments of the EU (COSAC). National parliamentarians meet to discuss and advocate for their interests vis-à-vis EU bodies and policies.

11. Nugent, *The Government and Politics of the European Union*, 127.

12. Readers who wish to examine how comitology works in detail can consult the lucid analysis provided by Simon Hix, *The Political System of the European Union*, 2nd ed. (London: Palgrave, 2005), 52–57.

13. For further analysis, see Youri Devuyst, *EU Decisionmaking after the Treaty Establishing a Constitution for Europe*, Policy Paper No. 9, Center for Western European Studies, University of Pittsburgh, July 2004.

14. Data drawn from *Bulletin Quotidien*, Parlement Européen: Elections Européennes de Juin 2004, 1–17, No. 2373, 16 Juillet 2004; Richard Corbett, Francis Jacobs, and Michael Shackleton, *The European Parliament*, 7th ed. (London: John Harper, 2005), 26; and www .elections2004.eu.int/ep-election/sites/en/results1306/turnout—ep/grahical.html.

15. For the leading and authoritative text on the context, actors, structure, and powers of the EP, see Corbett, Jacobs, and Shackleton, *The European Parliament*.

16. Devuyst, *EU Decisionmaking after the Treaty Establishing a Constitution for Europe*, 14.

17. However, since 1989 there has been a framework for cooperation between national parliaments and the EP known by its French acronym, COSAC, the Conference of Community and European Affairs Committees of Parliaments of the EU.

18. This analysis of post-Maastricht EP procedures on Commission confirmation hearings draws on an unpublished paper by Francis Jacobs, "The European Parliament's Role in Nominating the Members of the Commission: First Steps towards Parliamentary Government or US Senate-Type Confirmation Hearings."

19. Jacobs, "The European Parliament's Role in Nominating the Members of the Commission."

20. Jacobs, "The European Parliament's Role in Nominating the Members of the Commission."

21. The SEA introduced the cooperation procedure in order to speed decisionmaking with

regard to the 1992 single market program and to lend a more democratic representative dimension to governmental decisionmaking by giving the EP a say but not a veto in single market legislation. The procedure was complemented by increased use of QMV in the Council. However, the procedure has been largely eclipsed as the result of the TEU and subsequent Treaty revisions that introduced and expanded the use of codecision (where the EP does have a veto). The cooperation procedure today applies only to four areas of integration. For more information see Corbett, Jacobs, and Shackleton, *The European Parliament*, 213.

22. Prior to the SEA, the consultation procedure was the only decisionmaking procedure used for legislating in nonadministrative areas. The Commission accepts about three-quarters of all EP amendments. The Council, which accepts under half of EP amendments, is less accommodating.

In a strategy to maximize the EP's influence in the consultation procedure, MEPs vote in plenary sessions on the EP's own amendments to the Commission's legislative proposal but not on the draft proposal itself. The EP waits until the Commission states, as it must under EU procedures, whether it will or will not accept the EP amendments. If the Council does accept the amendments, the EP issues an opinion favoring the amended text, which is sent to the Council for its consideration. If some or none of the amendments are accepted by the Commission, the EP seeks to pressure the Commission to be more responsive by not issuing a favorable opinion and by sending the proposal back to the responsible EP committee. This consultation procedure puts the Commission and Council under pressure to consider EP preferences. See Nugent, *The Government and Politics of the European Union*, 344, for further analysis.

23. European Commission, *General Report on the Activities of the European Union, 2004: Technical Annex* (Luxembourg: Office for Official Publications of the European Communities, 2005), 366–403. The EP has the power of initiative in areas related to adoption of uniform procedures governing the elections of the EP as well as statutes governing the rules of the EP. On December 22, 2004, the Council extended codecision to certain areas of policy with regard in particular to free movement of people and immigration, effective January 1, 2005.

24. *General Report on the Activities of the European Union, 2008* (Brussels: European Commission, 2009), 228.

25. Nugent, *The Government and Politics of the European Union*, 349.

26. The convening of the conciliation committee, which occurs within six weeks, may be extended by another two weeks if the EP and Council so wish. The period for the joint text out of the conciliation committee to be approved by the EP and Council with no possibility of amendment may be extended from six to eight weeks if the EP and Council so wish.

27. Corbett, Jacobs, and Shackleton, *The European Parliament*, 6.

28. Mark A. Pollack, *The Engines of European Integration: Delegation, Agency, and Agenda Setting in the EU* (Oxford: Oxford University Press, 2003).

29. Devuyst, *EU Decisionmaking after the Treaty Establishing a Constitution for Europe*, 14. The Amsterdam Treaty provides for national parliaments to be informed of Commission legislative proposals.

30. Andrew Moravcsik, ed., *Europe without Illusions: The Paul-Henri Spaak Lectures, 1994–1999* (Lanham, Md.: University Press of America, 2005), 132.

31. For a thorough description of the budgetary process, with a focus on the EP's role, see chap. 13 in Corbett, Jacobs, and Shackleton, *The European Parliament*.

32. The EP Committee on Budgets may amend the proposal by reintroducing items and then recommend passage by the EP. If at the plenary the EP votes to adopt the budget (plus three-fifths of the votes cast), the EU has an approved annual budget. Rejection of the budget at this point requires an absolute majority and two-thirds of the votes cast. This has happened rarely since the 1980s because the EP and Council endeavor to iron out differences before the EP resorts to a budgetary veto, which is a blunt instrument of power the EP would likely use sparingly. For a lucid account of the EC budget process with a focus on the role of the EP, see Corbett, Jacobs, and Shackleton, *The European Parliament*.

33. "1992 Court of Auditors Report," *Bulletin Quotidien*, November 17, 1993, 9.

34. The Commission depends heavily on the national and subnational governments to administer EU programs, and it often depends on NGOs and international organizations to which it subcontracts the implementation of foreign aid programs. There are times when ignorance or confusion, not fraud, causes problems with the way EU programs and expenditures are handled by national and subnational governments or EU agents abroad. Still, in the end, the Commission is responsible for overseeing those who expend EU resources. Nugent summarizes the deferral by the EP of the discharge of the 1996 budget. See Nugent, *The Government and Politics of the European Union*, 279.

35. Leslie Friedman Goldstein, *Constituting Federal Sovereignty: The European Union in Comparative Context* (Baltimore: Johns Hopkins University Press, 2001), 15–16.

36. The author wishes to thank Professor Ronald P. Seyb, Department of Government, Skidmore College, for his helpful comments with regard to this section.

37. John McCormick, *The European Union: Politics and Policies* (Boulder, Colo.: Westview, 1999), 107.

38. Corbett, Jacobs, and Shackleton, *The European Parliament*, 196.

39. Corbett, Jacobs, and Shackleton, *The European Parliament*.

40. An example of an interinstitutional accord that subsequently assisted EU governmental decisionmaking was the 1999 Joint Declaration on Practical Arrangements for the New Codecision Procedure. See *Official Journal*, C148/1, May 28, 1999. Nugent provides a pithy critique of EU governmental decisionmaking. See Nugent, *The Government and Politics of the European Union*, 361–365.

Chapter 6: The Outputs of EU Governmental Decisionmaking

1. This insight is attributed to Kenny Olmstead, one of the author's three research assistants who helped research and write this chapter. The author expresses his gratitude to Kenny Olmstead, Joshua Hutchinson, and Mihaela David for their ideas that were incorporated into this chapter.

2. A Council decision occurs when the Council takes action on a specific issue, such as its decision to establish the European Civil Service Tribunal in 2005. A decision is legally binding on those to whom it is addressed. The Council and the EP issue Resolutions that express a concern or position or intent to act on an EU issue. For example, in 2005 the EP passed a resolution in support of the opening of accession negotiations with Turkey. In 2004 an EP resolution stressed the importance of maintaining a lead EU role in climate change negotiations and called on the EU to redouble its efforts to meet the Kyoto emission reductions targets and to set an example for the world.

The EP and Commission also issue opinions. For example, a Commission opinion is requested by the Council on issues such as enlargement. The Commission submits an opinion to the Council—a formal detailed document—that describes political and economic conditions in a country that has applied for admission to the EU and evaluates the ability of that country to become a member. The Commission opinion recommends whether or not to open negotiations with a prospective applicant.

In a negotiating directive, the Council instructs the Commission on the parameters of negotiations with non-EU countries on specific issues (e.g., the draft European Convention on Combating Trafficking in Human Beings). In a council conclusion, the Council issues a statement advocating (but not requiring) a position on an issue or admonishing the member states or other EU bodies to do something the Council deems necessary. In 2004 the Council adopted conclusions on the need for a strategic plan to combat organized cross-border crime.

The Council issues joint actions, common positions, and common strategies in CFSP and common positions in JHA. A joint action establishes the objectives, modalities, and time frame for a specific Council objective. For example, the EU Police Mission in Bosnia-Herzegovina was based on a 2002 CFSP Joint Action of the Council. A common position defines the approach of the EU regarding an international issue, region, or country or an issue of internal security and justice. In October 2004 the Council adopted a common position on negotiations for the draft European Convention on Combating Trafficking in Human Beings. A common strategy refers to the publication by the Council of a set of objectives with regard to a region of the world. The European Council adopted a Common Strategy for Africa in 2005.

A council framework decision is provided for by the Treaty to approximate member state laws and regulations within JHA (police and judicial cooperation in criminal matters). The results of a framework decision are binding on the member states, but national authorities are left to implement the decision. Framework decisions are similar to EC directives with a major exception. A framework decision does not produce direct effect. It does not confer individual rights that national courts must protect. Examples of framework decisions put into effect after the 9/11 attacks are the adoption of an EU-wide arrest warrant and measures to combat money laundering. The Treaty of Amsterdam replaced JHA Joint Actions with framework decisions and measures because they are a more flexible decisionmaking instrument.

In a competition ruling, the Commission determines if member governments or companies are in violation of EC antitrust rules. In a communication, the Commission issues a document that outlines general policy issues to generate public discussion in advance of possible legislative activity. For example, in 2005 the Commission issued a communication to the EP on its strategic objectives at the start of a new five-year Commission term. In a recommendation, the Commission issues suggestions to the Council that could lead to action plans or other legislative proposals. For example, in 2004 the Commission recommended to the Council new procedures for handling asylum requests.

In an action plan, the Commission drafts a set of goals in a specific policy area. The plan must be approved by the Council or European Council. For example, the Commission drafted an action plan designed to accelerate transposition of EC market legislation into domestic law by national governments; the European Council adopted the plan in 1997. In studies and reports, the Commission publishes documents (on its own initiative or at the request of the EP, the Council, or the European Council) that focus on specific issues or problem areas. In 2004 the Commission presented a study, requested by the European Council, on the impact of EU cooperation with third countries to combat illegal immigration into the EU.

White Papers are studies the Commission produces for discussion and action in specific areas. Green Papers are Commission studies that introduce ideas for public discussion and debate. The Commission's 2000 *White Paper on Reform of the Commission* improved the running of the Commission. A 1985 *Green Paper on Reform of the Common Agricultural Policy* was influential in the reform of the CAP in 1992.

3. The EC is concerned with cartels—groups of producers who agree to fix prices and share markets. For example, in 2004 the Commission imposed a fine of €19 million on four companies of a Swiss group for involvement in price fixing and market sharing as part of a secret cartel for sodium gluconate, a chemical used for cleaning metal and glass.

4. The Commission has the power to examine, approve, or prohibit mergers between companies if the results would adversely affect competition in the internal market. The Treaty explicitly provided for review of state aids and of firms whose agreements threatened competition in the internal market. Merger review and control evolved over time as an explicit authority of the Commission. In merger review and control, the ECJ, once again, drove integration. In the *Continental Can* decision (1974), the ECJ determined that the Commission had the authority to apply the Treaty's competition articles to some mergers even in the absence of a regulation issued by the Council. Over time, corporations considering mergers have increasingly asked the Commission for reviews of their plans. Moreover, competitors of firms considering mergers became more inclined to press the Commission to initiate a merger review. Companies have also pressed for EU regulations that would govern merger review and control,

offer legal certainty, and provide for transparent rules. After fifteen years of negotiations, the Council unanimously passed the Merger Regulation in 1989, providing the long-awaited increase in legal certainty for the Commission in this area. In the 1990s the Commission blocked some mergers and imposed strict conditions on others.

In merger review, the Commission first decides if a merger is within the scope of the Merger Regulation. It may then approve the merger or initiate proceedings against it. Within four months of review, the Commission decides to approve, offer conditional approval to, or prohibit a merger. Most mergers are approved. For example, the Commission authorized the creation of a Sony joint venture with Bertelsmann but agreed to keep a close watch on developments in the industry. The Commission worked closely with the U.S. Federal Trade Commission on this case.

EU Competition Policy has enormous impact on nonmember state firms doing business in the EU. The Commission twice blocked the mergers of American firms, first in 1997 when it blocked the merger of McDonnell Douglas and Boeing, and second in 2001 when it blocked the merger of GE and Honeywell. Since both mergers had been approved by the U.S. Federal Trade Commission, the U.S. Government lobbied the Commission to unblock them, but to no avail.

For more information, see forthcoming Tim Buthe, "The Politics of Competition in the European Union: The First Fifty Years," in *Making History: European Integration and Institutional Change at Fifty—The State of the European Union*, vol. 8, ed. Sophie Meunier and Kathleen McNamara (Oxford: Oxford University Press, 2007).

5. The Commission is charged by the Treaty to review state aids that threaten or infringe Treaty rules on competition. State aids include government subsidies, tax breaks, and other provisions that advantage recipient firms but distort competition. As a result of the SEA and the 1992 Project, the Commission grew sufficiently more confident in this area to reduce one of the biggest NTBs in the single market: government subsidies. The Commission either prohibits state aids or sets boundaries to them. For example, in 2005 the Commission proposed that temporary aid for the shipbuilding industry be extended to 2006 to permit more time for the sector to restructure in order to regain competitiveness. In a far more complicated and messier case, the Commission initially approved €160 million in Greek state aid (1994–2000) for an ailing airline (Olympic Airways). However, following complaints lodged at the Commission from rival airlines in 2000 and 2001, the Commission determined in 2002 that the aid it had previously approved would have to be recovered because the Greek Government had failed to restructure Olympic Airways. The ECJ upheld the Commission's ruling in 2005.

6. Simon Hix, *The Political System of the European Union* (New York: Palgrave Macmillan, 2005), 257–258.

7. Hix, *The Political System of the European Union*, 258–259.

8. For further analysis see Elliot Posner, "Financial Services," in *Making History*, ed. Meunier and McNamara.

9. If the EU members wished to impose a trade embargo on a third country considered an outlaw regime for violating basic human rights, they would have to do so through the CCP, which provides the legal basis for such actions, since individual member states do not have sovereign authority to act alone with regard to the terms of trade with nonmembers. There is one exception. As discussed in Chapter 3, the ECJ has ruled that a member state may undertake trade restrictions if it considers the absence of such action a threat to its national security.

10. Eve Fouilleux, "The Common Agricultural Policy," in *European Union Politics*, ed. Michelle Cini (Oxford: Oxford University Press, 2003), 251.

11. For the most recent studies on JHA, see John Occhipinti, *The Impact of Enlargement on Justice and Home Affairs*, paper presented to the 8th Biennial Conference, European Union Studies Association, Nashville, March 29, 2003, 6; John Occhipinti, "Policing across the Atlantic: EU–U.S. Relations and International Crime Fighting," *Bologna Center of International Affairs* 8 (Spring 2005): 1–12; and John Occhipinti, "Sovereignty's Last Stand: Exploring the Two Dimensions of European Integration in the Fight against Transnational Organized

Crime," Workshop on the Transformation of the Territorial State, International University of Bremen, June 2005.

12. Some of the important measures adopted by the Schengen members included: removing checks at common borders among signatories and replacing those checks with external border checks; common definition of the rules for crossing external borders; separation in air terminals and ports of persons traveling within the Schengen area from those arriving from countries outside the area; harmonization of rules governing conditions of entry and visas for short stays; coordination among administrators on surveillance of borders, including staff training and harmonization of instructions; drawing up rules for asylum seekers; introduction of rights of surveillance and of pursuit of illegal persons across internal borders; and creation of the Schengen Information System. Beginning in 1984, the JHA Ministers of the member governments began holding regular biannual meetings on police and customs cooperation and on the free movement of persons. Trevi, Schengen, and JHA ministerial meetings presaged the incorporation of JHA affairs into the Treaty framework a decade later.

13. Britain and Ireland cooperate closely with the other member states on many issues related to judicial cooperation and police cooperation. Schengen was an early example of a model of European integration based on a multiple-speed approach: members willing to intensify cooperation proceed, so long as others can jump on the train at a later time.

14. Occhipinti, *The Impact of Enlargement on Justice and Home Affairs*, 7.

15. Occhipinti, *The Impact of Enlargement on Justice and Home Affairs*.

16. See 2002/584/JHA: Council Framework Decision, June 13, 2002, on the European arrest warrant and the surrender procedures between member states.

Chapter 7: European Union Foreign Policy

1. This concept was first introduced and tested for explanatory relevance in Roy H. Ginsberg, *Foreign Policy Actions of the European Community: The Politics of Scale* (Boulder, Colo.: Lynne Rienner, 1989).

2. EUFP includes instances when one or more of the member governments act on behalf of the entire union (EU Council Presidency or the so-called EU3, Britain, France, and Germany, in dealing with Iranian nuclear development).

3. Ginsberg, *The European Union in International Politics*.

4. Javier Solana, *A Secure Europe in a Better World: European Security Strategy* (Brussels: Council of the European Union, 2003).

5. For an excellent analysis of the role of EUSRs in EUFP see Cornelius Adebahr, *Learning and Changing in European Foreign Policy: The Case of EU Special Representatives* (Baden-Baden: Nomos Verlagsgellschaft, 2009).

6. One study estimates that the transatlantic economy generates $3.75 trillion in total commercial sales annually and employs 14 million workers on both sides of the Atlantic. For more data on the EU-U.S. commercial relationship, see Daniel S. Hamilton and Joseph P. Quinlan, *The Transatlantic Economy 2009* (Washington: Center for Transatlantic Relations, 2009).

Chapter 8: The Internal Dimension of European Integration

1. Greenland, a part of Denmark, seceded from the EU in 1985 when the EU adopted a Common Fisheries Policy and the Greenlanders did not wish to share their rich fishing resources with the rest of the EU. Gaullist France boycotted the EC institutions for six months

in 1965–1966 but did not secede from the EC. The Lisbon Treaty features a new clause that provides for a member state to leave the EU.

2. Harald Badinger and Fritz Breuss, *What Has Determined the Rapid Post-War Growth of Intra-EU Trade?* (Vienna: University of Economics and Business Administration, 2003), 2.

3. The data presented were provided by Eurostat in 2009. For more information, visit the Eurostat database at http://epp.eurostat.ec.europa.eu/.

4. "Onward and Upward: Ten Years of the Euro," *The Financial Times*, December 31, 2008, 5.

5. "Reserve Currencies," *Economist*, October 1, 2005.

6. *Results of the 2009 Elections,* European Parliament, http://www.europarl.europa.eu/parl iament/archive/elections2009/en/index_en.html. For more information see Richard Corbett, Francis Jacobs, and Michael Shackleton, eds., *The European Parliament* (London: John Harper, 2000), 25.

7. For information on the ratification process as it occurred for the EU Constitutional Treaty, see http://europa.eu.int/constit/ratif_en.htm.

8. Eurobarometer 63 (2005), 153.

9. The results of the polls are found at http://europa.eu.int/comm/public_opinion. Readers interested in learning more about the methodology used by the pollsters contracted by Eurobarometer should refer to the annex of each standard report.

10. The author wishes to thank his research assistant, Mihaela David '10, for updating and analyzing Eurobarometer data used in this chapter. In addition, the author thanks Professor Robert Turner for his comments on this section of the chapter and for expressing his view of the value of Eurobarometer data, given the inexact science of polling citizens over time, country, and issue.

11. Eurobarometer 4 (1975) to Eurobarometer 38 (1992).

12. Eurobarometer 45 (1996), 1–2.

13. Eurobarometer 66 (2006), 195.

14. Eurobarometer 71 (2009), 95.

15. Eurobarometer 45 (1996), 14

16. Eurobarometer 71 (2009), 96.

17. Eurobarometer 15 (1981) to Eurobarometer 71 (2009).

18. Eurobarometer 71 (2009), 93.

19. Eurobarometer 00 to 60 (1971–2003).

20. Eurobarometer 45 (1996), 45.

21. Eurobarometer 71 (2009), 121.

22. Eurobarometer 68 (2007), 78.

23. Eurobarometer 68 (2007), 78.

24. Eurobarometer 68 (2009), 122.

25. Eurobarometer 68 (2007), 53.

26. Eurobarometer 63 (2005), 75.

27. Eurobarometer 63 (2005), 145.

28. Eurobarometer 68 (2007), 90–97

29. Eurobarometer 71 (2009), 114.

30. Eurobarometer 68 (2007), 90–97.

31. Eurobarometer 71 (2009), 111.

32. Eurobarometer 68 (2007), 90–97.

33. Eurobarometer 63 (2005), 118.

34. Eurobarometer 63 (2005), 119.

35. Eurobarometer 63 (2005), 118.

36. Eurobarometer 68 (2007), 84.

37. Eurobarometer 68 (2007), 84.

38. Eurobarometer 63 (2005), 150.

39. Eurobarometer 44 (1996), 55; Eurobarometer 63 (2005), 31;

Eurobarometer 70 (2008), 21.

40. Eurobarometer 71 (2009), European Elections 2009, 2–6.
41. Eurobarometer 63 (2005), 28
42. Eurobarometer 68 (2007), 114.
43. Eurobarometer 68 (2007), 109.
44. Special Eurobarometer 215 (2005), 57.
45. Eurobarometer 68 (2007), 109.
46. Special Eurobarometer 215 (2005), 23.
47. Special Eurobarometer 215 (2005), 21.
48. Eurobarometer 45 (1996) to Eurobarometer 58 (2002).
49. Eurobarometer 68 (2007), 117; Eurobarometer 71 (2009), 156.
50. Eurobarometer 71 (2009), 156.
51. Eurobarometer 71 (2009), 118.
52. Eurobarometer 45 (1996), 101.
53. Eurobarometer 44 (1996), 55.
54. Eurobarometer 71 (2009), European Elections 2009, 6.
55. Eurobarometer 44 (1996), 55.
56. Eurobarometer 47–57 (1997–2002).
57. Eurobarometer 71 (2009), European Elections 2009, 6.
58. Eurobarometer 68 (2007), 109.
59. Eurobarometer 68 (2007), 108–116.
60. Eurobarometer 215 (2005), 57.
61. Eurobarometer 215 (2005), 37.
62. Eurobarometer 63 (2005), 28, 31.
63. Eurobarometer 32–56 (1989–2001).
64. Eurobarometer 44 (1996), 101.
65. Eurobarometer 44 (1996).
66. Eurobarometer 47 (1997) to Eurobarometer 58 (2002).
67. Eurobarometer 61 (2004), 14
68. Eurobarometer 70 (2008), 21.
69. Eurobarometer 71 (2009), European Elections 2009, 6
70. Eurobarometer 61 (2004), 73.
71. Eurobarometer 63 (2005).
72. Eurobarometer 70 (2008), 136.

Chapter 9: The External Dimension of European Integration

1. Eurobarometer 68 (2007), 120.
2. Eurobarometer 68 (2007), 120–121.
3. Eurobarometer 68 (2007), 122–123.
4. Eurobarometer 63 (2005), 59.
5. Eurobarometer 63 (2005), 152.
6. Eurobarometer 66 (2006), 179–180.
7. Eurobarometer 68 (2007), 128–129.
8. Eurobarometer 61 (2004), 19.
9. This section is based on the author's prior works, principally Roy H. Ginsberg, *Foreign Policy Actions of the European Community: The Politics of Scale* (Boulder, Colo.: Lynne Rienner, 1989) and Roy H. Ginsberg, *The European Union in International Politics: Baptism by Fire* (Boulder, Colo.: Rowman & Littlefield, 2001).

10. This section draws on Roy H. Ginsberg and Susan E. Penksa, *The European Union in Global Security: The Politics of Impact* (London: Palgrave Macmillan, 2011).

11. For an analysis of the effects of the mission, see Winrich Kuehne *How the EU Organizes and Conducts Peace Operations in Africa* (Berlin: Center for International Peace Operations, 2009).

12. Based on interview in Brussels, June, 2009.

13. Based on an interview in the Council Secretariat, June, 2009.

14. The EU member states chose not to intervene directly in the humanitarian crisis in Darfur. However, since 2005 the EU has provided a program of assistance in support of AU peacekeeping and humanitarian efforts in Darfur—training, technical, and logistical support and equipment for the policing effort of the AU peacekeepers. The EU assists in the lifting of African battalions in Darfur, provides training in aerial observation, and offers financial assistance to support the salaries and insurance for AU troops. EU military experts and political advisors deployed to Addis Ababa to support the EUSR for Sudan in his cooperation with the AU.

Index

About the Author

Roy H. Ginsberg is Joseph C. Palamountain Jr. Chair in Government at Skidmore College in Saratoga Springs, New York. Cofounder and former chair of the European Union Studies Association of the United States, he received his Ph.D. in Political Science from The George Washington University. Before starting his academic career, he was an analyst in various federal agencies, including the Foreign Agricultural Service, the Office of Management and Budget, and the International Trade Commission. He was founding Director of Skidmore's International Affairs Program, Glaverbel Chair in European Politics at Catholic University of Louvain, Visiting Professor at New York University and the Paul H. Nitze School of Advanced International Studies, Fulbright Fellow at the Centre for European Policy Studies in Brussels, and Research Fellow in European Integration at the European Commission. Professor Ginsberg has submitted congressional testimony on transatlantic relations and conducts briefings for foreign policy agencies and institutes in Washington and Europe. He is author of *Foreign Policy Actions of the European Community: The Politics of Scale* and *The European Union in International Politics: Baptism by Fire*, as well as other books and articles on European integration and transatlantic relations. Professor Ginsberg speaks regularly on these topics in Europe and the United States and is a consultant to U.S. government agencies on European Union affairs and to U.S. universities on international studies education.

About the Book

Written by one of the premier scholars on the European Union and hailed as the best undergraduate text on the subject, this book has been thoroughly revised and updated to include the entry into force of the Lisbon Treaty. Clear and comprehensive, it "demystifies" one of the world's most important and least understood institutions. Roy H. Ginsberg contextualizes European integration through the foundation blocks of history, law, economics, and politics. He then breaks the EU down into its components so that they can be understood individually and in relation to the whole. Reconstructing the EU as a single polity, Ginsberg evaluates the EU's domestic and foreign policies and their effects on Europeans and non-Europeans alike. The author thus challenges students to see what the European Union truly represents: a unique experiment in regional cooperation and a remarkable model of conflict resolution for the world's troubled regions.